D1349327

# Total Quality Management

*For Susan, Jane and Robert*

# Total Quality Management

*The route to improving performance*

## Second edition

## John S. Oakland
PhD, CChem, MRSC, FIQA, FSS, MASQC

*Exxon Chemical Professor of*
*Total Quality Management,*
*European Centre for TQM,*
*Management Centre, University of Bradford*

Butterworth-Heinemann Ltd
Linacre House, Jordan Hill, Oxford OX2 8DP

A member of the Reed Elsevier plc group

OXFORD LONDON BOSTON
MUNICH NEW DELHI SINGAPORE SYDNEY
TOKYO TORONTO WELLINGTON

First published 1989
Reprinted 1989 (three times), 1990, 1991, 1992
Second edition 1993
Reprinted 1994, 1995

**British Library Cataloguing in Publication Data**
Oakland, John S.
  Total Quality Management: The route
  to improving performance. –
  2Rev. ed
  I. Title
  658.5

ISBN 0 7506 0993 1

Set by Hope Services (Abingdon) Ltd
Printed and bound in Great Britain by Clays, St Ives plc

# Contents

# Preface

When I wrote the first edition of this book in 1988, there were very few books on the subject of Total Quality Management. Since its publication, the interest in TQM and business process improvement has exploded. There are now many many texts on the subject and its various aspects.

So much has been learned during the last four to five years of TQM implementation that it has been necessary to rewrite this book. This edition is based on the first, but its structure and content have changed substantially to reflect the developments, current understanding, and experience gained of TQM.

Continuous cost reduction, productivity and quality improvement have proved essential for organizations to stay in operation. We cannot avoid seeing how quality has developed into the most important competitive weapon, and many organizations have realised that TQM is *the* way of managing for the future. TQM is far wider in its application than assuring product or service quality – it is a way of managing business processes to ensure complete 'customer' satisfaction at every stage, internally and externally.

This book is about how to manage in a total quality way. It is structured around five parts of a model for TQM. The core of the model is the *customer–supplier* interfaces, both externally and internally, and the fact that at each interface there lies a number of *processes*. This sensitive core must be surrounded by *commitment* to quality, meeting the customer requirements, *communication* of the quality message, and recognition of the need to change the *culture* of most organizations to create total quality. These are the soft FOUNDATIONS, to which must be added the SYSTEMS, the TOOLS, and the TEAMS – the hard management necessities.

Under these headings the essential steps for the successful IMPLE-MENTATION of TQM are set out in what I hope is a meaningful and practical way. Aimed at directors and managers in industrial, commercial, and service organizations, the book guides the reader through the language of TQM and sets down a clear way to proceed for the whole organization.

Many of the 'gurus' appear to present different theories of quality management. In reality they are all talking the same 'language' but they use different dialects; the basic principles of defining quality and taking it into account throughout all the activities of the 'business' are common. Quality has to be managed – it does not just happen. Understanding and commitment by senior management, effective leadership and teamwork are fundamental parts of the recipe for success. I have tried to use my extensive research and consultancy experience to take what is to many a jigsaw puzzle and assemble a comprehensive, practical, working model for total quality – the rewards of which are greater efficiencies, lower costs, improved reputation and greater market share.

In addition to helping senior managers to develop TQM within their organizations, this book should meet the requirements of the increasing number of students who need to understand the part it may play in their courses on science, engineering, or management. I hope that those engaged in the pursuit of professional qualifications in the management of quality assurance, such as membership of the Institute of Quality Assurance, the American Society of Quality Control, or the Australian Organization for Quality, will make this book an essential part of their library. With its companion book, *Statistical Process Control* (now in its second edition) *Total Quality Management* documents a comprehensive approach, one that has been used successfully in many organizations throughout the world.

I would like to thank my colleagues at the European Centre for TQM, Bradford, and in O&F Quality Management Consultants Ltd for the sharing of ideas and help in their development. The book is the result of many years of collaboration in assisting organizations to introduce good methods of management and embrace the concepts of total quality. I am most grateful to Barbara Shutt and Wendy Docherty who converted a patchwork quilt of scribble and typescript into error-free electronic form, and indebted to Susan, Jane and Robert, who put up with a 'distant' husband and father for yet another year.

*John Oakland*

# Part One
# The Foundations – A Model for TQM

Good order is the foundation of all good things.

*Edmund Burke*, 1791

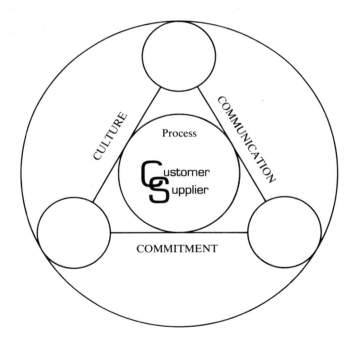

# 1 Understanding quality

## 1.1 Quality and competitiveness

There was a company outside Japan that tried to manufacture motor cars. Its name does not matter – it has changed its name now anyway – let's call it B. Motors. The company did a deal with a Japanese car manufacturer that allowed the Japanese-named cars, let's call them HO, to be manufactured by B. Motors. What happened in the boardroom of HO motor cars when that deal was announced can only be described as mass hara-kiri.

Clearly, rather a lot of depression had settled over those particular Japanese gentlemen. Why should they behave in this way? What was the difference between the two companies? In a word, image or reputation. Reputation for what? Reputation for quality, reliability, price, and delivery – all the things we *compete* on.

Whatever type of organization you work in – a hospital, a university, a bank, an insurance company, local government, an airline, a factory – competition is rife: competition for customers, for students, for patients, for resources, for funds. There are very few people around in most types of organization who remain to be convinced that quality is the most important of the competitive weapons. If you doubt that, just look at the way some organizations, even whole industries in certain countries, have used quality to take the heads off their competitors. And they are not only Japanese companies. British, American, French, German, Italian, Spanish, Swiss, Swedish organizations, and organizations from other countries, have used quality strategically to win customers, steal business resources or funding, and be competitive. Moreover, attention to quality improves performance in reliability, delivery, and price.

The reputation of Japanese companies once was anything but good. Not too long ago they were most famous for 'cheap oriental trash'. They have clearly *learned* something. This has not as much to do with differences in national cultures, as many people think it has. The Japanese culture, which is much older than most western cultures, has not changed significantly in 40–50 years.

One of the lessons many Japanese companies learned after the Second World War was to manage quality, and the other things on which we compete. They learned it from a handful of Americans – people like Joseph M. Juran and W. Edwards Deming, who have since reached fame as 'gurus' of quality management.

The company we called B. Motors also learned a thing or two about quality and competition. It lost market share, but started to put things right by a better understanding of quality management and the needs of its customers. Unfortunately its previous reputation was so bad that it is taking it many years to change people's view. It may never do so. Moreover, the country in which it operates gained a poor reputation for shoddy goods and services, in contrast to the 'Japanese', who seem to take so many industries by storm. Even the trains run on time there!

For any organization, there are several lessons to be learned about *reputation* from this story:

1  It is built upon the competitive elements of quality, reliability, delivery, and price, of which quality has become strategically the most important.
2  Once an organization acquires a poor reputation for quality, it takes a very long time to change it.
3  Reputations, good or bad, can quickly become national reputations.
4  The management of the competitive weapons, such as quality, can be learned like any other skill, and used to turn round a poor reputation in time.

Before anyone will buy the idea that quality is an important consideration, they would have to know what was meant by it.

### What is quality?

'Is this a quality watch?' Pointing to my wrist, I ask this question of a class of students – undergraduates, postgraduates, experienced managers – it matters not who. The answers vary:

- 'No, it's made in Japan.'
- 'No, it's cheap.'
- 'No, the face is scratched.'
- 'How reliable is it?'
- 'I wouldn't wear it.'

My watch has been insulted all over the world – London, New York, Paris, Sydney, Brussels, Amsterdam, Bradford! Very rarely am I told that the quality of the watch depends on what the wearer requires from a watch – perhaps a piece of jewellery to give an impression of wealth; a timepiece that gives the required data, including the date, in digital form; or one with the ability to perform at 50 metres under the sea? Clearly these requirements determine the quality.

Quality is often used to signify 'excellence' of a product or service – people talk about 'Rolls-Royce quality' and 'top quality'. In some engineering companies the word may be used to indicate that a piece of metal conforms to certain physical dimension characteristics often set down in the form of a particularly 'tight' specification. In a hospital it might be used to indicate some sort of 'professionalism'. If we are to define quality in a way that is useful in its *management*, then we must recognize the need to include in the assessment of quality the true requirements of the 'customer' – the needs and expectations.

*Quality* then is simply *meeting the customer requirements*, and this has been expressed in many ways by other authors:

- 'Fitness for purpose or use' – Juran.
- 'The totality of features and characteristics of a product or service that bear on its ability to satisfy stated or implied needs' – BS 4778, 1987 (ISO 8402, 1986) *Quality Vocabulary*: Part 1, *International Terms*.
- 'Quality should be aimed at the needs of the consumer, present and future' – Deming.
- 'The total composite product and service characteristics of marketing, engineering, manufacture and maintenance through which the product and service in use will meet the expectation by the customer' – Feigenbaum.
- 'Conformance to requirements' – Crosby.

Another word that we should define properly is *reliability*. 'Why do you buy a Volkswagen car?' 'Quality and reliability' comes back the answer. The two are used synonymously, often in a totally confused way. Clearly, part of the acceptability of a product or service will depend on its ability to function satisfactorily *over a period of time*, and it is this aspect of performance that is given the name *reliability*. It is the ability of the product or service to *continue* to meet the customer requirements. Reliability ranks with quality in importance, since it is a key factor in many purchasing decisions where alternatives are being considered. Many of the general management issues related to achieving product or service quality are also applicable to reliability.

It is important to realize that the 'meeting the customer require-ments' definition of quality is not restrictive to the functional charac-teristics of products or services. Anyone with children knows that the quality of some of the products they purchase is more associated with *satisfaction in ownership* than some functional property. This is also true of many items, from antiques to certain items of clothing. The requirements for status symbols account for the sale of some executive cars, certain bank accounts and charge cards, and even hospital beds! The requirements are of paramount importance in the assessment of the quality of any product or service.

By *consistently* meeting customer requirements, we can move to a different plane of satisfaction – *delighting the customer*. There is no doubt that many organizations have so well ordered their capability to meet their customers' requirements time and time again, that this has created a reputation for 'excellence'.

## 1.2   Understanding and building the quality chains

The ability to meet the customer requirements is vital, not only between two separate organizations, but within the same organization.

When the air hostess pulled back the curtain across the aisle and set off with a trolley full of breakfasts to feed the early morning travellers on the short domestic flight into an international airport, she was not thinking of quality problems. Having stopped at the row of seats marked 1ABC, she passed the first tray on to the lap of the man sit-ting by the window. By the time the second tray had reached the lady beside him, the first tray was on its way back to the air hostess with a complaint that the bread roll and jam were missing. She calmly replaced it in her trolley and reached for another – which also had no roll and jam.

The calm exterior of the girl began to evaporate as she discovered two more trays without a complete breakfast. Then she found a good one and, thankfully, passed it over. This search for complete breakfast trays continued down the aeroplane, causing inevitable delays, so much so that several passengers did not receive their breakfasts until the plane had begun its descent. At the rear of the plane could be heard the mutterings of discontent. 'Aren't they slow with breakfast this morning?' 'What is she doing with those trays?' 'We will have indigestion by the time we've landed.'

The problem was perceived by many to be one of delivery or service. They could smell food but they weren't getting any of it, and they were getting really wound up! The air hostess, who had suffered the embarrassment of being the purveyor of defective product and service, was quite wound up and flushed herself, as she returned to the curtain and almost ripped it from the hooks in her haste to hide. She was heard to say through clenched teeth, 'What a bloody mess!'

A problem of quality? Yes, of course, requirements not being met, but where? The passengers or customers suffered from it on the aircraft, but down in the bowels of the organization there was a little man whose job it was to assemble the breakfast trays. On this day the system had broken down – perhaps he ran out of bread rolls, perhaps he was called away to refuel the aircraft (it was a small airport!), perhaps he didn't know or understand, perhaps he didn't care.

Three hundred miles away in a chemical factory ... 'What the hell is Quality Control doing? We've just sent 15,000 litres of lawn weedkiller to CIC and there it is back at our gate – they've returned it as out of spec.' This was followed by an avalanche of verbal abuse, which will not be repeated here, but poured all over the shrinking Quality Control Manager as he backed through his office door, followed by a red faced Technical Director advancing menacingly from behind the bottles of sulphuric acid racked across the adjoining laboratory.

'Yes, what is QC doing?' thought the Production Manager, who was behind a door two offices along the corridor, but could hear the torrent of language now being used to beat the QC man into an admission of guilt. He knew the poor devil couldn't possibly do anything about the rubbish that had been produced except test it, but why should he volunteer for the unpleasant and embarrassing ritual now being experienced by his colleague – for the second time this month. No wonder the QC manager had been studying the middle pages of the *Telegraph* on Thursday – what a job!

Do you recognize these two situations? Do they not happen every day of the week – possibly every minute somewhere in manufacturing or the service industries? Is it any different in banking, insurance, the health service? The inquisition of checkers and testers is the last bastion of desperate systems trying in vain to catch mistakes, stop defectives, hold lousy materials, before they reach the external customer – and woe betide the idiot who lets them pass through!

Two everyday incidents, but why are events like these so common? The answer is the acceptance of one thing – *failure*. Not doing it right the first time at every stage of the process.

Why do we accept failure in the production of artefacts, the provision of a service, or even the transfer of information? In many walks of life we do not accept it. We do not say, 'Well, the nurse is bound to drop the odd baby in a thousand – it's just going to happen'. We do not accept that!

In each department, each office, even each household, there are a series of suppliers and customers. The typist is a supplier to her boss. Is she meeting his requirements? Does he receive error-free typing set out as he wants, it, when he wants it? If so, then we have a quality typing service. Does the air hostess receive from her supplier in the airline the correct food trays in the right quantity?

Throughout and beyond all organizations, whether they be manufacturing concerns, banks, retail stores, universities, hospitals or hotels, there is a series of *quality chains* of customer and suppliers (Figure 1.1) that may be broken at any point by one person or one piece of equipment not meeting the requirements of the customer, internal or external. The interesting point is that this failure usually finds its way to the interface between the organization and its outside customers, and the people who operate at that interface – like the air hostess – usually experience the ramifications. The concept of internal and external customers/suppliers forms the *core* of total quality.

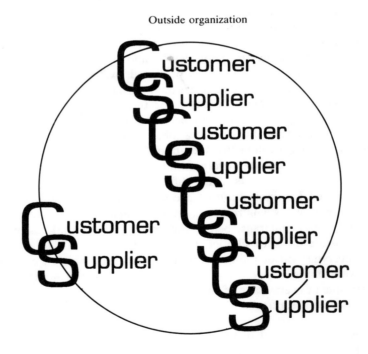

Figure 1.1 *The quality chains*

A great deal is written and spoken about employee motivation as a separate issue. In fact the key to motivation *and* quality is for everyone in the organization to have well-defined customers – an extension of the word beyond the outsider that actually purchases or uses the ultimate product or service to anyone to whom an individual gives a part, a service, information – in other words the results of his or her work.

Quality has to be managed – it will not just happen. Clearly it must involve everyone in the process and be applied throughout the organization. Many people in the support functions of organizations never see, experience, or touch the products or services that their organizations buy or provide, but they do handle or produce things like purchase orders or invoices. If every fourth invoice carries at least one error, what image of quality is transmitted!

Failure to meet the requirements in any part of a quality chain has a way of multiplying, and failure in one part of the system creates problems elsewhere, leading to yet more failure, more problems and so on. The price of quality is the continual examination of the requirements and our ability to meet them. This alone will lead to a 'continuing improvement' philosophy. The benefits of making sure the requirements are met at every stage, every time, are truly enormous in terms of increased competitiveness and market share, reduced costs, improved productivity and delivery performance, and the elimination of waste. The Japanese have called this 'company-wide quality improvement' or CWQI.

## Meeting the requirements

If quality is meeting the customer requirements, then this has wide implications. The requirements may include availability, delivery, reliability, maintainability and cost-effectiveness, among many other features. The first item on the list of things to do is find out what the requirements are. If we are dealing with a customer/supplier relationship crossing two organizations, then the supplier must establish a 'marketing' activity charged with this task.

The marketers must of course understand not only the needs of the customer but also the ability of their own organization to meet them. If my customer places a requirement on me to run 1,500 metres in 4 minutes, then I know I am unable to meet this demand, unless something is done to improve my running performance. Of course I may never be able to achieve this requirement.

Within organizations, between internal customers and suppliers, the transfer of information regarding requirements is frequently poor to totally absent. How many executives really bother to find out what their customers' – their secretaries' – requirements are? Can their handwriting be read, do they leave clear instructions, do the secretaries always know where the boss is? Equally, do the secretaries establish what their bosses need – error-free typing, clear messages, a tidy office? Internal supplier/customer relationships are often the most difficult to manage in terms of establishing the requirements. To achieve quality throughout an organization, each person in the quality chain must interrogate every interface as follows:

*Customers*
- Who are my immediate customers?
- What are their true requirements?
- How do or can I find out what the requirements are?
- How can I measure my ability to meet the requirements?
- Do I have the necessary capability to meet the requirements? (If not, then what must change to improve the capability?)
- Do I continually meet the requirements? (If not, then what prevents this from happening, when the capability exists?)
- How do I monitor changes in the requirements?

*Suppliers*
- Who are my immediate suppliers?
- What are my true requirements?
- How do I communicate my requirements?
- Do my suppliers have the capability to measure and meet the requirements?
- How do I inform them of changes in the requirements?

The measurement of capability is extremely important if the quality chains are to be formed within and without an organization. Each person in the organization must also realize that the supplier's needs and expectations must be respected if the requirements are to be fully satisfied.

To understand how quality may be built into a product or service, at any stage, it is necessary to examine the two distinct, but interrelated aspects of quality:

- Quality of design
- Quality of conformance to design.

**Quality of design**

We are all familiar with the old story of the tree swing (Figure 1.2), but in how many places in how many organizations is this chain of

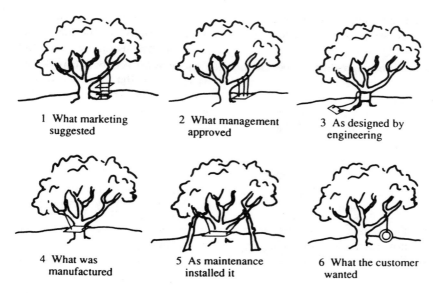

**Figure 1.2** *Quality of design*

activities taking place? To discuss the quality of, say, a chair it is necessary to describe its purpose. What it is to be used for? If it is to be used for watching TV for 3 hours at a stretch, then the typical office chair will not meet this requirement. The difference between the quality of the TV chair and the office chair is not a function of how it was manufactured, but its *design*.

Quality of design is a measure of how well the product or service is designed to achieve the agreed requirements. The beautifully presented gourmet meal will not necessarily please the recipient if he or she is travelling on the highway and has stopped for a quick bite to eat. The most important feature of the design, with regard to achieving quality, is the specification. Specifications must also exist at the internal supplier/customer interfaces if one is to pursue company-wide quality. For example, the company lawyer asked to draw up a contract by the sales manager requires a specification as to its content:

1   Is it a sales, processing or consulting type of contract?
2   Who are the contracting parties?
3   In which countries are the parties located?
4   What are the products involved (if any)?
5   What is the volume?
6   What are the financial, e.g. price, escalation, aspects?

The financial controller must issue a specification of the information he or she needs, and when, to ensure that foreign exchange fluctuations do not cripple the company's finances. The business of sitting down and agreeing a specification at every interface will clarify the true requirements and capabilities. It is the vital first stage for a successful total-quality effort.

There must be a corporate understanding of the organization's quality position in the market place. It is not sufficient that marketing specifies the product or service 'because that is what the customer wants'. There must be an agreement that the operating departments can achieve that requirement. Should they be incapable of doing so, then one of two things must happen: either the organization finds a different position in the market place or substantially changes the operational facilities.

**Quality of conformance to design**

This is the extent to which the product or service achieves the quality of design. What the customer actually receives should conform to the design, and operating costs are tied firmly to the level of conformance achieved. Quality cannot be inspected into products or services; the customer satisfaction must be designed into the whole system. The conformance check then makes sure that things go according to plan.

A high level of inspection or checking at the end is often indicative of attempts to inspect in quality. This may well result in spiralling costs and decreasing viability. The area of conformance to design is concerned largely with the quality performance of the actual operations. It may be salutory for organizations to use the simple matrix of Figure 1.3 to assess how much time they spend doing the right things right. A lot of people, often through no fault of their own, spend a good proportion of the available time doing the right things wrong. There are people (and organizations) who spend time doing the wrong things very well, and even those who occupy themselves doing the wrong things wrong, which can be very confusing!

## 1.3   Managing processes

Every day two men who work in a certain factory scrutinize the results of the examination of the previous day's production, and begin the ritual battle over whether the material is suitable for despatch to the customer. One is called the Production Manager, the other the Quality Control Manager. They argue and debate the evidence before them,

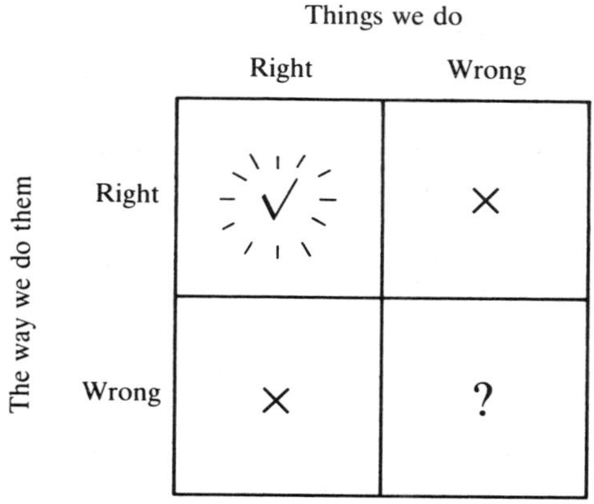

Things we do

**Figure 1.3** *How much time is spent doing the right things right?*

the rights and wrongs of the specification, and each tries to convince the other of the validity of his argument. Sometimes they nearly start fighting.

This ritual is associated with trying to answer the question, '*Have we done the job correctly?*', correctly being a flexible word, depending on the interpretation given to the specification on that particular day. This is not quality *control*, it is *detection* – wasteful detection of bad product before it hits the customer. There is still a belief in some quarters that to achieve quality we must check, test, inspect or measure – the ritual pouring on of quality at the end of the process. This is nonsense, but it is frequently practised. In the office one finds staff checking other people's work before it goes out, validating computer input data, checking invoices, typing, etc. There is also quite a lot of looking for things, chasing why things are late, apologising to customers for lateness, and so on. Waste, waste, waste!

To get away from the natural tendency to rush into the detection mode, it is necessary to ask different questions in the first place. We should not ask whether the job has been done correctly, we should ask first '*Are we capable of doing the job correctly?*' This question has wide implications, and this book is devoted largely to the various activities necessary to ensure that the answer is yes. However, we should realize straight away that such an answer will only be obtained by means of satisfactory methods, materials, equipment, skills and instruction, and a satisfactory 'process'.

**What is a process?**

As we have seen, quality chains can be traced right through the business or service processes used by any organization. A process is the transformation of a set of inputs, which can include actions, methods and operations, into outputs that satisfy customer needs and expectations, in the form of products, information, services or – generally – results. Everything we do is a process, so in each area or function of an organization there will be many processes taking place. For example, a finance department may be engaged in budgeting processes, accounting processes, salary and wage processes, costing processes, etc. Each process in each department or area can be analysed by an examination of the inputs and outputs. This will determine some of the actions necessary to improve quality. There are also functional processes

The output from a process is that which is transferred to somewhere or to someone – the *customer*. Clearly, to produce an output that meets the requirements of the customer, it is necessary to define, monitor and control the inputs to the process, which in turn may be supplied as output from an earlier process. At every supplier–customer interface then there resides a transformation process (Figure 1.4), and every single task throughout an organization must be viewed as a process in this way.

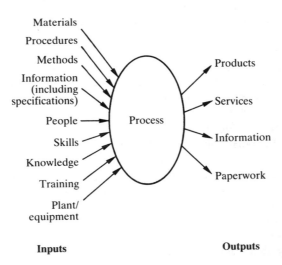

**Figure 1.4** *A process*

Once we have established that our process is capable of meeting the requirements, we can address the next question, '*Do we continue to do the job correctly?*', which brings a requirement to monitor the process and the controls on it. If we now re-examine the first question, 'Have we done the job correctly?', we can see that, if we have been able to answer the other two questions with a yes, we *must* have done the job correctly. Any other outcome would be illogical. By asking the questions in the right order, we have moved the need to ask the 'inspection' question and replaced a strategy of *detection* with one of *prevention.* This concentrates all the attention on the front end of any process – the inputs – and changes the emphasis to making sure the inputs are capable of meeting the requirements of the process. This is a managerial responsibility.

These ideas apply to every transformation process; they all must be subject to the same scrutiny of the methods, the people, skills, equipment and so on to make sure they are correct for the job. A person giving a lecture whose overhead projector equipment will not focus correctly, or whose teaching materials are not appropriate, will soon discover how difficult it is to provide a lecture that meets the requirements of the audience.

In every organization there are some very large processes – groups of smaller processes called *key, critical or business processes.* These are activities the organization must carry out especially well if its mission and objectives are to be achieved. This area will be dealt with in some detail in Chapter 15 on the implementation of TQM. It is crucial if the management of quality is to be integrated into the strategy for the organization.

The *control* of quality clearly can only take place at the point of operation or production – where the letter is typed, the sales call made, the patient admitted, or the chemical manufactured. The act of *inspection is not quality control.* When the answer to 'Have we done the job correctly?' is given indirectly by answering the questions of capability and control, then we have *assured* quality, and the activity of checking becomes one of *quality assurance* – making sure that the product or service represents the output from an effective *system* to ensure capability and control. It is frequently found that organizational barriers between departmental empires encourage the development of testing and checking of services or products in a vacuum, without interaction with other departments. These will be referred to in Chapter 11.

*Quality control* then is essentially the activities and techniques employed to achieve and maintain the quality of a product, process, or service. It includes a monitoring activity, but is also concerned with finding and eliminating causes of quality problems so that the requirements of the customer are continually met.

*Quality assurance* is broadly the prevention of quality problems through planned and systematic activities (including documentation). These will include the establishment of a good quality management system and the assessment of its adequacy, the audit of the operation of the system, and the review of the system itself.

## 1.4  Quality starts with 'marketing'

The author has been asked on more than one occasion if TQM applies to marketing. The answer to the question is not remarkable – it starts there!

The marketing function of an organization must take the lead in establishing the true requirements for the product or service. Having determined the need, marketing should define the market sector and demand, to determine such product or service features as grade, price, quality, timing, etc. For example, a major hotel chain thinking of opening a new hotel or refurbishing an old one will need to consider its location and accessibility before deciding whether it will be predominantly a budget, first-class, business or family hotel.

Marketing will also need to establish customer requirements by reviewing the market needs, particularly in terms of unclear or unstated expectations or preconceived ideas held by customers. Marketing is responsible for determining the key characteristics that determine the suitability of the product or service in the eyes of the customer. This may of course call for the use of market research techniques, data-gathering, and analysis of customer complaints. If possible, quasi-quantitative methods should be employed, giving proxy variables that can be used to grade the characteristics in importance, and decide in which areas superiority over competitors exists. It is often useful to compare these findings with internal perceptions of quality.

Excellent communication between customers and suppliers is the key to total quality; it will eradicate the 'demanding nuisance/idiot' view of customers, which pervades many organizations. Poor communications often occur in the supply chain between organizations, when neither party realizes how poor they are. Feedback from both customers and suppliers needs to be improved where dissatisfied customers and suppliers do not communicate their problems. In such cases non-conformance of purchased products or services is often due to customers' inability to communicate their requirements clearly. If these ideas are also used within an organization, then the internal supplier/customer interfaces will operate much more smoothly.

All the efforts devoted to finding the nature and timing of the demand will be pointless if marketing fails to communicate the requirements promptly, clearly, and accurately to the remainder of the organization. The marketing function should be capable of supplying the company with a formal statement or outline of the requirements for each product or service. This constitutes a preliminary set of *specifications*, which can be used as the basis for service or product design. The information requirements include:

1 Characteristics of performance and reliability – these must make reference to the conditions of use and any environmental factors that may be important.
2 Aesthetic characteristics, such as style, colour, smell, taste, feel, etc.
3 Any obligatory regulations or standards governing the nature of the product or service.

Marketing must also establish systems for feedback of customer information and reaction, and these systems should be designed on a continuous monitoring basis. Any information pertinent to the product or service should be collected and collated, interpreted, analysed, and communicated, to improve the response to customer experience and expectations. These same principles must also be applied inside the organization if continuous improvement at every transformation process interface is to be achieved. If one department of a company has problems recruiting the correct sort of staff, and personnel has not established mechanisms for gathering, analysing, and responding to information on new employees, then frustration and conflict will replace communication and co-operation.

One aspect of the analysis of market demand that extends back into the organization is the review of market readiness of a new product or service. Items that require some attention include assessment of:

1 The suitability of the distribution and customer-service systems.
2 Training of personnel in the 'field'.
3 Availability of spare parts or support staff.
4 Evidence that the organization is capable of meeting customer requirements.

All organizations receive a wide range of information from customers through invoices, payments, requests for information, letters of complaint, responses to advertisements and promotion, etc. An essential component of a system for the analysis of market demand is that this data is channelled quickly into the appropriate areas for action and, if necessary, response.

There are various techniques of market research, but they will not be described in detail in this book, for they are well documented elsewhere. Nevertheless it is worth listing some of the most common and useful general methods that should be considered for use, both externally and internally:

- Customer surveys.
- Quality panel or focus group techniques.
- In-depth interviews.
- Brainstorming and discussions.
- Role rehearsal and reversal.
- Interrogation of trade associations.

The number of methods and techniques for researching market demand is limited only by imagination and funds. The important point to stress is that the supplier, whether the internal individual or the external organization, keeps very close to the customer. Market research, coupled with analysis of complaints data, is an essential part of finding out what the requirements are, and breaking out from the obsession with inward scrutiny that bedevils quality.

## 1.5   Quality in all functions

For an organization to be truly effective, each part of it must work properly together. Each part, each activity, each person in the organization affects and is in turn affected by others. Errors have a way of multiplying, and failure to meet the requirements in one part or area creates problems elsewhere, leading to yet more errors, yet more problems, and so on. The benefits of getting it right first time everywhere are enormous.

Everyone experiences – almost accepts – problems in working life. This causes people to spend a large part of their time on useless activities – correcting errors, looking for things, finding out why things are late, checking suspect information, rectifying and reworking, apologizing to customers for mistakes, poor quality and lateness. The list is endless, and it is estimated that about one-third of our efforts are wasted in this way. In the service sector it can be much higher.

Quality, the way we have defined it as meeting the customer requirements, gives people in different functions of an organization a common language for improvement. It enables all the people, with different abilities and priorities, to communicate readily with one another, in pursuit of a common goal. When business and industry were local, the craftsman could manage more or less on his own. Business is now so complex and employs so many different specialist skills that everyone has to rely on the activities of others in doing their jobs.

Some of the most exciting applications of TQM have materialized from departments that could see little relevance when first introduced to its concepts. Following training, many different departments of organizations can show the use of the techniques. Sales staff can monitor and increase successful sales calls, office staff have used TQM methods to prevent errors in word-processing and improve inputting to computers, customer-service people have monitored and reduced complaints, the distribution department has controlled lateness and disruption in deliveries.

It is worthy of mention that the first points of contact for some outside customers are the telephone operator, the security people at the gate, or the person in reception. Equally the paperwork and support services associated with the product, such as invoices and sales literature and their handlers, must match the needs of the customer. Clearly TQM cannot be restricted to the production or operational areas without losing great opportunities to gain maximum benefit.

Managements that rely heavily on exhortation of the workforce to 'do the right job right the first time', or 'accept that quality is your responsibility', will not only fail to achieve quality but will create division and conflict. These calls for improvement infer that faults are caused only by the workforce and that problems are departmental when, in fact, the opposite is true – most problems are inter-departmental. The commitment of all members of an organization is a requirement of 'company-wide quality improvement'. Everyone must work together at every interface to achieve perfection. And that can only happen if the top management is really committed to quality improvement.

## Chapter highlights

### Quality and competitiveness

- The reputation enjoyed by an organization is built by quality, reliability, delivery and price. Quality is the most important of these competitive weapons.

- Reputations for poor quality last for a long time, and good or bad reputations can become national. The management of quality can be learned and used to improve reputation.
- Quality is meeting the customer requirements, and this is not restricted to the functional characteristics of the product or service.
- Reliability is the ability of the product or service to continue to meet the customer requirements over time.
- Organizations 'delight' the customer by consistently meeting customer requirements, and then achieve a reputation for 'excellence'.

**Understanding and building the quality chains**

- Throughout all organizations there are a series of internal suppliers and customers. These form the so-called 'quality chains', the core of company-wide quality improvement (CWQI).
- The internal customer/supplier relationships must be managed by interrogation, i.e. using a set of questions at every interface. Measurement of capability is vital.
- There are two distinct but interrelated aspects of quality, design and conformance to design. *Quality of design* is a measure of how well the product or service is designed to achieve the agreed requirements. *Quality of conformance to design* is the extent to which the product or service achieves the design. Organizations should assess how much time they spend doing the right things right.

**Managing processes**

- Asking the question 'Have we done the job correctly?' should be replaced by asking 'Are we capable of doing the job correctly?' and 'Do we continue to do the job correctly?'
- Asking the questions in the right order replaces a strategy of *detection* with one of *prevention*.
- Everything we do is a process, which is the transformation of a set of inputs into the desired outputs.
- In every organization there are some key, critical or business processes that must be performed especially well if the mission and objectives are to be achieved.
- Inspection is not *quality control*. The latter is the employment of activities and techniques to achieve and maintain the quality of a product, process or service.
- *Quality assurance* is the prevention of quality problems through planned and systematic activities.

**Quality starts with 'marketing'**

- Marketing establishes the true requirements for the product or service. These must be communicated properly throughout the organization in the form of specifications.

**Quality in all functions**

- All members of an organization need to work together on 'company-wide quality improvement'. The co-operation of everyone at every interface is required to achieve perfection.

# 2 Commitment and leadership

## 2.1 The total quality management approach

'What is quality management?' Something that is best left to the experts is often the answer to this question. But this is avoiding the issue, because it allows executives and managers to opt out. Quality is too important to leave to the so called 'quality professionals'; it cannot be achieved on a company-wide basis if it is left to the experts. Equally dangerous, however, are the uninformed who try to follow their natural instincts because they 'know what quality is when they see it'. This type of intuitive approach will lead to serious attitude problems, which do no more than reflect the understanding and knowledge of quality that are present in an organization.

The organization which believes that the traditional quality control techniques, and the way they have always been used, will resolve their quality problems is wrong. Employing more inspectors, tightening up standards, developing correction, repair and rework teams do not promote quality. Traditionally, quality has been regarded as the responsibility of the QC department, and still it has not yet been recognized in some organizations that many quality problems originate in the service or administrative areas.

Total Quality Management is far more than shifting the responsibility of *detection* of problems from the customer to the producer. It requires a comprehensive approach that must first be recognized and then implemented if the rewards are to be realized. Today's business environment is such that managers must plan strategically to maintain a hold on market share, let alone increase it. We have known for years that consumers place a higher value on quality than on loyalty to home-based producers, and price is no longer the major determining factor in consumer choice. Price has been replaced by quality, and this is true in industrial, service, hospitality, and many other markets.

TQM is an approach to improving the competitiveness, effectiveness and flexibility of a whole organization. It is essentially a way of planning, organizing and understanding each activity, and depends on each individual at each level. For an organization to be truly effective, each part of it must work properly together towards the same goals, recognizing that each person and each activity affects and in turn is affected by others. TQM is also a way of ridding people's lives of wasted effort by bringing everyone into the processes of improvement, so that results are achieved in less time. The methods and techniques used in TQM can be applied throughout any organization. They are equally useful in the manufacturing, public service, health care, education and hospitality industries. TQM needs to gain ground rapidly and become a way of life in many organizations.

The impact of TQM on an organization is, firstly, to ensure that the management adopts a strategic overview of quality. The approach must focus on developing a *problem-prevention* mentality; but it is easy to underestimate the effort that is required to change attitudes and approaches. Many people will need to undergo a complete change of 'mindset' to unscramble their intuition, which rushes into the detection/inspection mode to solve quality problems – 'We have a quality problem, we had better check every letter – take two samples out of each sack – check every widget twice', etc.

The correct mindset may be achieved by looking at the sort of barriers that exist in key areas. Staff will need to be trained and shown how to reallocate their time and energy to studying their processes in teams, searching for causes of problems, and correcting the causes, not the symptoms, once and for all. This will require of management a positive, thrusting initiative to promote the right-first-time approach to work situations. Through *quality improvement teams*, which will need to be set up, these actions will reduce the inspection-rejection syndrome in due course. If things are done correctly first time round, the usual problems that create the need for inspection for failure will disappear.

The managements of many firms may think that their scale of operation is not sufficiently large, that their resources are too slim, or that the need for action is not important enough to justify implementing TQM. Before arriving at such a conclusion, however, they should examine the existing quality performance by asking the following questions:

1  Is any attempt being made to assess the costs arising from errors, defects, waste, customer complaints, lost sales, etc.? If so, are these costs minimal or insignificant?
2  Is the standard of quality management adequate and are attempts being made to ensure that quality is given proper consideration at the design stage?
3  Are the organization's quality systems – documentation, procedures, operations etc. – in good order?

4 Have personnel been trained in how to prevent errors and quality problems? Do they anticipate and correct potential causes of problems, or do they find and reject?

5 Do job instructions contain the necessary quality elements, are they kept up-to-date, and are employees doing their work in accordance with them?

6 What is being done to motivate and train employees to do work right first time?

7 How many errors and defects, and how much wastage occurred last year? Is this more or less than the previous year?

If satisfactory answers can be given to most of these questions, an organization can be reassured that it is already well on the way to using adequate quality procedures and management. Even so, it may find that the introduction of TQM causes it to reappraise quality activities throughout. If answers to the above questions indicate problem areas, it will be beneficial to review the top management's attitude to quality. Time and money spent on quality-related activities are *not* limitations of profitability; they make significant contributions towards greater efficiency and enhanced profits.

## 2.2 Commitment and policy

To be successful in promoting business efficiency and effectiveness, TQM must be truly organization-wide, and it must start at the top with the Chief Executive or equivalent. The most senior directors and management must all demonstrate that they are serious about quality. The middle management have a particularly important role to play, since they must not only grasp the principles of TQM, they must go on to explain them to the people for whom they are responsible, and ensure that their own commitment is communicated. Only then will TQM spread effectively throughout the organization. This level of management must also ensure that the efforts and achievements of their subordinates obtain the recognition, attention and reward that they deserve.

The Chief Executive of an organization must accept the responsibility for and commitment to a quality policy in which he/she must really believe. This commitment is part of a broad approach extending well beyond the accepted formalities of the quality assurance function. It creates responsibilities for a chain of quality interactions between the marketing, design, production/operations, purchasing, distribution and service functions. Within each and every department of the organization at all levels, starting at the top, basic changes of attitude will be required to operate TQM. If the owners or directors of the organization do not recognize and accept their responsibilities for the initiation and operation of TQM, then these changes will not happen. Controls, systems and techniques are very important in TQM, but they are not the primary requirement. It is more an attitude of mind, based on pride in the job and teamwork, and it requires from the management total commitment, which must then be extended to all employees at all levels and in all departments.

Senior management commitment must be obsessional, not lip service. It is possible to detect real commitment; it shows on the shop floor, in the offices, in the hospital wards – at the point of operation. Going into organizations sporting poster-campaigning for quality instead of belief, one is quickly able to detect the falseness. The people are told not to worry if quality problems arise, 'just do the best you can', 'the customer will never notice'. The opposite is an organization where total quality means something can be seen, heard, felt. Things happen at this operating interface as a result of *real* commitment. Material problems are corrected with suppliers, equipment difficulties are put right by improved maintenance programmes or replacement, people are trained, change takes place, partnerships are built, continuous improvement is achieved.

**The quality policy**

A sound quality policy, together with the organization and facilities to put it into effect, is a fundamental requirement, if a company is to begin to implement TQM. Every organization should develop and state its policy on quality, together with arrangements for its implementation. The contents of the policy should be made known to all employees. The preparation and implementation of a properly thought out quality policy, together with continuous monitoring, make for smoother production or service operation, minimize errors and reduce waste.

Management must be dedicated to the regular improvement of quality, not simply a one-step improvement to an acceptable plateau. These ideas must be set out in a *quality policy* that requires top management to:

1 Establish an 'organization' for quality.
2 Identify the customer' needs and perception of needs.
3 Assess the ability of the organization to meet these needs economically.

4   Ensure that bought-in materials and services reliably meet the required standards of performance and efficiency.
5   Concentrate on the prevention rather than detection philosophy.
6   Educate and train for quality improvement.
7   Review the quality management systems to maintain progress.

The quality policy must be publicized and understood at all levels of the organization.

Given below are three examples of good company quality policies. Each has its own style and impact, and is consistent with the other policies within the companies.

*Quality policy A*

1   Quality improvement is primarily the responsibility of management.
2   In order to bring everyone in the organization into quality improvement, management must enable all employees to participate in the preparation, implementation and evaluation of improvement activities.
3   Quality improvement must be tackled and followed up in a systematic and planned manner. This applies to every part of our organization.
4   Quality improvement must be a continuous process.
5   The organization must concentrate more than ever on its customers and suppliers, both external and internal.
6   The performance of our competitors must be known to all relevant units.
7   Important suppliers will be closely involved in our quality policy. This relates to both external and internal suppliers of goods, resources, and services.
8   Widespread attention will be given to education and training activities, which will be assessed with regard to their contribution to the quality policy.
9   Publicity will be given to the quality policy in every part of the organization so that everyone may understand it. All available methods and media will be used for its internal and external promotion and communication.
10  Reporting on the progress of the implementation of the policy will be a permanent agenda item in management meetings.

*Quality policy B*

1   The goal of the organization is to achieve superior external and internal customer satisfaction levels. The directors are committed to

the implementation of supporting managerial and operating systems to realize that goal.

2  Quality is defined by the customer as products and services that throughout their life meet needs and expectations at a cost that represents value.

3  Quality will be achieved by preventing problems rather than by detecting and correcting them after they occur.

4  All work that is done by company employees, suppliers and product outlets is part of a process that creates a product or service for a customer. Each person will be able to influence some part of that process and affect the quality of its output and the ultimate customer' satisfaction.

5  Sustained quality excellence requires continuous improvement. This means, regardless of how good present performance may be, it can be improved.

6  People provide the intelligence and generate the actions that are necessary to realize improvements.

7  Each employee is a customer for work done by other employees or suppliers, with a right to expect good work from others and an obligation to contribute work of high calibre.

8  Each process owner is responsible for reviewing existing systems and procedures and for revising them, as required, in line with this policy statement.

*Quality policy C*

The policy of the company is that its products and services will meet the requirements of its customers at all times.

It is the company's intention to become and remain the market leader with respect to the quality of its products and services.

The company believes in the concept of customer–supplier working together and continually striving for improvements in quality.

All the company' employees will have a positive commitment to quality and respond quickly and effectively to achieve the performance standards required.

The quality policy is based on four fundamental principles:

- *Quality is defined* as conforming to requirements, once the needs of our customers, our suppliers and our own processes, have been very carefully specified.
- *The system of quality management* concentrates on prevention, looking at our processes, identifying the opportunities for errors and taking action to eliminate them.

- *The standard of quality* is 'no failures', everyone understanding how to do their job and the standards required, and doing it right first time.
- *The measurement of quality* is the cost of nonconformity and the eventual cost of getting it right.

Each department will develop its own quality policies, based on these principles, taking into account its own particular circumstances.

To ensure that the policy is fully implemented, each department is responsible for specifying the customer's requirements (the customer could be another department within the company), preparing adequate procedures, and providing the facilities to see that these requirements are met.

The quality policy is the concern of all employees, and the principles and objectives will be communicated as widely as possible. Practical assistance and training will be given, where necessary, to ensure the relevant knowledge and experience are acquired for successful implementation of this policy.

## 2.3   Creating or changing the culture

The culture within an organization is formed by a number of components:

1   Behaviours based on people interactions.
2   Norms resulting from working groups.
3   Dominant values adopted by the organization.
4   Rules of the game for getting on.
5   The climate.

Culture in any 'business' may be defined then as the beliefs that pervade the organization about how business should be conducted, and how employees should behave and should be treated. Any organization needs a vision framework that includes its *guiding philosophy, core values and beliefs* and a *purpose*. These should be combined into a *mission*, which provides a vivid description of what things will be like when it has been achieved.

The *guiding philosophy* drives the organization and is shaped by the leaders through their thoughts and actions. It should reflect the vision of an organization rather than the vision of a single leader, and should evolve with time, although organizations must hold on to the *core* elements.

The *core values and beliefs* represent the organization's basic principles about what is important in business, its conduct, its social responsibility and its response to changes in the environment. They should act as a guiding force, with clear and authentic values, which are focused on employees, suppliers, customers, society at large, safety, shareholders, and generally stakeholders.

The *purpose* of the organization should be a development from the core values and beliefs and should quickly and clearly convey how the organization is to fulfil its role.

The *mission* will translate the abstractness of philosophy into tangible goals that will move the organization forward and make it perform to its optimum. It should not be limited by the constraints of strategic analysis, and should be proactive not reactive. Strategy is subservient to mission, the strategic analysis being done after, not during, the mission setting process.

## Control

The effectiveness of an organization and its people depends on the extent to which each person and department perform their role and move towards the common goals and objectives. Control is the process by which information or feedback is provided so as to keep all functions on track. It is the sum total of the activities that increase the probability of the planned results being achieved. Control mechanisms fall into three categories, depending upon their position in the managerial process:

| *Before the fact* | *Operational* | *After the fact* |
|---|---|---|
| Strategic plan | Observation | Annual reports |
| Action plans | Inspection and correction | Variance reports |
| Budgets | Progress review | Audits |
| Job descriptions | Staff meetings | Surveys |
| Individual performance objectives | Internal information and data systems | Performance review |
| Training and development plans | Training programmes | Evaluation of training |

Many organizations use after-the-fact controls, causing managers to take a reactive rather than a proactive position. Such 'crisis-orientation' needs to be replaced by a more anticipative one in which the focus is on preventive or before-the-fact controls.

Attempting to control performance through systems, procedures, or techniques *external* to the individual is not an effective approach, since it relies on 'controlling' others; individuals should be responsible for their own actions. An externally based control system can result in a high degree of concentrated effort in a specific area if the system is overly structured, but it can also cause negative consequences to surface:

1   Since all rewards are based on external measures, which are imposed, the 'team members' often focus all their efforts on the measure itself, e.g. to have it set lower (or higher) than possible, to manipulate the information which serves to monitor it, or to dismiss it as someone else's goal not theirs. In the budgeting process, for example, distorted figures are often submitted by those who have learned that their 'honest projections' will be automatically altered anyway.
2   When the rewards are dependent on only one or two limited targets, all efforts are directed at those, even at the expense of others. If short-term profitability is the sole criterion for bonus distribution or promotion, it is likely that investment for longer-term growth areas will be substantially reduced. Similarly, strong emphasis and reward for output or production may result in lowered quality.
3   The fear of not being rewarded, or even being criticized, for performance that is less than desirable may cause some to withhold information that is unfavourable but nevertheless should be flowing into the system.
4   When reward and punishment are used to motivate performance, the degree of risk-taking may lessen and be replaced by a more cautious and conservative approach. In essence, the fear of failure replaces the desire to achieve.

The following problem situations have been observed by the author and his colleagues within companies that have taken part in research and consultancy on quality management:

• The goals imposed are seen or known to be unrealistic. If the goals perceived by the subordinate are in fact accomplished, then the subordinate has proved himself wrong. This clearly has a negative effect on the effort expended, since few people are motivated to prove themselves wrong!
• Where individuals are stimulated to commit themselves to a goal, and where their personal pride and self-esteem are at stake, then the level of motivation is at a peak. For most people the toughest critic and the hardest taskmaster they confront is not their immediate boss but themselves.

- Directors and managers are often afraid of allowing subordinates to set the goals for fear of them being set too low, or loss of control over subordinate behaviour. It is also true that many do not wish to set their own targets, but prefer to be told what is to be accomplished.

TQM is concerned with moving the focus of control from outside the individual to within, the objective being to make everyone accountable for their own performance, and to get them committed to attaining quality in a highly motivated fashion. The assumptions a director or manager must make in order to move in this direction are simply that people do not need to be coerced to perform well, and that people want to achieve, accomplish, influence activity, and challenge their abilities. If there is belief in this, then only the techniques remain to be discussed.

Total Quality Management is user-driven – it cannot be imposed from outside the organization, as perhaps can a quality standard or statistical process control. This means that the ideas for improvement must come from those with knowledge and experience of the processes, activities and tasks; this has massive implications for training and follow-up. TQM is not a cost-cutting or productivity improvement device in the traditional sense, and it must not be used as such. Although the effects of a successful programme will certainly reduce costs and improve productivity, TQM is concerned chiefly with changing attitudes and skills so that the culture of the organization becomes one of preventing failure – doing the right things, right first time, every time.

## 2.4   Effective leadership

Some management teams have broken away from the traditional style of management; they have made a 'managerial breakthrough'. Their new approach puts their organizations head and shoulders above competitors in the fight for sales, profits, resources, funding and jobs. Many service organizations are beginning to move in the same way, and the successful quality-based strategy they are adopting depends very much on effective leadership.

Effective leadership starts with the Chief Executive's vision, capitalizing on market or service opportunities, continues through a strategy that will give the organization competitive advantage, and leads to business or service success. It goes on to embrace all the beliefs and values held, the decisions taken and the plans made by anyone anywhere in the organization, and the focusing of them into effective, value-adding action.

Together, effective leadership and total quality management result in the company or organization doing the right things, right first time.

The five requirements for effective leadership are the following.

## 1  Developing and publishing clear documented corporate beliefs and objectives – a mission statement

Executives must express values and beliefs through a clear vision of what they want their company or organization to be, and through objectives – what they specifically want to achieve in line with the basic beliefs. Together, they define what the company or organization is all about. The senior management team will need to spend some time away from the 'coal face' to do this and develop their programme for implementation.

Clearly defined and properly communicated beliefs and objectives, which can be summarized in the form of a mission statement, are essential if the directors, managers and other employees are to work together as a winning team. The beliefs and objectives should address:

- The definition of the business, e.g. the needs that are satisfied or the benefits provided.
- A commitment to effective leadership and quality.
- Target sectors and relationships with customers, and market or service position.
- The role or contribution of the company, organization, or unit, e.g. example, profit-generator, service department, opportunity-seeker.
- The distinctive competence – a brief statement which applies only to that organization, company or unit.
- Indications for future direction – a brief statement of the principal plans which would be considered.
- Commitment to monitoring performance against customers' needs and expectations, and continuous improvement.

The mission statement and the broad beliefs and objectives may then be used to communicate an inspiring vision of the organization's future. The top management must then show *TOTAL COMMITMENT* to it.

**2   Developing clear and effective strategies and supporting plans for achieving the mission and objectives**

The achievement of the company or service objectives requires the development of business or service strategies, including the strategic positioning in the 'market place'. Plans for implementing the strategies can then be developed. Strategies and plans can be developed by senior managers alone, but there is likely to be more commitment to them if employee participation in their development and implementation is encouraged.

**3   Identifying the critical success factors and critical processes**

The next step is the identification of the *critical success factors* (CSFs), a term used to mean the most important subgoals of a business or organization. CSFs are what must be accomplished for the mission to be achieved. The CSFs are followed by the key, critical or business processes for the organization – the activities that must be done particularly well for the CSFs to be achieved. This process is described in some detail in Chapter 15 on implementation.

**4   Reviewing the management structure**

Defining the corporate objectives and strategies, CSFs and critical processes might make it necessary to review the organizational structure. Directors, managers and other employees can be fully effective only if an effective structure based on process management exists. This includes both the definition of responsibilities for the organization's management and the operational procedures they will use. These must be the agreed best ways of carrying out the critical processes.

The review of the management structure should include the establishment of a process quality improvement team structure throughout the organization.

**5   Empowerment – encouraging effective employee participation**

For effective leadership it is necessary for management to get very close to the employees. They must develop effective communications – up, down and across the organization – and take action on what is communicated; and they must encourage good communications between all suppliers and customers.

Particular attention must be paid to the following.

*Attitudes*

The key attitude for managing any winning company or organization may be expressed as follows: 'I will personally understand who my customers are and what are their needs and expectations of me; I will measure how well I am satisfying their needs and expectations and I will take whatever action is necessary to satisfy them fully. I will also understand and communicate my requirements to my suppliers, inform them of changes and provide feedback on their performance'. This attitude must start at the top – with the Chairman or Chief Executive. It must then percolate down, to be adopted by each and every employee. That will happen only if managers lead by example. Words are cheap and will be meaningless if employees see from managers' actions that they do not actually believe or intend what they say.

*Abilities*

Every employee must be able to do what is needed and expected of him or her, but it is first necessary to decide what is really needed and expected. If it is not clear what the employees are required to do and what standards of performance are expected, how can managers expect them to do it?

Train, train, train and train again. Training is very important, but it can be expensive if the money is not spent wisely. The training must be related to needs, expectations, and process improvement. It must be planned and *always* its effectiveness must be reviewed.

*Participation*

If all employees are to participate in making the company or organization successful (directors and managers included), then they must also be trained in the basics of disciplined management.

They must be trained to:

E   **Evaluate** – the situation and define their objectives.
P   **Plan** – to achieve those objectives fully.
D   **Do**, i.e. implement the plans.
C   **Check** – that the objectives are being achieved.
A   **Amend**, i.e. take corrective action if they are not.

The word 'disciplined' applied to people at all levels means that they will do what they say they will do. It also means that in whatever they do they will go through the full process of Evaluate, Plan, Do, Check and Amend, rather than the more traditional and easier option of starting by doing rather than evaluating. This will lead to a never-ending improvement helix (Figure 2.1)

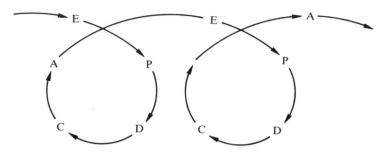

**Figure 2.1** *The helix of never-ending improvement*

This basic approach needs to be backed up with good project management, planning techniques and problem-solving methods, which can be taught to anyone in a relatively short period of time. The project management enables changes to be made successfully and the problem-solving helps people to remove the obstacles in their way. Directors and managers need this training as much as other employees.

## 2.5   Ten points for senior management – the foundations of the TQM model

The vehicle for achieving effective leadership is Total Quality Management. We have seen that it covers the entire organization, all the people and all the functions, including external organizations and suppliers. In the first two chapters, several facets of TQM have been reviewed, including:

* Recognizing customers and discovering their needs.
* Setting standards that are consistent with customer requirements.
* Controlling processes, including systems, and improving their capability.
* Management's responsibility for setting the guiding philosophy, quality policy, etc., and providing motivation through leadership and equipping people to achieve quality.
* Empowerment of people at all levels in the organization to act for quality improvement.

The task of implementing TQM can be daunting, and the Chief Executive and directors faced with it may become confused and irritated by the proliferation of theories and packages. A simplification is required. The *core* of TQM must be the customer–supplier interfaces, both internally and externally, and the fact that at each interface there are processes to convert inputs to outputs. Clearly, there must be commitment to building-in quality through management of the inputs and processes.

How can senior managers and directors be helped in their understanding of what needs to be done to become committed to quality and implement the vision? Some American and Japanese quality 'gurus' have each set down a number of points or absolutes – words of wisdom in management and leadership – and many organizations are using these to establish a policy based on quality. These have been distilled down and modified here to ten points for senior management to adopt.

*1   The organization needs long term COMMITMENT to constant improvement*

There must be a constancy of purpose, and commitment to it must start from the top. The quality improvement process must be planned on a truly organization-wide basis, i.e. it must embrace all locations and departments and must include customers, suppliers, and subcontractors. It cannot start in 'one department' in the hope that the programme will spread from there.

The place to start the quality process is in the boardroom – leadership must be by example. Then the process must *progressively* expand to embrace all parts of the organization. It is wise to avoid the 'blitz' approach to TQM implementation, for it can lead to a lot of hype but no real changes in behaviour.

*2   Adopt the philosophy of zero errors/defects to change the CULTURE to right first time*

This must be based on a thorough understanding of the customer's needs and expectations, and on teamwork, developed through employee participation and rigourous application of the EPDCA helix.

*3   Train the people to understand the CUSTOMER–SUPPLIER relationships*

Again the commitment to customer needs must start from the top, from the Chairman or Chief Executive. Without that, time and effort will be wasted. Customer orientation must then be achieved for each and every employee, directors and managers. The concept of internal customers and suppliers must be thoroughly understood and used.

*4  Do not buy products or services on price alone – look at the TOTAL COST*

Demand continuous improvement in everything, including suppliers. This will bring about improvements in product, service and failure rates. Continually improve the product or the service provided externally, so that the total costs of doing business are reduced.

*5  Recognize that improvement of the SYSTEMS needs to be managed*

Defining the performance standards expected and the systems to achieve them is a managerial responsibility. The rule has to be that the systems will be in line with the shared needs and expectations and will be part of the continuous improvement process.

*6  Adopt modern methods of SUPERVISION and TRAINING – eliminate fear*

It is all too easy to criticize mistakes, but it often seems difficult to praise efforts and achievements. Recognize and publicize efforts and achievements and provide the right sort of training, facilitation and supervision.

*7  Eliminate barriers between departments by managing the PROCESS – improve COMMUNICATIONS and TEAMWORK*

Barriers are often created by 'silo management', in which departments are treated like containers that are separate from one another. The customers are not interested in departments; they stand outside the organization and see slices through it – the *processes*. It is necessary to build teams and improve communications around the processes.

*8  Eliminate the following*:

- Arbitrary goals without methods.
- All standards based only on numbers.
- Barriers to pride of workmanship.
- Fiction. Get *FACTS* by using the correct *TOOLS*.

At all times it is essential to know how well you are doing in terms of satisfying the customers' needs and expectations. Help all employees to know *how* they will achieve their goals and how well they are doing.

Traditional piecework will not survive in a TQM environment, or *vice-versa*, because it creates barriers and conflict. People should be proud of what they do and not be encouraged to behave like monkeys being thrown peanuts.

Train people to measure and report performance in language that the people doing the job can understand. Encourage each employee to measure his/her own performance. Do not stop with measuring performance in the organization – find out how well other organizations (competitive or otherwise) are performing against similar needs and expectations (*benchmark* against best practice).

The costs of quality mismanagement and the level of firefighting are excellent factual indicators of the internal health of an organization. They are relatively easily measured and simple for most people to understand.

*9   Constantly educate and retrain – develop the 'EXPERTS' in the business.*

The experts in any business are the people who do the job every day of their lives. The 'energy' that lies within them can be released into the organization through education, training, encouragement and the chance to participate.

*10   Develop a SYSTEMATIC approach to manage the implementation of TQM*

TQM should not be regarded as a woolly-minded approach to running an organization. It requires a carefully planned and fully integrated strategy, derived from the mission. That way it will help any organization to realize its vision.

*Summary*

- Identify *customer supplier* relationships.
- Manage *processes*.
- Change the *culture*.
- Improve *communication*.
- Show *commitment*.

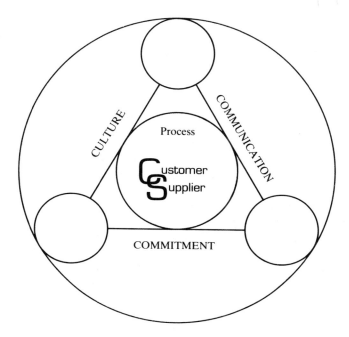

**Figure 2.2** *Total quality management model – the 'soft' outcomes*

These form the basis of the first part of a model for TQM – the 'soft' outcomes of TQM (Figure 2.2). The process core must be surrounded, however, by some 'hard' management necessities:

1 *Systems* (based on a good international standard, see Part 2 of this book).
2 *Tools* (for analysis, correlations, and predictions for action for continuous improvement to be taken, see Part 3 of this book).
3 *Teams* (the councils, quality improvement teams, quality circles, corrective action teams, etc., see Part 4 of this book).

The model now provides a multi-dimensional TQM 'vision' against which a particular company's status can be examined, or against which a particular approach to TQM implementation may be compared and weaknesses highlighted. It is difficult to draw in only two dimensions, but Figure 2.3 is an attempt to represent the major features of the model, the implementation of which is dealt with in Part Five.

One of the greatest tangible benefits of improved quality is the increased market share that results, rather than just the reduction in

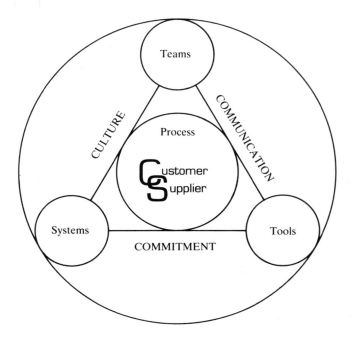

**Figure 2.3** *Total quality management model – major features*

quality costs. The evidence for this can already be seen in some of the major consumer and industrial markets of the world. Superior quality can also be converted into premium prices. Quality clearly correlates with profit. The less tangible benefit of greater employee participation in quality is equally, if not more, important in the longer term. The pursuit of continual improvement must become a way of life for everyone in an organization if it is to succeed in today's competitive environment.

## Chapter highlights

### The Total Quality Management approach

- TQM is a comprehensive approach to improving competitiveness, effectiveness and flexibility through planning, organizing and understanding each activity, and involving each individual at each level. It is useful in all types of organization.

- TQM ensures that management adopts a strategic overview of quality and focuses on prevention, not detection, of problems.
- It often requires a mindset change to break down existing barriers. Managements that doubt the applicability of TQM should ask questions about the operation's costs, errors, wastes, standards, systems, training and job instructions.

## Commitment and policy

- TQM starts at the top, where serious obsessional commitment to quality must be demonstrated. Middle management also has a key role to play in communicating the message.
- Every Chief Executive must accept the responsibility for commitment to a quality policy that deals with the organization for quality, the customer needs, the ability of the organization, supplied materials and services, education and training, and review of the management systems for never-ending improvement.

## Creating or changing the culture

- The culture of an organization is formed by the beliefs, behaviours, norms, dominant values, rules and climate in the organization.
- Any organization needs a vision framework, comprising its guiding philosophy, core values and beliefs, purpose, and mission.
- The effectiveness of an organization depends on the extent to which people perform their roles and move towards the common goals and objectives.
- TQM is concerned with moving the focus of control from the outside to the inside of individuals, so that everyone is accountable for his/her own performance.

## Effective leadership

- Effective leadership starts with the Chief Executive's vision and develops into a strategy for implementation.
- Top management must develop the following for effective leadership: clear beliefs and objectives in the form of a mission statement; clear and effective strategies and supporting plans; the critical success factors and critical processes; the appropriate management structure; employee participation through empowerment, and the EPDCA helix.

**Ten points for senior management – the foundations**

- Total quality is the key to effective leadership through commitment to constant improvement, a right first time philosophy, training people to understand customer–supplier relationships, not buying on price alone, managing systems improvement, modern supervision and training, managing processes through teamwork and improved communications, elimination of barriers and fear, constant education and 'expert' development, a systematic approach to TQM implementation.
- The core of TQM is the customer–supplier relationship, where the processes must be managed. The 'soft' outcomes of TQM – the culture, communications, and commitment provide the foundation for the TQM model.
- The process core must be surrounded by the 'hard' management necessities of systems, tools and teams. The model provides a framework against which an organization's progress towards TQM can be examined.

# 3 Design for quality

## 3.1 Innovation, design and improvement

All businesses competing on the basis of quality need to update their products, processes and services periodically. In markets such as electronics, audio and visual goods, and office automation, new variants of products are offered frequently – almost like fashion goods. While in other markets the pace of innovation may not be as fast and furious, there is no doubt that the rate of change for product, service and process design has accelerated on a broad front.

Innovation entails both the invention and design of radically new products and services, embodying novel ideas, discoveries and advanced technologies, *and* the continuous development and improvement of existing products, services, and processes to enhance their performance and quality. It may also be directed at reducing costs of production or operations throughout the life cycle of the product or service system.

In many organizations innovation is predominantly either technology-led, e.g. in some chemical and engineering industries, or marketing-led, e.g. in some food companies. What is always striking about leading product or service innovators is that their developments are market-led, which is different from marketing-led. The latter means that the marketing function takes the lead in product and service developments. But most leading innovators identify and set out to meet the existing and potential demands profitably, and therefore are market-led, constantly striving to meet the requirements even more effectively through appropriate experimentation.

Commitment to quality in the most senior management helps to build quality throughout the design process and to ensure good relationships and communication between various groups and functional areas. Designing customer satisfaction into products and services contributes greatly to competitive success. Clearly, it does not guarantee it, because the conformance aspect of quality must be present and the operational processes must be capable of producing to the design. As in the marketing/operations interfaces, it is never acceptable to design a product, service, system or process that the customer wants but the organization is incapable of achieving.

The design process, then, often concerns technological innovation in response to, or in anticipation of, changing market requirements and trends in technology. Those companies with impressive records of product- or service-led growth have demonstrated a state-of-the-art approach to innovation based on three principles:

- *Strategic balance* to ensure that both old and new product service developments are important. Updating old products, services and processes, ensures continuing cash generation from which completely new products may be funded.
- *Top management approach* to design to set the tone and ensure that commitment is the common objective by visibly supporting the design effort. Direct control should be concentrated on critical decision points, since over-meddling by very senior people in day-to-day project management can delay and demotivate staff.
- *Teamwork*, to ensure that once projects are under way, specialist inputs, e.g. from marketing and technical experts, are fused and problems are tackled simultaneously. The teamwork should be urgent yet informal, for too much formality will stifle initiative, flair and the fun of design.

The extent of the design activity should not be underestimated, but it often is. Many people associate design with *styling* of products, and this is certainly an important aspect. But for certain products and many service operations the *secondary design* considerations are vital. Anyone who has bought an 'assemble-it-yourself' kitchen unit will know the importance of the design of the assembly instructions, for example. Aspects of design that affect quality in this way are packaging, customer-service arrangements, maintenance routines, warranty details and their fulfilment, spare-part availability, etc.

An industry that has learned much about the secondary design features of its products is personal computers. Many of the problems of customer dissatisfaction experienced in this market have not been product design features but problems with user manuals, availability and loading of software, and applications. For technically complex products or service systems, the design and marketing of after-sales arrangements are an essential component of the design activity. The design of production equipment and its layout to allow ease of access for repair and essential maintenance, or simple use as intended, widens the management of design quality into suppliers and contractors and requires their total commitment.

Proper design of plant and equipment plays a major role in the elimination of errors, defectives, and waste. Correct initial design also obviates the need for costly and wasteful modifications to be carried out after the plant or equipment has been constructed. It is at the plant design stage that such important matters as variability, reproducibility, ease of use in operation, maintainability, etc. should receive detailed consideration.

**Designing**

If quality design is taking care of all aspects of the customer's requirements, including cost, production, safe and easy use, and maintainability of products and services, then *designing* must take place in all aspects of:

- Identifying the need (including need for change).
- Developing that which satisfies the need.
- Checking the conformance to the need.
- Ensuring that the need is satisfied.

Designing covers every aspect, from the identification of a problem to be solved, usually a market need, through the development of design concepts and prototypes to the generation of detailed specifications or instructions required to produce the artefact or provide the service. It is the process of presenting needs in some physical form, initially as a solution, and then as a specific configuration or arrangement of materials, resources, equipment, and people.

## 3.2 Quality function deployment (QFD) – the house of quality

The 'house of quality' is the framework of the approach to design management known as quality function deployment (QFD). It originated in Japan in 1972 at Mitsubishi's Kobe shipyard, but it has been developed in numerous ways by Toyota and its suppliers, and many other organizations. The house of quality (HOQ) concept, initially referred to as quality tables, has been used successfully by manufacturers of integrated circuits, synthetic rubber, construction equipment, engines, home appliances, clothing, and electronics, mostly Japanese. Ford and General Motors use it, and other organizations, including AT&T, Bell Laboratories, Digital Equipment, Hewlett-Packard,

Procter & Gamble, ITT, Rank Xerox, Jaguar, and Mercury have applications. In Japan its design applications include public services, retail outlets, and apartment layout.

Quality function deployment (QFD) is a 'system' for designing a product or service, based on customer demands, with the participation of members of all functions of the supplier organization. It translates the customer's requirements into the appropriate technical requirements for each stage. The activities included in QFD are:

1   Market research.
2   Basic research.
3   Invention.
4   Concept design.
5   Prototype testing.
6   Final-product or service testing.
7   After-sales service and trouble-shooting.

These are performed by people with different skills in a team whose composition depends on many factors, including the products or services being developed and the size of the operation. In many customer industries, such as cars, video equipment, electronics, and computers, 'engineering' designers are seen to be heavily into designing. But in other industries and service operations designing is carried out by people who do not carry the word 'designer' in their job title. The failure to recognize the design inputs they make, and to provide appropriate training and support, will limit the success of the design activities and result in some offering that does not satisfy the customer. This is particularly true of internal customers.

**The QFD team in operation**

The first step of a QFD exercise is to form a cross-functional QFD team. Its purpose is to take the needs of the market and translate them into such a form that they can be satisfied within the operating unit and delivered to the customers.

As with all organizational problems, the structure of the QFD Team must be decided on the basis of the detailed requirements of each organization. One thing, however, is clear – close liaison must be maintained at all times between the design, marketing and operational functions represented in the team.

The QFD team must answer three questions – WHO, WHAT and HOW, i.e.

*WHO* are the customers?
*WHAT* does the customer need?
*HOW* will the needs be satisfied?

WHO may be decided by asking 'Who will benefit from the success-ful introduction of this product, service, or process?' Once the cus-tomers have been identified, WHAT can be ascertained through an interview/questionnaire process, or from the knowledge and judgement of the QFD team members. HOW is more difficult to determine, and will consist of the attributes of the product, service, or process under development. This will constitute many of the action steps in a 'QFD strategic plan'.

WHO, WHAT, and HOW are entered into the QFD matrix or grid of 'house of quality', which is a simple 'quality table'. The *WHAT*s are recorded in rows and the HOWs are placed in the columns.

The house of quality provides structure to the design and develop-ment cycle, often likened to the construction of a house, because of the shape of matrices when they are fitted together. The key to building the house is the focus on the customer requirements, so that the design and development processes are driven more by what the customer needs than by innovations in technology. This ensures that more effort is used to obtain the vital customer information. It may increase the initial planning time in a particular development project, but the time, including design and redesign, taken to bringing a product of service to the market will be reduced.

This requires that marketing people, design staff (including engi-neers), and production/operations personnel work closely together from the time the new service, process, or product is conceived. It will need to replace in many organizations the 'throwing it over the wall' approach, where a solid wall exists between each pair of functions (Figure 3.1).

The HOQ provides an organization with the means for inter-depart-mental or inter-functional planning and communications, starting with the so-called customer attributes (CAs). These are phrases customers use to describe product, process, and service characteristics.

A complete QFD project will lead to the construction of a sequence of house of quality diagrams, which translate the customer require-ments into specific operational process steps. For example, the 'feel' that customers like on the steering wheel of a motor car may translate into a specification for 45 standard degrees of synthetic polymer hard-ness, which in turn translates into specific manufacturing process steps, including the use of certain catalysts, temperatures, processes, and additives.

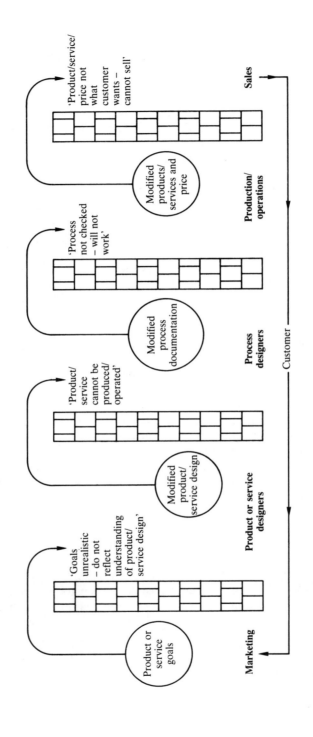

**Figure 3.1** *'Throw it over the wall.' The design and development process is sequential and walled into separate functions*

The first steps in QFD lead to a consideration of the product as a whole, and subsequent steps to consideration of the individual components. For example, a complete hotel service would be considered at the first level, but subsequent QFD exercises would tackle the restaurant, bedrooms and reception. Each of the sub-services would have customer requirements, but they all would need to be compatible with the general service concept.

**The QFD or house of quality tables**

Figure 3.2 shows the essential components of the quality table or HOQ diagram. The construction begins with the *customer requirements*, which are determined through the 'voice of the customer' – the marketing and market research activities. These are entered into the blocks to the left of the central relationship matrix. Understanding and prioritizing the customer requirements by the QFD team may require the use of competitive and compliant analysis, focus groups, and the analysis of market potential. The prime or broad requirements should lead to the detailed WHATs.

Once the customer requirements have been determined and entered into the table, the *importance* of each is rated and rankings are added. The use of the 'emphasis technique' or paired comparison may be helpful here (see Chapter 9).

Each customer requirement should then be examined in terms of customer rating; a group of customers may be asked how they perceive the performance of the organization's product or service versus those of competitors'. These results are placed to the right of the central matrix. Hence the customer requirements' importance rankings and competition ratings appear from left to right across the house.

The WHATs must now be converted into the HOWs. These are called the *technical design requirements* and appear on the diagram from top to bottom in terms of requirements, rankings (or costs) and ratings against competition (technical benchmarking, see Chapter 7). These will provide the 'voice of the process'.

The technical requirements themselves are placed immediately above the central matrix and may also be given a hierarchy of prime and detailed requirements. Immediately below the central relationship matrix appear the rankings of technical difficulty, development time, or costs. These will enable the QFD team to discuss the efficiency of the various technical solutions. Below the technical rankings on the diagram comes the benchmark data, which compares the technical processes of the organization against its competitors'.

The *central relationship matrix* is the working core of the house of

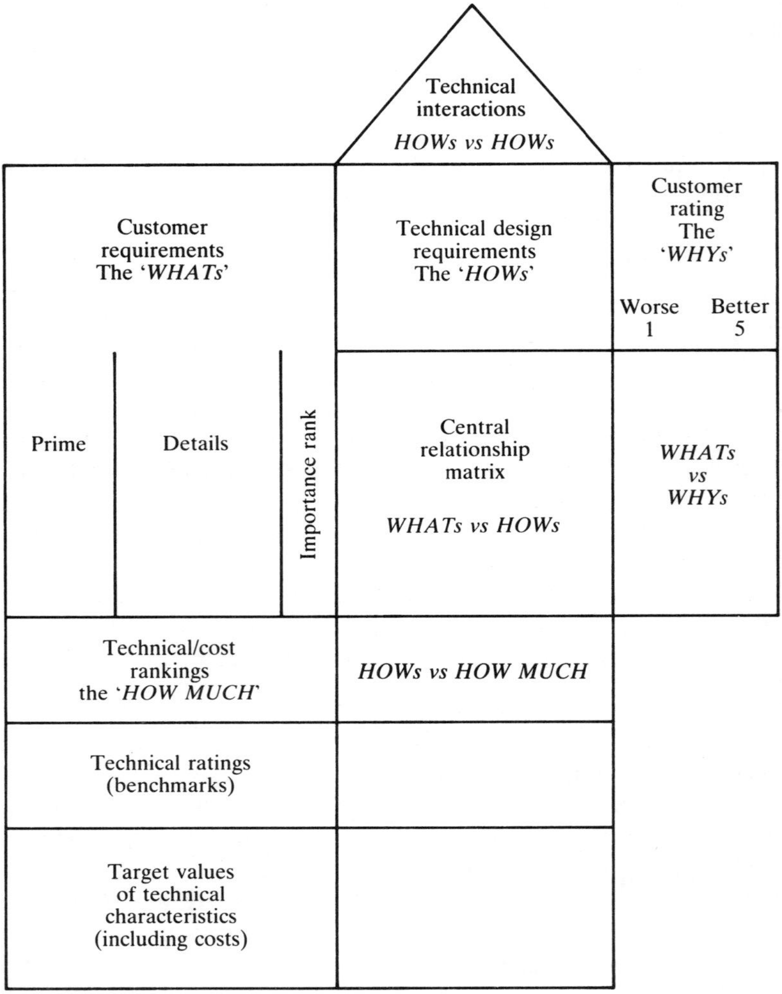

**Figure 3.2** *The house of quality*

quality diagram. Here the WHATs are matched with the HOWs, and each customer requirement is systematically assessed against each technical design requirement. The nature of any relationship – strong positive, positive, neutral, negative, strong negative – is shown by symbols in the matrix. The QFD team carries out the relationship estimation, using experience and judgement, the aim being to identify HOW the WHATs may be achieved. All the HOWs listed must be necessary and together sufficient to achieve the WHATs. Blank rows (customer requirement not met) and columns (redundant technical characteristics) should not exist.

The roof of the house shows the interactions between the technical design requirements. Each characteristic is matched against the others, and the diagonal format allows the nature of relationships to be displayed. The symbols used are the same as those in the central matrix.

The complete QFD process is time-consuming, because each cell in the central and roof matrices must be examined by the whole team. The team must examine the matrix to determine which technical requirement will need design attention, and the costs of that attention will be given in the bottom row. If certain technical costs become a major issue, the priorities may then be changed. It will be clear from the central matrix if there is more than one way to achieve a particular customer requirement, and the roof matrix will show if the technical requirements to achieve one customer requirement will have a negative effect on another technical issue.

The very bottom of the house of quality diagram shows the *target values* of the *technical characteristics*, which are expressed in physical terms. They can only be decided by the team after discussion of the complete house contents. While these targets are the physical output of the QFD exercise, the whole process of information-gathering, structuring, and ranking generates a tremendous improvement in the team's cross-functional understanding of the product/service design delivery system. The target technical characteristics may be used to generate the next level house of quality diagram, where they become the WHATs, and the QFD process determines the further details of HOW they are to be achieved. In this way the process 'deploys' the customer requirements all the way to the final operational stages. Figure 3.3 shows how the target technical characteristics at each level become the input to the next level matrix.

QFD progresses now through the use of the 'seven new planning tools' and other standard techniques such as value analysis,[1] experimental design,[2] statistical process control,[3] and so on. The seven new tools are described in Chapter 10.

### The benefits of QFD

The aim of the HOQ is to co-ordinate the inter-functional activities and skills within an organization. This should lead to products and services designed, produced/operated, and marketed so that customers will want to purchase them and continue doing so.

The use of competitive information in QFD should help to prioritize

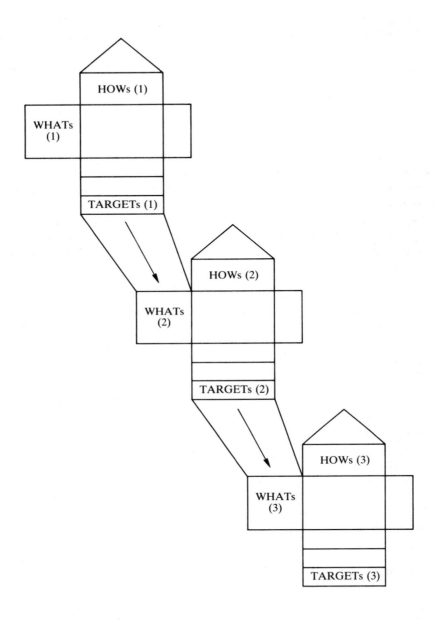

**Figure 3.3** *The 'deployment' of the 'voice of the customer' through quality tables*

resources and to structure the existing experience and information. This allows the identification of items that can be acted upon.

There should be reductions in the number of midstream design changes, and these reductions in turn will limit post-introduction problems and reduce implementation time. Because QFD is consensus-based, it promotes teamwork and creates communications at functional interfaces, while also identifying required actions. It should lead to a 'global view' of the development process, from a consideration of all the details.

If QFD is introduced systematically, it should add structure to the information, generate a framework for sensitivity analysis, and provide documentation, which must be 'living' and adaptable to change. In order to understand the full impact of QFD it is necessary to examine the changes that take place in the team and the organization during the design and development process. The main benefit of QFD is of course the increases in customer satisfaction, which may be measured in terms of, for example, reductions in warranty claims.

## 3.3 Design control and management

Design, like any other activity, must be carefully managed. A flow-chart of the various stages and activities involved in the design and development process appears in Figure 3.4.

By structuring the design process in this way, it is possible to:

* Control the various stages.
* Check that they have been completed.
* Decide which management functions need to be brought in and at what stage.
* Estimate the level of resources needed.

The design control must be carefully handled to avoid stifling the creativity of the designer(s), which is crucial in making design solutions a reality.

It is clear that the design process requires a range of specialized skills, and the way in which these skills are managed, the way they interact, and the amount of effort devoted to the different stages of the design and development process is fundamental to the quality, producibility, and price of the service or final product. A QFD team approach to the management of design can play a major role in the success of a project.

It is never possible to exert the same tight control on the design

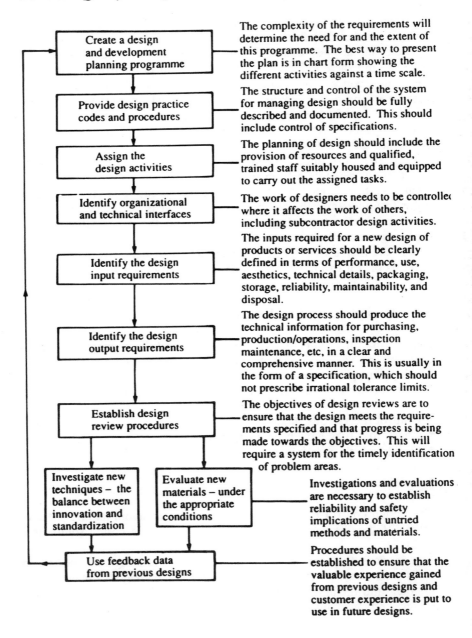

**Figure 3.4** *The design control process*

effort as on other operational efforts, yet the cost and the time used are often substantial, and both must appear somewhere within the organization's budget.

Certain features make control of design difficult:

1    No design will ever be 'complete' in the sense that, with effort, some modification or improvement cannot be made.
2    Few designs are entirely novel. An examination of most 'new' products, services or processes will show that they employ existing techniques, components or systems to which have been added a comparatively small novel element.
3    The longer the time spent on a design, the less the increase in the value of the design unless a technological breakthrough is achieved. This diminishing return from the design effort must be carefully managed.
4    External and/or internal customers will impose limitations on design time and cost. It is as difficult to imagine a design project whose completion date is not implicitly fixed, either by a promise to a customer, the opening of a trade show or exhibition, a seasonal 'deadline', a production schedule or, some other constraint, as it is to imagine an organization whose funds are unlimited, or a product whose price has no ceiling.

**Design review**

Design review is used to ensure that the process of designing progresses towards the objectives of the programme. It does this by studying the process and identifying problem areas systematically and in time for them to be solved. The aims of design reviews are to establish that:

- The design of the service or product will meet all the specified performance criteria.
- The product or service being designed can be produced, inspected, tested or checked, installed, operated, and maintained to provide satisfaction to the 'customer'.
- All possible design alternatives have been considered.
- Any statutory requirements will be met.
- There is adequate documentation to define the design and how the service or product is to be used and maintained.

Design reviews should cover all the quality-related factors, and checklists of these should be drawn up for each review. These are usually carried out at the preliminary, intermediate, and final stages of the design process, by people who represent the relevant disciplines or by a QFD team. The extent of the design review, the membership of the review team, and the methods used will depend on many factors, including:

1   Service or product application.
2   'State of the art'.
3   Complexity of the design,
4   Competence of the designers or originators.
5   Similarity with previous designs.
6   Degree of standardization.

The design review methods to be used should be identified and recorded, together with the results of the review. Techniques of value analysis, reliability engineering, and service- or product-testing may be incorporated. The main theme of the review must be objectivity, which often requires the use of experienced specialists, who take the formal design review meetings very seriously, with agendas, minutes, and action plans for follow-up.

### The use of computer-aided design (CAD) in quality

The tremendous speed and vast strorage capacity of a computer aids the design process in a number of ways:

1   Quantities of data can be held in the computer's store and withdrawn with such ease that it becomes possible to refer readily to previous designs and experience, and respond very quickly to the customer requirements.
2   Computer graphics may well permit a visual display of a design under various conditions, so that various ideas and changes can be immediately observed.
3   The computer can store the results of the design process and issue them in a useful form, often obviating the need for the preparation of drawings.
4   A library of 'ready-made' designs can be easily stored in and retrieved from a computer.
5   Frequently repeated, and long, tedious calculations can be carried out rapidly. Without a computer, a designer will reduce the need for calculations by using tables or graphs of 'established standards' or 'good practice'. These, to become manageable, are the abbreviated results either of a few calculations or of a series of trials, and in either case contain ample 'safety' factors, which usually over-

compensate for the inadequacies of the calculations. As a result, the design produced may not meet the requirements or may be unnecessarily costly in some way. The computer enables these calculations to be carried out as and when needed, reducing wasted effort. Some calculations are so lengthy that they cannot be carried out by hand. A computer may perform these if appropriate software is available.

6  The computer's abilities may be used to check the effect of modifications. The manual effort of examining the effect of changing one or another of the constituent parameters may be so great that no such examination is made. This may result in accepting a result which could be modified.

Computer-aided design is so common in some industries that organizations that intend to compete successfully for market share cannot avoid it as a way of life. In industries where it is less used breakthroughs will continually update the need for companies to adopt CAD in the most unlikely situations.

**Total design processes**

Quality of design, then, concerns far more than the product or service design and its ability to meet the customer requirements. It is also about the activities of design and development. The appropriateness of the actual *design process* has a profound influence on the quality performance of any organization, and much can be learned by examining successful organizations and how their strategies for research, design, and development are linked to the efforts of marketing and operations. In some quarters this is referred to as 'total design', and the term 'simultaneous engineering' has been used. This is an integrated approach to a new product or service introduction, similar in many ways to QFD in using multifunction teams or task forces to ensure that research, design, development, manufacturing, purchasing, supply, and marketing all work in parallel from concept through to the final launch of the product or service into the market place, including servicing and maintenance.

## 3.4  Specifications and standards

There is a strong relationship between standardization and specification. To ensure that a product or a service is *standardized* and may be repeated a large number of times in exactly the manner required, *specifications* must be written so that they are open to only one interpretation. The requirements, and therefore the quality, must be built into the design specification. There are national and international standards which, if used, help to ensure that specifications will meet certain accepted criteria of technical or managerial performance, safety, etc.

Standardization does not guarantee that the best design or specification is selected. It may be argued that the whole process of standardization slows down the rate and direction of technological development, and affects what is produced. If standards are used correctly, however, the process of drawing up specifications should provide opportunities to learn more about particular innovations and to change the standards accordingly.

It is possible to strike a balance between innovation and standardization. Clearly, it is desirable for designers to adhere where possible to past-proven materials and methods, in the interests of reliability, maintainability and variety control. Hindering designers from using recently developed materials, components, or techniques, however, can cause the design process to stagnate technologically. A balance must be achieved by analysis of materials, products and processes proposed in the design, against the background of their known reproducibility and reliability. If breakthrough innovations are proposed, then analysis or testing should be directed objectively, justifying their adoption in preference to the established alternatives.

One aspect of design specification that is often debated is the setting of realistic tolerances and the selection of appropriate standards. This is required for, and at, all stages of the design and development process, and is an important step in translating a design brief into specifications that can be used by production personnel or in the operation of the service system. The aim should be to reflect the tolerances that are the true requirements of the product or service function and are capable of being achieved. It is indicative of the lack of communication in many organizations that some production people claim that their colleagues in marketing or design set unnecessarily tight tolerances to make life in production more difficult. Sales people or designers, on the other hand, have been known to set tighter limits than necessary in order to encourage production to concentrate on 'controlling' the process and thereby achieve the true requirements. This conflict, which is explained quantitatively in Reference 3, leads only to increased variability of processes and greater mismatch between the specifications and the capability of the process.

The specification is the principal document in respect of attaining and maintaining quality, irrespective of the product or service.

Without it, there is no basis for the control of quality, and we cannot be sure that a pair of shoes of a certain size bought in the UK will be the same size as a pair bought in the USA, France, or Australia. We could never be confident that, by quoting a number, we may obtain a replacement part for a motor car that will fit perfectly, or that a bar code will register the same information each time it is scanned.

It is useful to define a specification. The International Standards Organization (ISO) defines it in ISO 8402 (1986) as 'The document that prescribes the requirements with which the product or service has to conform'. A document not giving a detailed statement or description of the requirements to which the product, service or process must comply cannot be regarded as a specification, and this is true of much sales literature.

The specification conveys the customer requirements to the supplier to allow the product or service to be designed, engineered, produced, or operated by means of conventional or stipulated equipment, techniques, and technology. The basic requirements of a specification are that it gives the:

* Performance requirements of the product of service.
* Parameters – such as dimensions, concentration, turn-round time – which describe the product or service adequately (these should be quantified and include the units of measurement).
* Materials to be used by stipulating properties or referring to other specifications.
* Method of production or operations.
* Inspection/testing/checking requirements.
* References to other applicable specifications or documents.

To fulfil its purpose the specification must be written in terminology that is readily understood, and in a manner that is unambiguous and so cannot be subject to differing interpretation. This is not an easy task, and one which requires all the expertise and knowledge available. Good specifications are usually the product of much discussion, deliberation and sifting of information and data, and represent tangible output from a QFD team.

## 3.5 Quality design in the service sector

The emergence of the services sector has been suggested by economists to be part of the natural progression in which economic dominance changes first from agriculture to manufacturing and then to services. It is argued that if income elasticity of demand is higher for services than it is for goods, then as incomes rise, resources will shift toward services. The continuing growth of services verifies this, and is further explained by changes in culture, health, fitness, safety, demography and life styles.

In considering the design of services it is important to consider the differences between goods and services. Some authors argue that the marketing and design of goods and services should conform to the same fundamental rules, whereas others claim that there is a need for a different approach to services because of the recognizable differences between the goods and services themselves.

In terms of design, it is possible to recognize three distinct elements in the service package – the physical elements or facilitating goods, the explicit service or sensual benefits, and implicit service or psychological benefits. In addition, the particular characteristics of service delivery systems may be itemized:

- Intangibility.
- Perishability.
- Simultaneously.
- Heterogeneity.

It is difficult, if not impossible, to design the intangible aspects of a service, since consumers often must use experience or the reputation of a service organization and its representatives to judge quality.

Perishability is often an important issue in services, since it is often impossible or undesirable to hold stocks of the explicit service element of the service package. This aspect often requires that service operation and service delivery must exist simultaneously.

Simultaneity occurs because the consumer must be present before many services can take place. Hence services are often formed in small and dispersed units, and it is difficult to take advantage of economies of scale. There is evidence that the emergence of computer and communications technologies is changing this in sectors such as banking, but contact continues to be necessary for the majority. Design considerations here include the environment and the systems used. Service facilities, procedures, and systems should be designed with the customer in mind, as well as the 'product' and the human resources. Managers need a picture of the total span of the operation, so that factors which are crucial to success are not neglected. This clearly means that the functions of marketing, design, and operations cannot be separated in services, and this must be taken into account in the design of the operational controls, such as the diagnosing of individual customer expectations. A QFD approach here is most appropriate.

Heterogeneity of services occurs in consequence of explicit and implicit service elements relying on individual preferences and perceptions. Differences exist in the outputs of organizations generating the same service, within the same organization, and even the same employee on different occasions. Clearly, unnecessary variation needs to be controlled, but the variety attributed to estimating, and then matching, the consumers' requirements is essential to customer satisfaction and must be designed into the systems. This inherent variability does, however, make it difficult to set precise quantifiable standards for all the elements of the service.

In the design of services it is useful to classify them in some way. Several sources from the literature on the subject help us to place services in one of five categories:

- Service factory.
- Service shop.
- Mass service.
- Professional service.
- Personal services.

Several service attributes have particular significance for the design of service operations:

1 *Labour intensity* – the ratio of labour costs incurred to the value of plant and equipment used (people versus equipment-based services).
2 *Contact* – the proportion of the total time required to provide the service for which the consumer is present in the system.
3 *Interaction* – the extent to which the consumer actively intervenes in the service process to change the content of the service; this includes customer participation to provide information from which needs can be assessed, and customer feedback from which satisfaction levels can be inferred.
4 *Customization* – which includes *choice* (providing one or more selections from a range of options, which can be single or fixed) and *adaptation* (the interaction process in which the requirement is decided, designed and delivered to match the need).
5 *Nature of service act* – either tangible, i.e. perceptible to touch and can be owned, or intangible, i.e. insubstantial.
6 *Recipient of service* – either people or things.

Table 3.1 gives a list of some services with their assigned attribute types and Table 3.2 shows how these may be used to group the services under the various classifications.

**Table 3.1** *A classification of selected services*

| Service | Labour intensity | Contact | Inter-action | Custom-ization | Nature of act | Recipient of service |
|---|---|---|---|---|---|---|
| Accountant | High | Low | High | Adapt | Intangible | Things |
| Architect | High | Low | High | Adapt | Intangible | Things |
| Bank | Low | Low | Low | Fixed | Intangible | Things |
| Beautician | High | High | High | Adapt | Tangible | People |
| Bus service | Low | High | Low | Choice | Tangible | People |
| Cafeteria | Low | High | High | Choice | Tangible | People |
| Cleaning firm | High | Low | Low | Fixed | Tangible | Things |
| Clinic | Low | High | High | Adapt | Tangible | People |
| Coach service | Low | High | Low | Choice | Tangible | People |
| Sports coaching | High | High | High | Adapt | Intangible | People |
| College | High | High | Low | Fixed | Intangible | People |
| Courier firm | High | Low | Low | Adapt | Tangible | Things |
| Dental practice | High | High | High | Adapt | Tangible | People |
| Driving school | High | High | High | Adapt | Intangible | People |
| Equip. hire | Low | Low | Low | Choice | Tangible | Things |
| Finance consult. | High | Low | High | Adapt | Intangible | Things |
| Hairdresser | High | High | High | Adapt | Tangible | People |
| Hotel | High | High | Low | Choice | Tangible | People |
| Leisure centre | Low | High | High | Choice | Tangible | People |
| Maintenance | Low | Low | Low | Choice | Tangible | Things |
| Nursery | High | Low | Low | Fixed | Tangible | People |
| Optician | High | High | High | Adapt | Tangible | People |
| Postal service | Low | Low | Low | Adapt | Tangible | Things |
| Rail service | Low | High | Low | Choice | Tangible | People |
| Repair firm | Low | Low | Low | Adapt | Tangible | Things |
| Restaurant | High | High | Low | Choice | Tangible | People |
| Service station | Low | High | High | Choice | Tangible | People |
| Solicitors | High | Low | High | Adapt | Intangible | Things |
| Take away | High | Low | Low | Choice | Tangible | People |
| Veterinary | High | Low | High | Adapt | Tangible | Things |

It is apparent that services are part of almost all organizations and not confined to the service sector. What is clear is that the service classifications and different attributes must be considered in any service design process.

(The author is grateful to the contribution made by John Dotchin to this section of Chapter 3.)

**Table 3.2** *Grouping of similar services*

| PERSONAL SERVICES | |
|---|---|
| Driving school | Sports coaching |
| Beautician | Dental practice |
| Hairdresser | Optician |

| SERVICE SHOP | |
|---|---|
| Clinic | Cafeteria |
| Leisure centre | Service station |

| PROFESSIONAL SERVICES | |
|---|---|
| Accountant | Architect |
| Finance consult. | Solicitors |
| Veterinary | |

| MASS SERVICES | |
|---|---|
| Hotel | Restaurant |
| College | Bus service |
| Coach service | Rail service |
| Take away | Nursery |
| Courier firm | |

| SERVICE FACTORY | |
|---|---|
| Cleaning firm | Postal service |
| Repair firm | Equip. hire |
| Maintenance | Bank |

## Chapter highlights

### Innovation, design and improvement

- All businesses need to update their products, processes and services.
- Innovation entails both invention and design, *and* continuous improvement of existing products, services, and processes.
- Leading product/service innovations are market-led. This requires a commitment at the top to building in quality throughout the design process. Moreover, the operational processes must be capable of achieving the design.
- State-of-the-art approach to innovation is based on a strategic balance of old and new, top management approach to design, and teamwork. The 'styling' of products must also be matched by secondary design considerations, such as operating instructions and software support.

### Quality function deployment (QFD) – the house of quality

- The 'house of quality' is the framework of the approach to design management known as quality function deployment (QFD). It provides structure to the design and development cycle, which is driven by customer needs rather than innovation in technology.
- QFD is a system for designing a product or service, based on customer demands, and bringing in all members of the supplier organisation.
- A QFD team's purpose is to take the needs of the market and translate them into such a form that they can be satisfied within the operating unit.
- The QFD team answers the following questions. WHO are the customers? WHAT do the customers need? HOW will the needs be satisfied?
- The answers to the WHO, WHAT and HOW questions are entered into the QFD matrix or quality table, one of the seven new tools of planning and design (Chapter 10).
- The foundations of the house of quality are the customer requirements; the framework is the central planning matrix, which matches the 'voice of the customer' with the 'voice of the processes' (the technical descriptions and capabilities); and the roof is the interrelationships matrix between the technical design requirements.
- The benefits of QFD include customer-driven design, prioritizing of resources, reductions in design changes and implementation time, and improvements in teamwork, communications, functional interfaces, and customer satisfaction.

### Design control and management

- Design must be managed and controlled through planning, practice codes, procedures, activities assignments, identification of organizational and technical interfaces and design input requirements, review investigation and evaluation of new techniques and materials, and use of feedback data from previous designs.
- Computers aid the design process (CAD) through handling large quantities of data, producing excellent graphics, storing designs, performing complex calculations, and predicting the effects of modifications.
- Total design or 'simultaneous engineering' is similar to QFD and uses multifunction teams to provide an integrated approach to product or service introduction.

**Specifications and standards**

- There is a strong relation between standardization and specifications. If standards are used correctly, the process of drawing up specifications should provide opportunities to learn more about innovations and change standards accordingly.
- The aim of specifications should be to reflect the true requirements of the product/service that are capable of being achieved.

**Quality design in the service sector**

- In the design of services three distinct elements may be recognized in the service package: physical (facilitating goods), explicit service (sensual benefits), and implicit service (psychological benefits). Moreover, the characteristics of service delivery may be itemized as intangibility, perishability, simultaneity, and heterogeneity.
- Services may be classified generally as service factory, service shop, mass service, professional service, and personal service. The service attributes that are important in designing services include labour intensity, contact interaction, customerization, nature of service act, and the direct recipient of the act.
- Use of this framework allows services to be grouped under the five classifications.

**References**

1  See K G Lockyer, A P Muhlemann and J S Oakland, *Production and Operations Management*, 6th edition, Pitman, 1992
2  See R Caulcutt, *Statistics in Research and Development*, 2nd edition, Chapman and Hall, 1991.
3  See J S Oakland and R F Followell, *Statistical Process Control*, 2nd edition, Butterworth-Heinemann, 1990.

# Part Two
# TQM – The Role of the Quality System

I must create a System or be enslaved by another man's.
*William Blake*, 1757–1827, from 'Jerusalem'

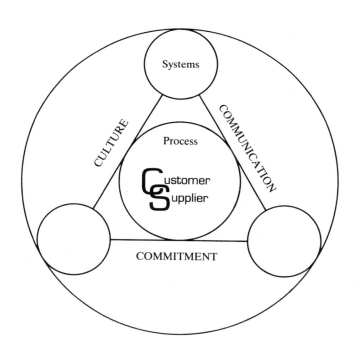

# 4 Planning for quality

## 4.1 Quality planning

Systematic planning is a basic requirement for effective quality management in all organizations. For quality planning to be useful, however, it must be part of a continuous review process that has as its objective zero errors or defectives, through a strategy of never ending improvement. Before an appropriate total quality management system can be developed, it is necessary to carry out a preliminary analysis to ensure that a quality organization structure exists, that the resources required will be made available, and that the various assignments will be carried out. This analysis has been outlined in the flowchart of Figure 4.1. The answers to the questions will generate the appropriate action plans.

In quality planning it is always necessary to review existing programmes within the organization's functional areas, and these may be compared with the results of the preliminary analysis to appraise the strengths and weaknesses in quality throughout the business or operation. When this has been done, the required systems and programmes may be defined in terms of detailed operating plans, procedures and techniques. This may proceed through the flowchart of Figure 4.2, which provides a logical approach to developing a multifunctional total quality management system.

### A quality plan

A quality plan is a document which is specific to each product, activity or service (or group) that sets out the necessary quality-related activities. The plan should include references to any:

- Purchased material or service specifications.
- Quality system procedures.
- Product formulation or service type.
- Process control.

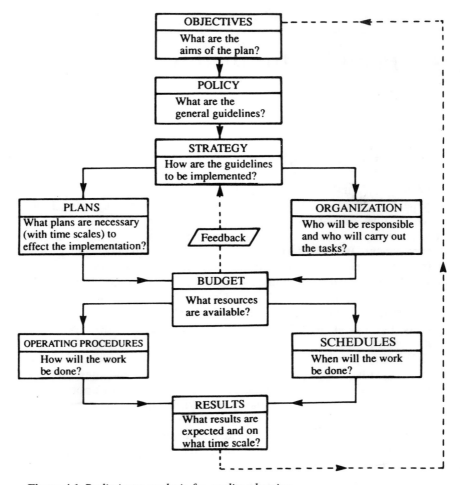

**Figure 4.1** *Preliminary analysis for quality planning*

- Sampling and inspection procedures.
- Packaging or distribution specifications.
- Miscellaneous, relevant procedures.

Such a quality plan might form part of a detailed operating procedure.

For projects relating to new products or services, or to new processes, written quality plans should be prepared to define:

1   Specific allocation of responsibility and authority during the different stages of the project.

2   Specific procedures, methods and instructions to be applied throughout the project.
3   Appropriate inspection, testing, checking, or audit programmes required at various defined stages.
4   Methods for changes or modifications in the plan as the project proceeds.

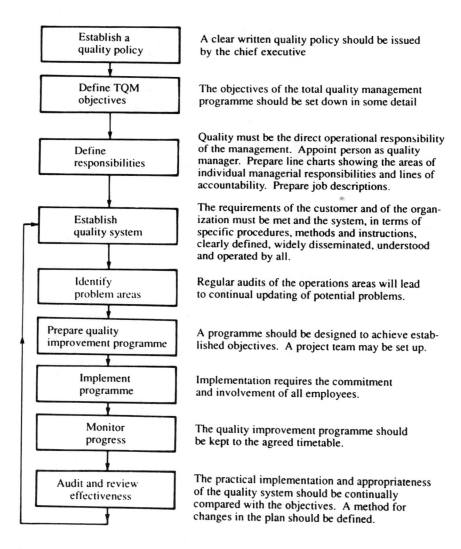

| | |
|---|---|
| Establish a quality policy | A clear written quality policy should be issued by the chief executive |
| Define TQM objectives | The objectives of the total quality management programme should be set down in some detail |
| Define responsibilities | Quality must be the direct operational responsibility of the management. Appoint person as quality manager. Prepare line charts showing the areas of individual managerial responsibilities and lines of accountability. Prepare job descriptions. |
| Establish quality system | The requirements of the customer and of the organization must be met and the system, in terms of specific procedures, methods and instructions, clearly defined, widely disseminated, understood and operated by all. |
| Identify problem areas | Regular audits of the operations areas will lead to continual updating of potential problems. |
| Prepare quality improvement programme | A programme should be designed to achieve established objectives. A project team may be set up. |
| Implement programme | Implementation requires the commitment and involvement of all employees. |
| Monitor progress | The quality improvement programme should be kept to the agreed timetable. |
| Audit and review effectiveness | The practical implementation and appropriateness of the quality system should be continually compared with the objectives. A method for changes in the plan should be defined. |

**Figure 4.2** *Plan for a quality system*

Some of the main points in the planning of quality relate very much to the *inputs* of processes:

*Plant/equipment* – the design, layout, and inspection of plant and equipment, including heating, lighting, storage, disposal of waste, etc.

*Processes* – the design and monitoring of processes to reduce to a minimum the possibility of malfunction and/or failure.

*Workplace* – the establishment and maintenance of suitable, clean and orderly places of work.

*Facilities* – the provision and maintenance of adequate facilities.

*Procedures* – the preparation of procedures for all operations. These may be in the form of general plans and guides rather than tremendous detail, but they should include specific operational duties and responsibilities.

*Training* – the provision of effective training in quality, technology, process and plant operation.

*Information* – the lifeblood of all quality management systems. All processes should be operated according to the simple rules:

(a)   no data collection without recording,
(b)   no recording without analysis,
(c)   no analysis without action (see also Chapter 5).

The quality plan should focus on providing action to prevent cash leaking away through waste. If the quality management system does not achieve this, then there is something wrong with the plan and the way it has been set up or operated – not with the principle. The whole approach should be methodical and systematic, and designed to function irrespective of changes in management or personnel.

The principles and practice of setting up a good quality-management system are set out in Chapters 5 and 6. The quality system must be planned and developed to take into account all other functions, such as design, development, production or operations, subcontracting, installation, maintenance, and so on. The remainder of this chapter is devoted to certain aspects of the quality-planning process that require specific attention or techniques.

## 4.2   Flowcharting

In the systematic planning or examination of any process, whether that be a clerical, manufacturing, or managerial activity, it is necessary to record the series of events and activities, stages and decisions in a form that can be easily understood and communicated to all. If improvements are to be made, the facts relating to the existing method must be recorded first. The statements defining the process should lead to its understanding and will provide the basis of any critical examination necessary for the development of improvements. It is essential therefore that the descriptions of processes are accurate, clear and concise.

The usual method of recording facts is to write them down, but this is not suitable for recording the complicated processes that exist in any organization, particularly when an exact record is required of a long process, and its written description would cover several pages requiring careful study to elicit every detail. To overcome this difficulty, certain methods of recording have been developed, and the most powerful of these is flowcharting. This method of describing a process owes much to computer programming, where the technique is used to arrange the sequence of steps required for the operation of the program. It has a much wider application, however, than computing.

Certain standard symbols are used on the chart, and these are shown in Figure 4.3. The starting point of the process is indicated by a circle. Each processing step, indicated by a rectangle, contains a description of the relevant operation, and where the process ends is indicated by an oval. A point where the process branches because of a decision is shown by a diamond. A parallelogram contains useful information but is not a processing step. The arrowed lines are used to

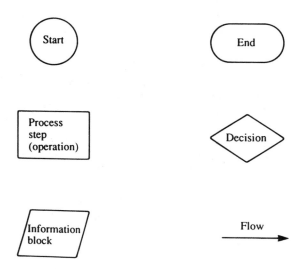

**Figure 4.3** *Flowcharting symbols*

connect symbols and to indicate direction of flow. For a complete description of the process all operation steps (rectangles) and decisions (diamonds) should be connected by pathways to the start circle and end oval. If the flowchart cannot be drawn in this way, the process is not fully understood.

It is a salutary experience for most people to sit down and try to draw the flowchart for a process in which they take part every working day. It is often found that:

* The process flow is not fully understood.
* A single person is unable to complete the flowchart without help from others.

The very act of flowcharting will improve knowledge of the process, and will begin to develop the teamwork necessary to find improvements. In many cases the convoluted flow and octopus-like appearance of the chart will highlight unnecessary movement of people and materials and lead to commonsense suggestions for waste elimination.

**Example of flowcharting in use**

*Improving a travel procedure*

We start by describing the original process for a male employee, though clearly it applies equally to females.

The process starts with the employee explaining his travel plans to his secretary. The secretary then calls the travel agent to inquire about the possibilities and gives feedback to the employee. The employee decides if the travel arrangements, e.g. flight numbers and dates, are acceptable and informs his secretary, who calls the agent to make the necessary bookings or examine alternatives. The administrative procedure, which starts as soon as the bookings have been made, is as follows:

1   The employee's secretary prepares the travel request (which is in four parts, A, B, C and D), and gives it to the secretary. The request is then sent to the employee's manager, who approves it. The manager's secretary sends it back to the employee's secretary.
2   The employee's secretary sends copies A, B and C to the agent and gives copy D to the employee. The travel agent delivers the ticket to the employee's secretary, together with copy B of the travel request. The secretary endorses copy B for receipt of the ticket, sends it to Accounting, and gives ticket to employee.
3   The travel agent bills the credit-card company, and sends

Accounting a pro-forma invoice with copy C of the travel request. Accounting matches copies B and C, and charges the employee's 181 account.

4  Accounting receives the monthly bill from the credit-card company, matches it against the travel request, then books and pays the credit-card company.

5  The employee reports the travel request on his expense statement. Accounting matches and books to balance the employee's 181 account.

The total time taken for the administrative procedure, excluding the correction of errors and the preparation of overview reports, is 23 minutes per travel request.

The flowchart for the process is drawn in Figure 4.4. A quality-improvement team was set up to analyse the process and make recommendations for improvement, using brainstorming and questioning techniques. They made the following proposal to change the procedure. The preparation for the trip remained the same but the administrative steps, following the bookings being made became:

1  The travel agent sends the ticket to the secretary, along with a receipt document, which is returned to the agent with the secretary's signature.

2  The agent sends the receipt to the credit-card company, which bills the company on a monthly basis with a copy of all the receipts. Accounting pays the credit-card company and charges the employee's 181 account.

3  The employee reports the travel on his expense statement, and Accounting books to balance the employee's 181 account.

The flowchart for the improved process is shown in Figure 4.5. The proposal reduced the total administrative effort per travel request (or per travel arrangement, because the travel request was eliminated) from 23 minutes to 5 minutes.

The details that appear on a flowchart for an existing process must be obtained from direct observation of the process, not by imagining what is done or what should be done. The latter may be useful, however, in the planning phase, or for outlining the stages in the introduction of a new concept. Such an application is illustrated in Figure 4.6 for the installation of statistical process control charting systems (see Chapter 10). Similar charts may be used in the planning of quality management systems.

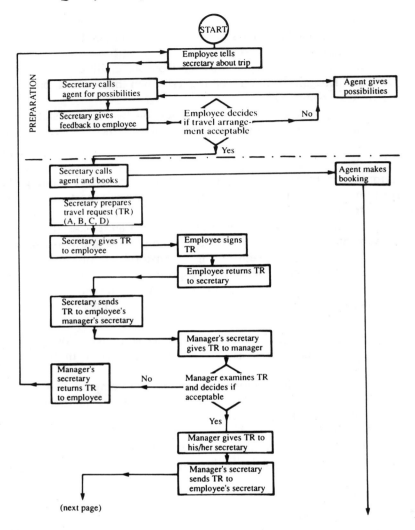

**Figure 4.4** *Original process for travel procedure*

It is surprisingly difficult to draw flowcharts for even the simplest processes, particularly managerial ones, and following the first attempt it is useful to ask whether:

• The facts have been correctly recorded.
• Any over-simplifying assumptions have been made.

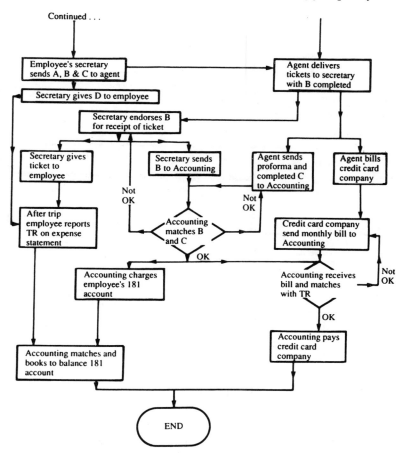

Continued . . .

**Figure 4.4** (*continued*)

• All the factors concerning the process have been recorded.

The author has seen too many process flowcharts that are so incomplete as to be grossly inaccurate.

## 4.3 Detailed flow process charts and flow diagrams

In these charts and diagrams, which are used in Industrial Engineering, the recording of detailed facts about a process is achieved by the use of five standard symbols, which together represent all the different

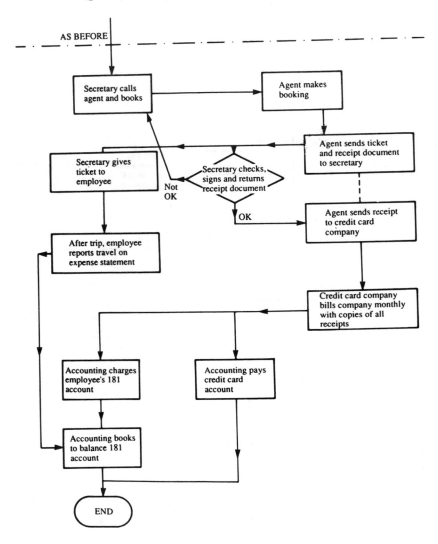

**Figure 4.5** *Improved process for travel procedure*

types of activity or event likely to be encountered. These are shown on a detailed flow process chart and a flow diagram, which *together* give a complete picture of the 'shape' of the flow and its components. The symbols provide a convenient, easily communicated shorthand and international language, saving much time and writing, which helps to

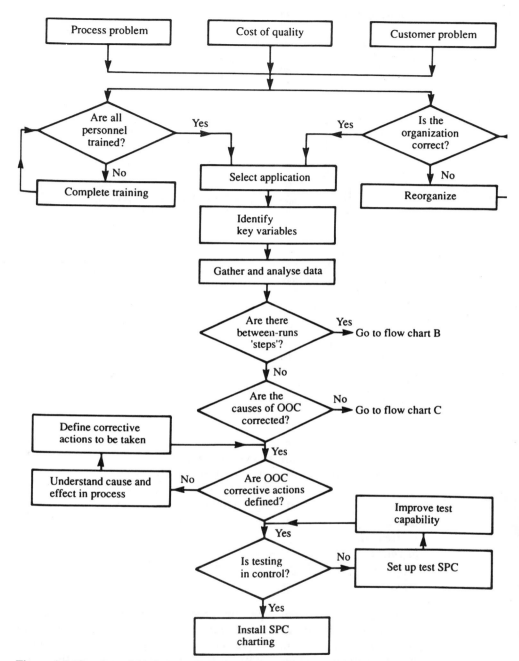

**Figure 4.6** *Flowchart (A) for installation of SPC charting systems. (The author is grateful to Exxon Chemical International for permission to use and modify this chart.)*

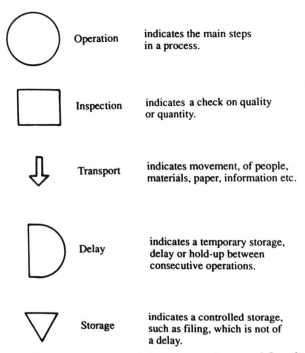

| | | |
|---|---|---|
| ◯ | Operation | indicates the main steps in a process. |
| ▢ | Inspection | indicates a check on quality or quantity. |
| ⬇ | Transport | indicates movement, of people, materials, paper, information etc. |
| D | Delay | indicates a temporary storage, delay or hold-up between consecutive operations. |
| ▽ | Storage | indicates a controlled storage, such as filing, which is not of a delay. |

**Figure 4.7** *Symbols used for detailed flow process charts and flow diagrams*

show exactly what happens, or needs to happen, in the correct sequence. The symbols are shown in Figure 4.7.

The charts and diagrams may be of four basic types:

*Person* – recording what people actually do.
*Material* – recording how material is handled (including paperwork) or treated.
*Equipment* – recording how equipment is used.
*Information* – recording how information flows and to whom or where.

Examples of a material type flow process chart and a flow diagram, using the symbols, are given in Figures 4.8 and 4.9 respectively. They describe the authorization to investigate following an insurance claim.

The flow diagram (Figure 4.9) shows the original layout of the property loss department of the company. The path of movement of the claims department request (Form 245) from the point of delivery to

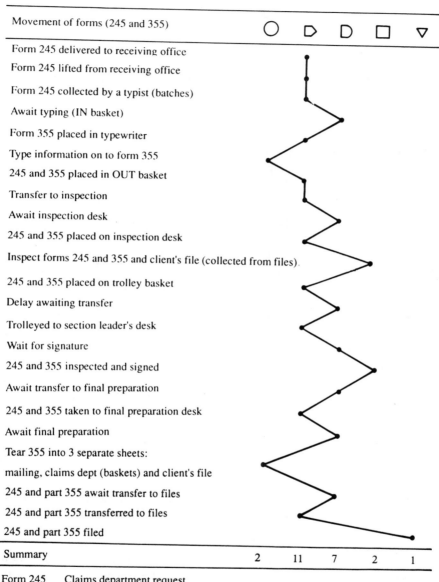

| Movement of forms (245 and 355) | ○ | ▷ | ◇ | □ | ▽ |
|---|---|---|---|---|---|
| Form 245 delivered to receiving office | | | | | |
| Form 245 lifted from receiving office | | | | | |
| Form 245 collected by a typist (batches) | | | | | |
| Await typing (IN basket) | | | | | |
| Form 355 placed in typewriter | | | | | |
| Type information on to form 355 | | | | | |
| 245 and 355 placed in OUT basket | | | | | |
| Transfer to inspection | | | | | |
| Await inspection desk | | | | | |
| 245 and 355 placed on inspection desk | | | | | |
| Inspect forms 245 and 355 and client's file (collected from files). | | | | | |
| 245 and 355 placed on trolley basket | | | | | |
| Delay awaiting transfer | | | | | |
| Trolleyed to section leader's desk | | | | | |
| Wait for signature | | | | | |
| 245 and 355 inspected and signed | | | | | |
| Await transfer to final preparation | | | | | |
| 245 and 355 taken to final preparation desk | | | | | |
| Await final preparation | | | | | |
| Tear 355 into 3 separate sheets: | | | | | |
| mailing, claims dept (baskets) and client's file | | | | | |
| 245 and part 355 await transfer to files | | | | | |
| 245 and part 355 transferred to files | | | | | |
| 245 and part 355 filed | | | | | |
| Summary | 2 | 11 | 7 | 2 | 1 |

Form 245    Claims department request
Form 355    Authorization to investigate

**Figure 4.8** *Flow process chart: method used for completing form to authorize investigation*

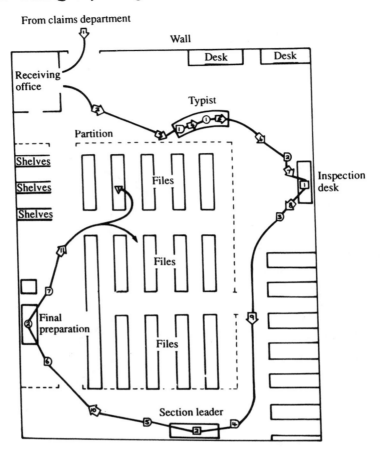

**Figure 4.9** *Flow diagram: completing form to authorize investigation*

the filing system is shown by the broad line. It will be noticed that the symbols for the various activities have been inserted at the proper places. This enables anyone looking at the diagram to imagine more readily the activities to which the forms are subjected.

A study of the flow diagram in Figure 4.9 shows immediately that the forms take a very long and roundabout path on their journey to the files. This could not have been seen from the flow process chart alone (Figure 4.8). The chart, however, enables the various activities to be recorded and summarized in a manner not conveniently possible on the diagram.

A critical examination of the two together is required, using a questioning technique that follows a well-established sequence to examine:

the PURPOSE for which  
the PLACE at which  
the SEQUENCE in which $\}$ the activities are undertaken  
the PEOPLE by which  
the METHOD by ·which

with a view to $\{$

    ELIMINATING  
    COMBINING  
    REARRANGING those  
    activities  
    or  
    SIMPLIFYING

*The questions that need to be answered in full are:*

PURPOSE:   What is actually done? (or What is actually achieved?)

    Why is the activity necessary at all?

    What else might be or should be done?

**ELIMINATE** unnecessary parts of the job.

PLACE:   Where is it being done?

    Why is it done at that particular place?

    Where else might or should it be done?

SEQUENCE: When is it done?

    Why is it done at that particular time?

    When might or should it be done?

**COMBINE** wherever possible and/or **REARRANGE** operations for more effective results or reduction in waste

PEOPLE:   Who does it?

    Why is it done by that particular person?

    Who else might or should do it?

METHOD:   How is it done?

Why is it done in that particular way?

} SIMPLIFY the operations

How else might or should it be done?

Questions such as these, when applied to the insurance authorization, raise many points demanding explanation, such as:

**Q** Why are the inspection, section leader and final preparation points so far apart?
**A** Because they happen to have been put there.
**Q** Where else could they be?
**A** They could be all together.
**Q** Where should they be?
**A** Together at the present inspection point.
**Q** Why do the forms and client's file have to go all round the building to reach the filing system?
**A** Because the door to the files is located at the opposite end from the delivery point.

No doubt if the flow diagram and the flow process chart are examined carefully there will be many other questions to ask. There is evidently much room for improvement. This is a real-life example of what happens when a series of activities is started without being properly planned. Examples with as much waste of time and effort can be found in offices all over the world.

The solution arrived at by the staff in this insurance company can be seen in the Figures 4.10 and 4.11. It is clear that among the questions they asked were those suggested above. The section leader's and final preparation desks have now been placed beside the inspection bench, so that the forms and file can be passed from hand to hand for inspection, signing and final preparation. It is evident that the investigators were led to ask 'Why do the forms and client's file have to go all round the building to reach the filing system?' Having received no satisfactory answer, they decided to make a new doorway into the files opposite the desks, so that the files could be taken in by the shortest route.

It will be seen from the summary on the new flow process chart (Figure 4.10) that the 'inspections' have been reduced from two to one, the 'transports' from eleven to six and the 'delays' (or temporary storages) from seven to two. The distance travelled was reduced from 56.2 to 32.2 metres.

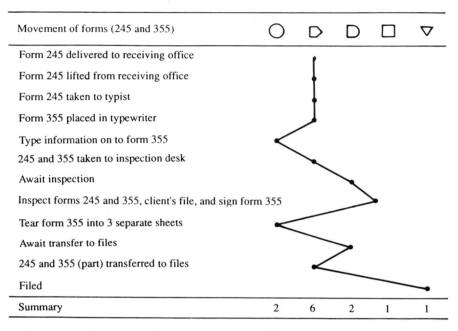

| Movement of forms (245 and 355) | ○ | ▷ | D | □ | ▽ |
|---|---|---|---|---|---|
| Form 245 delivered to receiving office | | | | | |
| Form 245 lifted from receiving office | | | | | |
| Form 245 taken to typist | | | | | |
| Form 355 placed in typewriter | | | | | |
| Type information on to form 355 | | | | | |
| 245 and 355 taken to inspection desk | | | | | |
| Await inspection | | | | | |
| Inspect forms 245 and 355, client's file, and sign form 355 | | | | | |
| Tear form 355 into 3 separate sheets | | | | | |
| Await transfer to files | | | | | |
| 245 and 355 (part) transferred to files | | | | | |
| Filed | | | | | |
| Summary | 2 | 6 | 2 | 1 | 1 |

**Figure 4.10** *Flow process chart: improved method for completing form to authorize investigation*

Summarizing, then, a flowchart is a picture of the steps used in performing a function. This function can be anything from a process step to accounting procedures, even preparing a meal. Lines connect the steps to show the flow of the various functions. Flowcharts provide excellent documentation and are useful trouble-shooting tools to determine how each step is related to the others. By reviewing the flowchart, it is often possible to discover inconsistencies and determine potential sources of variation and problems. For this reason, flowcharts are very useful in process improvement when examining an existing process to highlight the problem areas. A group of people, with the knowledge about the process, should take the following simple steps:

1  Draw a flowchart of existing process.
2  Draw a second chart of the flow the process could or should follow.
3  Compare the two to highlight the changes necessary.

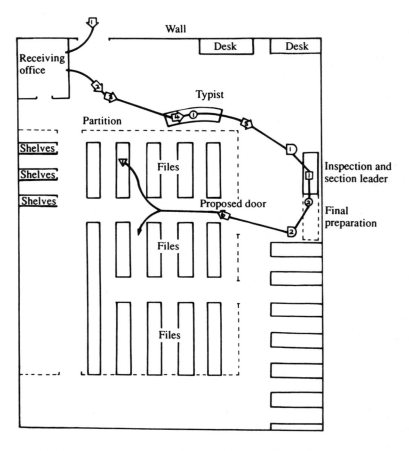

**Figure 4.11** *Flow diagram: improved method for completing form to authorize investigation*

## 4.4  Planning for purchasing

A company selling wooden products had a very simple purchasing policy: it bought the cheapest wood it could find anywhere in the world. Down in the workshops they were scrapping doors and window frames as if they were going out of fashion – warping, knots in the wood, 'flaking', cracking, splits, etc. When the purchasing manager was informed, he visited the workshops and explained to the supervisors how cheap the wood was and instructed them to 'do the best you can – the customer will never notice'. On challenging this policy, the author was told that it would not change until someone proved to the purchasing manager, in a quantitative way, that the policy was wrong. That year the company 'lost' £1 million worth of wood – in scrap and rework. You can go out of business waiting for such proof.

Very few organizations are self-contained to the extent that their products and services are all generated at one location, from basic materials. Some materials or services are usually purchased from outside organizations, and the primary objective of purchasing is to obtain the correct equipment, materials, and services in the right quantity, of the right quality, from the right origin, at the right time and cost. Purchasing also plays a vital role as the organization's 'window-on-the-world', providing information on any new products, processes, materials and services. It should also advise on probable prices, deliveries, and performance of products under consideration by the research, design and development functions.

The *total* cost of bought-in material and/or services usually forms a large proportion of the final selling price of an organization's products or services. Consequently, purchasing is an extremely important function, and its importance should never be underestimated. The value of purchases varies from industry to industry, but it averages 60 per cent of the turnover of all industries, and clearly the effects of good purchasing management on the profitability of a 'typical' manufacturing or service organization can be considerable.

Although purchasing is clearly an important area of managerial activity, it is often neglected by both manufacturing and service industries. The separation of purchasing from selling has, however, been removed in many large retail organizations, which have recognized that the purchaser must be responsible for the whole 'product line' – its selection, quality, specification, delivery, price, acceptability, and reliability. If any part of this chain is wrong, the purchasing function must resolve the problem. This concept is clearly very appropriate in retailing, where transformation activities on the product itself, between purchase and sale, are small or zero, but it shows the need to include market information in the buying decision processes in all organizations.

The purchasing system should be set out in a written manual which:

1 Assigns responsibilities for and within the purchasing function.
2 Defines the manner in which suppliers are selected, to ensure that they are continually capable of supplying the requirements in terms of material and services.
3 Indicates the purchasing documentation – written orders, specifications, etc. – required in any modern purchasing activity.

So what does an organization require from its suppliers? The goals are easy to state, but less easy to reach:

- Consistency – low variability.
- Centring – on target.
- Process evolution and development to continually reduce variability.
- Correct delivery performance.
- Speed of response.
- A *systematic* quality management approach to achieve the above.

Historically many organizations, particularly in the manufacturing industries, have operated an inspection-oriented quality system for bought-in parts and materials. Such an approach has many disadvantages. It is expensive, imprecise, and impossible to apply evenly across all material and parts, which all lead to variability in the degree of appraisal. Many organizations, such as Ford, have found that survival and future growth in both volume and variety demand that changes be made to this approach.

The prohibitive cost of holding large stocks of components and raw materials also pushed forward the 'just-in-time' (JIT) concept. As this requires that suppliers make frequent, on time, deliveries of small quantities of material, parts, components, etc., often straight to the point of use, in order that stocks can be kept to a minimum, the approach requires an effective supplier network – one producing goods and services that can be trusted to conform to the real requirements with a high degree of confidence.

**Commitment and involvement**

The process of improving suppliers' performance is complex and clearly relies very heavily on securing real commitment from the senior management of the supplier organizations. This may be aided by presentations made to groups of directors of the suppliers brought together to share the realization of the importance of their organizations' performance in the quality chains. The synergy derived from different suppliers meeting together, being educated, and discussing mutual problems, will be tremendous. If this can be achieved, within the constraints of business and technical confidentiality, it is always a better approach than separate meetings and presentations on the suppliers' premises.

The author recalls the benefits that accrued from bringing together suppliers of a photocopier, paper, and ring binders to explain to them the way their inputs were used to generate training-course materials and how they in turn were used during the courses themselves. The suppliers were able to understand the business in which their customers were engaged, and play their part in the whole process. A supplier of goods *or* services that has received such attention, education, and training, and understands the role its inputs play, is less likely knowingly to offer nonconforming materials and services, and more likely to alert customers to potential problems.

## Policy

One of the first things to communicate to any external supplier is the purchasing organization's policy on quality of incoming goods and services. This can include such statements as:

- It is the policy of this company to ensure that the quality of all purchased materials and services meets its requirements.
- Suppliers who incorporate a quality management system into their operations will be selected. This system should be designed, implemented and operated according to the International Standards Organization (ISO) 9000 series (see Chapter 5).
- Suppliers who incorporate statistical process control (SPC) methods into their operations (see Chapters 9 and 10) will be selected.
- Routine inspection, checking, measurement and testing of incoming goods and services will *not* be carried out by this company on receipt.
- Suppliers will be audited and their operating procedures, systems, and SPC methods will be reviewed periodically to ensure a never ending improvement approach.
- It is the policy of this company to pursue uniformity of supply, and to encourage suppliers to strive for continual reduction in variability. (This may well lead to the narrowing of specification ranges.)

## Quality system assessment certification

Many customers examine their suppliers' quality management systems themselves, operating a second party assessment scheme (see Chapter 6). Inevitably this leads to high costs and duplication of activity, for both the customer and supplier. If a qualified, independent third party is used instead to carry out the assessment, attention may be focused by the customer on any special needs and in developing closer partnerships with suppliers. Visits and dialogue across the customer/supplier interface are a necessity for the true requirements to be met, and for future growth of the whole business chain. Visits should be concentrated, however, on improving understanding and capability, rather than on close scrutiny of operating procedures, which is best left to experts, including those within the supplier organizations charged with carrying our internal system audits and reviews.

## Supplier approval and single sourcing

Most organizations have as an objective to obtain at least two 'approved' suppliers for each material or service purchased on a regular basis. It may be argued, however, that single sourcing – the development of an extremely close relationship with just one supplier for each item or service – encourages greater commitment and a true partnership to be created. This clearly needs careful management, but it is a sound policy, based on the premise that it is better to work together with a supplier to remove problems, improve capability, and generate a mutual understanding of the *real* requirements, than to hop from one supplier to another and thereby experience a different set of problems each time.

To become an 'approved supplier', it is usually necessary to pass through a number of stages:

1  *Technical approval* – largely to determine if the product/service meets the technical requirements. This stage should be directed at agreeing a specification that is consistent with the supplier's process capability.
2  *Conditional approval* – at this stage it is known that the product/service meets the requirements, following customer in-process trials, and there is a good commercial reason for purchase.
3  *Full approval* – when all the requirements are being met, including those concerning the operation of the appropriate management systems, SPC, etc.

## Supplier-capability audits and reviews

It is normal for organizations to carry out audits of their suppliers and to review their systems and process capabilities. These may take many forms. A questionnaire, visits to sites and premises, interviews with personnel, and simple calculations of indices are just a few of the many methods employed. The planning of the audit and review system is vital to successful co-operation with suppliers; and they must contribute to it, so that it is viewed as a desirable part of the collaboration between two organizations.

Often an organization that understands it cannot inspect quality into its products or services tries to inspect quality into its suppliers' systems. This manifests itself as a 'policeman' approach by the auditor, who arrives unannounced and determined to 'nail' the supplier with a few discrepancies. The aim should be to help the supplier identify problems, by acting as a fresh pair of outside eyes, and to offer advice in their solution. The penalty-issuing auditor will create a desire to cover up rather than expose difficulties. If exposure results in help and advice being offered, rather than business being withdrawn, then clearly the partnership will be fostered and develop to a strength which resists all attempts by men, materials and machines to interfere. The principles behind this are not new, but they are often not practised. Being rude to, irritating, or simply bullying your suppliers, whether internal or external ones, will achieve one thing – conflict – and there is no evidence that this breeds anything other than defeat and frustration. A firm hand is required, but it must be used to lead and support rather than beat into submission.

Any supplier-quality audit and review system should be designed to assess the quality and reliability of suppliers through a complete survey of the producing system. The objectives should be to improve the four Cs: communication, capability, confidence, and control. This will develop respect for each party and make sure that the frequency and organization of the audits are appropriate.

In the search for new suppliers the following questions are useful to see if there is even the chance of a partnership developing:

1 Do you have a quality system that meets the requirements of ISO 9000?
2 Do you have quality assured purchased materials and services?
3 Do you have a system for traceability?
4 Do you use statistical process control?
5 What are your process capabilities?
6 Have you set up quality improvement teams?
7 Do you operate total quality management?

A lack of understanding by potential suppliers of the meaning of any of these questions suggests much work will be required to bring them to the required standard. Once potential suppliers have been identified, the standards may become more insistent for the partnership to develop further:

- You *must* operate a quality system that meets the requirements of ISO 9000 (this could become, You must have certification of assessed capability against ISO 9000).

- We want to see your quality policy.
- We want to see your quality manual.
- We want to see your process control charts or their equivalent.
- We want to see your process capability indices.
- We want to carry out quality audits and system reviews with you.

As with so much in quality management, data will provide the objective evidence of supplier capability. But the records must be used with skill and sensitivity to forge long-term associations, built with trust and collaboration for continuity and mutual success.

## 4.5  Planning for just-in-time (JIT) management

There are so many organizations throughout the world that are looking at, introducing, or practising just-in-time (JIT) management principles that the probability of encountering it is very high. JIT, like many modern management concepts, is credited to the Japanese, who developed and began to use it in the late 1950s. It took approximately 20 years for JIT methods to reach Western hardgoods industries and a further 10 years before businesses realized the generality of the concepts.

Basically JIT is a programme directed towards ensuring that the right quantities are purchased or produced at the right time, and that there is no waste. Anyone who perceives it purely as a material-control system, however, is bound to fail with JIT. JIT fits well under the TQM umbrella, for many of the ideas and techniques are very similar and, moreover, JIT will not work without TQM in operation. Writing down a definition of JIT for all types of organization is extremely difficult, because the range of products, services and organization structures leads to different impressions of the nature and scope of JIT. It is essentially:

- A series of operating concepts that allows systematic identification of operational problems.
- A series of technology-based tools for correcting problems following their identification.

An important outcome of JIT is a disciplined programme for improving productivity and reducing waste. This programme leads to cost-effective production or operation and delivery of only the required goods or services, in the correct quantity, at the right time and place. This is achieved with the minimum amount of resources – facilities, equipment, materials, and people. The successful operation of JIT is dependent upon a balance between the suppliers' flexibility and the users' stability, and of course requires total management and employee commitment and teamwork.

## Aims of JIT

The fundamental aims of JIT are to produce or operate to meet the requirements of the customer exactly, without waste, immediately on demand. In some manufacturing companies JIT has been introduced as 'continuous flow production', which describes very well the objective of achieving conversion of purchased material or service receipt to delivery, i.e. from supplier to customer. If this extends into the supplier and customer chains, all operating with JIT, a perfectly continuous flow of material, information or service will be achieved. JIT may be used in non-manufacturing, in administration areas, for example, by using external standards as reference points.

The JIT concepts identify operational problems by tracking the following:

1 *Material movements* – when material stops, diverts or turns backwards, these always correlate with an aberration in the 'process'.
2 *Material accumulations* – these are there as a buffer for problems, excessive variability, etc., like water covering up 'rocks'.
3 *Process flexibility* – an absolute necessity for flexible operation and design.
4 *Value-added efforts* – much of what is done does not add value and the customer will not pay for it.

## The operation of JIT

The tools to carry out the monitoring required are familiar quality and operations management methods, such as:

• Flowcharting.
• Method study and analysis.
• Preventive maintenance.
• Plant layout methods.
• Standardized design.
• Statistical process control.
• Value analysis and value engineering.

But some techniques are more directly associated with the operation of JIT systems:

1   Batch or lot size reduction.
2   Flexible workforce.
3   Kanban or cards with material visibility.
4   Mistake-proofing.
5   Pull-scheduling.
6   Set-up time reduction.
7   Standardized containers.

In addition, joint development programmes with suppliers and customers will be required to establish long-term relationships and develop single sourcing arrangements that provide frequent deliveries in small quantities. These can only be achieved through close communications and meaningful certified quality.

There is clear evidence that JIT has been an important component of business success in the Far East and that it is used by Japanese companies operating in the West. Many European and American companies that have adopted JIT have made spectacular improvements in performance. These include:

• Increased flexibility (particularly of the workforce).
• Reduction in stock and work-in-progress, and the space it occupies.
• Simplification of products and processes.

These programmes are **always** characterized by a real commitment to continuous improvement. Organizations have been rewarded, however, by the low cost, low risk aspects of implementation, provided a sensible attitude prevails. The golden rule is to never remove resources – such as stock – before the organization is ready and able to correct the problems that will be exposed by doing so. Reduction of the water level to reveal the rocks, so that they may be demolished, is fine, provided that we can quickly get our hands back on the stock while the problem is being corrected.

Successive phases of JIT may well become self-financing by rapid simplification of systems and work flows, but JIT must never be regarded at the intermediate stage as the 'quick-fix'. Management must contemplate:

1   Long implementation times – typically 5–7 years.
2   A total or company-wide quality and just-in-time management programme.
3   Never ending improvement and reduction of waste.

The primary objective of JIT is the improvement of quality through elimination of waste. It demands that inventory is kept to a minimum, for inventory costs (insurance, interest, obsolescence, etc.) can be as high as 26 per cent of stock value, and significant improvements in costs and quality can be achieved by the reduction of inventory. Defective parts, materials, and workmanship are detected promptly and quickly fed back to the producing process, where the problems are identified and corrected on the spot. In addition to quality improvement, there is no requirement for a profusion of warehouses, fleets of forklift trucks, rows of racks, scores of employees, and piles of cash to purchase, handle, and move the inventory.

With low inventory in the system, any fluctuation in the final stage of production or operations creates variations in the requirements at preceding stages. This variation becomes larger for processes further away from the final stage. To prevent the variance in earlier stages, a minimum lot or batch size, ideally a lot size of one, should be chosen. Small lot sizes help to reduce nonconformities through the detection of problems and their rapid solution, before large quantities are generated.

In some engineering and process industry applications the major obstacle in producing small lots is the set-up times of equipment and machines. Long set-up times make the small lot size uneconomical so, clearly, cutting set-up times is one of the first tasks. This will also reduce equipment downtime; work-in-progress; costs associated with obsolescence, materials handling and control; and quality control. Shorter set-up times also result in shorter lead times, which provides greater flexibility for processes to adapt to changes in the market demand and requirements.

**The Kanban system**

Kanban is a Japanese word meaning visible record, but in the West it is generally taken to mean a card that signals the need to deliver or produce more parts or components. In manufacturing, various types of record cards, e.g. job orders or tickets and route cards, are used for ordering more parts in a *push* type, schedule-based system. In a push system a multi-period master production schedule of future demands is prepared, and a computer explodes this into detailed schedules for producing or purchasing the appropriate parts or materials. The schedules then *push* the production of the parts or components, out and onward. These systems, when computer-based, are usually called Material Requirements Planning (MRP) or the more recent Manufacturing Resource Planning (MRPII).

The main feature of the Kanban system is that it *pulls* parts and components through the production processes when they are needed.

Each material, component, or part has its own special container designed to hold a precise, preferably small, quantity. The number of containers for each part is a carefully considered management decision. Only standard containers are used, and they are always filled with the prescribed quantity. There are two cards or Kanbans for each container. The *production* or *P-Kanban* serves the work centre producing the part, whereas the *conveyance* or *C-Kanban* serves the work centre using it. Each container travels between the two work centres and one Kanban is exchanged for another along the way. No parts may be made at any work centre unless there is a P-Kanban to authorize it, and work centres may come to a halt rather than produce materials or parts not yet requested. The operators will engage in other activities, such as cleaning, maintenance, improvement or quality-circle project work when no P-Kanbans have been submitted. These hold-ups often help to identify and improve bottleneck situations.

A Kanban system provides parts when they are needed but without guesswork, and therefore without the excess inventory that results from bad guesses. The system will only work well, however, within the context of a JIT system in general, and the reduction of set-up times and lot sizes in particular. A JIT programme can succeed without a Kanban-based operation, but Kanbans will not function effectively independently of JIT.

### The implementation of JIT

If it has been decided to embark on JIT, then a pilot scheme should be implemented first. The key features of an appropriate pilot section will be that it is:

- Reasonably self-contained.
- Concerned with products or services that have established designs and stable markets for the foreseeable future.
- Staffed by people who are keen to try to implement JIT.

Clearly, if the pilot implementation is successful, it is appropriate to proceed to other areas of the business.

The implementation of JIT may be described as a two-stage process:

1  Establish foundations.
2  Introduce core techniques.

To establish foundations, the company must be organized and managed to achieve:

- Quality.
- Low cost.
- Minimum lead times.
- High flexibility.

The methods required to reach these goals will include:

1  TQM.
2  Focus on design.
3  Plant and equipment layout.
4  Set-up time reduction.
5  Lot or batch size reduction.
6  Work-in-progress and/or buffer stock reduction.
7  Flexible workforce.

Much of this will depend, obviously, on the type of industry and relative position of the company, e.g. many flow-production operations will already possess significant focus on standardization of design.

Core techniques often provide the most spectacular improvements and savings, but may be more difficult to implement. A satisfactory stage one foundation is essential for the introduction of:

- Pull scheduling.
- Visibility.
- JIT purchasing.
- Buffer stock removal.
- Multifunction workforce.
- Enforced improvement.

The implementation of JIT requires a planned and co-ordinated, company-wide JIT organization, which should incorporate three main features: a steering committee, a project manager, and project teams. This is so similar to the organization for TQM that the two may well be run in parallel, at least through stage one (see Chapter 11).

The steering committee should be a cross-functional group of personnel who meet regularly to direct and monitor the programme. Members of the committee may include people from marketing, design, purchasing, production or operations, quality, personnel, and possibly the workforce. It is beneficial to appoint a project manager to lead the implementation. His/her characteristics and training are vital to the duties of acquiring and organizing resources, facilitating and chairing meetings, internally publicizing results, and training. The project teams are established to implement specific JIT techniques. With help from the project manager, these 'working parties' should establish terms of reference at an early stage. Their membership should be cross-functional, but above all relevant to the JIT technique concerned. The reporting system should be from the teams through the project manager to the steering committee.

The emphasis throughout all stages of JIT or TQM implementation should be on the participation of all employees, especially those who will be directly affected by changes. This may require some 'enforced' delegation from specialists, such as quality and industrial engineers, to shop-floor personnel. The culture in which JIT will operate successfully will provide support to the project teams' recommendations for change.

**Just-in-time purchasing**

Purchasing is an important feature of JIT. The development of long-term relationships with a few suppliers, rather than short-term ones with many, leads to the concept of *co-producers* in networks of trust providing dependable quality and delivery of goods and services. Each organization in the chain of supply is encouraged to extend JIT methods to its suppliers. The requirements of JIT mean that suppliers are usually located near the purchaser's premises, delivering small quantities, often several times per day, to match the usage rate. Paperwork is kept to a minimum and standard quantities in standard containers are usual. The requirement for suppliers to be located near the buying organization, which places those at some distance at a competitive disadvantage, causes lead times to be shorter and deliveries to be more reliable.

It can be argued that JIT purchasing and delivery are suitable mainly for assembly line operations, and less so for certain process and service industries, but the reduction in the inventory and transport costs that it brings should encourage innovations to lead to its widespread adoption. Those committed to open competition and finding the lowest price will find most difficulty. Nevertheless, there must be a recognition of the need to develop closer relationships and to begin the dialogue – the sharing of information and problems – that leads to the product or service of the right quality, being delivered in the right quantity, at the right time.

# Chapter highlights

## Quality planning

- Systematic planning is a basic requirement for TQM.
- A quality plan sets out details for systems, procedures, purchased materials or services, products/services, plant/equipment, process control, sampling/inspection, training, packaging and distribution.

## Flowcharting

- Flowcharting is a method of describing a process in pictures, using symbols – rectangles for operation steps, diamonds for decision, parallelograms for information, and circles/ovals for the start/end points. Arrow lines connect the symbols to show the 'flow'.
- Flowcharting improves knowledge of the process and helps to develop the team of people involved.

## Detailed flow process charts and flow diagrams.

- Five standard symbols are used to represent all the different types of activity on detailed flowcharts and diagrams, which are used together.
- The flowcharts and diagrams may be of four basic types: person, material, equipment, information.
- The charts and diagrams should be examined by means of a questioning technique to determine purpose, place, sequence, people, and method, to eliminate, combine, rearrange, or simplify process steps.
- Flowcharts document processes and are useful as trouble-shooting tools and in process improvement. An improvement team would flowchart the existing process and the improved or desired process, comparing the two to highlight the changes necessary.

## Planning for purchasing

- The prime objective of purchasing is to obtain the correct equipment, materials, and services in the right quantity, of the right quality, from the right origin, at the right time and cost. Purchasing also acts as a 'window-on-the-world'.
- The separation of purchasing from selling has been eliminated in many retail organizations, to give responsibility for a whole 'product line'. Market information must be included in *any* buying decision.

- The purchasing system should be set out in a written manual, which gives responsibilities, the means of selecting suppliers, and the documentation to be used.
- An organization requires from its suppliers consistency, on target, process evolution, good delivery performance, speed of response, and systematic quality management.
- Improving supplier performance requires from the suppliers' senior management commitment, education, a policy, an assessed quality system, and supplier approval.
- Single sourcing – the close relationship with one supplier for each item or service – depends on technical, conditional, and full stages of approval.
- Supplier-capability audits and reviews should be carried out by one of the number of methods available. The methods should be designed to improve the partnership and not lead to conflict.

**Planning for just-in-time (JIT) management**

- JIT fits well under the TQM umbrella and is essentially a series of operating concepts that allow the systematic identification of problems, *and* tools for correcting them.
- JIT aims to produce or operate, in accordance with customer requirements, without waste, immediately on demand. Some of the direct techniques associated with JIT are batch or lot size reduction, flexible workforce, Kanban cards, mistake proofing, set up time reduction, standardized containers.
- JIT implementation requires the foundations of quality, low cost, minimum lead times, high flexibility, through the core techniques of pull scheduling, JIT purchasing, buffer stock removal, multifunction workforce and enforced improvement.
- As with TQM, a steering committee, a project manager and project teams are required for successful JIT implementation.
- Purchasing is an important feature of JIT. Long-term relationships with a few suppliers, or 'co-producers', are developed in networks of trust to provide quality goods and services.

# 5 System design and contents

## 5.1 Why a documented system?

In earlier chapters we have seen how the keystone of quality management is the concept of customer and supplier working together for their mutual advantage. For any particular organization this becomes 'total' quality management if the supplier/customer interfaces extend beyond the immediate customers, back inside the organization, and beyond the immediate suppliers. In order to achieve this, a company must organize itself in such a way that the human, administrative and technical factors affecting quality will be under control. This leads to the requirement for the development and implementation of a quality system that enables the objectives set out in the quality policy to be accomplished. Clearly, for maximum effectiveness and to meet individual customer requirements, the quality system in use must be appropriate to the type of activity and product or service being offered.

It may be useful to reflect on why such a device is necessary to achieve control of processes. The author remembers being at a table in a restaurant with eight people who all ordered the 'Chef's Special Individual Soufflé'. All eight soufflés arrived together at the table, magnificent in their appearance and consistency, each one exhibiting an almost identical size and shape – a truly remarkable demonstration of culinary skill. How had this been achieved? The chef had *managed* such consistency by making sure that, for each soufflé, he used the same ingredients (materials), the same equipment (plant), the same method (procedure) in exactly the same way every time. The process was under control. This is the aim of a good quality system, to provide the 'operator' of the process with consistency and satisfaction in terms of methods, materials, equipment, etc. (Figure 5.1). Two feedback loops are also required: the 'voice' of the customer (marketing activities) and the 'voice' of the process (measurement activities).

The chef's soufflés were not British Standard, NIST Standard, Australian Standard, or ISO Standard soufflés – they were the chef's special soufflés. It is not conceivable that the chef sat down with a blank piece of paper to invent a soufflé recipe. Why re-invent wheels?

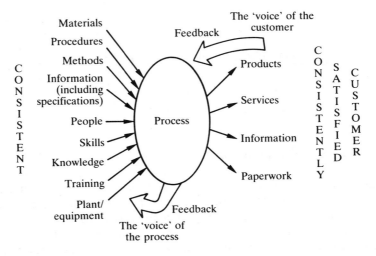

**Figure 5.1** *The systematic approach to process management*

He probably used a standard formula and changed it slightly to make it his own. This is exactly the way in which organizations must use the international standards on quality systems that are available. The 'wheel' has been invented but it must be built in a way that meets the specific organizational and product or service requirements. The International Standards Organization (ISO) Standard 9000 Series sets out the methods by which a management system, incorporating all the activities associated with quality, can be implemented in an organization to ensure that all the specified performance requirements and needs of the customer are fully met.

Let us return to the chef in the restaurant and propose that his success leads to a desire to open eight restaurants in which are served his special soufflés. Clearly he cannot rush from each one of these establishments to another every evening making soufflés. The only course open to him to ensure consistency of output, in all eight restaurants, is for him to write down in some detail the system he uses, and then make sure that it is used on all sites, every time a soufflé is produced. Moreover, he must periodically visit the different sites to ensure that:

1   The people involved are operating according to the documented system (a system audit).
2   The soufflé system still meets the requirements (a system review).

If in his system audits and reviews he discovers that an even better product or less waste can be achieved by changing the method or one of the materials, then he may wish to effect a change. To maintain consistency, he must ensure that the appropriate changes are made to the documented system, *and* that everyone concerned is issued with the revision and begins to operate accordingly.

A fully documented quality management system will ensure that two important requirements are met:

- *The customer's requirements* – for confidence in the ability of the organization to deliver the desired product or service consistently.
- *The organization's requirements* – both internally and externally, and at an optimum cost, with efficient utilization of the resources available – material, human, technological, and administrative.

These requirements can be truly met only if objective evidence is provided, in the form of information and data, which supports the system activities, from the ultimate supplier through to the ultimate customer.

A *quality system* may be defined, then, as an assembly of components, such as the organizational structure, responsibilities, procedures, processes and resources for implementing total quality management. These components interact and are affected by being in the system, so the isolation and study of each one in detail will not necessarily lead to an understanding of the system as a whole. Often the interactions between the components – such as materials and processes, procedures and responsibilities – are just as important as the components themselves, and problems can arise from these interactions as much as from the components. Clearly, if one of the components is removed from the system, the whole thing will change.

## 5.2 Quality system design

The quality system should apply to and interact with all activities of the organization. It begins with the identification of the requirements and ends with their satisfaction, at every transaction interface. The activities may be classified in several ways – generally as processing, communicating and controlling, but more usefully and specifically as:

1 Marketing.
2 Market research.
3 Design.
4 Specifying.

5   Development.
6   Procurement.
7   Process planning.
8   Process development and assessment.
9   Process operation and control.
10   Product- or service-testing or checking.
11   Packaging (if required).
12   Storage (if required).
13   Sales.
14   Distribution or installation/operation.
15   Technical service.
16   Maintenance.

These may be regarded as slats on a rotating drum rolling towards a satisfied customer, who becomes 'delighted' by the consistency of the product or service (Figure 5.2). The driving force of the drum is the centralized quality system, and the drum will not operate until the system is in place and working. The first step in getting the drum rolling is to prepare the necessary documentation. This means, in very basic terms, that procedures should be written down, preferably in such a way that the system conforms to one of the national or international standards. This is probably best done in the form of a quality manual (see Chapter 6).

It is interesting to bring together the concepts of Deming's Cycle of continuous improvement – PLAN DO CHECK ACT – and quality systems. A simplification of what a good quality system is trying to do is given in Figure 5.3, which follows the improvement cycle.

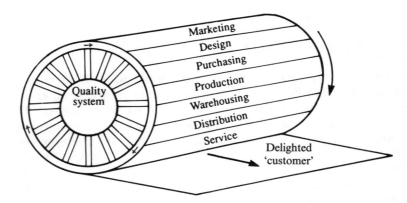

**Figure 5.2** *The quality system power unit to the delighted 'customer'*

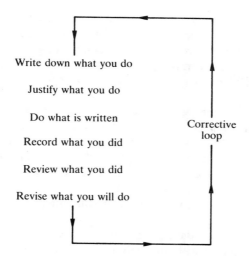

**Figure 5.3** *The quality system and never ending improvement*

In most organizations established methods of working already exist, and all that is required is the *writing down of what is currently done.* In some instances companies may not have procedures to satisfy the requirements of a good standard, and they may have to begin to devise them. Alternatively, it may be found that two people, supposedly performing the same task, are working in different ways, and there is a need to standardize the procedure. Some organizations use the effective slogan 'If it isn't written down, it doesn't exist'. This can be a useful discipline, provided it doesn't lead to paper bureaucracy.

*Justify* that the *system* as it is designed *meets the requirements of a good international standard,* such as ISO 9001. There are other excellent standards that are used, and these provide similar checklists of things to consider in the establishment of the quality system.

One of the best-documented quality systems the author has ever seen was in a small hand-tool manufacturing company. It possessed an excellent quality manual, beautifully laid out in sections covering each paragraph heading of ISO 9002. Each procedure described exactly how compliance with the standard was achieved, and identified the responsibilities and authorities of the individuals concerned – but it was a work of fiction! It did not bear any relation to *what actually happened.* There were two main reasons for this:

1  The quality manager had written the manual to describe how he wished things to happen or how he thought they happened, without discovering the reality before documenting the system.
2  The other people carrying out certain procedures had not been consulted or asked to write down how they operated.

Make sure that the system is a working one and the documents are well fingered in use. One person alone cannot document a quality system; the task is the job of all personnel who have responsibility for any part of it. The quality manual must be a *practical working document* – that way it ensures that consistency of operation is maintained and it may be used as a training aid.

In the operation of any process, a useful guide is:

- No process without data collection.
- No data collection without analysis.
- No analysis without decisions.
- No decisions without actions, which can include doing nothing.

This excellent discipline is built into any good quality system, primarily through the audit and review systems. The requirement to *audit or 'check'* that the system is functioning according to plan, and to *review* possible system improvements, utilizing audit results, should ensure that the *improvement cycle* is engaged through the *corrective action* procedures. The overriding requirement is that the systems must reflect the established practices of the organization, improved where necessary to bring them into line with current and future requirements.

## 5.3   Quality system requirements

The special methods and procedures that need to be documented and implemented will be determined by the nature of the process or processes carried out. Certain fundamental principles are applicable, however, throughout industry, commerce, and the services. These fall into generally well defined categories, as follows.

### 1  Management responsibility

*Quality policy (see Chapter 2)*

The organization should define and publish its quality policy, which forms one element of the corporate policy. Full commitment is required from the most senior management to ensure that the policy is communicated, understood, implemented and maintained at all levels in the organization. It should therefore be authorized by top management and signed by the Chief Executive, or equivalent, who must also ensure that it is updated as appropriate to meet organizational changes.

*Organization (see Chapter 11)*

Organizations should have an organization chart, and define the responsibilities of those shown in the chart, which should include all functions that affect quality. One manager with the necessary authority, resources, support, and ability should be given the responsibility to co-ordinate, implement, and monitor the quality system, resolve any problems and ensure prompt and effective corrective action. This includes responsibility for ensuring proper handling of the quality system. Those who control sales, service, processing, warehousing, delivery, and reworking of nonconforming product or service must also be identified.

*Management review (see Chapter 6)*

Management reviews of the system must be carried out, with records to indicate the actions decided upon. The effectiveness of these actions should be considered during subsequent reviews. Reviews typically include data on the internal quality audits, customer complaints, nonconforming materials, the performance of sub-contractors, and the training plan.

## 2  Quality system

The organization should prepare a quality plan and a quality manual that is appropriate for the 'level' of quality system required.

A *Level 1* system relates to design, production or operation, and installation, and applies when the customer specifies the goods or services in terms of how they are to perform, rather than in established technical terms.

A *Level 2* system is relevant when an organization is producing goods or services to a customer's or a published specification.

A *Level 3* system applies only to final production or service inspection, check, or test procedures.

The reader is referred to the International Standard, ISO 9000 (British Standard BS 5750, European Standard EN29,000) and Table 5.1.

**Table 5.1** *Quality systems ISO 9000 (BS5750) series*

| ISO Standard | BS5750 Part | Title |
|---|---|---|
| | 0 | Principal concepts and applications. |
| 9000 | 0.1 | Guide to selection and use. |
| 9001–3 | | Quality system specifications: |
| 9001 | 1 | for design/development, production, installation and servicing, |
| 9002 | 2 | for production and installation, |
| 9003 | 3 | for final inspection. |
| | 4 | Guide to the use of BS5750: Part 1 'Specification for design/development, production, installation and servicing', Part 2 'Specification for production and installation', Part 3 'Specification for final inspection and test' (NB: Parts 5 and 6 of BS5750 have been withdrawn). |
| 9004 | 0.2 | Guide to quality management and quality system elements. |
| 9004–1 | $7^{1,2}$ | General guidelines. |
| 9004–2 | 8 | Guide to quality management and quality system elements for services. |
| 9004–3 | $9^2$ | Guide for processed materials. |
| 9004–4 | $10^2$ | Guide to quality improvement. |
| 9004–5 | $11^2$ | Guide to use of quality plans. |
| 9004–6 | $12^2$ | Guide to configuration management. |
| 9000–3 | 13 | Guide to the application of BS5750: Part 1 to the development, supply, and maintenance of software. |

[1] Revision of Section 0.2.
[2] In preparation at time of printing.

Detailed recommendations for the development of a quality manual are given in Chapter 6 but, briefly, it should set out the general quality policies, procedures, and practices of the organization. In the quality manual for large organizations it may be convenient to indicate simply the existence and contents of other manuals, those containing the details of procedures and practices in operation in specific areas of the system.

Before an organization can agree to supply to a specification, it must ensure that:

(a) The processes and equipment (including any that are subcontracted) are capable of meeting the requirements.
(b) The operators have the necessary skills and training.
(c) The operating procedures are written down and not simply passed on verbally.

(d) The plant and equipment instrumentation is capable of measuring the process variables with the appropriate accuracy and precision.
(e) The quality-control procedures and any inspection, check, or test methods available, provide results to the required accuracy and precision, and are documented.
(f) Any subjective phrases in the specification, such as 'finely ground', 'low moisture content', 'in good time', are understood, and procedures to establish the exact customer requirements exist.

## 3 Contract review

It is difficult to over-emphasize the importance of this aspect of the system. Each accepted customer order should be regarded as a contract, and 'order entry procedures' should be developed and documented. These should ensure that:

(a) The customer requirements are absolutely clear and in writing, including the recording of any verbal communication, e.g. telephone instructions or orders.
(b) Differences between the order and any original enquiry and/or quotation are agreed or resolved.
(c) The terms of the order (contract) can be met, including verifying that dates promised to customers on acceptance of the contract can be met.

Clearly, a procedural dialogue should be established between customer and supplier with regard to the specification, interfaces and the communication of changes. The system must ensure that everyone in the organization understands the commitments, skills, and resources required to meet any particular contract, and that these have been scheduled.

## 4 Design control

Where a Level 1 system is required, there must be procedures that control and verify design of products or services to ensure that the customer requirements will be met. The translation of the information derived from market research into practical designs that are achievable by the operating units should be the core of the documented design-control system. This will include the following activities, which were dealt with in more detail in Chapter 3:

- Planning of research, design and development.
- Assignment of design activities to qualified staff.

- Identification of the organizational and technical interfaces between different groups.
- Preparation of a design brief relating to the requirements of the product or service (inputs).
- Production of clear and comprehensive technical data to enable complete operation of the service or production and delivery of the product, according to the requirements (outputs).
- Verification that the design outputs meet the requirements of the inputs.
- Identification and control of all design changes and modifications and the associated documentation.

Attention, in detail, to the above areas will form the basis of a research, design and development programme. With correct implementation it will maintain a balance between innovation and standardization, which encourages the use of new techniques whilst retaining reliable, proven designs, materials and methods.

## 5   Document control

All documents relating to quality, including the following, should be 'controlled':

(a) Quality manual and supplementary manuals.
(b) Departmental operating manuals.
(c) Written procedures.
(d) Purchasing specifications.
(e) Lists of approved suppliers.
(f) Product, parts, or service formulations and specifications.
(g) Intermediate, part, or component formulations and specifications.
(h) Service manuals.
(i) Relevant international and national standards.

'Control' is necessary to ensure that only the most up-to-date issues are used and referred to at the various locations. Clearly this will require records of what documents exist and/or are needed, and of who holds the documents; plus a written procedure for the issue of amendments and revisions, and for re-issues, together with some form of acknowledgement of receipt. Computerized techniques may be very helpful here. If additional copies of 'controlled' documents are produced for temporary purposes, procedures should exist to prevent their misuse. Sales literature is not usually regarded as controlled documentation, unless it forms the basis of a contract. In industries where continuous innovation, redesign and/or improvements are major features, good document change control is vital.


## 6 Purchasing (see also Chapter 4)

The objective of the purchasing system is very simple – to ensure that purchased products and services conform to the requirements of the organization. The means of achieving this should be concentrated on assessments of the suppliers' own quality systems, rather than by an elaborate scheme of checking, testing and inspection on receipt. The system should essentially consider the 'contract review' from the view of the purchaser.

Suppliers or subcontractors should be selected on the basis of their ability to meet the defined requirements, and objective documentary evidence will be required to show that the supplier:

(a) Has the capability to do so.
(b) Will do so reliably and consistently.

When the extent of *vendor appraisal* necessary has to be decided, the following factors should be taken into consideration:

- Feasibility of appraisal.
- Objective evidence, from records and analysis of acceptable past per-formance (not 'reputation', which is subjective).
- Any independent third-party quality system assessment, certification, or registration to a recognized standard, e.g. ISO 9000 series.
- Any assessments by means of questionnaires or visits, which should be documented.

Vendor appraisal of any product or service subcontractors is often necessary to ensure that their quality system matches the standard of the purchasing organization, and appraisal visits may form part of the corrective action following unsatisfactory performance. Purchasing documents were referred to in some detail in Chapter 4, but the basic requirements are that they:

(a) Are written.
(b) Include the specification, or reference to it, to describe clearly the product/service required.
(c) Are made available to the supplier.
(d) Are reviewed and approved by authorized personnel before issue.

Purchases can be made by telephone or computer means, but must refer to the appropriate purchasing documentation. The system should allow customers to impose quality-system requirments on their suppliers' suppliers, and so on, if specified in the contract. This may include independent third-party certification, assessment of products, services or records, or even the use of such specific techniques as statistical process control (SPC). See Chapter 9.

Records of acceptable suppliers and subcontractors should be maintained, together with their monitored performance.

### 7    Customer-supplied product or services

Where a customer supplies material or services on which further transformation work is required, it is necessary to have systems that ensure the material's suitability for use and that enable monitoring and traceability of the material or service through all processes and storage. Any material that is damaged, lost, or not suitable for use should be recorded and reported to the customer. Special consideration may be necessary when the customer supplies material that is to be used in a continuous process with other purchased material. Clearly a supplier cannot be held responsible for the quality of the customer's material handled, but he is responsible for maintaining its condition while it is in his care.

### 8    Identification and traceability

Identification and traceability from purchased materials to finished products and services are essential if effective methods of process control are to be applied and quality problems are to be related to cause. Materials in process or bulk storage should be identified, if necessary by virtue of their location and time, and the design of procedures and record-keeping should allow for this. Traceability requirements are an optional part of an agreed specification or contract, and may be the subject of special contract conditions. In a garage, for example, a system should be developed to identify any parts removed from vehicles as either for re-use, requiring repair, etc.

### 9    Process control

To control the operation of any process clearly requires some planning activity, i.e. careful consideration of the inputs to the process so that they become suitable for the purpose. This requirement covers the core of any operation. It may be difficult to imagine, but the author has seen too often the operation of processes about which too little is known in terms of the ability to meet the requirements.

To operate processes under controlled conditions, documented work instructions must be available to staff. These do not need to repeat the basic skills of the operator's profession, but they must contain sufficient detail to enable the process to be carried out under the specified conditions. A fully documented 'process manual' should contain, where appropriate:

(a) A description of the process, with appropriate technological information; this may be in the form of a process flowchart.
(b) A description of the plant or equipment required.
(c) Any special process 'set-up' or 'start-up' procedures.
(d) Reference to any instrumentation and calibration procedures related to control of the process.
(e) Simplified operator instructions or a summary that includes the quantity of materials required and the order in which the process is to be carried out. This may take the form of service handbooks or bulletins, etc.

For certain special processes, such as welding, plastic moulding, heat treatment, application of protective treatments, vehicle servicing, and cooking, where deficiencies may become apparent only after the product is in use, continuous monitoring of adherence to the documented procedures is the only effective method of process control.

## 10 Checking, measuring, inspecting and testing incoming materials and services

All need to be either inspected or otherwise verified. The amount of inspection is clearly a function of the situation, and might consist simply of:

- Checking a product label or delivery note against a purchase order.
- Visual examination for damage in transit.
- Checking the evidence from a certificate of conformity or of analysis.

These checks are valid only if an adequate assessment of the supplier's quality system has been carried out.

Whatever the system, it must be operated in accordance with the written procedures. If bought-in materials have to be released into production before adequate verification or checking can take place, the system should ensure that it is possible to identify the material and recall it if problems arise. This may prevent the acceptance of certain bulk materials without the appropriate receiving inspection.

*In process monitoring*

This answers the 'Are we doing the job OK?' question, which calls for some form of process monitoring and control. Ideally it is the actual process parameters, such as temperature, cutting speed, feederate, pressure, typing speed, flow rate, which should be monitored to ensure feedforward control of the process. The work instructions should also indicate the frequency of any in-process inspections or checks, and the action to be taken in the event of process parameters being found to be incorrect, or 'out-of-control'.

*Checking finished product and/or service*

Whatever final checking, inspecting or testing activities have been set out in the quality plan should be documented, including any delaying of despatch, or release of service, until the checks have been carried out. Records must be kept of all the checks, tests, mesurements, etc., carried out at inwards goods or services receipt, during operation of the process, or at the final product or service stage, which are required to demonstrate conformance to the requirements or specifications. These may include certificates of conformity or analysis, and evidence on plant records or in a computer that process control parameters were actually monitored. There should also be a statement of what records are kept, for how long, and by whom.

## 11　Measuring, inspection and test equipment

All measuring and the test equipment relevant to the quality system must be controlled, calibrated and maintained. This includes equipments used for in-process parameter measurements and control, such as temperature and pressure gauges, as well as that used in laboratories or test/measurement areas. Where equipment is used only for observation, safety, or fault diagnosis reasons, it may be excluded from the fully documented inspection calibration system.

　The system for the instrumentation should:

(a) Refer to the measurements to be made, their accuracy and precision, and the equipment to be used to ensure the necessary capability.
(b) Identify the equipment and ensure its calibration against the appropriate standard(s) with suitable procedures, and its correct handling, preservation, storage etc.

(c) Maintain calibration records for all inspection, measuring and test equipment.

(d) Allow, where appropriate, tracking back to national standards.

## 12 Inspection and test status

There are essentially three statuses for all materials and services – incoming, intermediate or in-process, and finished:

* Awaiting inspection, check or test.
* Passed requirements of inspection, check or test.
* Failed requirements of inspection, check or test.

The next status of material is identified by any suitable means: labels, location, stamps markings, position in the process, records (including computer), etc. These should be used to ensure that only material or services conforming to the requirements are passed on to the next stage, or despatched. The test or check carried out may of course refer to a process-control parameter.

## 13 Nonconforming products or services

To prevent inadvertent use or delivery of materials or provision of services that do not conform to the specified requirements, there should be a documented system that clearly identifies and, if possible, 'segregates' them. The procedures should also show how the nonconforming output will be reworked, disposed of, accepted with concession, or regraded, and what corrective action will take place.

## 14 Corrective action

This is a very important part of the system in any organization, since it provides the means to never ending improvement of process operation. Systematic planning is a basic requirement for effective corrective action programmes. The procedures for major corrective action should be in the form of general guidance and should define the duties of the managers, supervisors and key personnel. The detailed action to be taken will be dependent upon the circumstances prevailing at the time, and it is not therefore appropriate for the written procedures to be too detailed. All employees must be made fully aware of the general corrective action procedures appertaining to their own processes and activities. The written procedures for corrective action should be implemented when there are:

- Failures in *any* part of the quality system.
- Complaints from customers (internal or external).
- Complaints to suppliers (internal or external) and to subcontractors.

The underlying purpose of this part of the system is to eliminate the causes of nonconformance by initiation of investigations, analyses, and preventive actions. Controls must be built in to make sure that the corrective actions are taken, that they are effective, and that any necessary changes in procedures are recorded and implemented. The provision of *corrective action teams*, with regular training and updating, enables people to become used to working together to solve problems.

## 15   Protection of product or service quality

The sight of a warehouseman, in dirty wellington boots, climbing over clean sacks of finished product to count them, still remains in the author's memory. A great deal of damage can be done to products and services between their 'production' and their transfer to the customer. This highlights the need for the quality system to cover such things as handling, storage, packaging, transport, and delivery of final product or services. The written procedures should be aimed at preventing damage or deterioration. The use of the correct type of packaging and labelling may invoke national or international regulations and/or codes of practice. Where contract hauliers or outside transport are employed, their ability to meet the requirements of cleanliness, schedules, etc., should be established, and appropriate procedures documented.

## 16   Quality records

The records provide objective evidence that work is being carried out in accordance with the documented procedures. Attention should be paid to identifying which records need to be retained, and to their easy retrieval. One of the author's colleagues was, on one occasion, performing a vertical audit for traceability purposes in a garment manufacturer's. He selected some items from stock and, on attempting to trace back to purchased materials, discovered that final inspection records on certain items were missing. It transpired that one of the final inspectors spent 3 months in hospital, and the chief inspector, who insisted that she had stood in and carried out the necessary inspection, was too busy to write down the results. This represents a failure of the system to *demonstrate* compliance with its own requirements, and can be as serious as an ineffective procedure.

Records will have been established if the documented quality system has been set up as described above, but there must be procedures for the collection, indexing, filing or storage, retrieval, and disposition of records. Serious thought should be given to the retention time of records, which should then be stated in the documented system.

The quality records should include training and management audit and review records.

## 17 Quality-system audits and reviews

An internal *audit* sets out to establish whether the quality-management system is being operated according to the written procedures. A *review* addresses the much wider issue of whether the quality system actually meets the requirements, and aims to determine the system's effectiveness. Clearly the results of quality audits will be used in the reviews, for if procedures are not being operated according to plan, it may be that improvements in the system are required, rather than enforcing adherence to unsuitable methods. Organizations should plan to self-police the quality system by carrying out both internal audits and reviews, and the person responsible for organizing these is the manager with responsibility for co-ordinating and monitoring the whole quality system (see also Chapter 6). Auditor training is now recognized as a key element in quality-system implementation.

## 18 Training (see chapter 14)

For *all* staff, written procedures should be established and maintained for:

* Identifying and reviewing individual training needs.
* Carrying out the training.
* Keeping records of training, including qualifications.

On-the-job training may frequently be appropriate in meeting the training requirements. It should be possible to go to the training records and establish from them objectively whether an individual has been instructed to carry out the various tasks associated with his/her job.

Training procedures may also include methods of ensuring the quality policy is understood, implemented and maintained at all levels in the organization, for existing and new employees.

**19   Servicing**

If servicing is an important part of the customer requirement, e.g. in the provision of a burglar alarm service, procedures should be documented for its operation and to verify that it satisfies the needs. The servicing system may well include some or all of the contents of the quality system: design, documentation control, process control, training, review, etc. In particular it must ensure that:

(a) The servicing procedures are effectively carried out.
(b) Adequate resources are made available, in terms of people, time, equipment, materials, information, etc.
(c) Good interfaces exist for dealing with the customer, in terms of regular service contracts, items returned, customer complaints or call-outs.

**20   Statistical techniques (see Chapter 9)**

In most organizations it is necessary to measure and establish the so-called 'capability of the process'. In many industries this requires the use of certain procedures, which are grouped under the general heading of *statistical process control* (SPC).

In addition to measuring capability, controlling and improving processes through the use of statistical techniques, it might also be necessary to identify and classify lots of batches of material by their characteristics, select samples, determine any rules for acceptance or rejection of material or for adjusting the severity of inspection and the segregation and screening of rejected materials. The system should refer to the statistical procedures used, giving the areas for their application, but always remember that statistics is simply the collection and use of data.

In considering the detailed quality-system requirements, the system *must* be tailored to the needs of the 'business'. It must be seen to be an integral part of the way the business is run, and the system must be usable by all employees in never ending improvement.

## 5.4   Quality systems in the service sector, marketing and the environment

Historically, formal quality systems and procedures were confined to the manufacturing and process industries, but in recent years they have spread rapidly into the services sector, as organizations seek to enhance their reputations for supplying quality services. Against a background of escalating international competition and customer expectations, more and more customers of the service sector are demanding objective evidence of quality and consistency from their suppliers. This is increasingly taking the form of independent, third-party confirmation and certification to recognized standards.

The International Standard ISO 9000 series clearly has its origins in manufacturing industry, yet the principles it embodies are common to services. Having said that, however, we must recognize that the interpretation of the standard for the service sector is not so simple. It is for this reason that various 'guidance notes' have been generated for various sectors, e.g. education and training, and garages.

A key area of debate when applying quality-system standards to services is the use of the term 'product'. For an educational or training establishment, for example, it has been variously described as the course, the programme, the curriculum, and, perhaps more appropriately, the person who goes through the educational or training process. This has wide implications for quality-system design. In many services the 'product' is an individual who has benefited by the service. Therefore all functions and activities associated with student, patient and, generally, 'customer' care should be covered under 'purchaser supplied product'. In the case of students, for example, these should include joining instructions, health-care availability, career-counselling, personal safety, library, lodgings, etc. Similarly, 'product identification and traceability' in a hospital may start with patient records and 'who did what to whom, when and where', but could extend into similar records for medical and nursing staff.

Under the heading 'process control' the core of the service operation may include, for a training organization, course development, course evaluation, course planning and review, scheduling, registration/attendance recording procedures, course-delivery requirements for visual aids, course manuals, hand-outs, etc. In the service sector there is a sense in which the core processes are 'special processes' under the definition of the standard. Staff skill is often the key factor influencing the process, and documented selection and training procedures are a major need. Special processes in the service sector could also include those parts of the operation that impinge closely on the quality of the service 'experience', e.g. in an hotel. Where appropriate, these could include any arrangements for catering, residence, travel, car parking, cleaning and vacating premises. Some of these activities will also need to be covered in other sections, such as purchasing and in-process inspection.

Any service will require that some form of assessment, monitoring, testing or examination is laid down to evaluate the performance/progress of the service, student, patient, process, or customer. In the training/education area, for example, the evaluation method and criteria will depend on the type of course, and could be a range of methods from simple course-attendance records to a fully invigilated set of examinations. A key parameter is consistency of the evaluation method. As in any area, quality records, including those of audits and reviews, are a vital part of a service operation's quality system.

## Marketing Quality Assurance (MQA)

MQA is a third-party certification organization specializing in providing assessment services to organizations wishing to develop quality systems for their marketing, sales, and customer-service activities; in assessing companies in the services sector to the ISO 9000 series of Quality System Standards; and in developing third-party certification guidelines for specific service areas, such as public relations.

MQA has produced a quality assurance specification for marketing, sales and customer assurance. This is an associated document to the ISO 9000 series, and MQA offer registration to ISO 9001, EN 29001, BS5750 (Part 1) for an organization's marketing, sales and customer-service activities. MQA awards a certificate of excellence and the right to use the MQA mark, if companies achieve the required standard. The aim is to signal to customer, competitors and employees, that the certified organization is one that has achieved independent recognition of its marketing excellences.

The objectives of using the MQA approach are summarized in Figure 5.4. Its own quality specification deals with systems that apply specifically to marketing, sales and customer assurance. The specification defines a marketing audit, marketing strategy, customer assurance, code of conduct, and a marketing and sales quality system. The fifty-eight requirements of the specification are categorized under fifteen headings, which clearly relate to the ISO 9000 series:

- Quality policy.
- Business plans.
- Organization.
- Management representatives.
- Management review.
- Quality system.
- Marketing and sales plans.

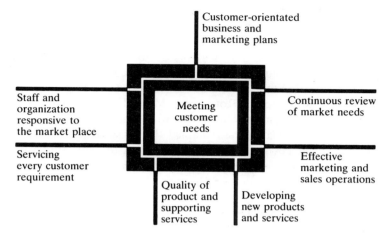

Customer-orientated
business and
marketing plans

Staff and
organization
responsive to
the market place

Meeting
customer
needs

Continuous review
of market needs

Servicing
every customer
requirement

Effective
marketing and
sales operations

Quality of
product and
supporting
services

Developing
new products
and services

**Figure 5.4** *MQA objectives*

- Code of conduct.
- Marketing and sales operations.
- Customer assurance.
- Purchasing.
- Resources, personnel, training, organization structure.
- Controls and procedures.
- Records.
- Quality audits.

Briefly, the specification states that *business plans* must exist and marketing inputs should have contributed to their development. There should be clearly defined processes for the *review of market needs*, which should identify and reassess customer needs and preference. The *marketing and sales* plans must relate to the business plans, and be understood and agreed by the contributing departments. The requirements under *marketing and sales operations* call for best practice in all the operational areas, including product or service development, promotion, pricing, selling, and distribution. All aspects of *customer assurance* should be covered to inspire confidence that the stated or implied needs are being satisfied. The specification sets down requirements, under *resources, personnel, training and organization structure*, for well-trained experienced staff who are responsive to the needs of the market place. All this and the more traditional areas are to be represented in a *documented quality system* that demonstrates the organization's capabilities in meeting customer requirements.

In 1991 Exxon Chemical International Marketing B.V. became the first organization to achieve registration to Marketing Quality Assurance (MQA) for the marketing, sales and customer-assurance activities of its Adhesives and Sealants Sector, which comprised seven offices throughout Europe. This Exxon Chemical industry sector achieved registration in seven assessed European offices in Cologne, Paris, Milan, Southampton, Rotterdam, Madrid and Brussels.

The European Business Unit General Manager claimed that the MQA Quality Specification had enabled the organization to further its commitment to achieving a quality culture, and to achieve registration to ISO 9000 in 'three of the most significant areas of any business'.


**Environmental management systems**

Organizations of all kinds are increasingly concerned to achieve and demonstrate sound environmental performance. Many have undertaken environmental audits and review to assess this. To be effective, these need to be conducted within a structured management system, which in turn is integrated with the management activities dealing with all aspects of desired environmental performance.

Such a system should establish procedures for setting environmental policy and objectives, and achieving compliance to them. It should be designed to place emphasis on the prevention of adverse environmental effects rather than on detection after occurrence. It should also identify and assess the environmental effects arising from the organization's existing or proposed activities, products, or services, and from incidents, accidents, and potential emergency situations. The system must identify the relevant regulatory requirements, the priorities, and pertinent environmental objectives and targets. It needs also to facilitate planning, control, monitoring, auditing and review activities to ensure that the policy is complied with, that it remains relevant, and that it is capable of evolution to suit changing circumstances.

In 1992 a British Standard BS7750 was prepared under the direction of the Environment and Pollution Standards Policy Committee in response to the increasing concerns about environmental protection and performance. It contains a specification for environmental management systems for ensuring and demonstrating compliance with stated policies and objectives. The standard is designed to enable any organization to establish an effective management system as a foundation for both sound environmental performance and participation in environmental auditing schemes.

BS7750 shares common management system principles with BS5750

**Table 5.2** *The links between BS7750 (1992) and BS5750: Part 1 (1987)*

A cell containing a • represents a connection between the relevant sub-clauses of the two standards.

| Requirement of BS5750: Part 1 Subclause | Requirement of BS7750 Subclause | | | | | | | | | | |
|---|---|---|---|---|---|---|---|---|---|---|---|
| | 4.1 | 4.2 | 4.3 | 4.4 | 4.5 | 4.6 | 4.7 | 4.8 | 4.9 | 4.10 | 4.11 |
| | Management system | Environmental policy | Organization and personnel | Environmental effects | Objectives and targets | Management programme | Manual and documentation | Operational control | Records | Audits | Reviews |
| **4.1** Management responsibility | • | • | • | | | | | | | • | |
| **4.2** Quality system | • | | | | | | • | | | | |
| **4.3** Contract review | | | | • | • | • | | | | | |
| **4.4** Design control | | | | | | • | • | • | | | |
| **4.5** Document control | | | | | | | • | | | | |
| **4.6** Purchasing | | | | • | | | | • | | | |
| **4.7** Purchaser supplied product | | | | • | | | | | | | |
| **4.8** Product identification | | | | | | | | | • | | |
| **4.9** Process control | | | | | | | | • | | | |
| **4.10** Inspection and testing | | | | | | | | • | | | |
| **4.11** Inspection, measuring and test equipment | | | | | | | | • | | | |
| **4.12** Inspection and test status | | | | | | | | • | | | |
| **4.13** Control of nonconforming product | | | | | | | | • | | | |
| **4.14** Corrective action | | | | | | | | • | | | |
| **4.15** Handling, storage, packaging and delivery | | | | • | | | | • | | | |
| **4.16** Quality records | | | | | | | | | • | | |
| **4.17** Internal quality audits | | | | | | | | | | • | |
| **4.18** Training | | | • | | | | | | | | |
| **4.19** Servicing | | | | • | | | | • | | | |
| **4.20** Statistical techniques | | | | | | | | • | | | |

*Source* – BS7750: 1992 (British Standards)

(EN 29000, ISO 9000), and organizations may elect to use an existing management system, developed in conformity with the ISO 9000 series, as a basis for environmental management. The new standard defines environmental policy, objectives, targets, effect, management, systems, manuals, evaluation, audits and reviews. It mirrors the ISO 9000 series requirements in many of its own eleven requirements, and it includes a guide to these in the informative Annex A.

The link to BS5750 (ISO 9000) is spelled out in a table that is reproduced in Table 5.2. The standard has also been developed in such a way as to complement the European Community ECO-Audit Regulations and as a foundation for registration under them.

Quality systems are needed in all areas of activity, whether large or small businesses, manufacturing, service or public sector. The advantages of systems in manufacturing are obvious, but they are just as applicable in areas such as marketing, sales, personnel, finance, research and development, as well as in the service industries and public sectors.

No matter where it is implemented, a good quality system will improve process control, reduce wastage, lower costs, increase market share (or funding), facilitate training, increase staff participation, and raise morale.

## 5.5   The rings of confidence

The activities to be addressed in the design and implementation of a good quality-management system may be considered to be attached to a 'ring of confidence', which starts and ends with the customer (Figure 5.5). It is possible to group these into two spheres of activities:

- Those directly interacting with the customer.
- Those concerning primarily the internal activities of the supplier.

The overlap necessary between customer and supplier is clearly illustrated by this model. Equally obvious is that separation will lead to disfunction and disaster.

It cannot be stated too often that the customer–supplier interactions, which generate satisfaction of needs, are just as necessary internally. The principles of quality-system design, documentation and implementation set out in this and the next chapter must apply to every single person, every department, every process transaction, and every type of organization. The vocabulary in the engineering factory system may be different

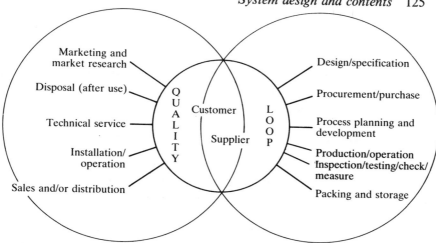

**Figure 5.5** *The rings of confidence*

from that used in the hotel, the hospital system will be set out differently to that of the drug manufacturer, but the underlying concepts will be the same.

It is not acceptable for the managers in industries, or parts of organizations, less often associated with standards on quality systems to find 'technological' reasons for avoiding the requirement to manage quality. The author and his colleagues have heard the excuse that 'our industry (or organization) differs from any other industry (or organization)', in almost every industry or organization with which they have come into contact. Clearly there are technological differences between all industries and nearly all organizations, but in terms of managing total quality there are hardly any at all.

Senior managers in every type and size of organization must take the responsibility for the adoption of the appropriate documented quality system. If this requires translation from 'engineering language', so be it – get someone from inside or outside the organization to do it. Do not wait for the message to be translated into different forms – inefficiencies, waste, high costs, crippling competition, loss of market.

# Chapter highlights

### Why a documented system?

- An appropriate documented quality system will enable the objectives set out in the quality policy to be accomplished.

- The International Standards Organization (ISO) 9000 series sets out methods by which a system can be implemented to ensure that the specified requirements are met.
- A quality system may be defined as an assembly of components, such as the organizational structure responsibilities, procedures, processes, and resources.

**Quality system design**

- Quality systems should apply to and interact with all activities of the organization. The activities are generally processing, communicating, and controlling. These should be documented in the form of a quality manual.
- The system should follow the PLAN DO CHECK ACT cycle, through documentation, implementation, audit and review.

**Quality system requirements**

- The general categories of ISO-based standards include management responsibility, quality system, contract review, design control, document control, purchasing, customer-supplied products or services, identification and traceability, process control, checking/measuring /inspecting of incoming materials or services, measuring/inspection/ test equipment, inspection/test status, nonconforming products or services, corrective action, protection of product or service quality, quality records, quality-system audits and reviews, training, servicing and statistical techniques.

**Quality systems in the service sector, marketing and the environment**

- There are 'guidance notes' for the use of ISO standards in the service sector, in which terms such as 'product' and 'process control' are given careful consideration.
- Marketing Quality Assurance (MQA) is a third-party certification organization specializing in assessment services for marketing, sales, customer-service activities, and the service sector.
- The MQA specification document is based on the ISO 9000 series and has fifty-eight requirements, categorized under fifteen headings. It addresses particularly the need for business plans, review of market needs, marketing and sales plans and operations, customer-assurance resources, personnel training and organization structure.
- Increasingly organizations are undertaking audits and reviews to assess environmental performance. These should be conducted

within a structured management system that sets policy, targets and objectives.
- The British Standard BS7750 contains a specification for environmental management systems for ensuring and demonstrating compliance with the stated policies and objectives, and acting as a base for auditing and review schemes. It shares common management-system principles with the ISO 9000 series.

**The rings of confidence**

- The activities needed in the design and implementation of a good quality system start and end with the customer, in two spheres – a customer sphere and a supplier sphere.
- Senior management in all types of industry must take responsibility for the adoption and documentation of the appropriate quality system in their organization.

# 6 System documentation, implementation and assessment

## 6.1 The quality system documentation

The quality manual is the document that explains how the organization carries out the quality policy. The author has visited many organizations in both the manufacturing and service sectors which, when asked to produce the quality manual, have required three people to carry it in, or pointed to a bank of filing cabinets. That volume of material is not a quality manual, it is usually a test and inspection procedures manual, a calibration and measurement system, a bank operating procedures manual, perhaps a purchasing system.

A good quality manual should be no longer than 25 to 30 pages. It is perhaps misnamed – it should be called the *management manual* – for it explains how the organization's management systems operate to achieve the general goals, the explanation being in the form of a series of simple statements of what is actually done, and it refers to where detailed procedures may be found, if necessary. There will be a section – a page – on how the purchasing system operates, one on what happens if customers complain, another on the organizational structure, with allocation of responsibility for the management of the quality system clearly stated, and so on. The *quality manual* then sets out the general policies, procedures, and practices of the organization, in a well-organized, comprehensive, and succinct manner.

### Planning a quality manual

There is no standard form for writing a quality manual, since each one must describe the particular policies and system to which it refers, and this must be the system that is actually operated, not the one the quality manager would like to see operating. Every organization produces and serves, and is organized in a unique way, and it is this that must be reflected in the documented system. All this means of course is that organizations must write their own quality manuals.

If an international standard, such as the ISO 9000 series, is being used as the framework for the quality system, it is necessary at this stage to decide which level or part of the standard will best suit the activities. It is not possible to move on to the detailed planning of the manual until this has been decided. The chosen standard and level should be mentioned in the quality manual at an early stage.

It is important to appreciate that there are various types of quality system and that the quality manual will reflect this. The ISO 9000 series specifies requirements for quality systems designed to generate products and services that meet the agreed specifications. Hence it addresses a limited number of activities, and differs from a system whose purpose is to achieve total quality management. For a TQM system, *every* activity in the organization must be included. Of course ISO 9000 series systems may be applied to every activity but a conscious effort must be made to interpret the standard in this way, and for it to be applied at every transformation interface. For example, it is not necessary to include the personnel or accounts department in an ISO 9000 series quality manual, but they must be included if the aim of the organization's quality policy is TQM.

The organization of the quality manual may reflect the standard chosen as the template, or it may be grouped under the managerial functions and activities. For example, one chemical company arranged its manual according to the latter, which generated the headings listed on the left-hand side of Table 6.1. These related to the requirements of ISO 9001 (also BS 5750, Part 1) according to the right-hand side of the table. Clearly, each organization will differ in some of these aspects, but the main requirement is to ensure that all the listed activities are covered by the documentation. These then provide headings under which more detailed statements are made. For the special operations undertaken by some organizations, other categories may be created. Some of the standard requirements appear in two or more of the functional areas; this is often necessary to ensure that the system operates effectively at functional or departmental interfaces.

## Writing a quality manual

Once the organization has been classified into groups of activities, and the requirements of any standard being used have been allocated to one or more groups, the construction of the quality manual may begin with the format. This should facilitate the incorporation of alterations or modifications as the organization, products, services, and processes change. A loose-leaf system obviously provides good flexibility, as does

**Table 6.1** *Arrangement of a quality manual by functional area*

| Section | Functional area | ISO 9000 requirement | Clause number |
|---|---|---|---|
| 1 | Quality management | Management responsibility | 4.1 |
| | | Quality system | 4.2 |
| | | Document control | 4.5 |
| | | Quality records | 4.16 |
| | | Internal quality system audits and reviews | 4.17 |
| | | Training | 4.18 |
| | | Corrective action | 4.14 |
| 2 | Marketing and sales | Contract review | 4.3 |
| | | Servicing | 4.19 |
| 3 | Product research and development | Design control | 4.4 |
| 4 | Purchasing and subcontracting | Purchasing | 4.6 |
| | | Purchaser-supplied product | 4.7 |
| | | Corrective action | 4.14 |
| | | Document control | 4.5 |
| | | Packaging | 4.15.4 |
| | | Delivery | 4.15.5 |
| 5 | Production | Product identification, traceability | 4.8 |
| | | Process control | 4.9 |
| | | In-process inspection and testing | 4.10.2 |
| | | Inspection, measuring and test equipment | 4.11 |
| | | Inspection and test status | 4.12 |
| | | Control of nonconforming product | 4.13 |
| | | Corrective action | 4.14 |
| | | Statistical techniques | 4.20 |
| 6 | Quality control | Inspection and testing | 4.10 |
| | | Inspection, measuring and test equipment | 4.11 |
| | | Inspection and test status | 4.12 |
| | | Control of nonconforming product | 4.13 |
| | | Quality records | 4.16 |
| | | Statistical techniques | 4.20 |
| | | Corrective action | 4.14 |
| 7 | Stock control (including warehousing, despatch, delivery and transport) | Product identification, traceability | 4.8 |
| | | Inspection and test status | 4.12 |
| | | Control of nonconforming product | 4.13 |
| | | Handling, storage, packaging and delivery | 4.15 |
| | | Corrective action | 4.14 |

a computerized system, if the ability to make changes is incorporated in the software.

The author has found a systematic questioning technique useful in setting out to help organizations to write a quality manual (see Chapter 4). The following questions should be asked with regard to each requirement being met:

- What is done? (to meet the requirement).
- Why is it done? (or why is it done that way?)
- Where is the requirement met?
- When is the requirement met?
- Who is responsible for ensuring that it is done?
- How is it done?

This sequence of questions is important if an organization wishes to review its working practices at the same time as writing the quality manual. If the second question receives the response 'Because it has always been done that way', then the last question may lead to better methods by developing into 'How else might it be done?'

The question relating to who is responsible should be answered by job titles not names, to avoid changes to the manual being required after every change of personnel. For the responsibilities to be clarified, the organizational structure must be set down. This is then amplified by listing, under the various divisions, the responsibilities and activities that may affect the quality. Chapter 11 of this book may prove helpful in this task. At this point it is worth mentioning that job descriptions or specifications should *not* appear in the quality manual, but may form part of the general documentation referred to in the manual.

Cross-references to detailed written procedures, such as test methods, process operation, and sales, will answer the 'How is it done?' question. It is not necessary for these to appear again in the quality manual. This applies also to commercially sensitive material or technical data, approved suppliers, details of processes, etc. These have no place in the manual, which needs to refer only to where the information is kept, who is responsible for it, when it must be referred to, and how it is used and updated. A test of a good quality manual with adequate cross-referencing is that it may be shown to a customer, potential customer, supplier or competitor, without revealing anything of a sensitive nature. It is usual somewhere at the front of the manual to define, again with cross-references, the terms common to the organization's industry, products, services, processes, etc.

**Large organizations**

Organizations with several thousand employees and/or many different sites will probably require a quality manual with several layers. Those organized into business groups may find it convenient to write a manual for each business, although in some very large companies even these will require further segregation – possibly on a site or unit basis. A multi-layer quality manual may take the following form:

*Layer 1   Overall quality policy manual*
          – usually very brief and extending the quality policy statement, it may be issued by 'headquarters'.
*Layer 2   Business group quality manual*
          – brief summary of one of the organization's multi-site business groups, it will probably address the issues related to managerial responsibilities.
*Layer 3   Site quality manual*
          – detailed description of how the standard requirements are actually met on the site generally, it will cross-reference any departmental manuals and procedures as necessary.
*Layer 4   Departmental or functional group quality manual*
          – detailed description of how the standard requirements are met at the local level, it will cross-reference product or service specifications, technical and operational procedures, and any commercially sensitive material.
*Layer 5   Detailed operational procedures*
          – details of how all methods pertaining to the business of the organization are performed, this layer will be the base point from which the documentation in support of the complete quality system is assembled.

In each layer the documentation must reflect what is actually done; thereby it serves the system, it does not master it.

**The system and the standard**

The questioning does not stop with the written manual, for it is necessary at this stage to ask if the system, accurately described in the written word, actually meets the requirements of the chosen standard. If the answer is no in one or more areas, then it must be ascertained whether the misalignment can be remedied by a minor change requiring *minimum paperwork*. It is far too easy to create 'additional forms' for every slight deviation, and so create a bureaucracy in which the dynamic quality system becomes completely bogged down. The act of writing a quality manual often proves a valuable means of exposing root causes of problems. It is necessary then of course to correct or remove those causes, rather than merely document them.

A Level 2 quality manual for one site of a large manufacturing group may have the following contents list:

Confidentiality of quality manual
Distribution list
Quality policy
Responsibility of manual holders to update record changes
Terms and definitions
Organization chart
Block diagram of process
Section 1:   Management responsibility
Section 2:   Quality system
Section 3:   Contract review
Section 4:   Purchasing
Section 5:   Purchaser supplied product
Section 6:   Product identification and traceability
Section 7:   Process control
Section 8:   Inspection and testing
Section 9:   Inspection, measuring and test equipment
Section 10:  Inspection and test status
Section 11:  Control of nonconforming product
Section 12:  Corrective action
Section 13:  Handling, storage, packaging and delivery
Section 14:  Quality records
Section 15:  Internal quality audits
Section 16:  Training
Section 17:  Statistical techniques

## 6.2   Quality information systems

In order to be sure of meeting customer requirements, and continuing to meet them, it is clearly necessary to create a quality information system. Computers may be used in such systems, since the tasks of collection, recording, and analysis of data and information are easily automated. This can save large amounts of human time otherwise expended in merely collecting and recording numbers and words. A microprocessor can form the basis of a small quality-information system, particulary if 'dedicated' use is required for a particular line of production or service.

Whatever the size and type of the computer system employed, it must:

- Provide 'real-time' computing.
- Be able to handle, or be linked into a sufficiently large database.

For rapid response and maximum availability, part of the computer system should be dedicated to quality information and data-handling. A computer that enables data to be collected in this way across the whole work base – the shop floor or office – allows relatively easy implementation of statistical process control (SPC).

Application software packages purpose-designed for quality information systems are now available. The basic requirement of any such package is for it to 'drive' the preventive model of quality management (Figure 6.1). It should include all the SPC techniques necessary to implement the process-control strategy and, when problems occur, operate a stepwise procedure to:

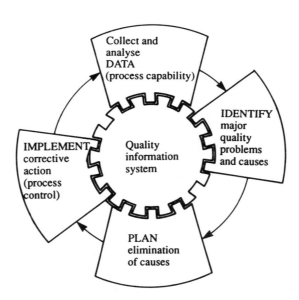

**Figure 6.1** *The quality information system helps 'drive' preventive quality management*

(a) Identify the problem.
(b) Identify the causes of the problem.
(c) Eliminate the causes of the problem.
(d) Continuously monitor the process for recurrence of the problem.

Clearly, human managerial decisions must interface with the package in this procedure, particularly during the elimination stage, but the efficient use of this type of data/information crunching power is invaluable in many complex process situations.

## System requirements

The information system should permit process and product information to be entered into a database. Ideally the user should then be able to employ a high level report generator to extract data, with various search criteria, then analyse and report it, preferably in graphic fashion. The functions of a good quality information system are visualized in Figure 6.2, the details of which are:

(a) *The database*. The structure of the database should be completely clear to the end-user. A standard database software sub-system,

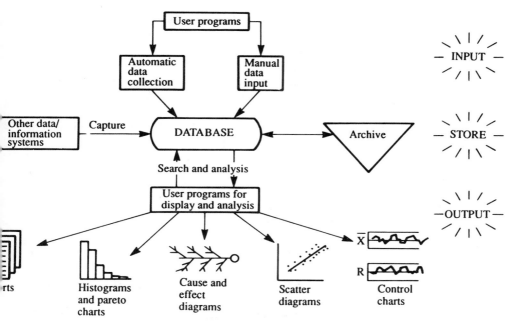

**Figure 6.2** *Quality information system requirements*

one that does not require optimization for different applications and allows the advanced user to access the database with self-written programs, should be used. The system should be capable of storing simultaneously, separately, all data and information introduced into the database. If the database should become corrupt or damaged, this will enable the entire database to be re-established. This important requirement for database integrity should not be neglected.

(b) *Data input*. It should be possible to input data in two different ways – automatically or manually. For automatic transmission into the database, no user intervention is necessary. Data may be provided by process control systems, data collectors and concentrators, measurement or test devices with local intelligence, or by a program running on the same computer. In applications where rapid evaluation of measured or counted data is required for control of the process to take place, the measurement or test control may be handled by a desk-top computer that transmits the results automatically to the database, via the automatic input route.

In the case of manual input the end-user enters data via appropriately designed terminals. The system should be capable of validating data and sending error messages. Bar-code input devices may ease the manual entry of data in applications, such as inwards goods receipt, sample test data input, and so on.

(c) *Report graph output*. Normally the output generator will consist of two parts: a configurator and an interpreter. The former provides the user with the means to build or adjust output reports and graphs, through screen instructions and menus, while the latter actually generates the desired output. Reports, tables, figures, graphs, etc., should be obtainable on a regular basis or by simple demand. The graphical reports most likely to be required include pie charts, histograms, Pareto charts, cause and effect diagrams, scatter diagrams, and various types of control charts (mean and range, proportion defective, cusum, etc). The choice of colour graphics may be desirable for presentation purposes.

## Computer-integrated operations

Computers are used increasingly in all parts of all types of organization. The advantages to be gained from linking computerized quality information to the rest of the computer network are substantial. Free movement of data around the whole system offers enormous flexibility and efficiency in the operational process. Considerable savings in staff time can be realized just in information transfer. The database can be shared by networks, and data entered into the system on one occasion instead of several. The time released may be put to more productive, higher level activities.

## 6.3 Implementation of the system

Even the most meticulous quality system design will not eliminate the need for people. Instructions to them must be clear, concise and precise. Supervisors must ensure that the instructions are followed and that the processes and plant are properly used and maintained, according to the system. The quality management system should be a living thing, not a bureaucracy or a paperwork model, and to make it come to life requires the co-operation of every person in the organization. This can only be achieved by effective communications about what the system is, how it operates, and what role each individual plays in it.

When organizations begin to document their quality systems, it is often necessary to ask people to change the habits of a lifetime. The author recalls some advisory work on a hand-tool manufacturer's premises in which all components and parts were identified with classification numbers and grade of material, until the very last process, where all identification mysteriously disappeared, leaving box after box of apparently identical products. When this was brought to the attention of the shop foreman, Jim, he pointed out that he had worked for the company for nearly 30 years and knew every product and grade by 'sight and sound'. Upon being asked what would happen if he was struck down by lightning while walking his dog one evening, he observed that his colleague Harry had worked in the same workshop for 25 years and knew almost as much as Jim. These are conscientious people – worth their weight in gold – but they need to be persuaded or to learn that part, product, or service identification can be reliable, transferable, and verifiable only if a properly documented system exists. When people have been working in a certain way for very long periods, it can be difficult for them to change and accept and adopt new procedures.

### Quality systems and small organizations

The increasing demands for fully documented quality systems are bound to have a marked effect on those firms employing less than 100 people, which are less likely to have a formal system than larger organizations. The small organization may be:

- Unaware of the implications of a quality management system, and how to meet the requirements of – say – ISO 9000.
- Unable to fend off or pass on pressure from customers,
- Subjected to increasing demands for vendor assessment, use of SPC, certification, etc.
- Subject to demands for verification of their quality system, the costs of which are out of proportion to the contract value.
- Unable to afford a specialist full-time quality manager.
- Inspection-oriented with respect to quality, with little feedback of information gathered.

Many small organizations that maintain a commendable flexibility in their operations and produce excellent service or quality products are frequently unable to demonstrate that they have maintained adequate process control throughout their operations. The reasons for the lack of documentation often lie in the belief that verbal communications will suffice. This is particularly true of tiny companies that have grown, with many employees continuing to carry out the same tasks on the same or similar product or service range. In such organizations formalized documentation is often seen as unnecessary or costly, with new employees being instructed verbally or by example.

Meeting the requirements of an international standard on quality management can be a formidable obstacle to small organizations, requiring from the management an appreciation of the standard(s), motivation, technical competence, and resources to achieve and implement the necessary changes. The motivation may arise from a philosophy of raising standards of quality management, but it is more likely to arise when the companies encounter new types of activity and behaviour from customers, competitors, and suppliers, which change the requirements. This can lead to anxiety and panic if certain customers or contracts may be retained only by compliance or registration.

The inability of the management of many small organizations to achieve the necessary standards may well be exposed by this type of pressure. Many will have little if any experience outside their own organization, and their multifunctional roles exacerbate the difficulties of setting aside time to contemplate, initiate, and implement the improvements. The mere clerical effort required to draw up manuals and operating procedures may be beyond their resources.

Where subsidized or grant-aided provision of outside help in the form of consultancy is available, perhaps through government schemes, this should be utilized to obtain a professional, objective view. Considerable help towards manual preparation and recommendations for system design and practice should then be forthcoming, but it may leave the residual problem of implementation and maintenance largely unsolved. One solution to this problem is for a group of small organizations to share a professional quality manager on an internal/external consultancy basis. This person reports to the chief executives of each of the collaborating partners in which he/she plays a functional role. Manuals can be prepared, changes implemented, audits and reviews carried out, and on a longer-term scale a continuous quality monitoring and improvement process established.

Whether the organization is large or small, whether the expertise comes from within or without, or is shared, there will be a requirement for some initial advisory work. This is best carried out in the form of a project.

## A quality system advisory project

In giving advice concerning a quality-management system it is seldom useful to do so in isolation. The services offered for such advisory projects should therefore be built round the specific requirements of a standard or recognized quality system. These include the British BS 5750 series, the American ANSI/ASQC Q90 series, and the equivalent International ISO 9000 series, as well as individual company requirements such as Ford's Q1.

Organizations should select a consultant who does not offer a standard package around which a company is asked to build or rebuild its Quality Systems. The systems must reflect the established practices of the company, modified if necessary to bring them into line with the requirements of the defined standard. The advice given during a project therefore begins with the current practices of the company. Where modifications are required, the company employees should be consulted to the maximum, consistent with the availability of in-house facilities. A standard set of procedures detailed by a third-party consultant is not embraced as the property of any organization and seldom becomes so – it is either a work of fiction or an alien and unwanted instruction.

A good advisory project covers one, or several, of a series of distinct phases.

*Phase one*

The initial phase, which should include a preliminary visit, is concerned with a clear, agreed and accepted definition of the work to be carried out. This should become the subject of written *terms of reference*, which include:

- An introduction, including the background to the enquiry for an advisory project.
- The objectives of the project.
- A brief description of the quality systems in use within the company.
- The programme of work to be carried out, including details of the areas where systems will need to be modified or expanded in order to meet the requirements of the quality-system standard chosen.
- A detailed estimate of the time required by the consultant in order to complete his part of the work.
- The general conditions and total costs for carrying out the following phases of the work.

*Phase two*

Once the terms of reference have been agreed and accepted by the company, the consultant should prepare an *interim report*. This report results from a more detailed interrogation of the company's actual systems and procedures, and includes sufficient detail to allow an *action plan* to be drawn up. The action plan shows the work to be undertaken both by the consultant and the company for each of the quality system's individual requirements, and the time likely to pass before a satisfactory, operational system can be installed. Guidance should be given on the revisions that will be required to the quality systems.

*Phase three*

This phase covers the consultant's work as outlined in the terms of reference and detailed in the interim report. A full, written *final report* of the consultant's findings and recommendations should be presented to the company, along with a *draft quality manual*, which includes as much of the quality systems as have been clearly defined at the time of presentation. This phase may also include arranging and holding a tripartite meeting with an assessment body, if some sort of independent third-party assessment will be sought.

*Phase four*

When the consultant and the company have both finished their work, it is often useful to invite the consultant to *audit* the systems during a short visit, and to report on any remaining deficiencies. A similar use of consultants may be made by a company considering its systems ready for assessment, without the advisory work.

*Estimated times*

Experience has demonstrated that a total input from the consultant of approximately 15 man–days is sufficient, in nearly all cases, to establish what has to be done, to participate in the vital elements of the work, to detail the remainder and to make a preliminary assessment of a site. The project must seek the views of company employees as much as possible in the detailed work of completing the quality systems, their documentation and implementation. There is seldom a requirement that exceeds 100 man–days of employees' time in order to complete the company's part of the work. The work of bringing quality systems into line with modern practices and standards will often encompass a period of at least 6 months but seldom requires more than 12 months.

## 6.4 Securing prevention by audit and review of the system

Error or defect prevention is the process of removing or controlling error/defect causes in the system. There are two major elements of this:

- Checking the system.
- Error/defect investigation and follow-up.

These have the same objectives – to find, record and report *possible* causes of error, and to recommend future corrective action.

### Checking the system

There are six methods in general use:

(a) *Quality audits and reviews*, which subject each area of an organization's activity to a systematic critical examination. Every component of the total system is included, i.e., quality policy, attitudes, training, process, decision features, operating procedures, documentation. Audits and reviews, as in the field of accountancy, aim to disclose the strengths and weaknesses and the main areas of vulnerability or risk.

(b) *Quality survey*, a detailed, in-depth examination of a narrower field of activity, i.e. major key areas revealed by quality audits, individual plants, procedures or specific problems common to an organization as a whole.

(c) *Quality inspection*, which takes the form of a routine scheduled inspection of a unit or department. The inspection should check standards, employee involvement and working practices, and that work is carried out in accordance with the procedures, etc.

(d) *Quality tour*, which is an unscheduled examination of a work area to ensure that, for example, the standards of operation are acceptable, obvious causes of errors are removed, and in general quality standards are maintained.

(e) *Quality sampling*, which measures by random sampling, similar to activity sampling, the error potential. Trained observers perform short tours of specific locations by prescribed routes and record the number of potential errors or defects seen. The results may be used to portray trends in the general quality situation.

(f) *Quality scrutinies*, which are the application of a formal, critical examination of the process and technological intentions for new or existing facilities, or to assess the potential for mal-operation or malfunction of equipment and the consequential effects on quality. There are similarities between quality scrutinies and FMECA studies (see Chapter 9).

The design of a prevention programme, combining all these elements, is represented in Figure 6.3.

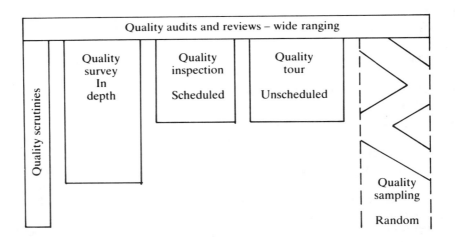

**Figure 6.3** *A prevention programme combining various elements of 'checking' the system*

**Error or defect investigations and follow-up**

The investigation of errors and defects can provide valuable error prevention information. The method is based on:

- *Collecting* data and information relating to the error or defect.
- *Checking* the validity of the evidence.
- *Selecting* the evidence without making assumptions or jumping to
  conclusions.

The results of the analysis are then used to:

- *Decide* the most likely cause(s) of the errors or defects.
- *Notify* immediately the person(s) able to take corrective action.
- *Record* the findings and outcomes.
- *Report* them to everyone concerned, to prevent a recurrence.

The investigation should not become an inquisition to apportion
blame, but focus on the positive preventive aspects. The types of follow-up to errors and their effects is shown in Table 6.2.

**Table 6.2** *Following up errors*

| System type | Aim | General effects |
|---|---|---|
| Investigation | To prevent a similar error or defect | *Positive:* identification notification correction |
| Inquisition | To identify responsibility | *Negative:* blame claims defence |

It is hoped that errors or defects are not normally investigated so
frequently that the required skills are developed by experience, nor are
these skills easily learned in a classroom. One suggested way to overcome this problem is the development of a programmed sequence of
questions to form the skeleton of an error or defect investigation questionnaire. This can be set out with the following structure:

(a) *Plant equipment* – description, condition, controls, maintenance, suitability, etc.
(b) *Environment* – climatic, space, humidity, noise, etc.
(c) *People* – duties, information, supervision, instruction, training, attitudes, etc.
(d) *Systems* – procedures, instructions, monitoring, control methods, etc.

### Internal and external quality-system audits and reviews

A good quality system will not function without adequate audits and reviews. The system reviews, which need to be carried out periodically and systematically, are conducted to ensure that the system achieves the required effect, while audits are carried out to make sure that actual methods are adhering to the documented procedures. The reviews should use the findings of the audits, for failure to operate according to the plan often signifies difficulties in doing so. A re-examination of the procedures actually being used may lead to system improvements unobtainable by other means.

A schedule for carrying out the *audits* should be drawn up, different activities perhaps requiring different frequencies. All procedures and systems should be audited at least once during a specified cycle, but not necessarily all at the same audit. For example, every 3 months a selected random sample of work instructions and test methods could be audited, with the selection designed so that each procedure is audited at least once per year. There must be, however, a facility to adjust this on the basis of the audit results.

A quality-system *review* should be instituted, perhaps every 6 months, with the aims of:

- Ensuring that the system is achieving the desired results.
- Revealing defects or irregularities in the system.
- Indicating any necessary improvements and/or corrective actions to eliminate waste or loss.
- Checking on all levels of management.
- Uncovering potential danger areas.
- Verifying that improvements or corrective action procedures are effective.

Clearly, the procedures for carrying out the audits and reviews and the results from them should be documented, and themselves be subject to review.

The assessment of a quality system against a particular standard or set of requirements by internal audit and review is known as a *first-*

*party* assessment or approval scheme. If an *external* customer makes the assessment of a supplier against either its own or a national or international standard, a *second-party* scheme is in operation. The external assessment by an independent organization not connected with any contract between customer and supplier, but acceptable to them both, is known as an *independent third-party* assessment scheme. The latter usually results in some form of certification or registration by the assessment body.

One advantage of the third-party schemes is that they obviate the need for customers to make their own detailed checks, saving both suppliers and customers time and money, and avoiding issues of commercial confidentiality. Just one knowledgeable organization has to be satisfied, rather than a multitude with varying levels of competence. This method often certifies suppliers for quality-assurance-based contracts without further checking.

Each certification body usually has its own recognized mark, which may be used by registered organizations of assessed capability in their literature, letter headings, and marketing activities. There are also publications containing lists of organizations whose quality systems and/or products and services have been assessed. To be of value, the certification body must itself be recognized and, usually, assessed and registered with a national or international accreditation scheme, such as the National Accreditation Council for Certification Bodies (NACCB) in the UK.

Many organizations have found that the effort of designing and implementing a written quality-management system good enough to stand up to external independent third-party assessment has been extremely rewarding in:

- Encouraging staff and improving morale.
- Better process control.
- Reduced wastage.
- Reduced customer service costs.

This is also true of those organizations that have obtained third-party registration and supply companies that still insist on their own second-party assessment. The reason for this is that most of the standards on quality systems, whether national, international, or company-specific, are now very similar indeed. A system that meets the requirements of the ISO 9000 series will meet the requirements of all other standards, with only the slight modifications and small emphases here and there required for specific customers. It is the author's experience, and that of his immediate colleagues, that an assessment carried out by one of the independent certified assessment bodies is at least as rigorous and delving as any carried out by a second-party representative.

Internal system audits and reviews must be positive, and conducted as part of the preventive strategy and not as a matter of expediency resulting from quality problems. They should not be carried out only before external audits, nor should they be left to the external auditor – whether second or third party. An external auditor discovering discrepancies between actual and documented systems will be inclined to ask why the internal review methods did not discover and correct them. As this type of behaviour in financial control and auditing is commonplace, why should things be different in the control of quality?

Managements anxious to display that they are serious about quality must become fully committed to operating an effective quality system for all personnel within the organization, not just the staff in the quality department. The system must be planned to be effective and achieve its objectives in an uncomplicated way. Having established and documented the procedures, an organization must ensure that they are working and that everyone is operating in accordance with them. The system once established is not static; it should be flexible, to enable the constant seeking of improvements or streamlining.

**Quality auditing standard**

There is a British Standard Guide to quality-systems auditing (BS 7229, 1989). This points out that audits are required to verify whether the individual elements making up quality systems are effective in achieving the stated objectives. The growing use of standards internationally emphasizes the importance of auditing as a management tool for this purpose. The guidance provided in the standard can be applied equally to any one of the three specific and yet different auditing activities:

(a) *First-party or internal audits*, carried out by an organization on its own systems, either by staff who are independent of the systems being audited, or by an outside agency.
(b) *Second-party audits*, carried out by one organization (a purchaser or its outside agent) on another with which it either has contracts to purchase goods or services or intends to do so.
(c) *Third-party audits*, carried out by independent agencies, to provide assurance to existing and prospective customers for the product or service.

BS 7229 covers audit objectives and responsibilities, including the roles of auditors and their independence, and those of the 'client' or auditee.

It provides the following detailed guidance on audit:

- *Initiation*, including its scope and frequency.
- *Preparation*, including review of documentation, the programme, and working documents.
- *Execution*, including the opening meeting, examination and evaluation, collecting evidence, observations, and closing the meeting with the auditee.
- *Report*, including its preparation, content and distribution.
- *Completion*, including report submission and retention.

Attention is given at the end of the standard to corrective action and follow-up, where it is stressed that the improvement process should be continued by the auditee after the publication of the audit report. This may include a call by the client for a verification audit of the implementation of any corrective actions specified.


## 6.5  Towards a TQM standard for assessment

'Total quality' is the goal of many organizations, but it is difficult to find a universally accepted definition of what this actually means. For some people TQM means SPC or quality systems, for others teamwork and involvement of the workforce. Clearly there are many different views on what constitutes the 'total quality organization' and, even with an understanding of the framework of TQM, there is the difficulty of calibrating the performance or progress of any organization towards it.

The philosophy of TQM recognizes that customer satisfaction, business objectives, safety, and environmental considerations are mutually dependent, and applicable in any organization. Clearly, the application of TQM calls for investment primarily in people and time; time to implement new concepts, time to train, time for people to recognize the benefits and move forward into new or different organizational cultures. But how will organizations know when they are getting close to TQM, or whether they are even on the right road? How will they *measure* their progress?

There have been many recent developments and there will continue to be many more, in the search for a TQM standard or framework against which organizations may be assessed or measure themselves, and carry out the so-called 'gap analysis'. To many companies the ability to judge their TQM progress against an accepted set of criteria would be most valuable and informative.

### The Malcolm Baldrige and other quality award criteria

Most TQM approaches strongly emphasize measurement, especially in the quality assurance and control areas. Some insist on the use of cost of quality. The recognition that total quality management is a broad culture change vehicle with internal and external focus embracing behavioural and service issues, as well as quality assurance and process control, prompted the United States to develop one of the most famous and now widely used frameworks for TQM – the Malcolm Baldrige National Quality Award (MBNQA). The award itself, which is composed of two solid crystal forms 14 inches high, is presented annually to recognize companies in the USA that have 'excelled in quality management and quality achievement'. Up to two awards may be given in each of three categories: manufacturing, service, and small businesses. But it is not the award itself, or even the fact that it is presented each year by the President of the USA, which has attracted the attention of most organizations. It is the excellent framework, which is one of the closest things we have to an international standard for TQM.

The value of a structured discipline using a points scoring system has been well established in quality and safety *assurance* systems (for example, ISO 9000/BS 5750, Vendor Auditing). The extension of this approach to a *total* quality-auditing process has been long established in the Japanese-based 'Deming Prize', which is perhaps the most demanding and intrusive auditing process. There are other excellent models and standards used throughout the world: the British Standard BS 7850 Guide to TQM, the Marketing Quality Assurance (MQA) Specification, the British Quality Award, the European Quality Award, and others not yet thought of.

In 1987 the MBNQA was introduced for US-based organizations, and, in terms of a universally accepted framework, it has few challengers. Many companies have realized the necessity to assess themselves against the Baldrige criteria, if not to enter for the Baldrige Award then certainly as an excellent basis for self-audit and review, to highlight areas for priority attention and provide internal and external benchmarking.

The MBNQA aims to promote:

- Awareness of quality as an increasingly important element in competitiveness.
- Understanding of the requirements for quality excellence.
- Sharing of information on successful quality strategies and the benefits to be derived from their implementation.

The award criteria are built upon ten core values and concepts:

1 Customer-driven quality.
2 Leadership.
3 Continuous improvement.
4 Employee participation and development.
5 Fast response.
6 Design quality and prevention.
7 Long-range outlook.
8 Management by fact.
9 Partnership by development.
10 Corporate responsibility and citizenship.

These are embodied in a criteria framework of seven first level categories, which are used to assess organizations. These are given in Table 6.3, along with the ten first level categories of the Deming Prize.

**Table 6.3** *The first-level categories of the Baldrige Award and the Deming Prize*

| Baldrige | Deming |
|----------|--------|
| 1 Leadership | 1 Policy |
| 2 Information and analysis | 2 Organization and management |
| 3 Strategic quality planning | 3 Education and dissemination |
| 4 Human resource development and management | 4 Collection, dissemination, and use of information on quality |
| 5 Management of process quality | 5 Analysis |
| 6 Quality and operational results | 6 Standardization |
| 7 Customer focus and satisfaction | 7 Control |
| | 8 Quality assurance |
| | 9 Results |
| | 10 Planning for the future |

Figure 6.4 shows how the framework connects and integrates the categories. This has four basic elements: driver, system, measures of progress, and goal. The driver is the senior executive leadership that creates the values, goals, and systems, and guides the sustained pursuit of quality and performance objectives. The system includes a set of well-defined and designed processes for meeting the organization's quality and performance requirements. Measures of progress provide a results-oriented basis for channelling actions to deliver ever-improving customer values and organizational performance. The goal is the basic aim of the quality process in delivering the above to the customers.

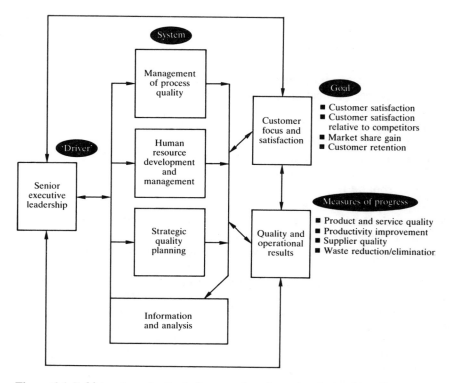

**Figure 6.4** *Baldrige Award criteria framework – dynamic relationships. Source: Malcolm Baldrige National Quality Award criteria, US National Institute of Standards and Technology*

The seven criteria categories are further subdivided into examination items and areas to address. These are described in some detail in the 'Award Criteria', available from the US National Institute of Standards and Technology.

In Europe it has also been recognized that the technique of quality self-appraisal is very useful for any organization wishing to develop and monitor its quality culture. The European Foundation for Quality Management (EFQM) has launched a European Quality Award, which can also be used for a systematic review and measurement of operations. The EC Award assessment model recognizes that *processes* are the means by which a company or organization harnesses and releases the talents of its *people* to produce *results*. Moreover, the processes and the people are the enablers which produce results.

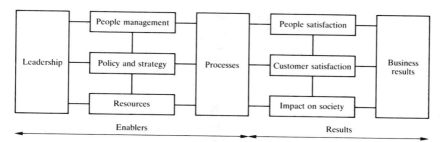

**Figure 6.5** *The European Quality Award assessment model. Source: Total Quality Management: The European Model for Self-Appraisal, EFQM*

Figure 6.5 displays graphically the principle of the European Quality Award. Essentially this claims that customer satisfaction, employee satisfaction, and impact on society are achieved through leadership driving policy and strategy, people management, resources, and processes, which lead ultimately to excellence in business results.

Using the MBNQA categories, supplemented with the European Award's additional categories of business results (financial) and impact on society (community), it is possible to build a model of criteria and a review framework against which an organization may face and measure itself, to examine any 'gaps'. Such a device is offered in Table 6.4, which also shows the links with Baldrige and the European Awards.

Many managers feel the need for a rational basis on which to measure TQM in their organization, especially in those companies 2 or 3 years 'into TQM' that would like the answers to questions such as 'Where are we now?' 'Where do we need/want to be?' and 'What have we got to do to get there?' These questions need to be answered from internal employees' views, the customers' views, and the views of suppliers. Table 6.5 is a proposed quality review process which uses the above TQM model criteria and lists questions that should be asked under each heading.

Clearly, it is necessary for any organization to rationalize all the criteria used by the various awards. There is great overlap between them, and the main components must be the organization's processes, quality management system, human-resource management, results and customer satisfaction.

Internal or self-assessments provide an organization with vital information in monitoring its progress towards its goals and total quality. The external assessments used in the processes of making awards must be based on those self-assessments that are performed as prerequisites for improvement.

**Table 6.4** *Total quality model criteria*

| | |
|---|---|
| 1 *Leadership and Behaviour* (Baldrige 1) | Senior managers provide clear *vision* and *values* that promote total quality. The *values* embrace suppliers, employees, customers, the community and shareholders of the organization. The senior managers provide an explicit total quality policy or mission as the underpinning process to realize the values and vision, and they direct and involve themselves in applying these to all work processes throughout the organization's operations to achieve customer satisfaction, on a zero error/defects basis. |
| | Management and all employees have and continue to change the ways things are done to encourage full participation and empower employees to share in teamwork, to pursue *customer satisfaction* both internally and externally. The culture values *'prevention heroes'* above *'firefighters'* and cross-departmental barriers have been dismantled. The structure and processes of the organization promote *communications*, including active listening and clear understanding of requirements, with an emphasis on teamwork and team leadership. |
| 2 *Strategic planning* (Baldrige 3) | Business strategies incorporate quality goals, and are understood throughout the organization. Overall strategy focuses on *critical success factors* and *critical processes* which give individuals and departments clear missions, purpose statements, and goals, arrived at by participation. |
| 3 *Techniques and continuous improvement* (Baldrige 3) | The company has effective data and information gathering processes on which the TQ analytical and measuring tools are used continuously, to drive the improvement process, via both ongoing work group activities and quality projects across the organization. |
| | Networking is actively promoted, data is accessible to all, to allow measured continuous improvement of all work. |
| 4 *People* (Baldrige 4) | The company maximizes opportunities for all employees to secure use of full potential through the processes of recruitment, training, development, motivation, involvement, responsibility and teamwork in an open environment. |

Recognition and reward reflect contribution of individuals and teams, based on performance. Communications encourage open behaviour, and active listening. Career progression promotes the values, and quality is seen as first among the equals of cost and schedule, in 'business as usual'.

5 *Quality assurance* (Baldrige 5)

The organization practises systematic assurance of quality in control of all operations, using documented traceable systems, which are integrated with continuous improvement, for all products and services.

6 *Quality and business results* (Baldrige 6 and EQA Business Results)

Effective measures are used to quantify results (and targets) in product supply and service as well as process improvement. These include project activity, corrective action, opportunities for involvement (O.F.Is), statistical control (and capability), costs of quality, supplier auditing, competitive benchmarking and measured customer satisfaction. The results are used to set priorities and update critical success factors. Suppliers are treated as partners in process improvement. Measures of customer satisfaction and financial performance are fed back to focus resources on process improvements to secure improved design and performance, in the long term.

7 *Customer satisfaction* (Baldrige 7)

The internal and external supplier/customer relationships are systematically managed to secure clear understanding of requirements to meet external customer needs. Where appropriate, customer and supplier partnerships are promoted on the basis of added value and joint strategies.

Service standards, determination and results are shared with customers and regularly updated.

8 *Community* (EQA Impact on Society)

All employees value and promote the organization within the community with special regard to communication and mutual education. The organization recognizes its societal responsibilities in balance with the demands of its shareholders, and is at the forefront of prevention based processes with well established systems for environmental management.

**Table 6.5** *Proposed quality review processes*

| Quality criteria | Maximum points score[1] | Areas for assessment |
|---|---|---|
| 1 Leadership and Behaviour | 120 | Are vision and values shared? Are leaders visible? Is TQ valued? Costs and benefits? Strengths, weaknesses, opportunities, threats. What's changed? How difficult? What stops change, me, them, it? Structure? Hierarchy? Dilemmas, Teamwork vs me? Successes – examples. |
| 2 Strategic planning | 100 | Do business plans promote TQ, and do TQ-derived critical success factors and priorities at least equal with conventional business criteria? Is there active use of participation in DPA to promote focus? |
| 3 Continuous improvement | 120 | Use of Ishikawa, Shewhart and SPC tools. Personal motivation for involvement in QITs, activities, projects. Examples of real changes to working processes. |
| 4 People | 120 | Views on TQ launch. Training and follow-up. Cross-company awareness and networking to share experiences. Knowledge of quality actions within job/task priorities. Team vs self vs task. |
| 5 Quality assurance | 140 | Are procedures enabling or bureaucratic? Value of ISO 9000 and Corrective Action. Are work systems clear? What's changed? Is internal auditing routine? |
| 6 Quality results | 120 | Will seek hard evidence of *data*, measuring projects, process, target-setting, CSFs, service and product improvement. Quality costs and savings. Market benefits, customer surveys. Has inspection reduced and prevention replaced it? |

| Quality criteria | Maximum points score[1] | Areas for assessment |
|---|---|---|
| 7 Customer satisfaction | 240 | *Internal* customer supplier chains – how well developed. Cross-functional projects. Involvement of *customers* in partnerships. Facts and views. Stories supported by facts. Supplier focus. Process emphasis to customer requirements. |
| 8 Community | 40 | Attitudes to social, environmental, and community affairs. School/university links. Apprenticeships. Local communications. Equal opportunities. |
| TOTAL | 1000 | |

## A few last words on self-assessment

TQM jargon is increasingly confused by a vast literature, spiced with acronyms, the generation of which often bend the meaning of words. There is also in the leadership of large organizations an ego-driven or publicity-seeking wish to invent new buzz words. It may be necessary to asses the status of TQM language before launching an assessment process. If recipients are not familiar with certain language, many propositions will be meaningless. A preliminary teach-in or awareness process may even be necessary.

Whatever are the main 'motors' for driving an organization towards its *vision* or *mission*, they must be linked to the five stakeholders embraced by the values of any organization, namely:

- Customers.                    and              - Shareholders.
- Employees.                                          - Community.
- Suppliers.

In any normal business or organization, measurements are continuously being made, often in retrospect, by the leaders of the organization to reflect the value put on the organization by its five stakeholders. Too often, these continuous readings are made by internal, biased agents with short-term priorities, not always in the best long-term interests of the organization or its customers, i.e. narrow firefighting scenarios that can blind the organization's strategic eye. Third-party agents, however, can carry out or facilitate periodic audits and reviews from the perspective of one or more of the key stakeholders, with particular emphasis on forward priorities and needs. These reviews will allow realignment of the principal driving motors to focus on the critical success factors for continuous improvement, to maintain a balanced and powerful general thrust that moves the whole organization towards the mission.

The relative importance of the five stakeholders may vary in time, but all are important. Customers, employees, and suppliers, which comprise the core value chain, are the *determinant* elements, where third-party audit and review are best applied. The application of TQM in this area will provide satisfaction as a *resultant* to the shareholders and the community. Thus, added value will benefit the community and the environment. The ideal is a long way off in most organizations, however, and active attention to the needs of the shareholders and/or community remain a priority for two reasons:

- They are the 'customers' of most organizational activities and are vital stakeholders.
- The world of consumerism has made perception, sentiment and imagery powerful components of the marketing process and the valuation of shares in the money markets.

Any instrument developed for third-party audit and review may be used at several stages in an organization's history;

1   *Before* starting TQM to identify needs and focus attention. At this stage a parallel cost of quality audit or assessment is a powerful way to overcome scepticism and get 'buy in'.
2   As part of a TQM launch, especially using a 'survey' instrument.
3   Every 2 to 3 years after the TQM launch, to steer and benchmark.

The systematic measurement and review of operations are two of the most important management activities of any TQM system. Self-assessment allows an organization clearly to discern its strengths and areas for improvement by focusing on the relationship between the people, processes, and results. Within any quality-conscious organization it should be a regular activity.

**Adding the systems to the TQM model**

In Chapters 1 and 2 the foundations for TQM were set down. The core of total quality was established as the customer/supplier chains that extend through and out from an organization. It was recognized that if the chains are 'cut' anywhere, processes that must be managed will be found. Within the TQM framework were identified the 'soft' outcomes of total quality, namely culture change, communication improvements and commitment.

To this foundation must be added the first hard management necessity – a quality system, based on any good international standard. This is shown in Figure 6.6.

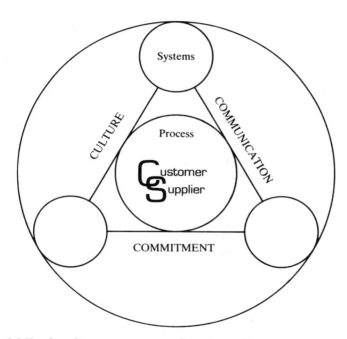

**Figure 6.6** *Total quality management model – the quality system*

## Chapter highlights

### The quality-system documentation

* The quality manual is the document in which it is explained how the organization carries out the quality policy. It should be no longer than 25 to 30 pages.

- The quality manual should reflect the type and level of quality system, and refer to the standard being used as the framework.
- The systematic questioning technique based on what, why, where, when, who, and how questions is useful in writing a quality manual. Detailed procedures should not appear in the manual, but be cross-referenced. Large organizations will have several quality manuals, or one with several layers.
- The written system must meet the requirements of the chosen standard.

## Quality information systems

- Computers may be used in creating a quality information system. Application software packages are now available for this purpose. These should drive the cycle of plan, implement, collect data, identify problem, and include all the SPC techniques required.
- The information system should permit process and product information to be entered into a database, and data to be extracted, searched, analysed and reported.

## Implementation of the system

- The quality system should be a living thing, not a bureaucracy or paperwork model, and this requires everyone's participation. It can be difficult for people to change to accept and adopt new procedures.
- Small organizations may see formalized quality-system documentation as unnecessary or costly, but often find that certain customers or contracts may be retained only by compliance or registration. One solution to this problem is for a group of small organizations to 'share' a professional quality manager on an internal/external consultancy basis.
- In using a consultant for quality-system advice, select one who does not offer a standard package. A good advisory project covers four phases: initial or terms of reference, interim report and action plan, final report and draft quality manual, audit.

## Securing prevention by audit and review of the system

- There are two major elements of error or defect prevention: checking the system, and error/defect investigations and follow-up. Six methods of checking quality systems are in general use: audits and reviews, surveys, inspections, tours, sampling and scrutinies.

Investigations proceed by collecting, checking and selecting data, and analysing it by deciding causes, notifying people, recording and reporting findings and outcomes.

* A good quality system will not function without adequate audits and reviews. Audits make sure the actual methods are adhering to documented procedures. Reviews ensure the system achieves the desired effect.

* System assessment by internal audit and review is known as first-party, by external customer as second-party, and by an independent organization as third-party certification. For the latter to be of real value the certification body must itself be recognized.

## Towards a TQM standard for assessment

* One of the most famous and widely used frameworks for TQM self-assessment is the Malcolm Baldrige National Quality Award (MBNQA) in the USA.

* The MBNQA criteria are built on ten core values and concepts, which are embodied on a framework of seven first level categories: leadership (driver), information and analyses, strategic quality planning, human resource development and management, management of process quality (system), quality and operational results (measure of focus), and customer focus and satisfaction (goal). These are comparable with the ten categories of the Japanese Deming Prize, and the nine components of the European Quality Award (EFQM).

* The various award criteria provide rational bases against which to measure progress towards TQM in organizations.

* The 'motors' driving an organization towards its mission must be linked to its five stakeholders: customers, employees, suppliers (determinants) and shareholders, community (resultants).

## The system and the TQM model

* To the foundation framework of the customer-supplier chain, processes and the 'soft' outcomes of TQM, must be added the first hard management necessity – a quality system based on a good international standard.

# Part Three
# TQM – The Tools and the
# Improvement Cycle

How doth the little busy bee
Improve each shining hour
And gather honey all the day
From every opening Flower?

*Isaac Watts*, 1674–1748, from 'Against idleness and mischief'

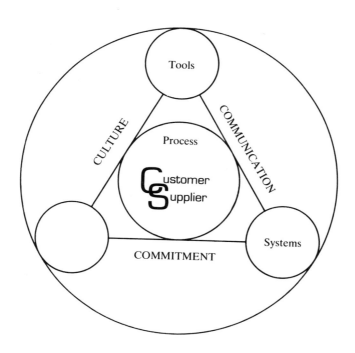

# 7 Measurement of quality

## 7.1 Measurement and the improvement cycle

Traditionally, performance measures and indicators have been derived from cost-accounting information, often based on outdated and arbitrary principles. These provide little motivation to support attempts to introduce TQM and, in some cases, actually inhibit continuous improvement because they are unable to map process performance. In the organization that is to survive over a long term, performance must begin to be measured by the improvements seen by the customer.

In the cycle of never ending improvement, measurement plays an important role in:

- Identifying opportunities for improvement (quality costing).
- Comparing performance against internal standards (process control and improvement).
- Comparing performance against external standards (benchmarking).

Measures are used in *process control*, e.g. control charts (see Chapter 9), and in *performance improvement*, e.g. quality improvement teams (see Chapters 11 and 12), so they should give information about how well processes and people are doing and motivate them to perform better in the future.

The author has seen many examples of so-called performance measurement systems that frustrated improvements efforts. Various problems include systems that:

1  Produce irrelevant or misleading information.
2  Track performance in single, isolated dimensions.
3  Generate financial measures too late, e.g. quarterly, for mid-course corrections or remedial action.
4  Do not take account of the customer perspective, both internal and external.
5  Distort management's understanding of how effective the organization has been in implementing its strategy.

6  Provide behaviour that *undermines* the achievement of the strategic objectives.

Typical harmful summary measures of local performance are purchase price, machine or plant efficiencies, direct labour costs, and ratios of direct to indirect labour. These are incompatible with quality-improvement measures such as process and throughput times, delivery performance, inventory reductions, and increases in flexibility, which are first and foremost *non-financial*. Financial summaries provide valuable information of course, but they should not be used for control. Effective decision-making requires direct physical measures for operational feedback and improvement.

One example of a 'measure' with these shortcomings is return on investment (ROI). ROI can be computed only after profits have been totalled for a given period. It was designed therefore as a single-period, long-term measure, but it is increasingly being used as a short-term one. Perhaps this is because most executive bonus 'packages' in the West are based on short-term measures. ROI tells us what happened, not what is happening or what will happen, and, for complex and detailed projects, ROI is inaccurate and irrelevant.

Many managers have a poor or incomplete understanding of their processes and products or services, and, looking for an alternative stimulus, become interested in financial indicators. The use of ROI, for example, for evaluating strategic requirements and performance can lead to a discriminatory allocation of resources. In many ways the financial indicators used in many businesses have remained static while the environment in which they operate has changed dramatically.

Traditionally, the measures used have not been linked to the processes where the value-adding activities take place. What has been missing is improvement measures that provide feedback to people in all areas of business operations. Of course TQM stresses the need to start with the process for fulfilling customer needs.

The critical elements of a good performance measurement and management effort look like any other list associated with total quality management:

* Leadership and commitment.
* Full employee involvement.
* Good planning.
* Sound implementation strategy.
* Measurement and evaluation.
* Control and improvement.
* Achieving and maintaining standards of excellence.

The Deming cycle of continuous improvement – PLAN DO CHECK ACT – clearly requires measurement to drive it, and yet it is a useful design aid for the measurement system itself:

PLAN:    establish performance objectives and standards.
DO:    measure actual performance.
CHECK: compare actual performance with the objectives and standards – determine the gap.
ACT:    take the necessary actions to close the gap and make the necessary improvements.

Before we use performance measurement in the improvement cycle, however, we should attempt to answer four basic questions:

1  Why measure?
2  What to measure?
3  Where to measure?
4  How to measure?

**Why measure?**

It has been said often that it is not possible to manage what cannot be measured. Whether this is strictly true or not, there are clear arguments for measuring. In a quality-driven, never ending improvement environment, the following are some of the main reasons *why measurement is needed* and why it plays a key role in quality and productivity improvement:

- To ensure customer requirements *have* been met.
- To be able to set sensible *objectives* and comply with them.
- To provide *standards* for establishing comparisons.
- To provide *visibility* and provide a 'score-board' for people to *monitor* their own performance levels.
- To highlight *quality problems* and determine which areas require *priority attention*.
- To give an indication of the *costs of poor quality* (see Chapter 8).
- To justify the *use of resources*.
- To provide *feedback* for driving the improvement effort.

It is also important to know the impact of TQM on improvements in business performance, on sustaining current performance, and perhaps on reducing any decline in performance.

## What to measure?

In the business of process improvement, process understanding, definition, measurement, and management are tied inextricably together. In order to assess and evaluate performance accurately, appropriate measurement must be designed, developed and maintained by people who *own* the processes concerned. They may find it necessary to measure effectiveness, efficiency, quality, impact, and productivity. In these areas there are many types of measurement, including direct output or input figures, the cost of poor quality, economic data, comments and complaints from customers, information from customer or employee surveys, etc., generally continuous variable measures (such as time) or discrete attribute measures (such as absentees). See Chapters 9 and 10.

No one can provide a generic list of what should be measured but, once it has been decided what measures are appropriate, they may be converted into indicators. These include ratios, scales, rankings, and financial and time-based indicators. Whichever measures and indicators are used by the process owners, they must reflect the true performance of the process in customer/supplier terms, and emphasize continuous improvement. Time-related measures and indicators have great value.

## Where to measure?

If true measures of the effectiveness of TQM are to be obtained, there are three components that must be examined – the human, technical and business components.

The human component is clearly of major importance and the key tests are that, wherever measures are used, they must be:

1   Understood by all the people being measured.
2   Accepted by the individuals concerned.
3   Compatible with the rewards and recognition systems.
4   Designed to offer minimal opportunity for manipulation.

Technically, the measures must be the ones that truly represent the controllable aspects of the processes, rather than simple output measures that cannot be related to process management. They must also be correct, precise and accurate.

The business component requires that the measures are objective, timely, and result-oriented, and above all they must mean something to those working in and around the process, *including the customers*.

**How to measure?**

Measurement, as any other management system, requires the stages of design, analysis, development, evaluation, implementation and review. The system must be designed to measure *progress*, otherwise it will not engage the improvement cycle. Progress is important in five main areas: effectiveness, efficiency, productivity, quality, and impact.

*Effectiveness*

Effectiveness may be defined as the percentage actual output over the expected output:

$$\text{Effectiveness} = \frac{\text{Actual output}}{\text{Expected output}} \times 100 \text{ per cent}$$

Hence effectiveness looks at the *output* side of the process and is about the implementation of the objectives – doing what you said you would do. Effectiveness measures should reflect whether the organization, group or process owner(s) are achieving the desired results, accomplishing the right things. Measures of this may include:

- Quality, e.g. a grade of product, or a level of service.
- Quantity, e.g. tonnes, lots, bedrooms cleaned, accounts opened.
- Timeliness, e.g. speed of response, product lead times, cycle time.
- Cost/price, e.g. unit costs.

*Efficiency*

Efficiency is concerned with the percentage resources actually used over the resources that were planned to be used:

$$\text{Efficiency} = \frac{\text{Resources actually used}}{\text{Resources planned to be used}} \times 100 \text{ per cent}$$

Clearly, this is a process *input* issue and measures performance of the process system management. It is, of course, possible to use resources 'efficiently' while being *ineffective*, so performance efficiency improvement must be related to certain output objectives.

All process inputs may be subjected to efficiency measurement, so we may use labour/staff efficiency, equipment efficiency (or utilization), material efficiency, information efficiency, etc. Inventory data and throughput times are often used in efficiency and productivity ratios.

*Productivity*

Productivity measures should be designed to relate the process outputs to its inputs:

$$\text{Productivity} = \frac{\text{Outputs}}{\text{Inputs}}$$

and this may be quoted as expected or actual productivity:

$$\text{Expected productivity} = \frac{\text{Expected output}}{\text{Resources expected to be consumed}}$$

$$\text{Actual productivity} = \frac{\text{Actual output}}{\text{Resources actually consumed}}$$

There is a vast literature on productivity and its measurement, but simple ratios such as tonnes per man–hour (expected and actual), pages of word-processing per operator–day, and many others like this are in use. Productivity measures may be developed for each input or a combination of inputs, e.g. sales/all employee costs.

*Quality*

This has been defined elsewhere of course (see Chapter 1). The *non-quality*-related measures include the simple counts of defect or error rates (perhaps in parts per million), percentage outside specification or Cp/Cpk values, deliveries not on time, or more generally as the costs of poor quality. When the positive costs of prevention of poor quality are included, these provide a balanced measure of the costs of quality (see Chapter 8).

The quality measures should also indicate positively whether we are doing a good job in terms of customer satisfaction, implementing the objectives, and whether the designs, systems, and solutions to problems are meeting the requirements. These really are voice-of-the-customer measures.

*Impact*

Impact measures should lead to key performance indicators for the business or organization, including monitoring improvement over time. Value-added management (VAM) requires the identification and elimination of all non-value-adding wastes, including time. Value added is simply the volume of sales (or other measure of 'turnover') minus the total input costs, and provides a good direct measure of the impact of the improvement process on the performance of the business. A related ratio, percentage return on value added (ROVA):

$$\text{ROVA} = \frac{\text{Net profits before tax}}{\text{Value added}} \times 100 \text{ per cent}$$

is another financial indicator that may be used.

Other measures or indicators of impact on the business are *growth*, in sales, assets, numbers of passengers/students, etc., and *asset-utilization* measures such as return on investment (ROI) or capital employed (ROCE), earnings per share, etc.

Some of the impact measures may be converted to people productivity ratios, e.g.:

$$\frac{\text{Value added}}{\text{Number of employees (or employee costs)}}$$

Activity-based costing (ABS) is an information system that maintains and processes data on an organization's activities and cost objectives. It is based on the activities performed being identified and the costs being traced to them. ABS uses various 'cost drivers' to trace the cost of activities to the cost of the products or services. The activity and cost-driver concepts are the heart of ABS.

Cost drivers reflect the demands placed on activities by products, services or other cost targets. Activities are processes or procedures that cause work and thereby consume resources. This clearly measures impact, both on and by the organization.

## 7.2 The metrics and the processes

In performance measurement the strategic objectives of the organization will be converted into desired standards of performance. This will lead to the development of metrics that will be used to compare the desired with the actually achieved standards. The gaps identified must be associated with the various practices and operation of the processes, if improved performance is to be achieved.

This separation of *process performance* from *process management* is important, for different questions need to be asked under these headings. Process performance is concerned with quantifying – the how often, how many, how big/small, how good/bad – while process management must concern itself with the what, why, where, when, who, and how.

It has already been stated that the performance metrics must relate to the particular process itself and the needs of the customer. It is possible, however, to give some examples of the sort of metrics/ratios used in various areas of human activity. What follows is a collection of these under various general headings (clearly each ratio given may be represented as a percentage).

## Marketing strategy

1  *Product strategy*
   Sales growth rate.
   Market share.
   Relative market share.
   Breadth of product lines, market coverage, degree of differentation.
   Rate of successful new product introductions.
   Product 'bundling'.
2  *Distribution strategy*
   Efficiency of distribution channels.
   Customer service levels.
   Distribution costs per channel.
   Distribution and salesforce productivity.
3  *Price strategy*
   Price sensitivity.
   Pricing of marketing mix.
4  *Promotion and advertising strategy*
   Product segmentation.
   Brand acceptance.
   Marketing intelligence: ability to anticipate customer needs and to detect changes in marketing trends.

## Innovation

Rate of new product development in net sales amount

$$= \frac{\text{Sales amount of new product in a given period}}{\text{Net sales amount in a given period}}$$

Rate of profitability of new product

$$= \frac{\text{Amount of profit gained by new product in a given period}}{\text{Total amount of profit in a given period}}$$

Rate of investment in research and development

$$= \frac{\text{Amount of investment in R \& D in a given period}}{\text{Net sales amount in a given period}}$$

## Research and Development

1 *Department cost*
  Cost vs budget.
  Cost of a standard procedure vs total cost per researcher, or total cost per research 'milestone'.
2 *Productivity*
  This is for staffing control and work-effectiveness:
     Project milestone per worker.
     Number of single vs multiple person projects.
     Unplanned personnel turnover.
     Frequency of utilization of pilot plant or other equipment.
3 *Market success*
     Project completion rate per period of time.
     Percentage improvements in project lead time.
     Number of new products released per period of time.
     Number of successful customer contacts per researcher.
     Product vs profitability ratios.
4 *Work in progress*
     Number and type of projects in relation to future strategic needs.
     Future market value of current project list.
     Next period's planned milestone vs long-term plan.
5 *On time*
  Number of products delivered to 'customers' on schedule vs total number of planned 'deliveries'.

  Percentage of milestones/deliverables on schedule vs backlog

  $$\frac{\text{Percentage emergency schedule interventions}}{\text{Total schedule bids}}$$
6 *Cycle time*

  $$\frac{\text{Number of projects undergone unnecessary queues/process time}}{\text{Total number of main procedures and routine projects}}$$
7 *Documentation*
  Percentage time spent recording findings vs total time available for project.

Time documentation made available vs time information was required.
Documentation availability vs effectiveness in its utilization (accuracy).

8   *Creativity and innovation*

$$\frac{\text{Number of awards given to organization/individual scientists}}{\text{Total number of projects carried out}}$$

Number of publications/presentations per individual/per period of time

$$\frac{\text{Percentage of staff exchanges between laboratories}}{\text{Number of laboratories available}}$$

Leads/lags vs competition in key R&D areas.

9   *High science (innovation)*

$$\frac{\text{Number of experiments/projects carried out by individuals}}{\text{Total number of projects reflecting state of art/practice}}$$

10  *Safety* (see also other safety metrics)

$$\frac{\text{Number of man hours lost due to accidents}}{\text{Total available man hours}}$$

$$\frac{\text{Costs of poor safety}}{\text{Total cost of all projects}}$$

$$\frac{\text{Number of hours lost per department due to poor safety}}{\text{Total number of hours lost due to poor safety}}$$

$$\frac{\text{Number of safety incidents per period of time}}{\text{Number of violations of safety regulations}}$$

## Manufacturing strategy

1   *Cost*
Total unit cost (manufacturer).
Total life-cycle cost (end customer).

2   *Delivery*
Percentage of on-time shipments.
Predictability of delivery dates.
Response time to demand changes.

3  *Quality*
   Performance.
   Features.
   Reliability.
   Conformance.
   Durability.
   Serviceability.
   Aesthetics.
   Rejection rates.
   Return rates.
   Cost and rates of field repair.
   Costs of quality.
4  *Flexibility to volume changes and new-product introduction*
   Response to product or volume changes.
   Product substitutability.
   Product options or variants.

## Performance measures for world-class manufacturing

1  *Quality*

$$\text{Supplier certification} = \frac{\text{Number of suppliers certified}}{\text{Total number of suppliers}}$$

$$\frac{\text{Volume of material received from certified suppliers}}{\text{Total volume received}}$$

$$\frac{\text{Number of shipments received accepted}}{\text{Number of shipments received}}$$

$$\frac{\text{Number of plant measurable processes under statistical process control (SPC)}}{\text{Total number of plant measurable processes}}$$

$$\frac{\text{Number of customer complaints}}{\text{Number of 'units' sold (or million!)}}$$

2  *Delivery*

$$\frac{\text{Number of orders delivered on time and complete for the period}}{\text{Number of orders delivered for the period}}$$

Schedule stability

$$= \frac{\text{Number of item schedule changes occurring within a week after the week has started (summed for the period)}}{\text{Number of items scheduled for the period}}$$

$$\frac{\text{Number of vendor deliveries early/late/on time}}{\text{Total number of vendor deliveries}}$$

3 *Production process time*

Production process time

$$= \frac{\text{Time first material is introduced into production process until finished}}{\text{product made with that material}}$$

Production delivery ratio

$$= \frac{\text{Total production lead time}}{\text{Total delivery lead time}}$$

or

$$= \frac{\text{Time to order and receive materials plus production time}}{\text{Time from customer order until goods received}}$$

4 *Flexibility*

Materials flexibility

$$= \frac{\text{Number of different materials used}}{\text{Number of different finished products made}}$$

Packing material flexibility

$$= \frac{\text{Number of different packing material components used}}{\text{Number of finished goods items produced}}$$

5 *Costs*

Materials days on hand

$$= \frac{\text{Tonnes of materials on hand in plant or company warehouses at end of period}}{\text{Average tonnes produced/day per period}}$$

Finished goods days on hand

$$= \frac{\text{Tonnes of finished goods on hand in plant or company warehouses at end of period}}{\text{Average tonnes produced/day for period}}$$

## Technology strategy

1 *Rate of technological innovation*

Progress through time

2 *R&D productivity*

$$\frac{\text{Improvement in performance of product/process}}{\text{Incremental investment in R\&D}}$$

3 *Rate of return in R&D Investment*

$$\text{R\&D Yield} = \frac{\text{Percentage profit generated by amount of R\&D investment}}{\text{Total amount of profit}}$$

4 *Resource allocated to R&D*

$$\frac{\text{Percentage expenditure on R\&D}}{\text{Total amount of expenditure}}$$

5 *Rate of new-product introduction*
Number of new products introduced per year/time period.

Number of patents obtained per time period

$$\frac{\text{Percentage of sales derived from new products}}{\text{Total amount of sales}}$$

## Purchasing

A good purchasing strategy based on TQM needs to be aimed at achieving the following goals:

Optimum quality.
Minimum final cost.
Effective supplier service.
Continuity of supply.
Strong supplier knowledge and competence.
Long-term supplier relations.

1 *Indicators for cost performance*
Costs of purchased goods vs standard costs.
Administrative cost of the purchasing department as a percentage of total purchase.
Total value added of purchased goods, as a percentage of total cost.
Inventory turnover ratios.
Cost savings.
2 *Indicators for service performance*
Percentage of on-time orders.
Average delay on delinquent orders.
3 *Indicators for quality performance*
Percentage orders meeting intended specifications.
Reliability of purchased goods.
Vendor quality.
Process capability indices such as Cp and Cpk.
4 *Indicators for vendor relationships*

## Maintenance Management

1 *Performance*
Maintenance cost as a percentage of sales value of production/operation.
Maintenance costs as a percentage of value added.
Maintenance cost per unit of output of product or service.
Maintenance man–hours as a percentage of total labour hours.
Maintenance man–hours per unit output of product or service.
2 *Downtime (by plant, area, unit and/or machine, etc)*
Downtime due to all causes as a percentage of total time.
Downtime due to maintenance as a percentage of total time.
Downtime due to maintenance as a percentage of time plant planned to be down.
3 *Analysis of work load*
Percentage of maintenance hours on planned maintenance vs corrective vs emergency vs reconditioning vs repairs vs capital and installation.
4 *Analysis of material*
Total annual maintenance materials spend.
Spend on materials as a percentage of maintenance labour spend.
5 *Equipment effectiveness measures*
Overall Equipment Effectiveness = Availability x performance rate x quality rate.

6   *Miscellaneous*
    Number of failures per period per category.
    Mean time between failures (MTBF) by category

$$\text{MTBF} = \frac{\text{Operating time}}{\text{Total number of stoppages}}$$

Mean time to repair (MTTR) by category.
Failure rate by category.

**Human resources management**

A wide variety of measures can be extracted in the area of human resources, covering any of the following aspects:

| | |
|---|---|
| Job satisfaction. | Job security. |
| Job performance. | Career prospects. |
| Turnover. | Psychological stress. |
| Absenteeism. | Safety/health conditions. |
| Motivation. | Income. |

For example, in absenteeism:

$$\text{Absence rate performance} = \frac{\text{Number of working days lost}}{\text{Total number of working days}}$$

**Safety**

Frequency rate = the number of disabling injuries per million
                 employee hours.

Incidence rates = number of recordable injuries and illnesses for every
                  200,000 hours worked by employees.

Severity rate = number of days charged for lost time injuries per
                million employee hours worked.

$$\frac{\text{Percentage investment on safety}}{\text{Percentage reduction in number of accidents}}$$

$$\frac{\text{Number of lost days}}{\text{Number of accidents}}$$

## 7.3   The implementation of performance measurement systems

It has already been established that a good measurement system will start with the customer and measure the right things. The value of any measure clearly needs to be compared with the cost of producing it. There will be appropriate measures for different parts of the organization, but everywhere they must relate process performance to the needs of the process customer. All critical parts of the process must be measured, and it is often better to start with simple measures and improve them.

There must be a recognition of the need to distinguish between different measures for different purposes. For example, an operator may measure time, various process parameters, and amounts, while at the management level measuring costs and delivery timeliness may be more appropriate.

Participation in the development of measures enhances their understanding and acceptance. Process-owners can assist in defining the required performance measures, provided that senior managers have communicated their mission clearly, defined the critical success factors, and identified the critical processes (see Chapter 15).

If all employees participate, and own the measurement processes, there will be lower resistance to the system, and a positive commitment towards future changes will be engaged. This will derive from the 'volunteered accountability', which will in turn make the individual contribution more visible. Involvement in measurement also strengthens the links in the customer–supplier chains and gives quality improvement teams much clearer objectives. This should lead to greater short-term and long-term productivity gains.

There are a number of possible reasons why measurement systems fail:

1   They do not define performance operationally.
2   They do not relate performance to the process.
3   The boundaries of the process are not defined.
4   The measures are misunderstood or misused or measure the wrong things.
5   There is no distinction between control and improvement.
6   There is a fear of exposing poor and good performance.
7   It is seen as an extra burden in terms of time and reporting.
8   There is a perception of reduced autonomy.
9   Too many measurements are focused internally and too few are focused externally.

10 There is a fear of the introduction of tighter management controls.

These and other problems are frequently due to poor planning at the implementation stage or a failure to assess current systems of measurement. Before the introduction of a total quality-based performance measurement system, an audit of the existing systems should be carried out. Its purpose is to establish the effectiveness of existing measures, their compatibility with the quality drive, their relationship with the processes concerned, and their closeness to the objectives of meeting customer requirements. The audit should also highlight areas where performance has not been measured previously, and indicate the degree of understanding and participation of the employees in the existing systems and the actions that result.

Generic questions that may be asked during the audit include:

- Is there a performance measurement system in use?
- Has it been effectively communicated throughout the organization?
- Is it systematic?
- Is it efficient?
- Is it well understood?
- Is it applied?
- Is it linked to the mission and objectives of the organization?
- Is there a regular review and update?
- Is action taken to improve performance following the measurement?
- Are the people who own the processes engaged in measuring their own performance?
- Have employees been properly trained to conduct the measurement?

Following such an audit, there are twelve basic steps for the introduction of TQM-based performance measurement. Half of these are planning steps and the other half implementation.

**Planning**

1 Identify the purpose of conducting the measurement, i.e. is it for:
   (a) Reporting, e.g. ROI reported to shareholders.
   (b) Controlling, e.g. using process data on control charts.
   (c) Improving, e.g. monitoring the results of a quality improvement team project.
2 Choose the right balance between individual measures (activity- or task-related) and group measures (process and sub-process-related) and make sure they reflect process performance.

3 Plan to measure all the key elements of performance, not just one, e.g. time, cost, and product quality variables may all be important.
4 Ensure that the measures will reflect the voice of the internal/external customers.
5 Carefully select measures that will be used to establish standards of performance.
6 Allow time for the learning process during the introduction of a new measurement system.

**Implementation**

7 Ensure full participation during the introductory period and allow the system to mould through participation.
8 Carry out cost/benefit analysis on the data generation, and ensure measures that have high 'leverage' are selected.
9 Make the effort to spread the measurement system as widely as possible, since effective decision-making will be based on measures from *all* areas of the busines operation.
10 Use *surrogate* measures for subjective areas where quantification is difficult, e.g. improvements in morale may be 'measured' by reductions in absenteeism or staff turnover rates.
11 Design the measurement systems to be as flexible as possible, to allow for changes in strategic direction and continual review.
12 Ensure that the measures reflect the quality drive by showing small incremental achievements that match the never ending improvement approach.

In summary the measurement system must be designed, planned and implemented to reflect customer requirements, give visibility to the processes and the progress made, communicate the total quality effort and engage the never ending improvement cycle. So it must itself be periodically reviewed.

## 7.4   Benchmarking

Product, service and process improvements can only take place in relation to established standards, with the improvements then being incorporated into the new standards. *Benchmarking*, one of the most transferable aspects of Rank Xerox's approach to total-quality management, and thought to have originated in Japan, measures an organization's operations, products and services against those of its competitors in a ruthless fashion. It is a means by which targets, priorities and operations that will lead to competitive advantage can be established.

The concept is based on the ancient Japanese quotation: 'If you know your enemy and know yourself, you need not fear the result of a hundred battles'. (Sun Tzu, *The Art of War, 500 BC*). In Japanese the word *dantotsu* (or benchmarking) means striving for the best of the best.

Benchmarking is the continuous process of measuring products, services and processes against those of industry leaders or the toughest competitors. This results in a search for best practices, those that will lead to superior performance, through measuring performance, continuously implementing change, and emulating the best.

There may be many reasons for carrying out benchmarking. Some of them are set against various objectives in Table 7.1. The links between benchmarking and TQM are clear – establishing objectives based on industry best practice should directly contribute to better meeting of the internal and external customer requirements.

There are four basic types of benchmarking:

*Internal* – a comparison of internal operations.
*Competitive* – specific competitor to competitor comparisons for a product or function of interest.

**Table 7.1** *Reasons for benchmarking*

| Objectives | Without benchmarking | With benchmarking |
|---|---|---|
| Becoming competitive | • Internally focused<br>• Evolutionary change | • Understanding of competition<br>• Ideas from proven practices |
| Industry best practices | • Few solutions<br>• Frantic catch up activity | • Many options<br>• Superior performance |
| Defining customer requirements | • Based on history or gut feeling<br>• Perception | • Market reality<br>• Objective evaluation |
| Establishing effective goals and objectives | • Lacking external focus<br>• Reactive | • Credible, unarguable<br>• Proactive |
| Developing true measures of productivity | • Pursuing pet projects<br>• Strength and weaknesses not understood<br>• Route of least resistance | • Solving real problems<br>• Understanding outputs<br>• Based on industry best practices |

*Functional* – comparisons to similar functions within the same broad industry or to industry leaders.

*Generic* – comparisons of business processes or functions that are very similar, regardless of the industry.

The evolution of benchmarking in an organization is likely to progress through four focuses. Initially attention will be concentrated on competitive products or services, including, for example, design, development and operational features. This should develop into a focus on industry best practices and may include, for example, aspects of distribution or service. The real breakthrough is when the organization focuses on all aspects of the total business performance, across all functions and aspects, and addresses current *and projected* performance gaps. This should lead to the final focus on true continuous improvement.

At its simplest, competitive benchmarking, the most common form, requires every department to examine itself against its counterpart in the best competing companies. This includes a scrutiny of all aspects of their activities. Benchmarks that may be important for *customer satisfaction*, for example, might include:

• Product or service consistency.
• Correct and on-time delivery.
• Speed of response or new product development.
• Correct billing.

For *impact* the benchmarks may be:

• Waste, rejects or errors.
• Inventory levels/work in progress.
• Costs of operation.
• Staff turnover.

The task is to work out what has to be done to improve on the competition's performance in each of the chosen areas.

At regular (say, weekly) meetings, managers should discuss the results of the competitive benchmarking, and on a daily basis departmental managers should discuss quality problems with staff. One afternoon may be set aside for the benchmark meetings, followed by a 'walkabout', when the manager observes the activities actually taking place and compares them mentally with the competitors' operations.

The process has fifteen stages, and these are all focused on trying to *measure* comparisons of competitiveness:

PLAN    Select department(s) or process group(s) for benchmarking.
        Identify best competitor, perhaps using customer feedback or industry observers.
        Identify benchmarks.
        Bring together the appropriate team.
        Decide information and data-collection methodology (do not forget desk research!).
        Prepare for any visits and interact with target organizations.
        Use data-collection methodology.

ANALYSE Compare the organization and its 'competitors', using the benchmark data.
        Catalogue the information and create a 'competency centre'.
        Understand the 'enabling processes' as well as the performance measures.

DEVELOP Set new performance level objectives/standards.
        Develop action plans to achieve goals and integrate into the organization.

IMPROVE Implement specific actions and integrate them into the business processes.

REVIEW  Monitor the results and improvements.
        Review the benchmarks and the ongoing relationship with the target organization.

Benchmarking is very important in the administrative areas, since it continuously measures services and practices against the equivalent operation in the toughest direct competitors or organizations renowned as leaders in the areas, even if they are in the same organization. An example of quantitative benchmarks in absenteeism is given in Table 7.2.

Technologies and conditions vary between different industries and markets, but the basic concepts of measurement and benchmarking are of general validity. The objective should be to produce products and services that conform to the requirements of the customer in a never ending improvement environment. The way to accomplish this is to use the continuous improvement cycle in all the operating departments – nobody should be exempt. Measurement and benchmarking are not separate sciences or unique theories of quality management, but rather strategic approaches to getting the best out of people, processes, products, plant, and programmes.

**Table 7.2** *Quantitative benchmarking in absenteeism*

| Organization's absence level (%) | Productivity opportunity |
| --- | --- |
| Under 3 | This level matches an aggressive benchmark that has been achieved in 'excellent' organizations. |
| 3–4 | This level may be viewed within the organization as a good performance – representing a moderate productivity opportunity improvement. |
| 5–8 | This level is tolerated by many organizations but represents a major improvement opportunity. |
| 9–10 | This level indicates that a serious absenteeism problem exists. |
| Over 10 | This level of absenteeism is totally unacceptable. |

### Acknowledgement

The author is grateful to his colleague Dr Mohamed Zairi, Unilever Lecturer at the European Centre for TQM, for his significant contribution to this chapter.

## Chapter highlights

### Measurement and the improvement cycle

- Traditional performance measures based on cost-accounting information provide little to support TQM, because they do not map process performance and improvements seen by the customer.
- Measurement is important in identifying opportunities, and comparing performance internally and externally. Measures, typically non-financial, are used in process control and performance improvement.
- Some financial indicators, such as ROI, are often inaccurate, irrelevant and too late to be used as measures for performance improvement.
- The Deming cycle of PLAN DO CHECK ACT is a useful design aid for measurement systems, but firstly four basic questions about measurement should be asked, i.e. why, what, where, and how.
- In answering the question 'how to measure?' progress is important in five main areas: effectiveness, efficiency, productivity, quality, and impact.

- Activity-based costing (ABS) is based on the activities performed being identified and costs traced to them. ABS uses cost drivers, which reflect the demands placed on activities.

## The metrics and the processes

- In TQM measurement, the strategic objectives will be converted into desired standards of performance, and metrics developed.
- The separation of process performance and process management is important, since it determines the type of questions to be asked, e.g. how much, how many *vs* what, where, why.

## The implementation of performance measurement systems

- The value of any measure must be compared with the cost of producing it. All critical parts of the process must be measured, but it is often better to start with the simple measures and improve them.
- Process-owners should take part in defining the performance measures, which must reflect customer requirements.
- Prior to introducing TQM measurement, an audit of existing systems should be carried out to establish their effectiveness, compatability, relationship and closeness to the customer.
- Following the audit, there are twelve basic steps for implementation, six of which are planning steps.

## Benchmarking

- Benchmarking measures an organization's operations, products, and services against those of its competitors. It will establish targets, priorities, and operations, leading to competitive advantage.
- There are four basic types of benchmarking: internal, competitive, functional, and generic. The evolution of benchmarking in an organization is likely to progress through four focuses towards continuous improvement.
- The implementation of benchmarking has fifteen stages, which are categorized into plan, analyse, develop, improve, and review.

# 8  Costs of quality

## 8.1    Cost effective quality management

Manufacturing a quality product, providing a quality service, or doing a quality job – one with a high degree of customer satisfaction – is not enough. The cost of achieving these goals must be carefully managed, so that the long-term effect of quality costs on the business or organization is a desirable one. These costs are a true measure of the quality effort. A competitive product or service based on a balance between quality and cost factors is the principal goal of responsible management. This objective is best accomplished with the aid of competent analysis of the costs of quality (COQ).

The analysis of quality related costs is a significant management tool that provides:

*   A method of assessing the effectiveness of the management of quality.
*   A means of determining problem areas, opportunities, savings, and action priorities.

The costs of quality are no different from any other costs. Like the costs of maintenance, design, sales, production/operations, and other activities, they can be budgeted, measured and analysed.

Having specified the quality of design, the operating units have the task of matching it. The necessary activities will incur costs that may be separated into prevention costs, appraisal costs and failure costs, the so-called P–A–F model first presented by Feigenbaum. Failure costs can be further split into those resulting from internal and external failure.

### Prevention costs

These are associated with the design, implementation and maintenance of the total quality management system. Prevention costs are planned and are incurred before actual operation. Prevention includes:

*Product or service requirements*

The determination of requirements and the setting of corresponding specifications (which also takes account of process capability) for incoming materials, processes, intermediates, finished products and services.

*Quality planning*

The creation of quality, reliability, and operational, production, supervision, process control, inspection and other special plans, e.g. pre-production trials, required to achieve the quality objective.

*Quality assurance*

The creation and maintenance of the quality system.

*Inspection equipment*

The design, development and/or purchase of equipment for use in inspection work.

*Training*

The development, preparation and maintenance of training programmes for operators, supervisors, staff, and managers both to achieve and maintain capability.

*Miscellaneous*

Clerical, travel, supply, shipping, communications and other general office management activities associated with quality.

Resources devoted to prevention give rise to the '*costs of doing it right the first time*'.

## Appraisal costs

These costs are associated with the supplier's and customer's evaluation of purchased materials, processes, intermediates, products and services to assure conformance with the specified requirements. Appraisal includes:

*Verification*

Checking of incoming material, process set-up, first-offs, running processes, intermediates and final products, services, including product or service performance appraisal against agreed specifications.

*Quality audits*

To check that the quality system is functioning satisfactorily.

*Inspection equipment*

The calibration and maintenance of equipment used in all inspection activities.

*Vendor rating*

The assessment and approval of all suppliers, of both products and services.
Appraisal activities result in the *'costs of checking it is right'*.


**Internal failure costs**

These costs occur when the results of work fail to reach designed quality standards and are detected before transfer to the customer takes place. Internal failure includes the following:

*Waste*

The activities associated with doing unnecessary work or holding stocks as the result of errors, poor organization or poor communications, the wrong materials, etc.

*Scrap*

Defective product, material or stationery that cannot be repaired, used or sold.

*Rework or rectification*

The correction of defective material or errors to meet the requirements.

*Re-inspection*

The re-examination of products or work that have been rectified.

*Downgrading*

A product that is usable but does not meet specifications may be downgraded and sold as 'second quality' at a low price.

*Failure analysis*

The activity required to establish the causes of internal product or service failure.

**External failure costs**

These costs occur when products or services fail to reach design quality standards but are not detected until after transfer to the consumer. External failure includes:

*Repair and servicing*

Either of returned products or those in the field.

*Warranty claims*

Failed products that are replaced or services re-performed under some form of guarantee.

*Complaints*

All work and costs associated with handling and servicing of customers' complaints.

*Returns*

The handling and investigation of rejected or recalled products or materials, including transport costs.

*Liability*

The result of product or service liability litigation and other claims, which may include a change of contract.

*Loss of goodwill*

The impact on reputation and image, which impinges directly on future prospects for sales.

External and internal failures produce the '*costs of getting it wrong*'.

Order re-entry, retyping, unnecessary travel and telephone calls, conflict, are just a few examples of the wastage or failure costs often excluded. Every organization must be aware of the costs of getting it wrong, and management needs to obtain some idea how much failure is costing each year.

Clearly, this classification of cost elements may be used to interrogate any internal transformation process. Using the internal customer requirements concept as the standard for failure, these cost assessments can be made wherever information, data, materials, service or artefacts are transferred from one person or one department to another. It is the 'internal' costs of lack of quality that lead to the claim that approximately one-third of *all* our efforts are wasted.

The relationship between the quality related costs of prevention, appraisal, and failure and increasing quality awareness and improve-

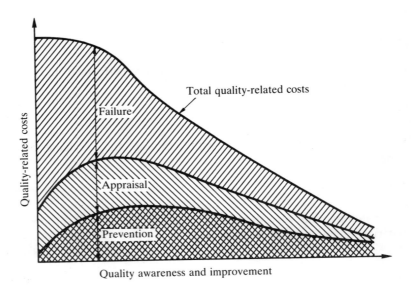

**Figure 8.1** *Increasing quality awareness and improvement activities. Source: British Standard BS6143, 1991*

ment in the organization is shown in Figure 8.1. Where the quality awareness is low, the total quality related costs are high, the failure costs predominating. As awareness of the cost to the organization of failure gets off the ground, through initial investment in training, an increase in appraisal costs usually results. As the increased appraisal leads to investigations and further awareness, further investment in prevention is made to improve design features, processes and systems. As the preventive action takes effect, the failure *and* appraisal costs fall and the total costs reduce.

The first presentations of the P–A–F model suggested there may be an optimum operating level at which the combined costs are at the minimum. The author however, has not yet found one organization in which the total costs have risen following investment in prevention.

## 8.2 Data and sources

The determination of the costs of quality is something organizations must pursue to make improvements in competitiveness. An assessment of the failure costs will create the thrust needed for a successful quality improvement programme. In the service sector the costs of failure or non-quality are sometimes difficult to measure, sometimes intangible, but they usually exceed the 10–15 per cent of turnover usually quoted for manufacturing industry. In some organizations they are as high as 35–40 per cent of volume.

In finding costs, one of the major pitfalls is isolating only those things that can be measured. The less easily quantified areas tend to be ignored or forgotten. Measuring only tangible items, such as scrap, wasted materials, direct people costs for dealing with complaints, reworking, mending or redoing, is a mistake many organizations make. It leads to the conclusion that the cost of failure is low – always far from the truth. Use of formulae that fail to provide the true costs of quality will generate complacency and lethargy, particularly in non-producing areas such as finance, personnel, legal services, computer systems, public relations, and purchasing.

The bulk of the costs associated with getting it wrong often lie in the non-producing sectors of an organization – the people who never touch the product or provide the service. A major source of such failure costs are the activities of the salesforce and marketing, who are responsible for defining the customers' requirements in terms sufficiently specific to develop suitable designs from which the producing departments can operate. This applies very much in non-manufacturing industries, where the customer needs are potentially more difficult to define and yet very noticeable when they are absent.

This type of communication problem can lead to cost creating difficulties in other parts of the organization. For example, materials-management problems frequently accompany poor marketing information. Companies with inventories nearly as high as turnover may restrict their investigations to the systems for inventory control, never getting to the real causes of high stocks, and all the time the competitive edge is being blunted by high operating costs. Such companies can go out of business with full order books.

Progressive managers, always anxious to reduce costs, should be looking closely at the costs of achieving and maintaining conformance to a predetermined design quality. Most of those who have attempted to do so have found ample scope for economies. It is necessary for effective management control that these expenditures be detailed and displayed. Yet efforts to discover the extent of quality costs prevailing in many organizations have met with frustration for a variety of reasons. Quality costing tends to cut across normal accounting methods, and cannot simply be secured by asking the accounting department for them. This may well elicit the response, 'We don't keep the books that way'.

The information must be pieced together, by using the 'books' where possible and resorting to estimates and finding new data when necessary. Successful quality costing requires working closely with the accountants and with the supervisors of the various departments to evaluate and estimate the costs associated with various activities. Table 8.1 is a generic quality cost report pro-forma, based on the P–A–F model, which is offered as a basis for modification to meet specific requirements of the user's own operations. It is based primarily on each department's contribution to quality costs, and should enable the sharing of quality costs between groups. It is not fully comprehensive; further cost areas may need to be added and some of the sections may be omitted, some may be too small to warrant inclusion, too difficult to isolate from a larger category, or not determined with sufficient accuracy to be valid. Particular care must be taken to avoid double counting.

Many useful documents and reports may exist within an organization, and these should aid the quality costing process, for example:

- People or equipment utilization reports.
- Material usage and review reports or records.
- Field or salesmen's reports.
- Analysis of credit notes, warranty claims, etc.

**Table 8.1** *Proforma for reporting quality-related costs*

| | Salaries and wages | Consumable materials | Capital equipment depreciation | Others | Total |
|---|---|---|---|---|---|
| *Quality assurance* | | | | | |
| Prevention costs | | | | | |
|   Quality planning | | | | | |
|   Training personnel | | | | | |
| Appraisal costs | | | | | |
|   Receiving and process appraisal | | | | | |
|   Final product or service appraisal | | | | | |
| Failure costs | | | | | |
|   Internal failure | | | | | |
|   External failure | | | | | |
| | | | | | |
| *Research, design and development* | | | | | |
| Prevention costs | | | | | |
|   Setting specifications (incl. services, materials, processes and products) | | | | | |
|   Pre-production/operation and prototype trials | | | | | |
| Appraisal costs | | | | | |
|   Inspection equipment | | | | | |
|   • maintenance of | | | | | |
|   • design and specifications for | | | | | |
| Failure costs | | | | | |
|   Rework and rectification | | | | | |
|   Downgrading of products and services | | | | | |
|   Product or service complaints and warranty claims | | | | | |
| | | | | | |
| *Production/operations* | | | | | |
| Prevention costs | | | | | |
|   Training – including supervisor training | | | | | |
|   Preproduction/operation and prototype trials | | | | | |
|   Special handling and storage during production or operations | | | | | |
|   Supervision of quality at all stages | | | | | |
| Appraisal costs | | | | | |
|   Line or process inspection (by production/operations personnel) | | | | | |
|   Finished product inspection or service checking (by production/operations personnel) | | | | | |

**Table 8.1** (*continued*)

| | Salaries and wages | Consumable materials | Capital equipment depreciation | Others | Total |
|---|---|---|---|---|---|

**Failure costs**
Full cost of scrap or wasted
    effort
Rework or rectification
Replacement of rejected product
    or repeating service
Downgrading of products,
    materials and services

*Marketing and sales*
**Prevention costs**
Setting of product or service
    specifications
**Appraisal costs**
Analysis of degree of acceptance
    of goods and services

**Failure costs**
Downgrading of products and
    services
Customer complaints, liaison and
    compensation
Warranty claims and replacements
    or refunds

*Purchasing*
**Prevention costs**
Supplier approval
**Appraisal costs**
Vendor rating
**Failure costs**
Incorrect choice of supplier(s)

*Service department*
**Prevention costs**
Product or service specification evaluation
Preproduction/operations and prototype trials
Planning of in-process control procedures
**Appraisal costs**
Finished product or service performance
    evaluation
**Failure costs**
Customer complaints
Product or customer service
Returned material investigations and repairs

**Table 8.1** (*continued*)

| | Salaries and wages | Consumable materials | Capital equipment depreciation | Others | Total |
|---|---|---|---|---|---|

*Personnel*
Prevention costs
  Recruitment of appropriate personnel
  Competencies analysis
Appraisal costs
  Operation of staff appraisal systems
Failure costs
  Dealing with results of poor recruitment process
  Disciplinary procedures

*Stores, transport and distribution*
Prevention costs
  Special handling and storage

Appraisal costs
  Receiving and checking materials,
    bought-out items or services
  Checking and despatching finished
    products and/or services
Failure costs
  Sorting of reject finished goods in
    stock
  Receiving and checking returned reject
    goods
  Checking and despatching replacement
    goods

*Material control*
Prevention costs
  Ordering correct materials
  Inventory system
Appraisal costs
  Checking stock levels
Failure costs
  Scrap material control
  Ordering of material or services for
    rework and rectification
  Ordering of material or services and
    finished goods for replacement

*Maintenance*
Prevention costs
  Prototype processes and equipment
  Planning and maintenance of plant
    equipment and inspection
    equipment

**Table 8.1** (*continued*)

| | Salaries and wages | Consumable materials | Capital equipment depreciation | Others | Total |
|---|---|---|---|---|---|
| **Appraisal costs** | | | | | |
| Equipment reliability monitoring | | | | | |
| **Failure costs** | | | | | |
| Investigations and repairs following complaints, return of goods and warranty claims | | | | | |
| | | | | | |
| *Finance* | | | | | |
| **Prevention costs** | | | | | |
| Establishment of good financial systems | | | | | |
| **Appraisal costs** | | | | | |
| Auditing accounts | | | | | |
| Determination of quality-related costs | | | | | |
| **Failure costs** | | | | | |
| Investigations and rework, following failure in the system | | | | | |
| | | | | | |
| **Total quality costs** | | | | | |

- Analysis of rework, repair, replacement, or refund records or authorizations.
- Salaries and wages analyses.
- Production or operations costing reports.
- Scrap reports.
- Travel expense claims.
- Inspection, check, test, and verification records.

A pilot study should establish the preliminary figures from a small area of the organization or a single product line or service operation. The aim of the pilot programme is to determine the scope of the work and to gain management approval and commitment to a total quality costing system. The quality related cost categories and the cost elements to be used should also be defined at this stage. A first estimate of the costs of quality in an organization may be made by combining data from such reports with estimates derived from discussions with appropriate managers and supervisors. Each assumption and estimate used in this first quality cost computation should be published in a document that is circulated to selected managers. This will produce heated arguments about whether certain costs are part of quality related costs. It is unimportant whether these 'grey' items are included or not; provided that there is consistency in including or excluding the debatable categories, the opportunities for reducing costs are not affected.

## 8.3   Assumptions, risks and benefits

### Some assumptions

One danger in recording and reporting quality related costs is that managers become too concerned with accuracy in their determination – a number-crunching exercise that will consume resources disproportionately. For many organizations or their parts, particularly the non-profit-making ones, it may be sufficient to assess the amount or proportion of time spent on work related to errors and their appraisal. This can always be equated to financial measures later. In quality costing, as in all areas of management, the skewed Pareto distribution (see Chapter 9) applies, and it is likely that 20 per cent of the cost elements result in 80 per cent of the total costs. Clearly, the isolation of this 'vital few' will focus attention on the areas in need of improvements. The following may be done to gather pertinent quality related cost data throughout the whole organization:

- The percentage of time spent by each person is categorized as prevention, appraisal or failure, the individuals being asked initially to give estimates of the percentages for each category.
- The percentage of total costs expended for each category is determined for each month.

The percentage values characteristic of most organizations without TQM are failure, about 65 per cent, and appraisal, about 25 per cent, of the total quality related costs, with prevention much lower, at 10 per cent.

Quality related costs may be 'normalized' if a standard costing system is established. This neutralizes any inflation effects. For each category an index of the quality related cost per £1,000 or $1,000 standard cost may be calculated, using the formula:

$$\text{Category index} = \frac{\text{Quality related cost in category}}{\text{Standard cost}} \times 100$$

For example, if the December standard cost of production was £2,250,000, and the total prevention cost for December was £39,250, the 'prevention index' is:

$$\text{Prevention index} = \frac{39{,}250 \times 100}{2{,}250{,}000} = 1.7 \text{ per cent}$$

Calculation of separate index values for scrap, rework or repeated work, may show trends in the value of the 'scrap index' (in terms of standard cost). Analysis of various improvement programmes or changes should show whether the results manifest themselves in the percentage of total costs attributable to failure. It is essential that the preventive-cost category is also monitored throughout any study period.

Several methods may be used to analyse quality costs, including the process cost model, which is introduced in Section 8.4. The objective of the exercise is to observe any trends and to relate the results to the management turnover and style. A complete analysis would include an assessment of the effects of any reorganization in personnel, increased workloads, or changes in communication methods; including the introduction of quality management systems. Any changes from appraisal to prevention should be recorded, and their effects noted. Other indicators should be included in the analysis, some with both advantages and disadvantages, e.g. fluctuations in total output. In this case the various indices give a better idea of trends in quality related costs as they are normalized. Weak quality assurance programmes, or management that believes that tighter control means more measuring to detect and redo faulty work, will be highlighted by this type of index quality related cost system.

**Risks**

Quality costs must not become a measure of competition between departments. This will serve to bury the real issues and causes of quality problems, which often lie *between* people or departments. The competitive use of quality costing will prevent individuals or managers from taking ownership of the processes and responsibility for failure – particularly if its resolution will have a more favourable impact on someone else or another department. Co-operation rather than competition is the essential component in reducing costs through TQM.

It is important to realize that the cost measurement process is like any other process, and will improve with use and experience. Hence, it is most likely that the second and third assessments of quality related costs will be more accurate than the first, and capture more sources of cost. It is not uncommon for senior management to interpret this as a sign of deterioration, which may also correspond with the introduction of TQM! Clearly, like must be compared with like and factors of time, use, and experience must be considered in the interpretation of quality cost data.

**Benefits**

There is no short cut to reducing the costs of quality, but once everyone recognizes that these high costs are reducing the organization's competitiveness, they should become committed to making total quality part of their working lives. The loss of the competitive edge through not meeting the customer requirements, sustaining high costs, or failing to deliver, reduces the number of options for human resource management. When shown, most people recognize the logical arguments that growth and job security derive from maintaining or increasing sales, which brings us back to the competitive edge. In this way a demonstrated high percentage quality related cost figure will often catalyse a TQM programme.

Some of the first actions that might result from this are:

- The initiation of a special study to determine error or defect sources, training needs, etc. This will, of course, initially increase prevention costs.
- Special efforts to improve communication at the internal supplier–customer interfaces and between departments such as marketing, design, production/operations, and purchasing.
- The continued collection, analysis, and reporting of quality related cost information by personnel in finance and quality management.
- The establishment and maintenance of quality objectives, in terms of costs, for the entire organization and for specific areas.

Clearly, expenditure on prevention and improvement activities is an investment from which a return is expected. Effective quality improvement should result in a future stream of benefits in the form of reduced failure costs, lower appraisal costs, increased market share, more students, etc. A financial model of the investments in and the savings from the implementation of TQM should be developed.

Perhaps the most important benefit that will be derived is the appreciation by top management that they construct the quality image and performance of the whole operation. It may come as a surprise to some managers to read that such lessons may be learned from a simple quality related cost reporting system, but its implementation will be truly effective *only* if it measures the real quality related costs within the organization. As stated, many organizations will have true quality related costs in excess of 15 per cent of sales revenue; effective quality improvement can reduce this considerably, thereby making a direct contribution to profits.

Total quality related costs, and their division between the categories of prevention, appraisal, internal failure and external failure, vary considerably from industry to industry and from plant to plant. The average figure for quality related costs of 10 per cent of sales turnover means that the average organization contains a 'ghost operation' amounting to approximately one-tenth of capacity. This is devoted to producing errors, waste, scrap, rework, correcting errors, replacing defective goods, apologizing for poor service, and so on. Thus, there is a direct link between quality and productivity, and there is no better way to improve productivity than to convert this ghost resource to truly productive use.

## 8.4   The process model for quality costing

The P–A–F model for quality costing has a number of drawbacks. In TQM, prevention of problems, defects, errors, waste, etc., is one of the prime functions, but it can be argued that everything a well managed organization does is directed at preventing quality problems. This makes separation of *prevention costs* very difficult. There are clearly a range of prevention activities in any manufacturing or service organization that are integral to ensuring quality but may never be included in the schedule of quality related costs.

It is probably impossible and unnecessary to categorize costs into the three categories of P–A–F. For example, a design review may be considered a prevention cost, an appraisal cost, or even a failure cost, depending on how and where it is used in the process. Another criticism of the P–A–F model is that it focuses attention on cost reduction and plays down, or in some cases even ignores, the positive contribution made to price and sales volume by improved quality.

The most serious criticism of the original P–A–F model presented by Feigenbaum and used in, for example, British Standard 6143 (1981) 'Guide to the determination and use of quality related costs', is that it implies an acceptable 'optimum' quality level above which there is a trade-off between investment in prevention and failure costs. Clearly, this is not in tune with the never ending improvement philosophy of

TQM. The key focus of TQM is on process improvement, and a cost categorization scheme that does not consider process costs, such as the P–A–F model, has limitations.

In a total quality related cost system that focuses on processes rather than products or services, the operating costs of generating customer satisfaction will be of prime importance. The so-called 'process cost model', now described in the revised BS6143 (1991) 'Guide to economics of quality', Part 1, sets out a method for applying quality costing to any process or service. It recognizes the importance of process ownership and measurement, and uses process modelling to simplify classification. The categories of the cost of quality (COQ) have been rationalized into the cost of conformance (COC) and the cost of non-conformance (CONC):

COQ = COC + CONC

The cost of conformance (COC) is the process cost of providing products or services to the required standards, by a given specified process in the most effective manner, i.e. the cost of the ideal process where every activity is carried out according to the requirements first time, every time. The cost of nonconformance (CONC) is the failure cost associated with a process not being operated to the requirements, or the cost due to variability in the process. Part 2 of BS6143 (1991) still deals with the P–A–F model, but without the 'optimum'/minimum cost theory (see Figure 8.1).

Process cost models can be used for any process within an organization and developed for the process by flowcharting. This will identify the key process steps and the parameters that are monitored in the process. The process cost elements should then be identified and recorded under the categories of product/service (outputs), and people, systems, plant or equipment, materials, environment, information (inputs). The COC and CONC for each stage of the process will comprise a list of all the parameters monitored.

**Steps in process cost modelling**

Process cost modelling is a methodology that lends itself to stepwise analysis, and the following are the key stages in building the model. The author is grateful to his colleagues Les Porter and Paul Rayner for the example used below:

1 Choose a key process to be analysed, identify and name it, e.g. Retrieval of Medical Records (Acute Admissions).

2 Define the process and its boundaries.
3 Construct the process diagram:
  (a) Identify the outputs and customers (for example see Figure 8.2).
  (b) Identify the inputs and suppliers (for example see Figure 8.3).

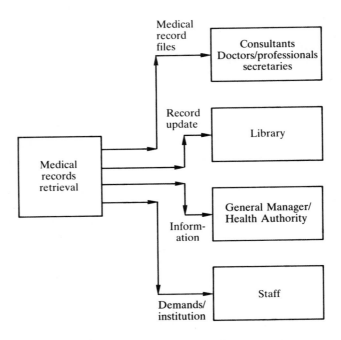

**Figure 8.2** *Building the model: identify outputs and customers*

  (c) Identify the controls and resources (for example see Figure 8.4).
4 Flowchart the process and identify the process owners (for example see Figure 8.5). Note, the process owners will form the improvement team.
5 Allocate the activities as COC or CONC (see Table 8.2).
6 Calculate or estimate the quality costs (COQ) at each stage (COC + CONC). Estimates may be required where the accounting system is unable to generate the necessary information.
7 Construct a process cost report (see Table 8.3). The report summary and results are given in Table 8.4.

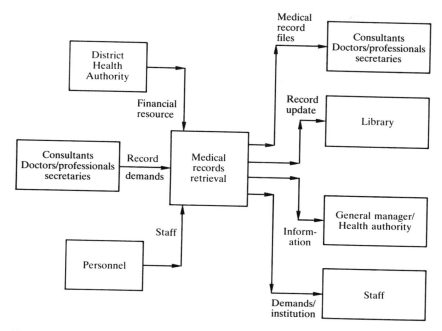

**Figure 8.3** *Building the model: identify inputs and suppliers*

There are three further steps carried out by the process owners – the improvement team – which take the process forward into the improvement stage:

8 Prioritize the failure costs and select the process stages for improvement through reduction in costs of nonconformance (CONC). This should indicate any requirements for investment in prevention activities. An excessive cost of conformance (COC) may suggest the need for process redesign.
9 Review the flowchart to identify the scope for reductions in the cost of conformance. Attempts to reduce COC require a thorough process understanding, and a second flowchart of what the new process should be may help (see Chapter 4).
10 Monitor conformance and nonconformance costs on a regular basis, using the model and review for further improvements.

The process cost model approach must be seen as more than a simple tool to measure the financial implications of the gap between the actual and potential performances of a process. The emphasis given to

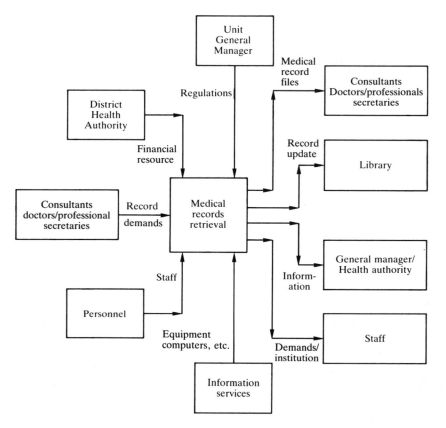

**Figure 8.4** *Building the model: identify controls and resources*

the process, improving the understanding, and seeing in detail where the costs occur, should be an integral part of quality improvement.

## 8.5    Managing the quality cost system

Good working knowledge of all the processes and experience of the organization's accounting systems are clearly essential for the successful management of a quality related cost system. The costs cut across conventional accounting boundaries in most organizations, so it is important to set down the objectives of the system at the start. This will prevent difficulties later and influence the strategy employed.

The main aim of the system, initially, may be to identify high cost

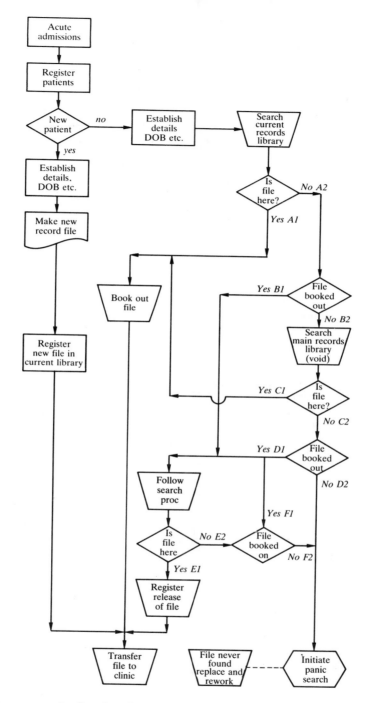

**Figure 8.5** *Present practice flowchart for acute admissions, medical records retrieval*

**Table 8.2** *Building the model: allocate activities as COC or CONC*

| Key activities | COC | CONC |
|---|---|---|
| Search for files | Labour cost incurred finding a record while adhering to standard procedure | Labour cost incurred finding a record while unable to adhere to standard procedure |
| Make up new files | New patient files | Patients whose original files cannot be located |
| Rework | | Cost of labour and materials for all rework files/records never found as a direct consequence of . . . |
| Duplication | | Cost incurred in duplicating existing files |

**Table 8.3** *Building the model: process cost report*

Process cost report
Process medical records retrieval (acute admissions)
Process-owner: various
Time allocation: 4 days (96 hrs)

| Process COC | Process CONC | Cost details Act | Synth | Definition | Source | |
|---|---|---|---|---|---|---|
| | Labour cost incurred finding records | # ref. sample | | Cost of time required to find missing records | Medical records | £98 |
| | Cost incurred making up replacement files | | # | Labour and material costs multiplied by number of files replaced | Medical records | £40 |
| | Rework | | # | Labour and material cost of all rework | Medical records | £50 |
| | Duplication | | # | | Medical records | £9 |

**Table 8.4** *Process cost model: report summary*

Labour cost
    13.75 hrs × £5.80/hr = £80
    £80 × overhead and contribution factor 22%
    = £98

Replacement costs
    No of files unfound 9
    Cost to replace each file £4.50
    Overall cost £40

Rework costs
    2 × Pathology reports to be retyped £50

Duplication costs
    No of files duplicated 2
    Cost per file £4.50
    Overall cost £9

                TOTAL COST £197

RESULTS
Acute admissions operated 24 hrs/day 365 days/year
This project established a cost of nonconformance of
approx. £197
This equates to £197 × 365/4 + £17,976
or two personnel fully employed for 12 months

problem areas, in which case approximate costs will suffice. Subsequently, the system should broaden and perhaps set a percentage cost reduction target on the organization's total quality related costs. This eventually requires the identification and measurement of all the contributing cost elements in order to be sure that the costs are actually reduced and not simply transferred elsewhere.

The key words – prevention, appraisal, internal failure and external failure – and the detailed checklists are helpful, but do not replace the need for knowledge and experience of the business processes and the whole operation.

How and to what depth of detail an organization wishes to apply the various techniques of quality costing will be determined by how far the organization is along the road of TQM and the establishment of a never-ending improvement culture. In general terms there are three levels of the organization at which support for and commitment to the quality costing system must be obtained:

- The executive/senior management.
- Functional or line management.
- The remainder of the staff.

In drawing up a quality costing strategy, the following should be considered:

1 At what stage is the organization in its awareness/understanding/ commitment to quality? If there is already a well understood and planned approach to process control, it may be necessary to examine the business direction, establish the critical activities and understand better the internal and external customer–supplier requirements and expectations.

2 How is the organization going to obtain an approximate order of quality related costs in order to:
   (a) Convince management that there is a great deal to be gained from a better approach?
   (b) Highlight probable candidates for more detailed analyses?
   For this, a baseline of performance must be established, and the right parameters for assessing and monitoring progress chosen.

3 How will the critical cost areas be analysed and who will be involved?

4 What data will be required and in what form, and how will it be collected? It will also be useful to know what data are already available in order to determine what additional information might be beneficial. At this stage types of incidents/failures and frequencies and methods of establishing *factual* data should also be considered.

5 What are the time scales and the review dates for the implementation of the quality costing system?

6 How is the cost of quality measurement to be built into the general quality awareness and communication strategy?

7 How will success be demonstrated? Within any organization many areas will contribute to quality related costs. It is recommended that the initial concentration is on the key business processes and that the support activities are left for a second phase.

**The system**

The checklist of quality cost elements in Table 8.1 stresses that total quality costing requires much more than the check, inspection and test functions. Every person, in every department of an organization, bears the responsibility for ensuring that the customers' requirements are met, and the costs associated with making sure they are must be included. Prevention costs, especially in small companies, are the most difficult to identify, and slavish adherence to any method or checklist may result in a great deal of effort being expended in chasing insignificant costs.

The stages in establishing a quality costing system are:

- Identify the cost elements, using a checklist or the process cost model.
- Begin the collection of quality cost data.
- Calculate the costs attributable directly to the 'quality function', including staff costs, pension costs, portion of accommodation costs – rent, rates, insurance, heating, lighting, security, canteen, office services and administration costs, etc.
- Calculate costs incurred by all other departments and organizations in a similar manner.
- Calculate the costs of the 'budgeted' failure. For example, it may be a company's practice to begin producing 1,100 articles for every 1,000 actually required, to be certain of achieving that number.
- Calculate the internal costs of unplanned failure, for which there is no allowance in the initial planning. Related costs may include material scrapped and repeated work, and they should be found either in the process causing failure or the one rectifying it.
- Pay particular attention to the identification and calculation of the costs of failures that fall between departments, including time spent on investigations by the quality and other departments; these costs will rarely appear in existing systems, and an initial estimate may need to be made.

All the data should be entered in a 'memorandum account' of quality related costs.

**Reporting**

Data extracted from source documents should be coded for easy tabulation, so that all cost data are reported by code. The use of coding permits consistency of collection, regardless of the source or size of the costs. Where actual costs cannot be directly associated with specific elements, it may be necessary to make an allocation by arbitration. If these costs are significant, the necessary records should be established, in order to record the data factually.

Quality costs may be collated and reported initially by the 'quality department', based on data collected by the accounts department. The separate roles most likely to be established are that the accounts department collects quality cost data, produces an operating report, allocates quality costs to agreed accountable areas or processes, and provides comparative bases for quality related cost assessment. The quality department analyses quality related costs and takes appropriate action by initiating the investigation of causes and making recommendations for improvements, co-ordinates inter-departmental activity to achieve quality cost objectives, pursues a policy for quality cost reduction and control, and arbitrates on the allocation of responsibility for quality failure costs.

For each organization there will be certain important aspects of the management of the quality costing system, e.g. the valuation of scrapped products and allocation of overhead costs. In the example of scrapped products it will be important to reach agreement early in the exercise on whether they should be costed as materials plus added value to the point in the process they had reached, or whether they should be valued at the cost when completed, and whether the cost to produce or the selling price should be used.

It may also be necessary to have a policy on how overhead costs should be included in the quality costing system. Many quality related costs are normally included as part of the overhead, while others are treated as direct costs and attract a proportion of overheads. Failure to clarify this issue can lead to a gross distortion of the picture derived from quality related cost analyses. It is also easy to fall into the trap of double counting.

Following identification of where costs are incurred and their magnitude, action can be taken to control and reduce them. Quality related costs should be collected and reported separately and not absorbed into a variety of overheads, or otherwise hidden, e.g. debits in one area that are balanced by credits in another. A financial report should be presented to management to give it an accurate statement of the costs of failure and the costs of operating quality controls. In order to have sufficient impact, this report should be presented separately but in a similar style to other management accounts, and should be supported by financial ratios and trend analyses related to the business of the organization to enable managment to allocate the relevant financial resources. It is essential that the classification of cost data is relevant and consistent with other accounting practices within the organization, so that comparisons may be made between costing periods or related activities.

The report format and frequency will depend upon the nature of the business and the level of management to which the information is presented. The reports must be relevant to the business objectives and should therefore have a consistent basis against which true comparisons can be made. Several measurement bases for the quality related cost reports may be useful for presentation. They should represent the business from different viewpoints and be sensitive to changes. The following bases may be appropriate:

- People costs, e.g. internal failure costs/direct labour costs.
- Manufacturing cost, e.g. total failure costs/manufacturing costs.
- Sales or turnover, e.g. total quality costs/net sales.
- Value added, e.g. total prevention costs/value added.
- Unit, e.g. test or inspection costs/units of output.

Quality related cost per unit produced (or patient, or student, or guest, etc.) has many advantages, but it is always necessary to take into account the effect of product/service mix, volume and value. The most generally used base is sales volume or turnover, which has the great advantage of being understood by all as a measure of an organization's activity. A change in the quality cost to turnover ratio can be immediately converted into an effect on the organization's pre-tax profitability. For a given industry, the profit to turnover ratio is one of the indices of financial success, so its close relationship to the quality related costs to turnover ratio is another reason for favouring volume as the base for quality related cost reporting.

Known or forecast changes, such as any of the following, can affect the choice of base:

1 Direct labour to be replaced by automation.
2 The use of alternative materials or methods of processes affecting costs.
3 Changes in selling prices, distribution costs, market demand, product/service mix or gross margins.

In reporting quality related costs, the scope for misinterpretation of the findings should be considered very carefully. The relationships between the total quality related costs and the costs of prevention, appraisal and failure, should be clearly seen. Ideally, quality costs should be recorded and reported on a regular period basis on a running scoreboard. An annual once-off survey is a poor alternative.

Quality cost reductions cannot be dictated by management, they have to be earned through the processes of problem solving and improvement. The identification of quality problems or opportunities – areas of significantly high quality costs – must be conducted within the framework of an appropriate quality policy. The approach adopted by any particular organization will depend on many factors, but there are common elements to all successful quality related cost systems. These include the following:

1 Management commitment – real commitment of the management to finding the true costs of quality throughout the organization.
2 A quality costing system – the design and implementation of a system for the identification, reporting and analysis of quality related costs.
3 Quality related costs management – the formation of a cost of quality management team responsible for direction and co-ordination of the quality costing system, and for ensuring that realistic targets are set and met.
4 Training – the inclusion of quality costing as an integral part of all training schemes to enable everyone to understand the financial implications of quality.
5 Quality related cost promotion – the presentation of significant costs of quality in readily understandable terms to all personnel, e.g. displays of defective products carrying price tags, or charts of errors and their costs. If possible, the promotion material should indicate courses of remedial action.
6 Quality related cost participation – the introduction of suitable schemes for achieving maximum participation of employees in this area, including means for promoting, initiating, receiving, discussing, appreciating and actioning ideas. Cost of quality action groups, quality circles, corrective action teams, or quality improvement groups, organized throughout the company, may well meet this purpose.

These are the fundamental steps in setting up a system for the measurement and analysis of quality related costs. Once established, the system itself should become dynamic, and the data derived and actions resulting from its use should impact on the achievement of the mission and objectives of the organization. If not, it just adds to the bureaucracy.

**Acknowledgement**

The author gratefully acknowledges the significant contribution to this chapter made by his colleague Dr Les Porter, Tioxide Lecturer at the European Centre for TQM.

# Chapter highlights

## Cost effective quality management

- A competitive product or service based on a balance between quality and cost factors is the principal goal of responsible management.
- The analysis of quality related costs provide a method of assessing the effectiveness of the management of quality and of determining problem areas, opportunities, savings, and action priorities.
- Total quality costs may be categorized into prevention, appraisal, internal failure, and external failure costs, the P–A–F model.
- Prevention costs are associated with doing it right the first time, appraisal costs with checking it is right, and failure costs with getting it wrong.
- When quality awareness in an organization is low, the total quality related costs are high, the failure costs predominating. After an initial rise in costs, mainly through the investment in training and appraisal, increasing investment in prevention causes failure, appraisal and total costs to fall.

## Data and sources

- In manufacturing industries the costs of failure can be 10–15 per cent of turnover, and in the service sector higher at 35–40 per cent of volume.
- In finding costs, one of the pitfalls is isolating only those things that can be easily measured, such as scrap, wasted materials, direct people costs, reworking, redoing, etc. The bulk of failure costs often lie in the non-producing sectors of an organization.
- Successful quality costing requires working closely with accountants and supervisors. Specific documents and reports should aid the quality costing process, e.g. utilization reports, material usage or sales records, analysis of rework, repair, etc., and even travel expense claims.
- A pilot study should be used to establish preliminary figures from a small area of the organization to determine the scope of the work required.

## Assumptions, risks and benefits

- For many organizations it may be sufficient to assess the proportion of time spent on errors and their appraisal, rather than become too concerned with financial accuracy. Quality cost indices or ratios are useful in reporting.

• Quality costs must not become a measure of competition between departments.

• The cost measurement process will improve with time and capture more actual costs. Care must be used in interpreting this as a worsening situation.

• A financial model of the investments in and the savings from TQM should be developed. Perhaps the greatest benefit from quality costing will be the quantification of the 'ghost operation' devoted to failure.

**The process model for quality costing**

• The P–A–F model for quality costing has a number of drawbacks, mainly due to estimating the prevention costs, and its association with an 'optimized' or minimum total cost.

• An alternative – the process cost model – rationalizes costs of quality (COQ) into the cost of conformance (COC) and the cost of nonconformance (CONC). COQ = COC + CONC at each process stage.

• Process cost modelling calls for choice of a process and its definition; construction of a process diagram; identification of outputs and customers, inputs and suppliers, controls and resources; flowcharting the process and identifying owners; allocating activities as COC or CONC; and calculating the costs. A process cost report with summaries and results is produced.

• The failure costs or CONC should be prioritized for improvements.

**Managing the quality cost system**

• Working knowledge of an organization's processes and accounting systems is essential for successful quality costing.

• A quality costing strategy should start with an assessment of the organization's quality management capability. Following this, the critical cost areas should be analysed, using the right data, time scales, system, and reporting mechanisms.

• It requires commitment, a system, management, training, promotion, and participation, and must impact on the mission of the organization.

# 9 Tools and techniques for quality improvement

## 9.1 A systematic approach

In the never-ending quest for improvement in the ways processes are operated, numbers and information will form the basis for understanding, decisions and actions; and a thorough data gathering, recording and presentation system is essential.

In addition to the basic elements of a quality system that provide a framework for recording, there exists a set of methods the Japanese quality guru Ishikawa has called the seven basic tools. These should be used to interpret and derive the maximum use from data. The simple methods listed below, of which there are clearly more than seven, will offer any organization means of collecting, presenting, and analysing most of its data:

* Process flowcharting – what is done?
* Check sheets/tally charts – how often is it done?
* Histograms – what do overall variations look like?
* Scatter diagrams – what are the relationships between factors?
* Stratification – how is the data made up?
* Pareto analysis – which are the big problems?
* Cause and effect analysis and Brainstorming (including CEDAC, NGT, and the five whys) – what causes the problems?
* Force-field analysis – what will obstruct or help the change or solution?
* Emphasis curve – which are the most important factors?
* Control charts – which variations to control and how?

Sometimes more sophisticated techniques, such as analysis of variance, regression analysis, and design of experiments, need to be employed.

The effective use of the tools requires their application by the people who actually work on the processes. Their commitment to this will be possible only if they are assured that management cares about improving quality. Managers must show they are serious by establishing a systematic approach and providing the training and implementation support required.

Improvements cannot be achieved without specific opportunities, commonly called problems, being identified or recognized. A focus on improvement opportunities leads to the creation of teams whose membership is determined by their work on and detailed knowledge of the process, and their ability to take improvement action. The teams must then be provided with good leadership and the right tools to tackle the job.

The systematic approach mapped out in Figure 9.1 should lead to the use of factual information, collected and presented by means of proven techniques, to open a channel of communications not available to the many organizations that do not follow this or a similar approach to problem solving and improvement. Continuous improvements in the quality of products, services, and processes can often be obtained without major capital investment, if an organization marshals its resources, through an understanding and breakdown of its processes in this way.

By using reliable methods, creating a favourable environment for team based problem solving, and continuing to improve using systematic techniques, the never-ending improvement helix (see Chapter 2) will be engaged. This approach demands the real time management of data, and actions on processes and inputs, not outputs. It will require a change in the language of many organizations from percentage defects, percentage 'prime' product, and number of errors, to *process capability*. The climate must change from the traditional approach of 'If it meets the specification, there are no problems and no further improvements are necessary'. The driving force for this will be the need for better internal and external customer satisfaction levels, which will lead to the continuous improvement question, 'Could we do the job better?'

## 9.2    Some basic tools and techniques

Understanding processes so that they can be improved by means of the systematic approach requires knowledge of a simple kit of tools or techniques. What follows is a brief description of each technique, but a full description and further examples of some of them may be found in reference.[1]

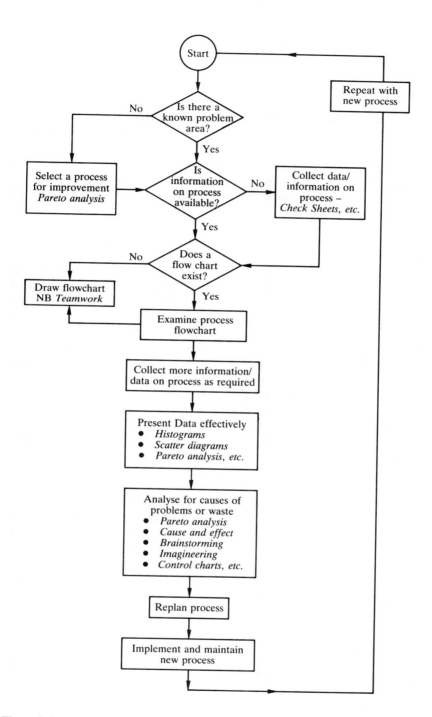

**Figure 9.1** *Strategy for process improvement*

**Process flowcharting**

The use of this technique, which is described fully in Chapter 4, ensures a full understanding of the inputs and flow of the process. Without that understanding, it is not possible to draw the correct flowchart of the process. In flowcharting it is important to remember that in all but the smallest tasks no single person is able to complete a chart without help from others. This makes flowcharting a powerful team forming exercise.

**Check sheets or tally charts**

A check sheet is a tool for data gathering, and a logical point to start in most process control or problem solving efforts. It is particularly useful for recording direct observations and helping to gather in facts rather than opinions about the process.

In the recording process it is essential to understand the difference between data and numbers. Data are pieces of information, including numerical information, that are useful in solving problems, or provide knowledge about the state of a process. Numbers alone often represent meaningless measurements or counts, which tend to confuse rather than to enlighten. Numerical data on quality will arise either from counting or measurement.

Data from counting can occur only at definite points or in 'discrete' jumps. There can be only 0, 1, 2, etc., errors in an invoice page; there cannot be 2.46 errors. The number of pens that fail to write properly give rise to discrete data called ATTRIBUTES. As there is only a two-way classification to consider, right or wrong, present or not present, attributes give rise to counted data, which necessarily vary in jumps.

Data from measurement can occur anywhere at all on a continuous scale, and are called VARIABLE data. The weight of a capsule, the diameter of a piston, the tensile strength of a piece of rod, the time taken to process an insurance claim, are all variables, the measurement of which produces continuous data.

Check sheets are prepared by following four steps:

1   Select and agree on the exact event to be observed.
2   Decide on the data collection time period. This includes both how often the data are to be obtained (frequency) and for how long they will be collected (duration).
3   Design a form that is simple, easy to use and large enough to record the information. Each column must be clearly labelled.

4 Collect the data and fill in the check sheet. Be honest in recording the information and allow enough time for it to be collected and recorded.

Follow up the recording by some analysis or presentation of the data.

The use of simple check sheets or tally charts aids the collection of data of the right type, in the right form, at the right time. The objectives of the data collection will determine the design of the record sheet used. Two examples of tally charts for different purposes are shown in Figures 9.2 and 9.3. These give rise to *frequency distributions*.

| Observer  F. Oldsman   Computer No.  148 | | | | Date 26 June | |
|---|---|---|---|---|---|
| Number of observations   95 | | | | Total | Percentage |
| Computer in use | | LHT  LHT  LHT  LHT  LHT  LHT  LHT  LHT  LHT  LHT  LHT | | 55 | 57·9 |
| Computer idle | Repairs | LHT | | 5 | 5·3 |
| | No work | LHT  LHT  II | | 12 | 12·6 |
| | Operator absent | LHT  LHT | | 10 | 10·5 |
| | System failure | LHT  LHT  III | | 13 | 13·7 |

**Figure 9.2** *Activity sampling record in an office*

A technique that is related to the check sheet is the so-called *measles chart*. On a process flowchart, engineering drawing, or map of an area, are marked errors, defects or problems. The accumulation of crosses or other marks on the document indicates where the major or more frequently occurring incidents may be found (e.g. Figure 9.4). The method is very simple to use, it avoids written descriptions or numbers, and it should lead to the rapid identification of real problems. Extensions of the technique are possible with the inclusion of times, amounts and the use of different symbols for different types of error or operators.

| Truck turn round time (minutes – rounded to nearest 5) | Tally | Number of trucks (frequency) |
|---|---|---|
| 10 | I | 1 |
| 15 | III | 3 |
| 20 | JHT I | 6 |
| 25 | JHT IIII | 9 |
| 30 | JHT JHT JHT JHT JHT JHT JHT JHT II | 42 |
| 35 | JHT JHT JHT JHT JHT JHT JHT JHT JHT JHT JHT JHT JHT JHT JHT JHT JHT JHT JHT JHT JHT II | 107 |
| 40 | JHT JHT JHT JHT JHT JHT JHT JHT JHT JHT JHT JHT JHT JHT JHT JHT JHT JHT JHT JHT JHT JHT JHT JHT JHT JHT JHT JHT JHT JHT JHT JHT JHT JHT | 170 |
| 45 | JHT JHT JHT JHT JHT JHT JHT JHT JHT JHT JHT JHT JHT JHT JHT JHT JHT JHT JHT JHT JHT JHT | 100 |
| 50 | JHT JHT JHT JHT JHT JHT JHT III | 38 |
| 55 | JHT JHT JHT I | 16 |
| 60 | JHT | 5 |
| 65 | II | 2 |
| 70 | I | 1 |
| | Total | 500 |

**Figure 9.3** *Tally chart and frequency distribution for truck turnround times*

## Histograms

Histograms show, in a very clear pictorial way, the frequency with which a certain value or group of values occurs. They can be used to display both attribute and variable data, and are an effective means of letting the people who operate the process know the results of their efforts. The data gathered on the tally chart of Figure 9.3 is drawn as a histogram in Figure 9.5.

## Scatter diagrams

Depending on the technology, it is frequently useful to establish the association, if any, between two parameters or factors. A technique to begin such an analysis is a simple X–Y plot of the two sets of data. The resulting grouping of points on scatter diagrams (e.g. Figure 9.6) will reveal whether or not a strong or weak, positive or negative, correlation exists between the parameters. The diagrams are simple to construct and easy to interpret, and the absence of correlation can be as revealing as finding that a relationship exists.

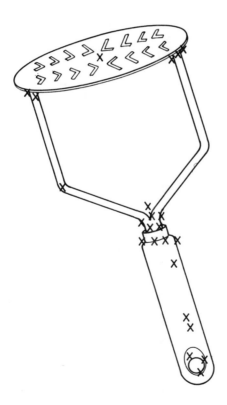

**Figure 9.4** *Measles chart of defects on a batch of potato mashers*

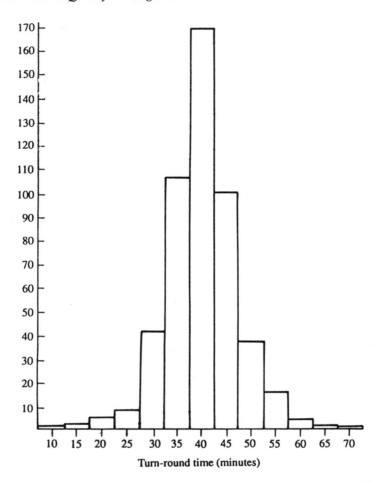

**Figure 9.5** *Frequency distribution for truck turnround times (histogram)*

### Stratification

Stratification is simply dividing a set of data into meaningful groups. It can be used to great effect in combination with other techniques, including histograms and scatter diagrams. If, for example, three shift teams are responsible for the output described by the histogram (a) in Figure 9.7, 'stratifying' the data into the shift groups might produce histograms (b), (c) and (d), and indicate process adjustments that were taking place at shift change overs.

Figure 9.8 shows the scatter diagram relationship between advertising investment and revenue generated for all products. In diagram (a) all the data are plotted, and there seems to be no correlation. But if the data are stratified according to product, a correlation is seen to exist. Of course the reverse may be true, so the data should be kept together and plotted in different colours or symbols to ensure all possible interpretations are retained.

## Pareto analysis

If the symptoms or causes of defective output or some other 'effect' are identified and recorded, it will be possible to determine what percentage can be attributed to any cause, and the probable result will be that the bulk (typically 80 per cent) of the errors, waste, or 'effects', derive from a few of the causes (typically 20 per cent). For example, Figure 9.9 shows a *ranked frequency distribution* of incidents in the distribution of a certain product. To improve the performance of the distribution process therefore, the major incidents (broken bags/drums, truck scheduling, temperature problems) should be tackled first. An analysis of data to identify the major problems is known as *Pareto analysis*, after the Italian economist who realized that approx 90 per cent of the wealth in his country was owned by approx 10 per cent of the people. Without an analysis of this sort, it is far too easy to devote

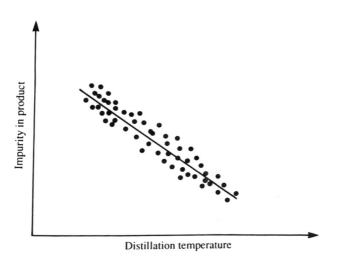

**Figure 9.6** *Scatter diagram showing a negative correlation between two variables*

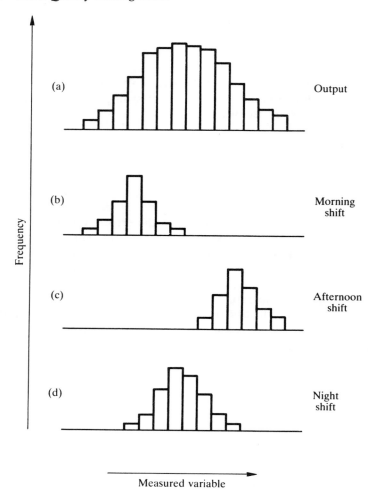

Figure 9.7 *Stratification of data into shift teams*

resources to addressing one symptom only because its cause seems immediately apparent.

**Cause and effect analysis and brainstorming**

A useful way of mapping the inputs that affect quality is the *cause and effect diagram*, also known as the Ishikawa diagram (after its origina-tor) or the fishbone diagram (after its appearance, Figure 9.10). The

(a)

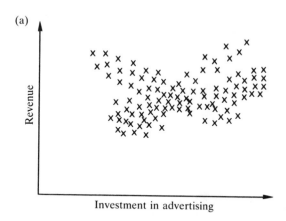

(b)

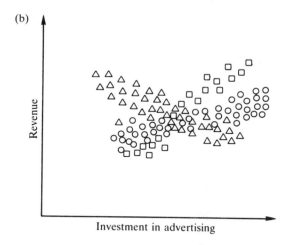

**Figure 9.8** *Scatter diagrams of investment in advertising vs. revenue: (a) without stratification; (b) with stratification*

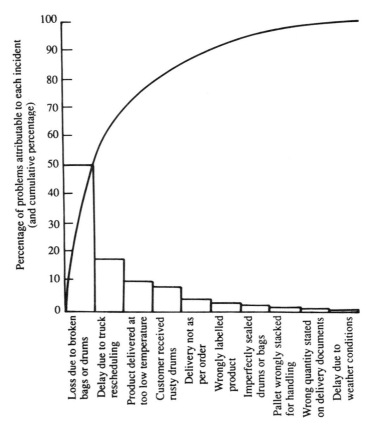

**Figure 9.9** *Incidents in the distribution of a chemical product*

effect or incident being investigated is shown at the end of a horizontal
arrow. Potential causes are then shown as labelled arrows entering the
main cause arrow. Each arrow may have other arrows entering it as
the principal factors or causes are reduced to their sub-causes, and
sub-sub-causes by *brainstorming*.

Brainstorming is a technique used to generate a large number of
ideas quickly, and may be used in a variety of situations. Each member of a group, in turn, may be invited to put forward ideas concerning a problem under consideration. Wild ideas are safe to offer, as
criticism or ridicule is not permitted during a brainstorming session.
The people taking part do so with equal status to ensure this. The
main objective is to create an atmosphere of enthusiasm and original-
ity. All ideas offered are recorded for subsequent analysis. The process
is continued until all the conceivable causes have been included. The

proportion of non-conforming output attributable to each cause, for example, is then measured or estimated, and a simple Pareto analysis identifies the causes that are most worth investigating.

A useful variant on the technique is negative brainstorming and cause/effect analysis. Here the group brainstorms all the things that would need to be done to ensure a negative outcome. For example, in the implementation of TQM, it might be useful for the senior management team to brainstorm what would be needed to make sure TQM *was not* implemented. Having identified in this way the potential road blocks, it is easier to dismantle them.

*CEDAC*

A variation on the cause and effect approach, which was developed at Sumitomo Electric and now is claimed to be used by major Japanese corporations across the world, is the cause and effect diagram with addition of cards (CEDAC).

The effect side of a CEDAC chart is a quantified description of the problem, with an agreed and visual quantified target and continually updated results on the progress of achieving it. The cause side of the CEDAC chart uses two different coloured cards for writing *facts* and

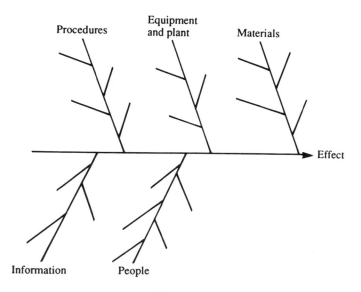

**Figure 9.10** *The cause-and-effect, Ishikawa or fishbone diagram*

*ideas*. This ensures that the facts are collected and organized before solutions are devised.

The basic diagram for CEDAC has the classic fishbone appearance. It is drawn on a large piece of paper, with the effect on the right and causes on the left. A project leader is chosen to be in charge of the CEDAC team, and he/she sets the improvement target. A method of measuring and plotting the results on the effects side of the chart is devised so that a visual display of the target and the quantified improvements are provided (for example, see Figure 9.11).

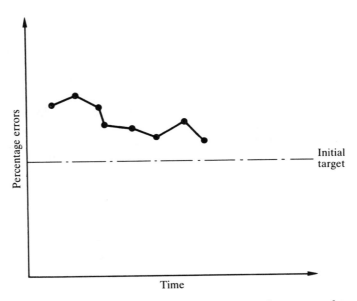

**Figure 9.11** *The effects side of a CEDAC chart showing the target and quantified improvements.*

The *facts* are gathered and placed on the left of the spines on the cause side of the CEDAC chart (Figure 9.12). The people in the team submitting the fact cards are required to initial them. Improvement *ideas* cards are then generated and placed on the right of the cause spines (Figure 9.13). The ideas are then selected and evaluated for substance and practicality. The test results are recorded on the effect side of the chart. The successful improvement ideas are incorporated into the new standard procedures.

Clearly, the CEDAC programme must start from existing standards and procedures, which must be adhered to if improvements are to be

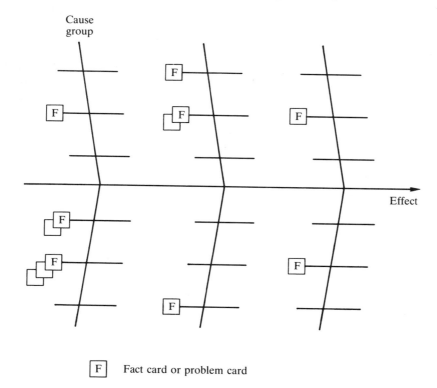

|F| Fact card or problem card

**Figure 9.12** *The CEDAC diagram with fact cards*

made. CEDAC can be applied to any problem that can be quantified – scrap levels, paperwork details, quality problems, materials usage, sales figures, insurance claims, etc. It is another systematic approach to marshalling the creative resources and knowledge of the people concerned. When they own and can measure the improvement process, they will find the solution.

*Nominal group technique (NGT)*

The nominal group technique (NGT) is a particular form of team brainstorming used to prevent domination by particular individuals. It has specific application for multi-level, multi-disciplined teams, where communication boundaries are potentially problematic.

In NGT a carefully prepared written statement of the problem to be tackled is read out by the facilitator (F). Clarification is obtained by questions and answers, and then the individual participants (P) are

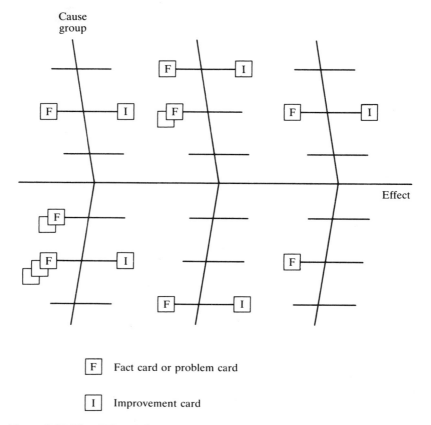

Figure 9.13 *The CEDAC diagram with fact and improvement cards*

asked to restate the problem in their own words. The group then dis-
cusses the problem until its formulation can be satisfactorily expressed
by the team (T). The method is set out in Figure 9.14.

About 15 minutes is then allowed for *silent idea generation*, in which
the participants think quietly about their responses and suggestions for
the problem statement. In a *round-robin* process each member of the
team is asked in turn to put forward one suggestion or idea. New
additional ideas, stimulated by others' suggestions, are also collected
on flip charts. As with any form of brainstorming, no criticism is
allowed by team members or facilitator. The round robin continues
until no more ideas/suggestions are forthcoming.

The *clarification* stage begins with the facilitator going through each
suggestion in turn for explanation, as necessary. Long detailed discus-

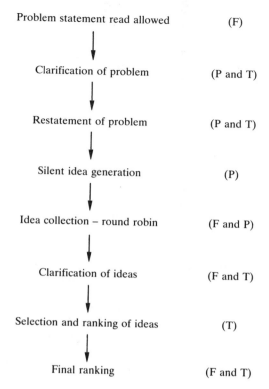

Problem statement read allowed    (F)

Clarification of problem    (P and T)

Restatement of problem    (P and T)

Silent idea generation    (P)

Idea collection – round robin    (F and P)

Clarification of ideas    (F and T)

Selection and ranking of ideas    (T)

Final ranking    (F and T)

**Figure 9.14** *Nominal group technique (NGT)*

sions and the premature working of issues by the team must be controlled by the facilitator. After any deletions and/or rephrasing, *selection and ranking* take place by means of cards issued to all team members. On these the members are asked to write, in silence, their top five or six ideas, with rankings. The facilitator collects the cards and transfers the results on to a new flip chart. The ranking scores are summed to give a *final ranking*. The result is a set of ranked ideas that are close to a team consensus view, obtained without domination by one or two individuals.

Even greater discipline may be brought to brainstorming by the use of 'Soft systems methodology (SSM)', developed by Peter Checkland.[2] The component stages of SSM are gaining a 'rich understanding' through 'finding out', input/output diagrams, root definition (which includes the so-called CATWOE analysis: customers, 'actors', transformations, 'world-view', owners, environment), conceptualization, comparison, and recommendation.

*The five whys*

This is a systematic questioning approach to ensure that the root causes of a problem are sought out. It consists merely of asking 'why?' several times in succession. The originators of the method, Toyota, suggested that 'why?' be asked successively at least five times to ensure the root cause is truly established.

An example from the author's own experience illustrates the method. Page 8 was missing from the contents of all the manuals used on a particular training course on quality. Why? Because the manuals had been assembled incorrectly. Why? Because the output from the photocopying machine was faulty – with page 8 missing from the first section. Why? Because the photocopying machine was sticking periodically and, following the unjamming, page 8 was left out of the process. Why was the machine sticking/jamming? Because the paper being used was of the wrong specification. Why? Because the supplier of the paper had been unable to supply the correct paper and had supplied a different type in its place. There may be even more whys. Why did the supplier not inform its customer of the change of paper type? Why did the stock of correct paper fall so low? The five-why analysis can assist any group of people to perform the detective work necessary to trace problems to their root cause. This is clearly a simple but powerful part of the continuous improvement tool kit.

**Force field analysis**

Force field analysis is a technique used to identify the forces that either obstruct or help a change that needs to be made. It is similar to negative brainstorming–cause/effect analysis and helps to plan how to overcome the barriers to change or improvement. It may also provide a measure of the difficulty in achieving the change.

The process begins with a team describing the desired change or improvement, and defining the objectives or solution. Having prepared the basic force field diagram, it identifies the favourable/positive/driving forces and the unfavourable/negative/restraining forces, by brainstorming. These forces are placed in opposition on the diagram and, if possible, rated for their potential influence on the ease of implementation. The results are evaluated. Then comes the preparation of an action plan to overcome some of the restraining forces, and increase the driving forces. Figure 9.15 shows a force field diagram produced by a senior management team considering the implementation of TQM in its organization.

**The emphasis curve**

This is a technique for ranking a number of factors, each of which cannot be readily quantified in terms of cost, frequency of occurrence, etc., in priority order. It is almost impossible for the human brain to make a judgement of the relative importance of more than three or four non-quantifiable factors. It is, however, relatively easy to judge which is the most important of two factors, using some predetermined criteria. The emphasis curve technique uses this fact by comparing only two factors at any one time.

The procedural steps for using the emphasis curve chart (Table 9.1) are as follows:

1   List the factors for ranking under 'Scope'. The number may be extended to more than ten by extending the matrix.
2   Compare factor 1 with factor 2 and rank the most important. To assist in judging the relative importance of two factors, it may help to use weightings, e.g. degree of seriousness, capital investment, speed of completion etc., on a scale of 1 to 10.
3   Compare factor 1 with 3, 1 with 4, 1 with 5 and so on – ringing the most important number in the matrix.
4   Having compared factor 1 against the total scope, proceed to compare factor 2 with 3, 2 with 4 and so on.
5   Count the number of 'ringed' number 1s in the matrix and put the total in the right-hand (RH) column against Number 1. Next count the total number of 2s in the matrix and put total in RH column against Number 2 and so on.
6   Add up the numbers in the RH column and check the total, using the formula $\{n(n-1)\}/2$, where n is the number of entries in the RH column. This check ensures that all numbers have been 'ringed' in the matrix.
7   Proceed to rank by putting number 1 in the box number along the bottom of the form, which equates to the number in the RH column entered against Number 1 and so on.
8   When two or more numbers appear in one box, check the matrix to see which factor is judged to be the most important and use the original decision to give absolute ranking.
9   Generally the length of time to make a judgement between two factors does not significantly affect the outcome; therefore the rule is 'accept the first decision, record it and move quickly onto the next pair'.

**Table 9.1** *The emphasis technique proforma*

Emphasis Curve to Assess ...................................................................

Assessment by ............................................. Date ............................

|   |   |   |   |   |   |   |   |   | No. | No. of rings |
|---|---|---|---|---|---|---|---|---|-----|--------------|
| 1 | 1 | 1 | 1 | 1 | 1 | 1 | 1 | 1 | 1   |              |
| 2 | 3 | 4 | 5 | 6 | 7 | 8 | 9 | 10|     |              |
|   | 2 | 2 | 2 | 2 | 2 | 2 | 2 | 2 | 2   |              |
|   | 3 | 4 | 5 | 6 | 7 | 8 | 9 | 10|     |              |
|   |   | 3 | 3 | 3 | 3 | 3 | 3 | 3 | 3   |              |
|   |   | 4 | 5 | 6 | 7 | 8 | 9 | 10|     |              |
|   |   |   | 4 | 4 | 4 | 4 | 4 | 4 | 4   |              |
|   |   |   | 5 | 6 | 7 | 8 | 9 | 10|     |              |
|   |   |   |   | 5 | 5 | 5 | 5 | 5 | 5   |              |
|   |   |   |   | 6 | 7 | 8 | 9 | 10|     |              |
|   |   |   |   |   | 6 | 6 | 6 | 6 | 6   |              |
|   |   |   |   |   | 7 | 8 | 9 | 10|     |              |
|   |   |   |   |   |   | 7 | 7 | 7 | 7   |              |
|   |   |   |   |   |   | 8 | 9 | 10|     |              |
|   |   |   |   |   |   |   | 8 | 8 | 8   |              |
|   |   |   |   |   |   |   | 9 | 10|     |              |
|   |   |   |   |   |   |   |   | 9 | 9   |              |
|   |   |   |   |   |   |   |   | 10|     |              |
|   |   |   |   |   |   |   |   |   | 10  |              |

Scope

......................................

......................................

......................................

......................................

......................................

......................................

......................................

......................................

Check total $= \dfrac{n(n-1)}{2} =$

RANKING – Highest to lowest

| 10 | 9 | 8 | 7 | 6 | 5 | 4 | 3 | 2 | 1 | 0 |
|----|---|---|---|---|---|---|---|---|---|---|
|    |   |   |   |   |   |   |   |   |   |   |

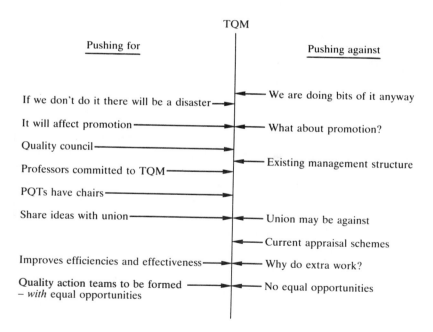

TQM

Pushing for                                                      Pushing against

If we don't do it there will be a disaster → | ← We are doing bits of it anyway

It will affect promotion ────→ | ← What about promotion?

Quality council ─────── |

Professors committed to TQM ───→ | ← Existing management structure

PQTs have chairs ──────── |

Share ideas with union ─────→ | ← Union may be against

| ← Current appraisal schemes

Improves efficiencies and effectiveness ──→ | ← Why do extra work?

Quality action teams to be formed ──→ | ← No equal opportunities
– *with* equal opportunities

**Figure 9.15** *Force-field analysis*

An interesting exercise is to tackle the type of question often used for competitions in the national press, such as 'Rank in order of importance the following features you consider when making a decision on which motor car to buy':

1   Style.
2   Colour.
3   Central locking.
4   Anti-lock braking.
5   Power steering.
6   Heated seats.
7   Electric sun roof.
8   Four-wheel drive.
9   Heated windscreen.
10  Fuel injection.
11  Five-speed manual transmission.
12  Lead-free fuel.
13  Four-speed automatic transmission.
14  Collapsible steering wheel.
15  Six-speaker radio/cassette.

Attempt to rank the features initially without the use of the emphasis curve, then use the technique and compare your results.

The author is grateful to his colleague Jim Borrill of O & F Quality Management Consultants Ltd for the information on this technique.

**Control charts**

A control chart is a form of traffic signal whose operation is based on evidence from the small samples taken at random during a process. A green light is given when the process should be allowed to run. All too often processes are 'adjusted' on the basis of a single measurement, check or inspection, a practice that can make a process much more variable than it is already. The equivalent of an amber light appears when trouble is possibly imminent. The red light shows that there is practically no doubt that the process has changed in some way and that it must be investigated and corrected to prevent production of defective material or information. Clearly, such a scheme can be introduced only when the process is 'in control'. Since samples taken are usually small, there are risks of errors, but these are small, calculated risks and not blind ones. The risk calculations are based on various frequency distributions.

These charts should be made easy to understand and interpret and they can become, with experience, sensitive diagnostic tools to be used by operating staff and first-line supervision to prevent errors or defective output being produced. Time and effort spent to explain the working of the charts to all concerned are never wasted.

The most frequently used control charts are simple run charts, where the data is plotted on a graph against time or sample number. There are different types of control charts for variables and attribute data: for variables mean ($\bar{X}$) and range ($R$) charts are used together; number defective or **np** charts and proportion defective or **p** charts are the most common ones for attributes. Other charts found in use are moving average and range charts, number of defects (**c** and **u**) charts, and cumulative sum (cusum) charts. The latter offer very powerful management tools for the detection of trends or changes in attributes and variable data.

The cusum chart is a graph that takes a little longer to draw than the conventional control chart, but gives a lot more information. It is particularly useful for plotting the evolution of processes, because it presents data in a way that enables the eye to separate true changes from a background of random variation. Cusum charts can detect small changes in data very quickly, and may be used for the control of variables and attributes. In essence, a reference or 'target value' is subtracted from each successive sample observation, and the result accumulated. Values of this cumulative sum are plotted, and 'trend lines' may be drawn on the resulting graphs. If they are approximately horizontal, the value of the variable is about the same as the target value. A downward slope shows a value less than the target, and an upward slope a value greater. The technique is very useful, for example, in comparing sales forecast with actual sales figures.

Figure 9.16 shows a comparison of an ordinary run chart and a cusum chart that have been plotted from the same data – errors in samples of 100 invoices. The change, which is immediately obvious on the cusum chart, is difficult to detect on the conventional control chart.

The range of type and use of control charts is now very wide, and within the present text it is not possible to indicate more than the basic principles underlying such charts. See reference.[3]

## 9.3  Failure mode, effect and criticality analysis (FMECA)

It is possible to analyse products, services and processes to determine possible modes of failure and their effects on the performance of the product or operation of the process or service system. Failure mode

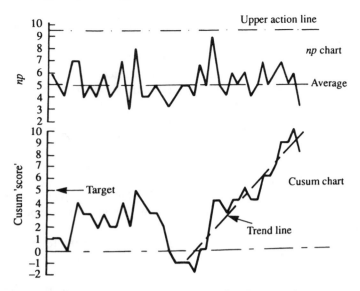

**Figure 9.16** *Comparison of cusum and np charts for the same data*

and effect analysis (FMEA) is the study of potential failures to determine their effects. If the results of an FMEA are ranked in order of seriousness, then the word CRITICALITY is added to give FMECA. The primary objective of a FMECA is to determine the features of product design, production or operation and distribution that are critical to the various modes of failure, in order to reduce failure. It uses all the available experience and expertise, from marketing, design, technology, purchasing, production/operation, distribution, service, etc., to identify the importance levels or criticality of potential problems and stimulate action to reduce these levels. FMECA should be a major consideration at the design stage of a product or service (see Chapter 3).

The elements of a complete FMECA are:

- *Failure mode* – the anticipated conditions of operation are used as the background to study the most probable failure mode, location and mechanism of the product or system and its components.
- *Failure effect* – the potential failures are studied to determine their probable effects on the performance of the whole product, process, or service, and the effects of the various components on each other.
- *Failure criticality* – the potential failures in the various parts of the product or service system are examined to determine the severity of each failure effect in terms of lowering of performance, safety hazard, total loss of function, etc.

FMECA may be applied at any stage of design, development, production/operation or use, but since its main aim is to prevent failure, it is most suitably applied at the design stage to identify and eliminate causes. With more complex product or service systems, it may be appropriate to consider these as smaller units or sub-systems, each one being the subject of a separate FMECA.

Special FMECA pro-formas are available (for example, see Table 9.2), and they set out the steps of the analysis as follows:

1  Identify the product or system components, or process function.
2  List all possible failure modes of each component.
3  Set down the effects that each mode of failure would have on the function of the product or system.
4  List all the possible causes of each failure mode.
5  Assess numerically the failure modes on a scale from 1 to 10. Experience and reliability data should be used, together with judgement, to determine the values, on a scale 1–10, for:
   **P**  the probability of each failure mode occurring (1 = low, 10 = high).
   **S**  the seriousness or criticality of the failure (1= low, 10 = high).
   **D**  the difficulty of detecting the failure before the product or service is used by the consumer (1 = easy, 10 = very difficult).

See also Table 9.3 on page 244.

6  Calculate the product of the ratings, C = P × S × D, known as the criticality index or risk priority number (RPN) for each failure mode. This indicates the relative priority of each mode in the failure prevention activities.
7  Indicate briefly the corrective action required and, if possible, which department or person is responsible and the expected completion date.

When the criticality index has been calculated, the failures may be ranked accordingly. It is usually advisable therefore to determine the value of C for each failure mode before completing the last columns. In this way the action required against each item can be judged in the light of the ranked severity and the resources available.

*Moments of truth* (MoT) is a concept that has much in common with FMEA. The idea was created by Jan Carlzon,[4] CEO of Scandinavian Airlines (SAS) and was made popular by Albrecht and Zemke.[5] An MoT is the moment in time when a customer first comes into contact with the people, systems, procedures, or products of an

**Table 9.2** *Failure mode, effect and criticality analysis (FMECA)*

Part name: emission assembly

| Process/ function (1) | Possible failure mode (2) | Effect(s) of failure (3) | Possible cause(s) of failure (4) | (5) P | S | D | (6) C | Corrective action (7) |
|---|---|---|---|---|---|---|---|---|
| Inspection of inwards goods | Base material incorrect | Early failure in service | Wrong selection of material by supplier | 1 | 8 | 9 | 72 | None |
| | Dimensions incorrect | Loose or tight fit on spigot and in moulding | Extrusion process out of statistical control | 8 | 5 | 7 | 280 | Supplier to certify and is applying in process controls |
| | Label incorrect regarding size | Wrong part supplied to customer | Specification incorrect | 2 | 5 | 7 | 70 | None |
| | Faulty moulding | Inability to assemble. | Incorrect inspection | 2 | 5 | 5 | 50 | None |
| | | Early failure in service | | 2 | 8 | 6 | 96 | |
| Washing | Not washed sufficiently | Line marking becomes indistinct and adhesion values reduced | Detergent not added to washer | 3 | 2 | 6 | 36 | None |
| | | | Water not changed | 2 | 6 | 6 | 72 | None |
| Air blow | Omitted | Blocked hose. | Operator error | 2 | 8 | 6 | 96 | Positive release system |
| | | Wet hose could affect sintered disc | | 2 | 8 | 6 | 96 | of passed tubing being investigated |

**Table 9.2** (continued)

Part name: emission assembly

| Process/ function (1) | Possible failure mode (2) | Effect(s) of failure (3) | Possible cause(s) of failure (4) | (5) P S D | (6) C | Corrective action (7) |
|---|---|---|---|---|---|---|
| Storage | Not stored correctly | Wet hose could affect sintered disc | Incorrect packaging | 2 8 6 | 96 | Drying facility under investigation Sept. |
| | Dirt in component | Incorrect operation | Bad storage | 1 8 9 | 72 | None |
| | | | Human error operator | 2 8 6 | 96 | None |
| Stripe application | Wrong colour | Incorrect fitment in assembly | Incorrectly planned | 2 8 6 | 96 | None |
| | Incomplete | Cosmetic rejection | Machine malfunction | 8 2 6 | 96 | Co-extruded stripe under investigation Sept. Target date |
| Cut to length | Short | Cannot assemble at customer or in plant | Machine capability incorrect | 5 9 7 | 315 | New design cutting machine to be evaluated Sept. |
| | Long | Fouls on fitment; in house difficulty to perform next operation | | 4 3 7 | 84 | |

**Table 9.2** (continued)

*Part name: emission assembly*

| Process/ function (1) | Possible failure mode (2) | Effect(s) of failure (3) | Possible cause(s) of failure (4) | (5) P | S | D | (6) C | Corrective action (7) |
|---|---|---|---|---|---|---|---|---|
| Storage awaiting assembly | Mixed parts | Incorrect length supplied to assembler | Parts mixed during transit | 2 | 5 | 7 | 70 | None |
| | Incorrect labelling | Incorrect length supplied to assembler | Operator error | 2 | 8 | 6 | 96 | Assembly boards and attribute charts to be introduced |
| Subassembly of mouldings | Incorrect units assembled. | Customer cannot fit unit | Incorrect selection | 2 | 8 | 6 | 96 | None |
| | Bonding | Leaks. Failing vacuum requirement affects driveability | Incorrect bonding agent preparation, overage material | 2 | 8 | 7 | 112 | Improved adhesive application under evaluation |
| | Fit incorrect length of tubing | Long and short lengths can result in customer being unable to assemble | Incorrect selection | 2 | 8 | 6 | 96 | Increased use of inspection boards as per sampling plan |
| | | | | 2 | 3 | 6 | 36 | |

**Table 9.2** (continued)

*Part name: emission assembly*

| Process/ function (1) | Possible failure mode (2) | Effect(s) of failure (3) | Possible cause(s) of failure (4) | P (5) | S | D | C (6) | Corrective action (7) |
|---|---|---|---|---|---|---|---|---|
| Assembly | Assembly fitted circuit broken | Short length unable to join components | | 2 | 8 | 7 | 112 | |
| | Missed parts | Failure of unit to function on vehicle | Operator error | 6 | 6 | 6 | 216 | Increased use of inspection boards in hand |
| | Valve orientation incorrect | Failure of unit to function on vehicle | Operator error | 2 | 7 | 6 | 84 | Increased use of inspection boards in hand |
| | Fuel trap orientation incorrect | Failure of unit to function on vehicle | Operator error | 2 | 8 | 6 | 96 | Increased use of inspection boards in hand |
| | Rubber elbow orientation incorrect | Will not fit on vehicle | Operator error | 2 | 6 | 6 | 72 | Increased use of inspection boards in hand |
| Packaging | Label omitted | Wrong part supplied | Operator error | 2 | 8 | 6 | 96 | Increased use of inspection boards in hand |
| | Incorrect label | Parts sent to wrong destination | Human error, incorrect data | 5 | 7 | 9 | 315 | Improved labelling system is being introduced |
| | Incorrect container | Rejected at customer | Human error, incorrect data | 2 | 5 | 6 | 60 | None |

**Table 9.3** *Probability and seriousness of failure and difficulty of detection*

| VALUE | 1 | 2 | 3 | 4 | 5 | 6 | 7 | 8 | 9 | 10 |
|-------|---|---|---|---|---|---|---|---|---|----|

| P | low chance of occurrence ————————— almost certain to occur |
|---|---|
| S | not serious, minor nuisance ———————— total failure, safety hazard |
| D | easily detected ——————————————— unlikely to be detected |

organization, which leads to the customer making a judgement about the quality of the organization's services or products.

In MoT analysis the points of potential dissatisfaction are identified proactively, beginning with the assembly of process flow chart type diagrams. Every small step taken by a customer in his/her dealings with the organization's people, products, or services is recorded. It may be difficult or impossible to identify all the MoTs, but the systematic approach should lead to a minimization of the number and severity of unexpected failures, and this provides the link with FMEA.

## 9.4   Statistical process control

The responsibility for quality in any transformation process must lie with the operators of that process. To fulfil this responsibility, however, people must be provided with the tools necessary to:

* Know whether the process is capable of meeting the requirements.
* Know whether the process is meeting the requirements at any point in time.
* Make correct adjustments to the process or its inputs when it is not meeting the requirements.

The techniques of statistical process control (SPC) will greatly assist in these stages.

To begin to monitor and analyse any process, it is necessary first of all to identify what the process is, and what the inputs and outputs are. Many processes are easily understood and relate to known procedures, e.g. drilling a hole, compressing tablets, filling cans with paint, polymerizing a chemical using catalysts. Others are less easily identifiable, e.g. servicing a customer, delivering a lecture, storing a product in a warehouse, inputting to a computer. In many situations it can be extremely difficult to define the process. For example, if the process is inputting data into a computer terminal, it is vital to know if the scope of the process includes obtaining and refining the data, as well as inputting. Process definition is so important because the inputs and outputs change with the scope of the process.

Once the process is specified, the inputs and suppliers, outputs and customers can also be defined, together with the requirements at each of the interfaces. The most difficult areas in which to do this are in non-manufacturing organizations or parts of organizations, but careful use of the questioning method, introduced in Chapter 1, should release the necessary information. Examples of outputs in non-manufacturing include training courses or programmes, typed letters, statements of intent (following a decision process), invoices, share certificates, deliveries of consignments, reports, serviced motor cars, purchase orders, wage slips, forecasts, material requirements plans, legal contracts, design change documents, clean offices, recruited trainees, and advertisements. The list is endless. Some processes may produce primary and secondary outputs, such as a telephone call answered *and* a message delivered.

If the requirements are not clarified or quantified, they are often assumed or estimated. Even if this does not lead to direct complaints, it will lead to waste – lost time, confusion – and perhaps lost customers. It is salutary for some suppliers of internal customers to realize that the latter can sometimes find new suppliers if their true requirements are not properly identified and/or repeatedly not met.

Inputs to processes include:

1  Equipment, tools, or plant required.
2  Materials – including paper.
3  Information – including the specification for the outputs.
4  Methods or procedures – including instructions.
5  People (and the inputs they provide, such as skills, training, knowledge, etc.).
6  Records.

Again this is not an exhaustive list.

Prevention of failure in any transformation is possible only if the process definition, flow, inputs, and outputs are properly documented and agreed. The documentation of procedures will allow reliable data about the process itself to be collected, analysis to be performed, and action to be taken to improve the process and prevent failure or non-conformance with the requirements. The target in the operation of any process is the total avoidance of failure. If the idea of no failures or error free work is not adopted, at least as a target, then it certainly will never be achieved.

All processes can be monitored and brought 'under control' by gathering and using data – to measure the performance of the process and provide the feedback required for corrective action, where necessary. Statistical process control (SPC) methods, backed by management commitment and good organization, provide objective means of *controlling* quality in any transformation process, whether used in the manufacture of artefacts, the provision of services, or the transfer of information.

SPC is not only a tool kit, it is a strategy for reducing variability, the cause of most quality problems: variation in products, in times of deliveries, in ways of doing things, in materials, in people's attitudes, in equipment and its use, in maintenance practices, in everything. Control by itself is not sufficient. Total quality management requires that the processes should be improved continually by reducing variability. This is brought about by studying all aspects of the process, using the basic question: 'Could we do this job more consistently and on target?' The answer drives the search for improvements. This significant feature of SPC means that it is not constrained to measuring conformance, and that it is intended to lead to action on processes that are operating within the 'specification' to minimize variability.

Process control is essential, and SPC forms a vital part of the TQM strategy. Incapable and inconsistent processes render the best design impotent and make supplier quality assurance irrelevant. Whatever process is being operated, it must be reliable and consistent. SPC can be used to achieve this objective.

In the application of SPC there is often an emphasis on techniques rather than on the implied wider managerial strategies. It is worth repeating that SPC is not only about plotting charts on the walls of a plant or office, it must become part of the company-wide adoption of TQM and act as the focal point of never-ending improvement. Changing an organization's environment into one in which SPC can operate properly may take several years rather than months. For many companies SPC will bring a new approach, a new 'philosophy', but the importance of the statistical techniques should not be disguised. Simple presentation of data using diagrams, graphs, and charts should become the means of communication concerning the state of control of processes. It is on this understanding that improvements will be based.

**The SPC system**

A systematic study of any process through answering the questions:

Are we capable of doing the job correctly?
Do we continue to do the job correctly?
Have we done the job correctly?
Could we do the job more consistently and on target?[6]

provides knowledge of the *process capability* and the sources of non-conforming outputs. This information can then be fed back quickly to marketing, design, and the 'technology' functions. Knowledge of the current state of a process also enables a more balanced judgement of equipment, both with regard to the tasks within its capability and its rational utilization.

Statistical process control procedures exist because there is variation in the characteristics of all material, articles, services, and people. The inherent variability in every transformation process causes the output from it to vary over a period of time. If this variability is considerable, it is impossible to predict the value of a characteristic of any single item or at any point in time. Using statistical methods, however, it is possible to take meagre knowledge of the output and turn it into meaningful statements that may then be used to describe the process itself. Hence statistically based process control procedures are designed to divert attention from individual pieces of data and focus it on the process as a whole. SPC techniques may be used to measure and control the degree of variation of any purchased materials, services, processes, and products, and to compare this, if required, to previously agreed specifications. In essence, SPC techniques select a representative, simple, random sample from the 'population', which can be an input to or an output from a process. From an analysis of the sample it is possible to make decisions regarding the current performance of the process.

**The quality system and SPC in improving processes**

The impact of an efficient quality management system and SPC together is that of gradually reducing process variability to achieve never-ending improvement. The requirement to set down defined procedures for all aspects of an organization's operations, and to stick to them, will reduce the variations introduced by the numerous different ways often employed of doing things. Go into any factory without a well defined and managed quality system in operation and ask to see the operators' 'black book' of plant operation and settings. Of course each shift has a different black book, each with slightly different settings and ways of operating the process. Is it any different in office work or for sales people in the field? Do not be fooled by the perceived simplicity of a process into believing that there is only one way of operating it. There are an infinite variety of ways of carrying out the simplest of tasks – the author recalls seeing various course participants finding fourteen different methods for converting A4 size paper into A5 size (half A4) in a simulation of a production task. The ingenuity of human beings needs to be controlled if these causes of variation are not to multiply together to render processes completely incapable of consistency or repeatability.

The role of the quality system here is to define and control process procedures and methods. Continual system audit and review will ensure that procedures are either followed or corrected, thus eliminating assignable or special causes of variation in materials, methods, equipment, information, etc. to ensure a 'Could we do this job with more consistency?' approach.

## 9.5   Quality improvement techniques in non-manufacturing

Organizations that embrace the TQM concepts should recognize the value of SPC techniques in areas such as sales, purchasing, invoicing, finance, distribution, training, and in the service sector generally. These are outside the *traditional areas* for SPC use but SPC needs to be seen as an organization-wide approach to reducing variation, with the specific techniques integrated into a programme of change throughout. A Pareto analysis, a histogram, a flowchart, or a control chart is a vehicle for communication. Data are data and, whether the numbers represent defects or invoice errors, weights or delivery times, or the information relates to machine settings, process variables, prices, quantities, discounts, sales or supply points, is irrelevant – the techniques can always be used.

In the author's experience, some of the most exciting applications of SPC have emerged from organizations and departments which, when first introduced to the methods, could see little relevance in them to their own activities. Following appropriate training, however, they have learned how to, for example:

- *Pareto Analyse* errors on invoices to customers and industry injury data.

- *Brainstorm* and *cause and effect analyse* reasons for late payment and poor purchase invoice matching.
- *Histogram* defects in invoice matching and arrival of trucks at certain times during the day.
- *Control chart* the weekly demand of a product.

Distribution staff have used control charts to monitor the proportion of late deliveries, and Pareto analysis and force field analysis to look at complaints about the distribution system. Word processor operators have been seen using cause and effect analysis, NGT and histograms to represent errors in the output from their service. Moving average and cusum charts have immense potential for improving processes in the marketing area.

Those organizations that have made most progress in implementing continuous improvement have recognized at an early stage that SPC is for the whole organization. Restricting it to traditional manufacturing or operational activities means that a window of opportunity for improvement has been closed. Applying the methods and techniques outside manufacturing will make it easier, not harder, to gain maximum benefit from an SPC programme.

*Sales, marketing and customer-service* are areas often resistant to SPC training on the basis that it is difficult to apply. Personnel in these vital functions need to be educated in SPC methods for two reasons:

1 They need to understand the way the manufacturing or service producing processes in their organizations work. This will enable them to have more meaningful dialogues with customers about the whole product/service/delivery system capability and control. It will also enable them to influence customers' thinking about specifications and create a competitive advantage from improving process capabilities.

2 They will be able to improve the marketing processes and activities. A significant part of the sales and marketing effort is clearly associated with building relationships, which are best built on facts (data) and not opinions. There are also opportunities to use SPC techniques directly in such areas as forecasting demand levels and market requirements, monitoring market penetration, marketing control, and product development, all of which must be viewed as processes.

SPC has considerable applications for non-manufacturing organizations, including universities! Data and information on patients in hospitals, students in universities, polytechnics, colleges and schools, people who pay (and do not pay) tax, draw social security benefit, shop at Sainsbury's or Macy's, are available in abundance. If the information were to be used in a systematic way, and all operations treated as processes, far better decisions could be made concerning past, present, and future performances of some service sectors.

**Adding the tools to the TQM model**

Having looked at some of the many tools and techniques of measurement and improvement, we see that the generic term 'tools' may be added, as the second hard management necessity, to the TQM model (Figure 9.17). The systems manage the processes, and the tools are used to progress further round the improvement cycle by measuring how well they may be improved to create better customer–supplier relationships, both externally and internally. They provide the means for analysis, correlation and prediction of what *action* to take on the systems.

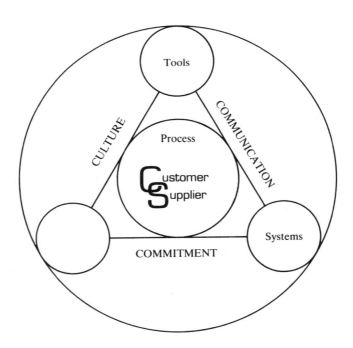

**Figure 9.17** *Total quality management model – the basic tools*

# Chapter highlights

## A systematic approach

- Numbers and information will form the basis for understanding, decisions, and actions in never ending improvement.
- A set of simple tools is needed to interpret fully and derive maximum use from data. More sophisticated techniques may need to be employed occasionally.
- The effective use of the tools requires the commitment of the people who work on the processes. This in turn needs management support and the provision of training.

## Some basic tools and techniques

The basic tools and the questions answered are:

| | | |
|---|---|---|
| Process flow charting | – | what is done? |
| Check/tally charts | – | how often is it done? |
| Histograms | – | what do variations look like? |
| Scatter diagrams | – | what are the relationships between factors? |
| Stratification | – | how is the data made up? |
| Pareto analysis | – | which are the big problems? |
| Cause and effect analysis and brainstorming (also CEDEC, NGT and the five whys) | – | what causes the problem? |
| Force-field analysis | – | what will obstruct or help the change or solution? |
| Emphasis curve | – | which are the most important factors? |
| control charts (including cusum) | – | which variations to control and how? |

## Failure mode, effect and criticality analysis (FMECA)

- FMEA is the study of potential product, service, or process failures and their effects. When the results are ranked in order of criticality, the technique is called FMECA. Its aim is to reduce the probability of failure.
- The elements of a complete FMECA are to study failure mode,

effect, and criticality. It may be applied at any stage of design, development, production/operation, or use.
- Moments of truth (MoT) is a similar concept to FMEA. It is the moment in time when a customer first comes into contact with an organization, leading to a judgement about quality.

## Statistical process control

- People operating a process must know whether it is capable of meeting the requirements, know whether it is actually doing so at any time, and make correct adjustments when it is not. SPC techniques will help here.
- Before using SPC, it is necessary to identify what the process is, what the inputs/outputs are, and how the suppliers and customers and their requirements are defined. The most difficult areas for this can be in non-manufacturing.
- All processes can be monitored and brought 'under control' by gathering and using data. SPC methods, with management commitment, provide objective means of controlling quality in any transformation process.
- SPC is not only a toolkit, it is a strategy for reducing variability, part of never ending improvement. This is achieved by answering the following questions:

> Are we capable of doing the job correctly?
> Do we continue to do the job correctly?
> Have we done the job correctly?
> Could we do the job more consistently and on target?

This provides knowledge of process capability.
- The impact of a quality system and SPC together is the gradual reduction of the variability in the ways things are done.

## Quality improvement techniques in non-manufacturing

- SPC techniques have value in the service sector and in the non-manufacturing areas, such as marketing and sales, purchasing, invoicing, finance, distribution, training and personnel.

## Adding the tools to the TQM model

A second hard management necessity – the tools – be added, with the systems, to the TQM model to progress further round the never-ending improvement cycle.

## References

1  See J S Oakland and R. F. Followell, *Statistical Process Control*, 2nd edition, Butterworth-Heinemann, Oxford, 1990.
2  Peter Checkland, *Soft Systems Methodology in Action*, Wiley, 1990.
3  See Oakland and Followell, *op. cit.*
4  Jan Carlzon, *Moments of Truth*, Harper & Row, 1987.
5  Albrecht, K. and Zemke, R., *Service America! – doing business in the new economy*, Dow Jones-Irwin, Homewood, Ill. (USA), 1985.
6  This system for process capability and control is based on Frank Price's very practical framework for thinking about quality in manufacturing:

Can we make it OK?
Are we making it OK?
Have we made it OK?
Could we make it better?

which he presented in his excellent book *Right First Time*.

# 10 Some additional techniques for design, reliability, maintenance, and process improvement

## 10.1 Seven new tools for quality design

Seven new tools may be used as part of quality function deployment (see Chapter 3) to improve the innovation processes. These do not replace the basic systematic tools described in Chapter 9, neither are they extensions of these. The new tools are systems and documentation methods used to achieve success in design by identifying objectives and intermediate steps in the finest detail. The seven new tools are:

1  Affinity diagram.
2  Interrelationship diagraph.
3  Tree diagram.
4  Matrix diagram or quality table.
5  Matrix data analysis.
6  Process decision programme chart (PDPC).
7  Arrow diagram.

The tools are interrelated, as shown in Figure 10.1. The promotion and use of the tools by the QFD Team should obtain better designs in less time. They are summarized below.

### 1  Affinity diagram

This is used to gather large amounts of language data (ideas, issues, opinions) and organizes them into groupings based on the natural relationship between the items. In other words, it is a form of brainstorming. One of the obstacles often encountered in the quest for improvement is past success or failure. It is assumed that what worked or failed in the past will continue to do so in the future. Although the lessons of the past should not be ignored, unvarying patterns of

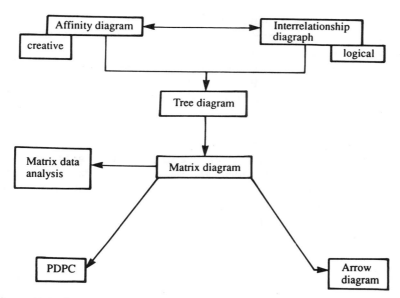

**Figure 10.1** *The seven new tools of quality design*

thought, which can limit progress, should not be enforced. This is especially true in QFD, where *new* logical patterns should always be explored.

The affinity diagram, like other brainstorming methods, is part of the creative process. It can be used to generate ideas and categories that can be used later with more strict, logic-based tools. This tool should be used to 'map the geography' of an issue when:

- Facts or thoughts are in chaos and the issues are too large or complex to define easily.
- Breakthroughs in traditional concepts are needed to replace old solutions and to expand a team's thinking.
- Support for a solution is essential for successful implementation.

The affinity diagram is not recommended when a problem is simple or requires a very quick solution.

The steps for generating an affinity diagram are as follows:

1  Assemble a group of people familiar with the problem of interest. Six to eight members in the group works best.
2  Phrase the issue to be considered. It should be vaguely stated so as not to prejudice the responses in a predetermined direction. For

example, if you are brainstorming on why issues are not followed up in an organization, it would be best to state the question as 'Why do issues remain unresolved?' rather than 'Why don't people take the responsibility to complete their assignments?'

3   Give each member of the group a stack of cards and allow 5–10 minutes for everyone in the group to record ideas on the cards, one per card. During this time the objective is to write down as many ideas as possible, as concisely as possible. There should be no communication between members of the group during the 5–10 minutes.

4   At the end of the 5–10 minutes each member of the group, in turn, reads out one of his/her ideas and places it on the table for everyone to see. There should be no criticism or justification of ideas, and it is allowable to write new ideas during this time if fresh thoughts are generated.

5   When all ideas are presented, members of the group place together all cards with related ideas. This process is repeated until the ideas are in approximately ten groups.

6   Look for one card in each group that captures the meaning of that group.

The output of this exercise is a compilation of a maximum number of ideas under a limited number of major headings (see, for example, Figure 10.2). This data can then be used with other tools to define areas for attack. One of these tools is the interrelationship digraph.

## 2   Interrelationship digraph

This tool is designed to take a central idea, issue or problem, and map out the logical or sequential links among related factors. While this still requires a very creative process, the interrelationship digraph begins to draw the logical connections that surface in the affinity diagram.

In designing, planning, and problem solving it is obviously not enough to just create an explosion of ideas. The affinity diagram allows some organized creative patterns to emerge but the interrelationship digraph lets *logical* patterns become apparent. The digraph is based on a principle that the Japanese frequently apply regarding the natural emergence of ideas. This tool starts therefore from a central concept, leads to the generation of large quantities of ideas, and finally to the delineation of observed patterns. To some this may appear to be like reading tealeaves, but it works incredibly well. Like the affinity diagram, the interrelationship digraph allows unanticipated ideas and connections to rise to the surface.

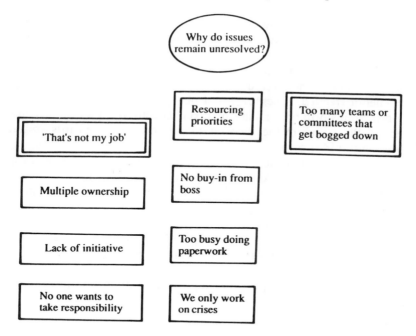

**Figure 10.2** *Example of an affinity diagram*

The interrelationship digraph is adaptable to both specific operational issues and general organizational questions. For example, a classic use of this tool at Toyota focused on all the factors behind the establishment of a 'billboard system' as part of their JIT programme. On the other hand, it has also been used to deal with issues underlying the problem of getting top management support for TQM.

In summary, the interrelationship digraph should be used when:

(a) An issue is sufficiently complex that the interrelationship between ideas is difficult to determine.
(b) The correct sequencing of management actions is critical.
(c) There is a feeling or suspicion that the problem under discussion is only a symptom.
(d) There is ample time to complete the required reiterative process and define cause and effect.

The interrelationship digraph can be used by itself, or it can be used after the affinity diagram, using data from the previous effort as input. The steps for using this tool are:

1   Clearly define one statement that describes the key issue to be discussed. Record this statement on a card and place it on the wall or a table, in the centre of a large sheet of paper. Mark this card in some way so that it can be easily identified as the central idea, e.g. use a double circle around the text.
2   Generate related issues or problems. This may be done in wide open brainstorming, or may be taken directly from an affinity diagram. Place each of the ideas on a card and place the cards around the central idea card.
3   Use arrows to indicate which items are related and what leads to what. Look for possible relationships between all items.
4   Look for patterns of arrows to determine key factors or causes. For example, if one card has seven arrows coming from it to other issues, the idea on that card is a key factor or cause. Mark these key areas in some way, e.g. by using a double box.
5   Use the key factors in a tree diagram for further analysis.

Figure 10.3 gives an example of a simple interrelationship digraph.

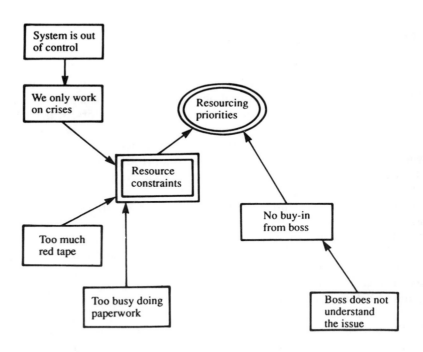

**Figure 10.3** *Example of the interrelationship digraph*

## 3   Systems flow/tree diagram

The systems flow/tree diagram (usually referred to as a tree diagram) is used to systematically map out the full range of activities that must be accomplished in order to reach a desired goal. It may also be used to identify all the factors contributing to a problem under consideration. As mentioned above, major factors identified by an interrelationship digraph can be used as inputs for a tree diagram. One of the strengths of this method is that it forces the user to examine the logical and chronological link between tasks. This assists in preventing a natural tendency to jump directly from goal or problem statement to solution (Ready . . . Fire . . . Aim!).

The tree diagram is indispensable when a thorough understanding of what needs to be accomplished is required, together with how it is to be achieved, and the relationships between these goals and methodologies. It has been found to be most helpful in situations when:

(a) Very ill-defined needs must be translated into operational characteristics, and to identify which characteristics can presently be controlled.
(b) All the possible causes of a problem need to be explored. This use is closest to the cause and effect diagram or fishbone chart.
(c) Identifying the first task that must be accomplished when aiming for a broad organizational goal.
(d) The issue under question has sufficient complexity and time available for solution.

Depending on the type of issue being addressed, the tree diagram will be similar to either a cause and effect diagram (Chapter 9) or a flowchart (Chapter 4), although it may be easier to interpret because of its clear linear layout. If a problem is being considered, each branch of the tree diagram will be similar to a cause and effect diagram. If a general objective is being considered, each branch may represent chronological activities, in which case the diagram will be similar to a flowchart. Although this tool is similar to other tools, suggestions on the stepwise procedure are included below. The procedure is based on trying to accomplish a goal, but it can be easily modified for use in problem solving:

1   Start with one statement that clearly and simply states the issue or goal. Write the idea on a card and place it on the left side of a flip chart or table.

2   Ask 'What method or task is needed to accomplish this goal or purpose?' Use the interrelationship digraph to find ideas that are most closely related to that statement, and place them directly to the right of the statement card.

3   Look at each of these 'second tier' ideas and ask the same question. Place these ideas to the right of the ones that they relate to. Continue this process until all the ideas are gone. Note: if none of the existing ideas on the interrelationship digraph can adequately answer the question, new ideas may be developed so as not to leave holes in the tree diagram.

4   Review the entire tree diagram by starting on the right and asking 'If this is done, will it lead to the accomplishment of the next idea or task?' The diagram produced will be similar to an organization chart.

An example is shown in Figure 10.4.

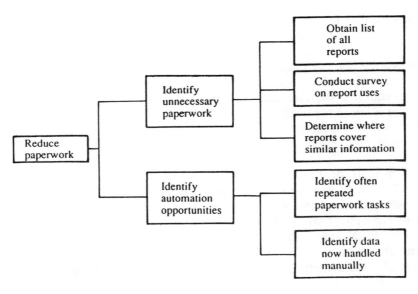

**Figure 10.4** *An example of the tree diagram*

## 4   Matrix diagrams

The matrix diagram is the heart of the seven new tools and the house of quality described in Chapter 3. The purpose of the matrix diagram is to outline the interrelationships and correlations between tasks, functions or characteristics, and to show their relative importance. There are many versions of the matrix diagram, but the most widely used is a simple L-shaped matrix known as the *quality table*.

## L-shaped matrix diagram

This is the most basic form of matrix diagram. In the L-shape two interrelated groups of items are presented in line and row format. It is a simple two-dimensional representation that shows the intersection of related pairs of items as shown in Figure 10.5. It can be used to display relationships between items in *all* operational areas, including administration, manufacturing, personnel, R&D etc., to identify all the organizational tasks that need to be accomplished and how they should be allocated to individuals. In a QFD it is even more interesting if each person completes the matrix individually and then compares the coding with everyone in the work group.

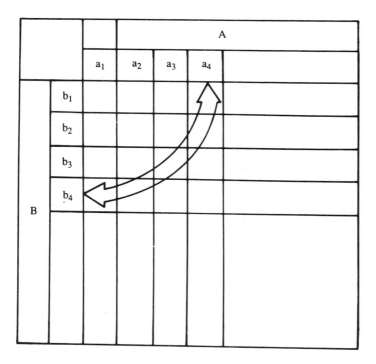

**Figure 10.5** *L-shaped matrix*

*Quality table*

In a *quality table* customer demands (the whats) are analysed with respect to substitute quality characteristics (the hows). See Figure 10.6. Correlations between the two are categorized as strong, moderate and possible. The customer demands shown on the left of the matrix are determined in co-operation with the customer. This effort requires a kind of a verbal 'ping-pong' with the customer to be truly effective: ask the customer what he wants, write it down, show it to him and ask him if that is what he meant, then revise and repeat the process as necessary. This should be done in a joint meeting with the customer, if at all possible. It is often of value to use a tree diagram to give structure to this effort.

The right side of the chart is often used to compare current performance to competitors' performance, company plan, and potential sales points with reference to the customer demands. Weights are given to these items to obtain a 'relative quality weight', which can be used to identify the key customer demands. The relative quality weight is then used with the correlations identified on the matrix to determine the key quality characteristics.

A modification that is added to create the house of quality table is a second matrix that explores the correlations between the quality characteristics. This is done so that errors caused by the manipulation of variables in a one-at-a-time fashion can be avoided. This also gives indications of where designed experiments would be of use in the design process. In the training required for use of this technique, several hours should be dedicated to a detailed explanation of the steps in the construction of a quality table, and the system to be used to compare numerically the various items.

*T-shaped matrix diagram*

The T-shaped matrix is nothing more than the combination of two L-shaped matrix diagrams. As can be seen in Figure 10.7, it is based on the premise that two separate sets of items are related to a third set. Therefore A items are somehow related to both B and C items.

Figure 10.8 shows one application. In this case it shows the relationship between a set of courses in a curriculum and two important sets of considerations: who should do the training for each course and which would be the most appropriate functions to attend each of the courses? It has also been widely used to develop new materials by simultaneously relating different alternative materials to two sets of desirable properties.

Substitute quality characteristics

| | MFR | Ash | Importance | Current | Best competitor | Plan | IR | SP | RQW |
|---|---|---|---|---|---|---|---|---|---|
| No film-breaks | ○ 17 | ▲ 6 | 4 | 4 | 4 | 4 | 1 | ○ | 5.6 |
| High rates | ◉ 23 | | 3 | 3 | 4 | 4 | 1.3 | | 4.6 |
| Low gauge variability | ◉ 37 | ▲ 7 | 4 | 3 | 4 | 4 | 1.3 | ○ | 7.3 |

Customer demands

◉ Strong correlation
○ Some correlation
▲ Possible correlation
IR Improvement ratio
SP Sales point
RQW Relative quality weight

**Figure 10.6** *An example of the matrix diagram (quality table)*

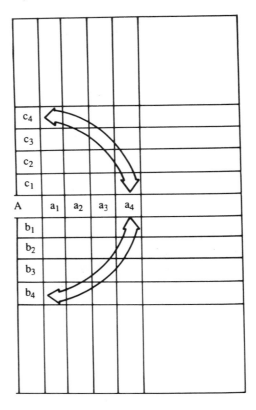

**Figure 10.7** *T-shaped matrix*

There are other matrices that deal with ideas such as product or service function, cost, failure modes, capabilities, etc., and there are at least forty different types of matrix diagrams available.

## 5   Matrix data analysis

Matrix data analysis is used to take data displayed in a matrix diagram and arrange them so that they can be more easily viewed and show the strength of the relationship between variables. It is used most often in marketing and product research. The concept behind matrix data analysis is fairly simple, but its execution (including data gathering) is complex.

A good idea of the uses and value of the construction of a chart for matrix data analysis may be shown in a simple example in which types of pain relievers are compared based on gentleness and effectiveness (Figure 10.9). This information could be used together with some type of demographic analysis to develop a marketing plan. Based on the information, advertising and product introduction could be effectively tailored for specific areas. New product development could also be carried out to attack specific niches in markets that would be profitable.

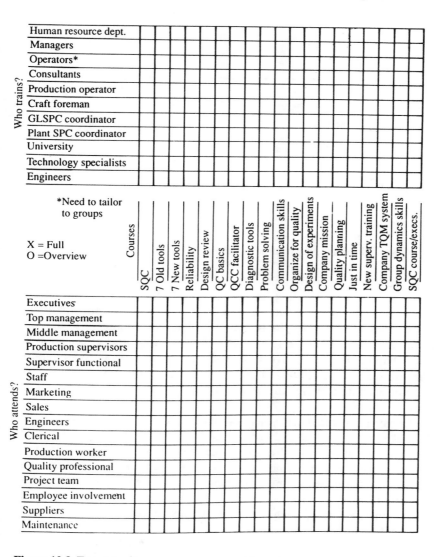

**Figure 10.8** *T-matrix diagram on company-wide training*

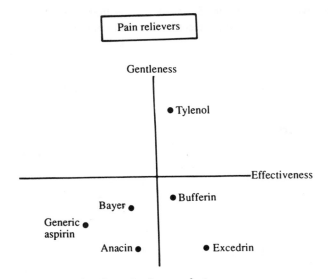

**Figure 10.9** *An example of matrix data analysis*

## 6   Process decision programme chart

A process decision programme chart (PDPC) is used to map out each event and contingency that can occur when progressing from a problem statement to its solution. The PDPC is used to anticipate the unexpected and plan for it. It includes plans for counter-measures on deviations. The PDPC is related to a failure mode and effect analysis (see Chapter 9) and its structure is similar to that of a tree diagram. (An example of the PDPC is shown in Figure 10.10.) Suggested steps for constructing a PDPC are as follows:

1   Construct a tree diagram as described previously.
2   Take one major branch of the tree diagram (an item just to the right of the main goal or purpose). Ask 'What could go wrong at this step?' or 'What other path could this step take?'
3   Answer the questions by branching off the original path in 'organization chart' manner.
4   Off to the side of each step, list actions or counter-measures that could be taken.
5   Continue the process until the branch is exhausted.
6   Repeat with other main branches.

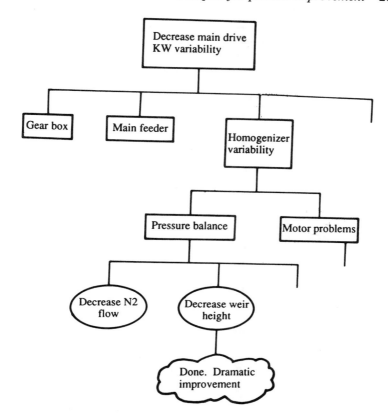

**Figure 10.10** *Process decision programme chart*

The PDPC is very simply an attempt to be proactive in the analysis of failure and to construct, on paper, a 'dry run' of the process so that the 'check' part of the improvement cycle can be defined in advance. PDPC is likely to enjoy widespread use because of increasing attention to product liability.

## 7 Arrow diagram

The arrow diagram is used to plan or schedule a task. To use it, one must know the sub-task sequence and duration. This tool is essentially the same as the standard Gantt chart shown in Figure 10.11. Figure 10.12 is the same sequence shown as an arrow diagram. Although it is a simple and well known tool for planning work, it is surprising how often it is ignored. The arrow diagram is useful in analysing a

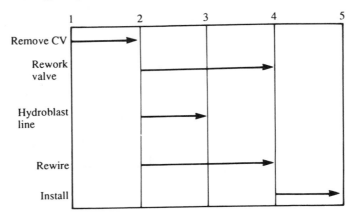

**Figure 10.11** *Gantt chart*

repetitive job in order to make it more efficient. Some suggestions on constructing arrow diagrams are:

1   Use a team of people working on a job or project, e.g. a QFD team, to list all the tasks necessary to complete the job, and write

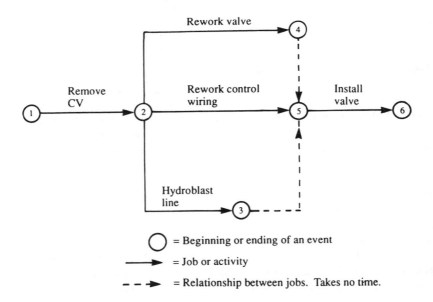

**Figure 10.12** *The arrow diagram*

them on individual cards. On the bottom half of the card, write the time required to complete the task.

2  Place related tasks together. Place them in chronological order.
3  Summarize the cards on a chart similar to Figure 10.12.

Refinements and modifications can be applied to make the arrow diagram more detailed or to account for contingency. The technique is used widely on project planning, where it is known as critical path analysis (CPA). It is easily computerized and has led to further developments, such as programme evaluation and review technique (PERT).

**Summary**

What has been described in this section is a system for improving the design of products, processes, and services by means of seven new tools, sometimes called the quality function deployment tools. For the most part the seven tools are neither new nor revolutionary, but rather a compilation and modification of some tools that have been around for a long time. The tools do not replace statistical methods or other tools, but they are meant to be used together as part of the design process.

The tools work best when representatives from all parts of an organization take part in their use and execution of the results. Besides the structure that the tools provide, the co-operation between functions or departments that is required will help break down barriers within the organizations.

While designers and marketing personnel will see the most direct applications for these tools, proper use of the 'philosophy' behind them requires participation from all parts of an organization. In addition, some of the seven new tools can be used in problem solving activities not directly related to design.

# 10.2  Measuring quality with time – reliability

Quality is a property that may change with the age of the product or service. Clearly, part of the acceptability of a product will depend on its ability to function satisfactorily *over a period of time*. This aspect of performance has been given the name *reliability*, which is the ability to continue to meet the customer requirements over time.

Reliability ranks with quality in importance. It is a key factor in many purchasing decisions where alternatives are being compared, and many of the general management issues related to achieving quality are also applicable to reliability.

Clearly, every product or service will eventually fail, although in some cases the possibility is small enough for the product to be effectively infinitely reliable. With the pressures to reduce cost, and with the need for increasing complexity, the probability of a product or service failing within the user's anticipation of its working life is likely to be finite. As reliability is an exceedingly important aspect of competitiveness, there is a need to plan and design reliability into products and services. Unfortunately, the testing of a design to assess its reliability is difficult, sometimes impossible, and the designer must therefore invest in any insurance that is practicable, such as simple, proven or fail-safe designs, reliable components, redundant parts, and proven methods.

**Failure**

In the discussion of reliability it is important to be clear about what is meant by *failure*. When a product, system, component or service no longer performs its required function, it is said to have failed. This definition assumes that the required function is known exactly. A motor car could be described as either working perfectly or broken down completely, but there could be something in between. It may, for example, achieve lower miles to the gallon than when new. Whether the latter is regarded as failure depends entirely on what is defined as the required function, and this in turn may depend on the use of the product or service. To assist in the definition of failure, it may be useful to consider the various types and causes of failure:

*Total failure* – this results in a complete lack of ability of the product or service to perform the required function.

*Partial failure* – the item does not work, or the service is not provided, as well as expected, but it has not completely failed.

*Gradual failure* – this takes place progressively over a period of time and could possibly be anticipated by some sort of examination.

*Sudden failure* – occurs very quickly and is not easily predicted by investigation or examination.

Clearly, there are many causes of product and/or service system failure, but two main general causes are common:

*Weakness* – this is inherent in the product or service itself and, when subject to the normal stresses of use, results in one of the types of failure described above. Weakness is usually introduced by poor or wrong design, materials, processes, or operation.

*Misuse*  – this represents the application of stresses which are outside the usual capability of the product or service system.

## Measures and analysis of reliability

All measures of reliability are time-dependent. The *reliability (Rt)* of a product or service is the probability that it will be still functioning at time t. This may be calculated for a product as follows:

$$R_t = \frac{\text{Number surviving at time t}}{\text{Number existing at t} = 0}$$

There is another important measure of reliability in use – the *failure or hazard rate ($\phi_t$)*:

$$\phi_t = \frac{\text{Number failing in unit time at time t}}{\text{Number surviving at time t}}$$

The curve from the plot of failure or hazard rate ($\phi_t$) against time is known as the 'bath tub curve', from its shape, and it is extremely useful in the analysis of product reliability. This shape is characteristic of the failure rate curve of many well designed products and components, including the human body (Figure 10.13).

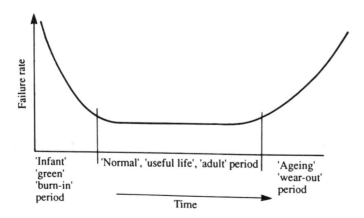

**Figure 10.13** *The bath tub curve*

It is obviously desirable that the initial 'infant' phase should be as short as possible, and to this end manufacturers may 'load' or 'burn-in' their products before sending them to the user, so that the consumer meets the product at the beginning of its 'adult' or 'useful' life. When the failure rate has increased to a value twice that of the constant failure rate period, the 'wear-out' phase is said to start. Knowledge of when this begins is vital if warranty or guarantee periods are to be determined on the basis of the product reliability.

Reliability, like all other properties of products and services, will not just happen, it must be planned, designed and built in, using systematic methods and techniques. These include establishing a quantified reliability specification, techniques for failure prediction, testing, data-collection, and analysis. Reliability can be influenced by everyone in the producing organization from marketing right through to delivery and after-sales service, and those outside it concerned with the supply of goods and services.

## 10.3   Improving maintenance performance

The maintenance of plant and equipment in working order is essential to achieve total quality, reliability, and efficient working. The 'best' equipment will not work satisfactorily unless it is cared for, and the cost of a breakdown in the system can be very high, not only in financial terms but also in poor staff morale and bad relations with customers – the internal as well as the external ones. The people and the materials must also be 'maintained', through training, motivation, health care and even entertainment for the people, and proper storage and handling of materials.

Within the context of maintenance, failure is defined as an inability to produce work in the appropriate manner rather than an inability to produce any work. Thus a piece of plant or equipment that deteriorates and consequently produces work of bad quality or at too high a cost is said to fail. Work carried out before failure is said to be overhaul, or preventive maintenance work, while that carried out after failure is emergency, breakdown or recovery work (Figure 10.14). It is worth noting that work can sometimes actually proceed while a plant has 'failed' but continues to produce: for example, some types of overhauls may be carried out at a power station while electricity is still being generated, though at an enhanced cost. The maintenance system exists within and as a part of the operating system as a whole.

As in all other areas of management, the 'most satisfactory' maintenance policy is unlikely to occur by chance. Data must be systemati-

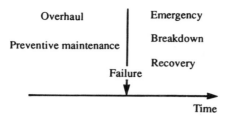

**Figure 10.14** *The time of failure*

cally gathered and analysed. The costs associated with failure and the costs of corrective action should be compared and a maintenance plan prepared – one that offers a satisfactory match of costs and equipment availability. In this sense *all* maintenance work should be *planned*.

Historically, the term 'planned maintenance' has been misguidedly restricted to the overhaul work, but this is better described as *preventive*. There are many cases where the best policy is to allow the equipment to fail before carrying out maintenance work. Such work is undoubtedly 'planned', even though the timing of the work is uncertain.

There are, then, broadly two types of maintenance policy:

- Repair or replacement due to failure.
- Preventive maintenance.

The first type is an emergency based policy, in which the plant or equipment is operated until it fails and then it is maintained. Formal preventive maintenance may take four different forms:

1  *Time-based*, which means doing maintenance at regular intervals – say every 2 months. It is easy to monitor time, and this form is used when deterioration is likely to be time rather than usage-dependent, or when usage cannot easily be measured.
2  *Work-based*, which is maintenance after a set number of operating hours of volume of work produced, e.g. every 40,000 photocopies. Usage can be more difficult than time to monitor, and some form of 'auto-counting' of output should be used, if possible.
3  *Opportunity-based*, where repair or replacement takes place when the equipment or system is available, e.g. during a holiday closure. This can extend the interval between maintenance to an unacceptable level, but it may be suitable for equipment that has intermittently heavy use.

4   *Condition-based*, which often relies on planned inspection to reveal when maintenance is prudent, e.g. replace a brake pad when it has worn to 2mm thickness. This is dependent on monitoring equipment condition, which can be difficult and out of the question if a time consuming strip down precedes any examination or inspection.

These various types of policy often operate together, overlap or coincide. For example, time-based and work-based maintenance will coincide if the rate of work is constant; and condition-based replacement may occur during a time, work or opportunity-based maintenance activity.

**The need for data**

Choice between the various policies needs to be made on objective grounds, and this underlines the need for good data collection and analysis. It is not easy to try to discover the actual time taken and the work necessary when carrying out a maintenance task, particularly when the plant is large and/or complex and the maintenance work carried out far from simple. Rational policies, however, need to be based on data, and the need for the collection and analysis of reliability and maintenance information cannot be over-emphasized. Furthermore, it is invaluable to feed particular problems and difficulties back to the designer or supplier of equipment, since it may be possible to reduce downtimes and overhaul times on new equipment.

**Total preventive maintenance (TPM)**

Well designed preventive maintenance plans can reduce the incidence of emergency maintenance. In the production of standardized product design along flow lines, where there is little if any work-in-progress between adjacent operations, an equipment breakdown at one operation will quickly cause all other downstream operations to come to a standstill. This situation can arise just as easily in the supply of cheeseburgers in a 'burger-bar', and the preparation of letters of credit in a bank, as in the assembly of motor cars. An extensive total preventive maintenance (TPM) programme is essential to reduce the frequency and severity of process flow interruption in these situations.

In automated production environments, again not restricted to manufacturing, TPM should be part of the operating quality policy. Where automated equipment operates continuously, without the need for operatives, human intervention will be required in the form of a maintenance unit to keep the equipment operating in good condition. As automation increases throughout various types of operation, we shall see a need to move to smaller production workforces and larger maintenance crews. Hence some of the production operatives replaced by robotics and computer aided production systems will require retraining to provide the necessary increase in maintenance staff.

As we see the increasing introduction of just-in-time (JIT) methods, in which in-process stocks and batch sizes are reduced to very low levels, the near absence of work-in-progress will focus attention on equipment and system failure. JIT demands perfect equipment maintenance, since breakdowns cannot be tolerated. It is not sufficient to speed up repairs to minimize downtime; breakdowns must be eliminated through an effective prevention strategy.

Where people are employed in production or service operations, this strategy requires their total concentration. They must be given the responsibility for preventing equipment and process failure by conducting checks, inspecting, and adjusting their own equipment or process, with meticulous attention to detail. Just as in the achievement of quality of conformance, people must be given the tools to do this, and this means providing the appropriate training to be able to detect, find and eliminate potential causes of trouble before they manifest themselves in a system failure.

Technology is increasingly more complex, with electronics, robotics and computer control now influencing every walk of life. These have clearly led to many changes in maintenance activities. Special and continuous training programmes are required to provide the necessary knowledge, understanding and skills to service the increasingly specialized equipment, and to keep up with the developments in the field.

Specialist organizations have developed to provide maintenance services on a subcontract basis, and transport vehicles, computers, office equipment and medical support systems are often serviced by outside companies. The specialized technical knowledge and skills are frequently more economical to acquire on a call-in fee basis than by the use of an in-house team. The advances in technology have enabled the development of systems that reduce the cost of maintenance while improving operational performance.

Total preventive maintenance management is far more than repairing and servicing equipment. The perspectives of maintenance planning must be broadened to the long range performance aspects of the complete customer service system. Failure of any component in that system can cause total disaster, and the functioning of the whole organization is dependent on adopting a TPM approach in the policies, plans and operations.

## 10.4   Further techniques for process improvement

### Poka-Yoke

Shigeo Shingo is the inventor of the SMED (single minute exchange of die) system, in which set-up times are reduced from hours to minutes, and the *Poka-Yoke* (mistake proofing) system. He was a key developer of the Toyota production system and likes to be known as 'Dr Improvement'.

Shingo teaches three interrelated aspects of quality control. *Zero quality control* is the ideal production system, in which no defects or errors are produced. To achieve this, two things are required: *Poka-Yoke* and *source inspections*.

In *Poka-Yoke* defects are examined, the production system stopped and immediate feedback given so that the root causes of the problems may be identified and prevented from occuring again.

Poka-Yoke recognizes that people are human, fallible and will on occasions inadvertently forget or do a thing wrongly. To counter this, Shingo suggests the incorporation of 'checklists', i.e., a Poka-Yoke, into the operation, so that if a worker forgets something, the device will signal that fact, thereby preventing errors or defects from occurring. This is similar to the checklist the author uses to make sure he has all the equipment necessary when leaving for the golf course!

The Poka-Yoke concept is based on the same idea as the badly named 'foolproofing', an approach often used for preserving the safety of operations, and one in which assembly, manufacture, or operation can be performed in only one way – the correct way. This clearly has large implications for product and process design.

In *source inspections* errors are looked at before they become defects, and the system is either stopped for correction or the error condition automatically adjusted to prevent it from becoming a defect. Ordinary inspection systems stimulate feedback and action in response to defects that have been produced. Source inspections are based on discovering errors in conditions that can give rise to defects, feeding back and taking action at the error stage to prevent the errors from turning into defects. This requires the clear distinction between errors and defects. Defects arise because errors are made, and there is a cause and effect relationship between the two. If this is so, then clearly errors will not turn into defects if feedback and action take place at the error stage.

*Zero QC* systems are set up by combining source inspections with 100 per cent inspections and providing immediate feedback and action.

According to Shingo, a zero quality control system is based on the following basic ideas:

(a) Use source inspections to prevent defects, by applying control functions at the error stage where defects originate, and eliminate them completely.
(b) Use 100 per cent inspections rather than sampling inspections.
(c) Minimize the time it takes to carry out corrective action when abnormalities appear.
(d) Recognize that human workers are not infallible, and set up Poka-Yoke devices accordingly.

Using Poka-Yoke and source inspection systems has enabled companies such as Toyota virtually to eliminate the need for acceptance sampling methods.

## Taguchi methods

Genichi Taguchi is a noted Japanese engineering specialist who has advanced 'quality engineering' as a technology to reduce costs and improve quality simultaneously. The popularity of Taguchi methods today testifies to the merit of his philosophies on quality. The basic elements of Taguchi's ideas, which have been extended here to all aspects of product, service and process quality, may be considered under four main headings.

### 1   Total loss function

An important aspect of the quality of a product or service is the total loss to society that it generates. Taguchi's definition of product quality as 'the loss imparted to society from the time a product is shipped', is rather strange, since the word *loss* denotes the very opposite of what is normally conveyed by using the word *quality*. The essence of his definition is that the smaller the loss generated by a product or service from the time it is transferred to the customer, the more desirable it is.

There are two particular problems with this idea:

• It does not include losses to society during manufacture of the product or operation of the service.
• It is rather profound and requires much thought, data collection, and analysis to be useful in the detailed business of quality management.

Its main advantage is that it encourages a new way of thinking about investment in quality improvement projects, which become attractive when the resulting savings to customers are greater than the cost of improvements.

Taguchi claims, with some justification, that any variation about a target value for a product or process parameter causes loss to the customer. The loss may be some simple inconvenience, but it can represent actual cash losses, owing to rework or badly fitting parts, and it may well appear as loss of customer goodwill and eventually market share. The loss (or cost) increases exponentially as the parameter value moves away from the target, and is at a minimum when the product or service is at the target value (Figure 10.15).

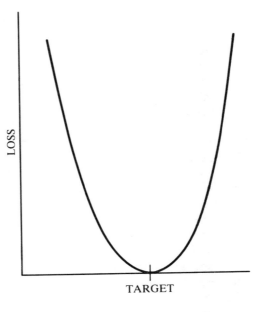

**Figure 10.15** *The Taguchi loss function*

Taguchi calculates an average loss to customers by a statistically based averaging process, which associates a quadratic approximation of loss with the values of the parameter being measured. This concept is also used to characterize process capability independently from specification limits, which Taguchi sees as no more than tentative cut-off points. These ideas emphasize the importance of continuously reducing process variability.

## 2   Design of products, services and processes

In any product or service development three stages may be identified: product or service design, process design, and production or operations. Each of these overlapping stages has many steps, the output of one often being the input to others. The output/input transfer points between steps clearly affect the quality and cost of the final product or service. The complexity of many modern products and services demands that the crucial role of design be recognized. Indeed the performance of the quality products from the Japanese automotive, banking, camera, and machine tool industries can be traced to the robustness of their product and process designs.

The prevention of problems in using products or services under varying operating and environmental conditions must be built in at the design stage. Equally, the costs during production or operation are determined very much by the actual manufacturing or operating process. Controls, including SPC methods, added to processes to reduce imperfections at the operational stage are expensive, and the need for controls *and* the production of non-conformance can be reduced by correct initial design of the process itself.

Taguchi distinguishes between *off-line* and *on-line* quality control methods, 'quality control' being used here in the very broad sense to include quality planning, analysis and improvement. Off-line QC uses technical aids in the *design* of products and processes, whereas on-line methods are technical aids for controlling quality and costs in the *production* of products or services. Too often the off-line QC methods focus on evaluation rather than improvement. The belief by some people (often based on experience!) that it is unwise to buy a new model of a motor car 'until the problems have been sorted out' testifies to the fact that insufficient attention is given to improvement at the product and process design stages. In other words, the bugs should be removed *before* not after product launch. This may be achieved in some organizations by replacing detailed quality and reliability evaluation methods with approximate estimates, and using the liberated resources to make improvements.

## 3   Reduction on variation

The objective of a continuous quality improvement programme is to reduce the variation of key product performance characteristics about their target values. The widespread practice of setting specifications in terms of simple upper and lower limits conveys the wrong idea that the customer is satisfied with all values inside the specification band, but is suddenly not satisfied when a value slips outside one of the limits. The practice of stating specifications as tolerance intervals only can lead manufacturers to produce and despatch goods whose parameters are just inside the specification band. Owing to the interdependence of many parameters of component parts and assemblies, this is likely to lead to quality problems.

The target value should be stated and specified as the ideal, with known variability about that mean. For those performance characteristics that cannot be measured on a continuous scale, the next best thing is an ordered categorical scale such as excellent, very good, good, fair, unsatisfactory, very poor, rather than the binary classification of 'good' or 'bad' that provides meagre information with which the variation reduction process can operate.

Taguchi has introduced a three-step approach to assigning nominal values and tolerances for product and process parameters:

(a) *System design* – the application of scientific engineering and technical knowledge to produce a basic functional prototype design. This requires a fundamental understanding of the needs of the customer *and* the production environment.

(b) *Parameter design* – the identification of the settings of product or process parameters that reduce the sensitivity of the designs to sources of variation. This requires a study of the whole process system design to achieve the most robust operational settings, in terms of tolerance to ranges of the input variables. This is similar to the experiments needed to identify the plant varieties that can tolerate variations in weather conditions, soil and handling. Manual processes that can tolerate the ranges of dimensions of the human body provide another example.

(c) *Tolerance design* – the determination of tolerances around the nominal settings identified by parameter design. This requires a trade-off between the customer's loss due to performance variation and the increase in production or operational costs.

## 4   Statistically planned experiments

Taguchi has pointed out that statistically planned experiments should be used to identify the settings of product and process parameters that will reduce variation in performance. He classifies the variables that affect the performance into two categories: design parameters and sources of 'noise'. As we have seen earlier, the nominal settings of the *design parameters* define the specification for the product or process. The *sources of noise* are all the variables that cause the performance characteristics to deviate from the target values. The *key* noise factors are those that represent the major sources of variability, and these should be identified and included in the experiments to design the parameters at which the effect of the noise factors on the performance is minimum. This is done by systematically varying the design parameter settings and comparing the effect of the noise factors for each experimental run.

Statistically planned experiments may be used to identify:

(a) The design parameters that have a large influence on the product or performance characteristic.
(b) The design parameters that have no influence on the performance characteristics (the tolerances of these parameters may be relaxed).
(c) The settings of design parameters at which the effect of the sources of noise on the performance characteristic is minimal.
(d) The settings of design parameters that will reduce cost without adversely affecting quality.[1]

Taguchi methods have stimulated a great deal of interest in the application of statistically planned experiments to product and process designs. The use of 'design of experiments' to improve industrial products and processes is not new – Tippett used these techniques in the textile industry more than 50 years ago. What Taguchi has done, however, is to acquaint us with the scope of these techniques in off-line quality control.

Taguchi's methods, like all others, should not be used in isolation, but be an integral part of continuous improvement.

# Chapter highlights

### Seven new tools for quality design

- Seven new tools may be used as part of quality function deployment (QFD, see Chapter 3) to improve the innovation processes. These are systems and documentation methods for identifying objectives and intermediate steps in the finest detail.
- The seven new tools are: affinity diagram, interrelationship digraph, tree diagram, matrix diagrams or quality table, matrix data analysis, process decision programme chart (PDPC), and arrow diagram.

- The tools are interrelated and their promotion and use should lead to better designs in less time. They work best when people from all parts of an organization are using them. Some of the tools can be used in problem solving activities not related to design.

### Measuring quality with time – reliability

- Reliability is the ability to meet the customer requirements over time. It ranks with quality in importance as a key factor in many purchasing decisions.
- When a product or service no longer performs its required function, it has failed. There are four types of failure – total, partial, gradual and sudden – and two main causes of failure – weakness and misuse.
- The measured reliability (Rt) of a product or service is the probability that it will be functioning at time t. The failure or hazard rate $\phi_t$ is the probability of failure in unit time, at a time t.
- The curve from the plot of failure or hazard rate against time is called the 'bath-tub curve' – from its shape. This shows clearly the infant or early life, adult or constant failure rate, and ageing or wear-out phases. It is useful in assessing warranty periods.

### Improving maintenance performance

- The maintenance of plant and equipment in working order is essential to achieve total quality and reliability. The people and materials must also be 'maintained'.
- Work carried out before failure is overhaul or preventive maintenance; after failure it is emergency, breakdown or recovery. All maintenance should have a policy and be planned – even breakdown, although the timing may be uncertain.
- There are two types of maintenance policy: repair/replacement due to failure, and preventive. The latter may take four forms – time-, work-, opportunity-, or condition-based. These often operate together.
- The choice between the policies should be made on data based objective grounds.
- Extensive total preventive maintenance (TPM) is essential to reduce frequency and severity of process flow interruption. TPM is a strategy for bringing people into the process and giving them responsibility for preventing equipment and process failure.

## Further techniques for process improvement

* Shigeo Shingo invented the SMED (single minute exchange of die) and the Poka-Yoke (mistake proofing) systems.
* Shingo teaches three interrelated aspects of quality control: zero quality control, Poka-Yoke, and source inspections. Using Poka-Yoke and source inspections to achieve zero quality control has enabled companies such as Toyota to eliminate acceptance sampling.
* Genichi Taguchi has advanced 'quality engineering' as a technology to reduce costs and make improvements.
* Taguchi's approach may be classified under four headings: total loss function; design of products, services and processes; reduction in variation; and statistically planned experiments.
* Shingo and Taguchi methods, like all others, should not be used in isolation, but as an integral part of continuous improvement.

## Reference

1  See Roland Caulcutt, *Statistics in Research and Development*, 2nd edition, Chapman and Hall, London 1991.

# Part Four
# TQM – The Organizational, Communication and Teamwork Requirements

Dust as we are, the immortal spirit grows
Like harmony in music; there is a dark
Inscrutable workmanship that reconciles
Discordant elements, makes them cling together
In one society.

*William Wordsworth, 1770–1850*

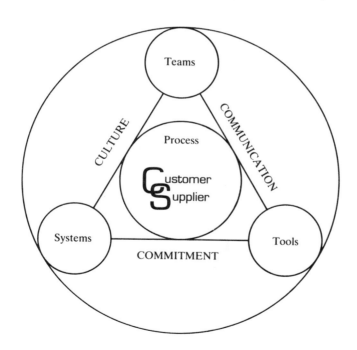

# 11 Organization for quality

## 11.1 People and the organizational structure

A company in the mechanical engineering industry had developed the outline organizational structure shown in Figure 11.1. The great big crack down the middle did not appear on the paper version, only in the reality.

Contrary to some opinion, the way we set down an organization on paper *does* affect the way people behave. It casts them in roles, sets them with or against others, and even provides them with short-term objectives. When the role of the quality function clearly appears on paper as a high ranking police force, set up to stop defective produce reaching the external customer, it is usually a reflection of the message that has been transmitted to the producing departments – output, output, output. It is this message alone that causes responsible, honourable people to behave in a quite peculiar way, and try to send or transfer to the 'customer' defective material, poor service, and error-ridden information, paperwork, invoices, etc., in order to reach output targets. Human beings will respond, like any other animal, to various stimuli. If these are all related to quantity, then quality will be seen to be of secondary importance.

Unfortunately, this will have far wider ranging effects than merely creating conflict between the producers and 'quality control'. It will strip the whole organization of the opportunity to manage quality at every interface, at every level, within and across all functional areas.

Clearly, the only point at which true responsibility for quality can lie is with the person or group of people that actually does the job. Abdication of this responsibility can be generated easily by the creation of a separate and elitist army of inspectors, checkers, measurers and testers. To make sure that the responsibility stays where it belongs, it is first necessary to arrange the people in their roles on the organizational table. Of course this simple act will not ensure a quality-ever-after life together, but it will give people and the organization a chance.

The organization of many companies reflects their concentration on

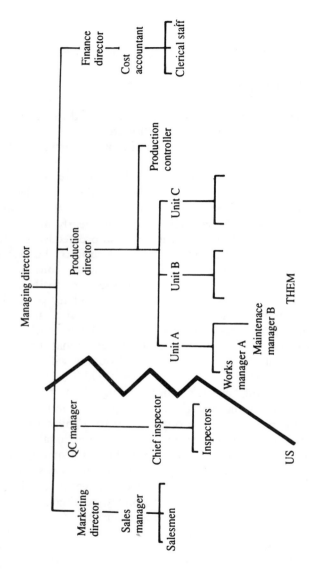

**Figure 11.1** *The us and them organization for quality*

the relatively narrow area of inspection- or checking-oriented quality assurance. The very title 'quality manager' is a misnomer when it is associated solely with the management of product or service quality. There is no way that one person or one department can manage quality, but one person – the Chief Executive – must take on the responsibility. A major thrust of TQM is to have the quality 'department' spending more time helping to prevent, rather than inspecting for or correcting, errors. Resources can then be redeployed from firefighting activities, and the organizational culture can gradually change to reflect the *error-free-work* method of operation.

To transform quality into a strategic business planning and management dimension, a new role must be created for the quality function, a role similar to that of a navigator on a ship. After preparing a course for the Chief Executive (the captain), the navigator 'manages' the route and the progress. When the ship is off course, he does not stride on to the bridge, elbow the helmsman in the ribs and start turning the ship's wheel. That is not his role. He is the provider of systems and guidance, but responsibility lies firmly and squarely on the shoulders of the captain and each of his colleagues for doing their job right the first time.

## 11.2  Responsibilities and performance management

The establishment of positive quality policy objectives within an organization must be accompanied by the clear allocation of responsibilities within the management structure. It is generally accepted that the primary operational responsibility for ensuring that the quality chain does not break must rest with line management, and in particular there are two key areas that require attention:

(a) *Senior executive level.* Direct responsibility for the general management of quality should be included in the duties of one of the senior executives in the same way that a director may be allocated responsibility for finance, production/operations, marketing, or safety. Undivided line management responsibility for quality often stops at some point in the middle management ladder; further up the responsibility tends to become diffused and uncertain. Quality must be treated like any other major managerial function, with a clear line of responsibility and command running up to an accountable individual at the top of the organization.

(b) *First-line supervision level.* The other critical level is the supervisor, who is 'on the spot' and in a position to know whether the supplier/customer interfaces are working satisfactorily in practice, and his/her influence can be dramatic. The promotion of quality is first and foremost a matter of efficient management. The first level supervision has a responsibility to:

- Instruct subordinates in the appropriate methods and procedures.
- Inform them of likely causes of errors or defects and the preventive methods necessary.
- Supervise the arrangement of such methods and instructions in the quality system.
- Initiate or facilitate any steps necessary to improve methods, equipment, materials, conditions, in the work area for which he/she is responsible.

Line managers and supervisors can improve their effectiveness as 'instructors' if they themselves have been trained in 'how to instruct'.

As with other areas, such as productivity and safety, real progress in quality improvement is impossible without the full co-operation and commitment of all employees. If they are to accept their full share of responsibility, however, they must be able to participate fully in the making and monitoring of arrangements for achieving the requirements at their place of work. Some organizations have arrangements whereby all employees in a particular unit meet periodically for discussions about quality – sometimes called 'quality circles' or Kaizen teams. This approach stresses the need for the participation of every individual employee.

The feeling of responsibility must be engendered in all employees to:

(a)   Follow the agreed written procedures.
(b)   Use materials and equipment correctly and as instructed.
(c)   Draw attention to existing or potential quality problems and report all errors, defects and waste.
(d)   Suggest ways in which risks of errors or quality problems could be reduced.
(e)   Assist in the training of new entrants and young people, particularly by setting a good example.

An effective method of achieving general co-operation, interest and involvement in quality should be established by formal arrangements for quality improvement teams. This will vary from organization to organization, and depend on particular circumstances on the site, e.g. its size and location, the composition of the workforce, and processes operated.

## The process of performance management

Managers are in control only when they have created a system and climate in which their subordinates can exercise self-control. Mechanisms may then be created to provide clear performance standards in all areas, backed by appropriate job descriptions and training, to ensure those standards are achieved. The process of performance management consists then of:

- Clarifying responsibilities.
- Developing performance indicators and objectives.
- Preparing action plans.

### 1 Clarifying responsibilities

If job descriptions have been written for the organization, they may serve as a starting point for clarifying each individual's role. It should be emphasized, however, that these need to be updated and reviewed with each subordinate to ensure their relevancy. The format for job descriptions is not of critical importance, although it must be standardized for a particular organization. Job descriptions should contain a statement of the purpose of the job, reporting relationships, responsibility and priorities. Agreement must be reached on the priorities – frequently managers or directors expect the major emphasis to be on activities 2, 5, 6, and 7, when the subordinate perceives the critical areas to be 1, 3, 4 and 8.

Organizational problems requiring role clarification will not be resolved by the introduction of job descriptions alone. Some of the other factors that prevent groups from functioning smoothly are:

(a) Poor communication of information to other departments, groups or individuals in time for it to be useful.
(b) Lack of understanding of where decisions are taken or goals set.
(c) Low involvement of other departments, groups or individuals in reaching decisions.
(d) Lack of appreciation of the role of other departments, groups or individuals in reaching goals or targets.
(e) Failure to identify and use systems, methods, or techniques for specific activities.
(f) Absence of corrective action following identification of weaknesses and problems.
(g) Lack of recognition of role of training and follow-up.

The important aspect of methods used to counter these is the team-building impact within each operational group. All participants must have the opportunity to review their current roles, seek to change those aspects for which they perceive valid cause, and do more in those areas where they feel their inputs would have merit.

## 2 Developing performance indicators and objectives

Although the responsibilities should clarify what is to be performed, they do not define *how well* the tasks are expected to be performed. Performance indicators therefore are the means by which performance will be evaluated. To be meaningful they must be:

(a) *Measurable* – indicators must lead to performance objectives which are quantifiable and tangible. Achievements in these areas must be recordable, verifiable, and observable. Areas such as quantity or quality of output, time schedules, costs, ratios, or percentages would be examples of measurable indicators (see also Chapter 7).

(b) *Relevant* – indicators must serve as a linkage between specific areas of responsibilities and the individual performance objectives to monitor achievement. They must describe what is the expected role of the position – the critical areas of performance.

(c) *Important* – indicators need not be defined for every area of responsibility. They should be developed for those activities that have a significant impact on the results for the individual, department, and organization.

The establishment of performance objectives provides clear direction and communication of expected levels of achievement. The process is a joint one – an interaction between the manager and his/her subordinates. If full commitment on the part of both parties is to be realized, the targets should be negotiated in the form of a performance 'contract'. Once the indicators have been agreed, the specific results desired need to be decided. The greater the participation, the greater the motivation to achieve. Agreed performance objectives should therefore contain the following ingredients:

- Be participatively developed.
- Be challenging but attainable.
- Be clear statements of performance expectations.
- Lie within the individual's scope of control.

(a) *Participation* – an interaction which leads to mutual agreement provides a good exchange of ideas between the manager and his/her subordinates. The results are not a compromise but should be the outcome of a persuasive but logical presentation of why such an outcome is plausible. Discussions should be analytical, not emotional, and deal with both sides of an issue if there are significant differences. The crucial factors in examining the advantages of this approach are:

Involvement→Commitment→Personal responsibility→Higher drive to achieve

*rather than*

Imposition→Lack of acceptance→External responsibility→Lower drive to achieve

(b) *Challenge* – a well set performance objective is one that is attainable but yet requires stretching for. The achiever sets targets that are moderately risky. When the likelihood of success is 65 per cent to 85 per cent, the inner sense of challenge is at its peak. As the probability decreases or increases from this range, the motive to achieve is reduced. The former makes the risk too great, since the target becomes perceived as unrealistic and self-esteem is lowered. The latter sets the risk too low and, if success is 'guaranteed', the pay-off value attached to attainment is reduced.

When individuals press for objectives that are either too low or too high, they tend to be motivated more by a fear of failure than the need to achieve. Those in this category either want the target to be fail-safe and, hence, be assured of success, or else want to set a target so high that no one really takes their goals seriously.

To deal most effectively with either of these personalities, the performance objectives established should be of three levels: minimally acceptable, above average, and excellent. A person need not negotiate the minimal acceptable level, since this is the least level of performance to maintain employment. The other levels can be discussed to arrive at realistic but challenging targets. Once they have been agreed upon, the choice of which path to follow is that of the subordinate – and the rewards can be similarly distributed.

(c) *Clarity of expectation* – the target should be objectively expressed and be tied to a specific time framework. Expressions such as 'approximate, minimum, maximum, adequate, none, as soon as possible,' are vague and should be avoided. Descriptive, evaluative terms such as 'frequently, seldom, usually,' etc. are also open to misinterpretation.

(d) *Scope of control* – the performance of the responsibility must be within the limits of authority that have been delegated. An individual cannot be reasonably held responsible for activities that cannot be directly controlled or influenced. For example, a production manager's performance objective of reviewing and accounting for the variation between budgeted and actual performance by the fifth working day of the month may not be adequately expressed, since the input for review may originate in data-processing or accounting rather than the manager's own department. If this is so, he may have no control over the budgeting data being available in time for a review on that date. A better indicator might be the time from receipt of the input to the submission of the analysis and recommendation.

### 3 Preparing action plans

The process of planning is dealt with in detail in Chapter 4. It is clear that some form of action plan, perhaps in the form of a flowchart, bar chart or Gantt chart, is required to enable the objectives to be reached. The plans should stipulate action by the individuals concerned, and be reviewed periodically against the milestones set down.

For quality to have top priority, it must receive the greatest weight in the evaluation of the performance of managers. The planning stage may require new thinking with respect to dealing with activities not previously subject to quality evaluation. For example:

- How will contributions made by individuals in team projects be evaluated?
- What action will be required to improve job performance?
- What are the criteria for promotion?
- What are the training needs to improve performance or prepare for promotion?
- What are the changes in the goals for the next performance period?

In order to manage performance effectively, an organization must have a performance management system for all its levels. The true translation of goals from the top to the bottom of the organization requires that one level's HOWs become the next level's WHATs. This interlocking or goal translation process should ensure the whole organization is working towards the same achievable mission. It is described fully in Chapter 15.

## Total quality management and financial incentive schemes

While it is desirable to introduce a TQM initiative or sustain an established one without direct financial incentives, it is possible to do so in the context of a pay structure with an incentive component, provided that the motivational impact of the incentive does not undermine the total quality aims. There would be, however, a major conflict between trying to create a total quality culture and trying to maintain a payment structure that was focused strongly on motivating individuals to maximize their output volume.

This conflict goes beyond a simple trade-off between quality and quantity. It is not resolved by the assertion that payment-by-result schemes reward only output that meets specified quality standards. The benefits of TQM come not from meeting a predetermined quality standard, but from a culture in which the efforts of everyone in the organization, working in groups or teams to identify and remove barriers to quality, are directed towards never-ending improvements in the delivery of the customers' requirements, to the benefit of the business.

Even in the crudest piecework systems, only that output meeting the specified tolerances should attract payment, but any 'rate-fixing' environment is clearly pulling in the opposite direction to TQM, which may not survive where piecework is the norm.

Particular difficulties flowing from output related incentives can include:

- A disincentive to share improved or more efficient methods, because this can result in a reduced job value – the longer an individual or work group can keep an improvement to themselves, the greater the benefit to them.
- An incentive not to fulfil the specification, especially in areas that are not easily examined, e.g. work below ground that is subsequently covered.
- Resistance or delay to the introduction of improved methods, because of the impact on job values and the consequential effect on earnings, particularly where work load is limited.
- The generation of distrust between management and the workforce, where the groups are motivated to 'outsmart' each other, and the associated waste of significant resources on this counter-productive activity.
- Conflict within work groups and between individuals and management over the allocation of 'good' and 'bad' jobs.

In the longer term the achievement of the full potential of a total quality culture requires a withdrawal from incentives focusing on output volume. A commitment to TQM accordingly needs, as a minimum, to be accompanied by a strategy to achieve a reward structure that does not conflict with it. Without such a strategy there is a risk that the existing benefits of output related incentives will be diluted and few benefits from TQM secured. More probably the inertia of the embedded culture would condemn any initiative to disrepute and failure.

If it is clearly impracticable to remove, in the short term, a current incentive scheme arrangement, measures should be taken to reduce the potential conflict with TQM. These should include:

* Reducing the proportion of earnings flowing from incentive bonus.
* Moving from individual or very small group schemes to larger group schemes.
* Introducing multi-factor schemes that balance the emphasis on volume against some measure of quality or quality improvement.
* Discontinuing the introduction of piecework type 'alternative' schemes.

Unless the potential conflicts are addressed, it is unlikely that the real benefits of TQM will be achieved. There may even be opportunities to refocus incentives in ways that remove barriers to TQM and demonstrate practical commitment to the individual and organizational values implicit in a never-ending improvement.

## 11.3   Departmental purpose analysis

'Quality is everyone's business' is an often quoted cliché, but 'Everything is everyone's business', and so quality often becomes nobody's business. The responsibility for quality begins with the determination of the customer's quality requirements and continues until the service or product is accepted by a satisfied customer. The department purpose analysis (DPA) technique, developed by IBM, helps to define the real purpose of each department, with the objective of improving performance and breaking down departmental barriers. It leads to an understanding and agreement on the key processes of each group. The department can then liaise with its immediate 'suppliers' and 'customers', often internally, to identify potential or actual problem areas and simultaneously carry out an analysis of what proportion of time is spent on the key activities. This begins the change from departmental to process management thinking.

Group discussions during the DPA process usually yield many good ideas for improvement, either eliminating wasteful activity or improving the quality of output from the department. Everyone becomes and should then remain aware of the prime purpose of the department, and the focus on efficiency and reducing waste usually carries through to all work activities. The manager of the department, who should run the exercise, must understand the DPA process and why it is necessary and important. He/she needs to be open minded towards change, and to encourage departmental staff to question whether all their activities add value to the product, service, or business. One of the greatest barriers to improvements through DPA is the 'but we've always done it that way' response.

The basic steps of DPA are:

1 Form the DPA group.
2 Brainstorm to list all the departmental tasks (see Chapter 9).
3 Agree which are the five main tasks.
4 Define the position and role of the departmental manager.
5 Review the main activities, and for each one identify the 'customer(s)' and 'supplier(s)'.
6 Consult the customer(s) and supplier(s) by means of a suitable questionnaire, an example of which is given in Figure 11.2. This is very similar to the list of questions suggested in Chapter 1 for interrogating any customer/supplier interface.
7 Review the customer/supplier survey results and brainstorm how improvements can be made.
8 Prioritize improvements to list those to be tackled first, and plan how.
9 Implement the improvement action plan, maintaining encouragement and support.
10 Review the progress made and repeat the DPA.

As with any new group activity, some successes are desirable early in the programme, if the department is to build confidence in its ability to make improvements and solve problems. For this reason DPA should confine itself, initially at least, to resolving issues that are within its control. It is unlikely, for example, that a sales team will be successful in getting a product redesigned in its first improvement project. Experience at IBM shows that, as confidence builds through continued management encouragement, the DPA groups will tackle increasingly difficult business processes and problems, with an increasing return of the investment in time.

Part 1

| Function/Business Unit | Dept: | No: |
|---|---|---|
|  |  |  |

| Task Ref. | Task list | Proportion of time taken |
|---|---|---|
| 1 |  |  |
| 2 |  |  |
| 3 |  |  |
| 4 |  |  |
| 5 |  |  |
| 6 |  |  |
| 7 |  |  |
| 8 |  |  |
| 9 |  |  |
| 10 |  |  |
| 11 |  |  |
| 12 |  |  |
| 13 |  |  |
| 14 |  |  |
| 15 |  |  |
| Misc. |  |  |
|  | Total (must be <100%) |  |

**Figure 11.2** *Department purpose analysis (DPA) questionnaire*

## 11.4    The quality function and the quality director or manager

In many organizations management systems are viewed in terms of the internal dynamics between marketing, design, sales, production/operations, distribution, accounting, etc. A change is required from this to a larger system that encompasses and integrates the business interests of customers and suppliers. Management needs to develop an in-depth understanding of these relationships and how they may be used to cement the partnership concept. The quality function should be the organization's focal point in this respect, and should be equipped to

Part 2

| Activity | Dept No. | Date |
|---|---|---|

### Customer

Have you seen your customer recently to determine their needs?

Yes          No

What are they?

---

How do you/should you measure your output quality?

---

What is the impact of non-conformity?

### Supplier

Have you seen your supplier recently to determine your needs?

Yes          No

What are they?

---

How do you/should you measure your input quality?

---

What is the impact of non-conformity?

gauge internal and external customers' expectations and degree of satisfaction. It should also identify quality deficiencies in all business functions, and promote improvements.

The role of the quality function is to make quality an inseparable aspect of every employee's performance and responsibility. The transition in many companies from quality departments with line functions will require careful planning, direction, and monitoring. Quality professionals have developed numerous techniques and skills, focused on product or service quality. In many cases there is a need to adapt these to broader applications. The first objectives for many 'quality managers' will be to gradually disengage themselves from line activities, which will then need to be dispersed throughout the appropriate operating departments. This should allow quality to evolve into a 'staff' department at a senior level, and to be concerned with the following throughout the organization:

- Encouraging and facilitating quality improvement.
- Monitoring and evaluating the progress of quality improvement.
- Promoting the 'partnership' in quality, in relations with customers and suppliers.
- Planning, managing, auditing, and reviewing quality systems.
- Planning and providing quality training and counselling or consultancy.
- Giving advice to management on:

  (a) Establishment of quality systems and process control.
  (b) Relevant statutory/legislative requirements with respect to quality.
  (c) Quality improvement programmes necessary.
  (d) Inclusion of quality elements in all job instructions and procedures.

Quality directors and managers have an initial task, however, to help those who control the means to implement this concept – the leaders of industry and commerce – to really believe that quality must become an integral part of all the organization's operations.

The author has a vision of quality as a strategic business management function that will help organizations to change their cultures. To make this vision a reality, quality professionals must expand the application of quality concepts and techniques to all business processes and functions, and develop new forms of providing assurance of quality at every supplier–customer interface. They will need to know the entire cycle of products or services, from concept to the *ultimate* end user.

An example of this was observed in the case of a company manufacturing pharmaceutical seals, whose customer expressed concern about excess aluminium projecting below and round a particular type of seal. This was considered a cosmetic defect by the immediate customer, the Health Service, but a safety hazard by a blind patient – the *customer's customer*. The prevention of this 'curling' of excess metal meant changing practices at the mill that rolled the aluminium – at the *supplier's supplier*. Clearly, the quality professional dealing with this problem needed to understand the supplier's problems and the ultimate customer's needs, in order to judge whether the product was indeed capable of meeting the requirements.

The shift in 'philosophy' will require considerable staff education in many organizations. Not only must people in other functions acquire quality related skills, but quality personnel must change old attitudes and acquire new skills – replacing the inspection, calibration, specification-writing mentality with knowledge of defect prevention, wide ranging quality systems design and audit. Clearly, the challenge for many quality professionals is not so much making changes in their organization as recognizing the changes required in themselves. It is more than an overnight job to change the attitudes of an inspection police force into those of a consultative, team-oriented improvement force. This emphasis on prevention and improvement-based systems elevates the role of quality professionals from a technical one to that of general management. A narrow departmental view of quality is totally out of place in an organization aspiring to TQM, and typical quality managers will need to widen their perspective and increase their knowledge to encompass all facets of the organization.

To introduce the concepts of operator self-inspection required for TQM will require not only a determination to implement change but sensitivity and skills in industrial relations. This will depend very much of course on the climate within the organization. Those whose management is truly concerned with co-operation and concerned for the people will engage strong employee support for the quality manager or director in his catalytic role in the quality improvement implementation process. Those with aggressive, confrontational management will create for the quality professional impossible difficulties in obtaining support from the 'rank and file'.

## TQM appointments

Many organizations have realized the importance of the contribution a senior, qualified director of quality can make to the prevention strategy. Smaller organizations may well feel that the cost of employing a full-time quality manager is not justified, other than in certain very high risk areas. In these cases a member of the management team should be appointed to operate on a part-time basis, performing the quality management function in addition to his/her other duties. To obtain the best results from a quality director/manager, he/she should be given sufficient authority to take necessary action to secure the implementation of the organization's quality policy, and must have the personality to be able to communicate the message to all employees, including staff, management and directors. Occasionally the quality director/manager may require some guidance and help on specific technical quality matters, and one of the major attributes required is the knowledge and wherewithal to acquire the necessary information and assistance.

In large organizations, then, it may be necessary to make several specific appointments or to assign details to certain managers. The following actions may be deemed to be necessary.

### Assign a TQM director, manager or co-ordinator

This person will be responsible for the planning and implementation of TQM. He or she will be chosen first for project management ability rather than detailed knowledge of quality assurance matters. Depending on the size and complexity of the organization, and its previous activities in quality management, the position may be either full or part-time, but it must report directly to the Chief Executive.

### Appoint a quality management adviser

A professional expert on quality management will be required to advise on the 'technical' aspects of planning and implementing TQM. This is a consultancy role, and may be provided from within or without the organization, full or part-time. This person needs to be a persuader, philosopher, teacher, adviser, facilitator, reporter and motivator. He or she must clearly understand the organization, its processes and interfaces, be conversant with the key functional languages used in the business, and be comfortable operating at many organizational levels. On a more general level this person must fully understand, and be an effective advocate and teacher of, TQM, be flexible and become an efficient agent of change.

## 11.5 Selection of people

To obtain the appropriate people for the organization and to carry out the tasks necessary for TQM, the phases and activities of a comprehensive selection procedure should be followed, as set out in Figure 11.3. The key processes in this procedure are represented in Figure 11.4 in which A, B and C are products of the initial conceptual phase of a selection procedure, i.e. developing a person specification. In the subsequent recruitment, screening and selection phases predictive information (D) is collected, compared for 'fit' (E) with the person specification, and decision (F) is made.

## 11.6 Councils, committees and teams

Devising and implementing total quality management for an organization take considerable time and ability. It must be given the status of a senior executive project. The creation of cost effective quality improvement is difficult, because of the need for full integration with the organization's strategy, operating philosophy and management systems. It may require an extensive review and maybe substantial revision of existing systems of management and ways of operating. Fundamental questions may have to be asked, such as 'Do the managers have the necessary authority, capability, and time to carry this through?'

Any review of existing management and operating systems will inevitably 'open many cans of worms' and uncover problems that have been successfully buried and smoothed over – perhaps for years. Authority must be given to those charged with following TQM through with actions that they consider necessary to achieve the goals. The commitment will be continually questioned and will be weakened, perhaps destroyed, by failure to delegate authoritatively.

The following steps are suggested in general terms. Clearly, different types of organization will have need to make adjustments to the detail, but the component parts are the basic requirements.

A disciplined and systematic approach to continuous improvement may be established in a quality council (Figure 11.5). The council should meet at least monthly to review strategy, implementation progress, and improvement. It should be chaired by the Chief Executive, who must attend every meeting – only death or serious illness should prevent him/her being there. Clearly, postponement may be necessary occasionally, but the council should not carry on

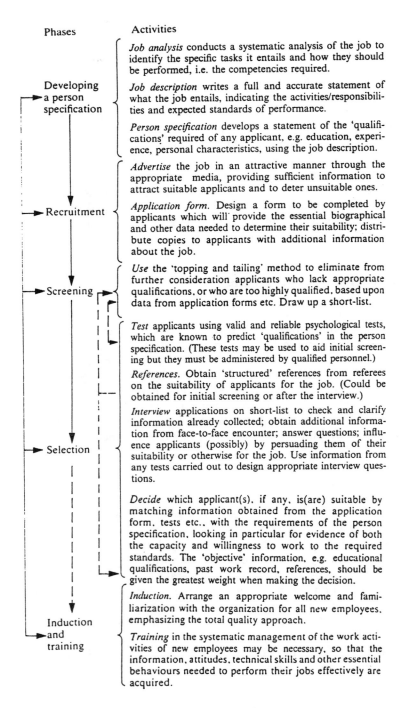

| Phases | Activities |
| --- | --- |

**Developing a person specification**

*Job analysis* conducts a systematic analysis of the job to identify the specific tasks it entails and how they should be performed, i.e. the competencies required.

*Job description* writes a full and accurate statement of what the job entails, indicating the activities/responsibilities and expected standards of performance.

*Person specification* develops a statement of the 'qualifications' required of any applicant, e.g. education, experience, personal characteristics, using the job description.

**Recruitment**

*Advertise* the job in an attractive manner through the appropriate media, providing sufficient information to attract suitable applicants and to deter unsuitable ones.

*Application form.* Design a form to be completed by applicants which will provide the essential biographical and other data needed to determine their suitability; distribute copies to applicants with additional information about the job.

**Screening**

*Use* the 'topping and tailing' method to eliminate from further consideration applicants who lack appropriate qualifications, or who are too highly qualified, based upon data from application forms etc. Draw up a short-list.

*Test* applicants using valid and reliable psychological tests, which are known to predict 'qualifications' in the person specification. (These tests may be used to aid initial screening but they must be administered by qualified personnel.)

*References.* Obtain 'structured' references from referees on the suitability of applicants for the job. (Could be obtained for initial screening or after the interview.)

**Selection**

*Interview* applications on short-list to check and clarify information already collected; obtain additional information from face-to-face encounter; answer questions; influence applicants (possibly) by persuading them of their suitability or otherwise for the job. Use information from any tests carried out to design appropriate interview questions.

*Decide* which applicant(s), if any, is(are) suitable by matching information obtained from the application form, tests etc., with the requirements of the person specification, looking in particular for evidence of both the capacity and willingness to work to the required standards. The 'objective' information, e.g. educational qualifications, past work record, references, should be given the greatest weight when making the decision.

**Induction and training**

*Induction.* Arrange an appropriate welcome and familiarization with the organization for all new employees, emphasizing the total quality approach.

*Training* in the systematic management of the work activities of new employees may be necessary, so that the information, attitudes, technical skills and other essential behaviours needed to perform their jobs effectively are acquired.

**Figure 11.3** *Phases and activities in people selection*

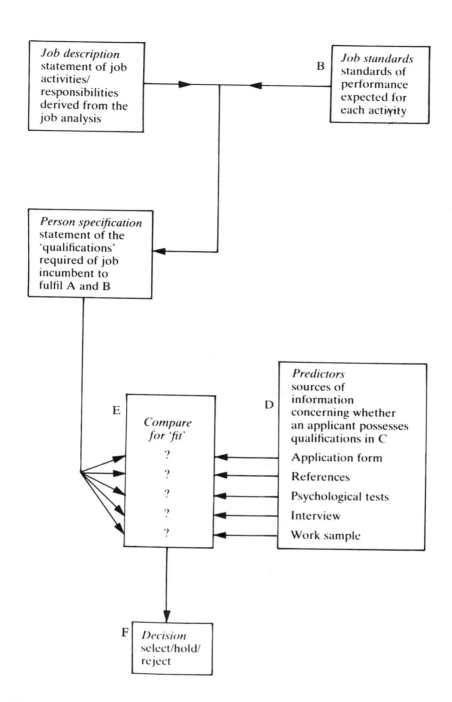

**Figure 11.4** *Key processes in the people selection procedure*

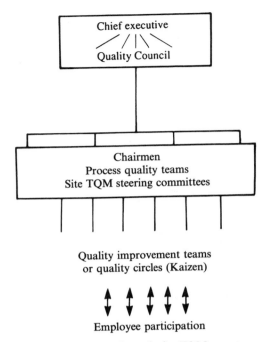

Quality improvement teams
or quality circles (Kaizen)

Employee participation

**Figure 11.5** *Employee participation through the TQM structure*

meetings without the Chief Executive present. The council members should include the top management team and the chairmen of any 'site' TQM steering committees or process quality teams, depending on the size of the organization. The objectives of the council are to:

* Provide strategic direction on TQM for the organization.
* Establish plans for TQM on each 'site'.
* Set up and review the process quality teams that will own the key or critical business processes.
* Review and revise quality plans for implementation.

The process quality teams (PQTs) and any site TQM steering committees should also meet monthly, shortly before the council meetings. Every senior manager should be a member of at least one PQT. This system provides the 'top-down' support for employee participation in process management and development, through either a quality improvement team or a quality circle programme. It also ensures that the commitment to TQM at the top is communicated effectively through the organization.

The three-tier approach of quality council, process quality teams (PQTs) and quality improvement teams (QITs) allows the first to concentrate on quality strategy, rather than become a senior problem solving group. Progress is assured if the PQT chairmen are required to present a status report at each meeting.

The process quality teams or steering committees will control the QITs and have responsibility for:

- The selection of projects for the QITs.
- Providing an outline and scope for each project to give to the QITs.
- The appointment of team members and leaders.
- Monitoring and reviewing the progress and results from each QIT project.

As the focus of this work will be the selection of projects, some attention will need to be given to the sources of nominations. Projects may be suggested by:

(a) Council members representing their own departments, process quality teams, their suppliers or their customers, internal and external.
(b) Quality improvement teams.
(c) Quality circles (if in existence).
(d) Suppliers.
(e) Customers.

The PQT members must be given the responsibility and authority to represent their part of the organization in the process. The members must also feel that they represent the team to the rest of the organization. In this way the PQT will gain knowledge and respect and be seen to have the authority to act in the best interests of the organization, with respect to their process.

## Quality improvement teams

A quality improvement team (QIT) is a group of people with the appropriate knowledge, skills, and experience who are brought together specifically by management to tackle and solve a particular problem, usually on a project basis. They are cross functional and often multi-disciplinary.

The 'task force' has long been a part of the culture of many organizations at the 'technology' and management levels. But quality improvement teams go a step further; they expand the traditional definition of 'process' to cover the entire production or operating system. This includes paperwork, communication with other units, operating procedures, and the process equipment itself. By taking this broader view, the teams can address new problems.

The actual running of quality improvement teams calls several factors into play:

- Team selection and leadership.
- Team objectives.
- Team meetings.
- Team assignments..
- Team dynamics.
- Team results and reviews.

### Team selection and leadership

The most important element of a QIT is its members. People with knowledge and experience relevant to solving the problem are clearly required; however, there should be a limit of five to ten members to keep the team small enough to be manageable but allow a good exchange of ideas. Membership should include appropriate people from groups outside the operational and technical areas directly 'responsible' for the problem, if their presence is relevant or essential. In the selection of team members it is often useful to start with just one or two people concerned directly with the problem. If they try to draw flowcharts (see Chapter 4) of the relevant processes, the requirement to include other people, in order to understand the process and complete the charts, will aid the team selection. This method will also ensure that all those who can make a significant contribution to the improvement process are represented.

The team leader has a primary responsibility for team management and maintenance, and his/her selection and training is crucial to success. The leader need not be the highest ranking person in the team, but must be concerned about accomplishing the team objectives (this is sometimes described as 'task concern') and the needs of the members (often termed 'people concern'). Weakness in either of these areas will lessen the effectiveness of the team in solving problems. Team leadership training should be directed at correcting deficiencies in these crucial aspects.

### Team objectives

At the beginning of any QIT project and at the start of every meeting the objectives should be stated as clearly as possible by the leader. This can take a simple form: 'This meeting is to continue the discussion from last Tuesday on the provision of current price data from sales-men to invoice preparation, and to generate suggestions for improve-ment in its quality'. Project and/or meeting objectives enable the team members to focus thoughts and efforts on the aims, which may need to be restated if the team becomes distracted by other issues.

*Team meetings*

An agenda should be prepared by the leader and distributed to each team member before every meeting. It should include the following information:

- Meeting place, time and how long it will be.
- A list of members (and co-opted members) expected to attend.
- Any preparatory assignments for individual members or groups.
- Any supporting material to be discussed at the meeting.

Early in a project the leader should orient the team members in terms of the approach, methods, and techniques they will use to solve the problem. This may require a review of the:

1 Systematic approach (Chapter 9).
2 Procedures and rules for using some of the basic tools, e.g. brain-storming – no judgement of initial ideas.
3 Role of the team in the continuous improvement process.
4 Authority of the team.

A team secretary should be appointed to take the minutes of meet-ings and distribute them to members as soon as possible after each meeting. The minutes should not be formal, but reflect decisions and carry a clear statement of the action plans, together with assignments of tasks. They may be handwritten initially, copied and given to team members at the end of the meeting, to be followed later by a more for-mal document that will be seen by any member of staff interested in knowing the outcome of the meeting. In this way the minutes form an important part of the communication system, supplying information to other teams or people needing to know what is going on.

*Team assignments*

It is never possible to solve problems by meetings alone. What must come out of those meetings is a series of action plans that assign specific tasks to team members. This is the responsibility of the team leader. Agreement must be reached regarding the responsibilities for individual assignments, together with the time scale, and this must be made clear in the minutes. Task assignments must be decided while the team is together and not by separate individuals in after meeting discussions.

*Team dynamics*

In any team activity the interactions between the members are vital to success. If solutions to problems are to be found, the meetings and ensuing assignments should assist and harness the creative thinking process. This is easier said than done, because many people have either not learned or been encouraged to be innovative. The team leader clearly has a role here to:

- Create a 'climate' for creativity.
- Encourage all team members to speak out and contribute their own ideas or build on others.
- Allow differing points of view and ideas to emerge.
- Remove barriers to idea generation, e.g. incorrect preconceptions, which are usually destroyed by asking 'Why?'
- Support all team members in their attempts to become creative.

In addition to the team leader's responsibilities, the members should:

(a) Prepare themselves well for meetings, by collecting appropriate data or information (*facts*) pertaining to a particular problem.
(b) Share ideas and opinions.
(c) Encourage other points of view.
(d) Listen 'openly' for alternative approaches to a problem or issue.
(e) Help the team determine the best solutions.
(f) Reserve judgement until all the arguments have been heard *and* fully understood.
(g) Accept individual responsibility for assignments and group responsibility for the efforts of the team.

Further details of teamworking are given in Chapter 12.

*Team results and reviews*

A QIT approach to problem solving functions most effectively when the results of the projects are communicated and acted upon. Regular feedback to the teams, via their leaders, will assist them to focus on project objectives, and review progress.

Reviews also help to deal with certain problems that may arise in teamwork. For example, certain members may be concerned more with their own personal objectives than those of the team. This may result in some manipulation of the problem solving process to achieve different goals, resulting in the team splitting apart through self interest. If recognized, the review can correct this effect and demand greater openness and honesty.

A different type of problem is the failure of certain members to contribute and take their share of individual and group responsibility. Allowing other people to do their work results in an uneven distribution of effort, and leads to bitterness. The review should make sure that all members have assigned and specific tasks, and perhaps lead to the documentation of duties in the minutes. A team roster may even help.

A third area of difficulty, which may be improved by reviewing progress, is the ready-fire-aim syndrome of action before analysis. This often results from team leaders being too anxious to deal with a problem. A review should allow the problem to be redefined adequately and expose the real cause(s). This will release the trap the team may be in of doing something before they really know what should be done. The review will provide the opportunity to rehearse the steps in the systematic approach:

| | |
|---|---|
| *Record* data | – all processes can and should be measured. |
| | – all measurements should be recorded. |
| *Use* data | – if data are recorded and not used they will be abused. |
| *Analyse* data systematically | – data analysis should be carried out by means of the seven basic tools (Chapter 9) |
| *Act* on the results | – recording and analysis of data without action leads to frustration. |

## Quality circles

One of the most publicized aspects of the Japanese approach to quality has been quality circles. The quality circle may be defined as a group of workers doing similar work who meet:

- Voluntarily.
- Regularly.

- In normal working time.
- Under the leadership of their 'supervisor'.
- To identify, analyse, and solve work related problems.
- To recommend solutions to management.

Where possible quality circle members should implement the solutions themselves.

The quality circle concept first originated in Japan in the early 1960s, following a postwar reconstruction period during which the Japanese placed a great deal of emphasis on improving and perfecting their quality control techniques. As a direct result of work carried out to train foremen during that period, the first quality circles were conceived, and the first three circles registered with the Japanese Union of Scientists and Engineers (JUSE) in 1962. Since that time the growth rate has been phenomenal. The concept has spread to Taiwan, the USA and Europe, and circles in many countries have become successful. Many others have failed.

It is very easy to regard quality circles as the magic ointment to be rubbed on the affected spot, and unfortunately many managers in the West have seen them as a panacea for all ills. There are no panaceas, and to place this concept into perspective, Juran, who has been an important influence in Japan's improvement in quality, has stated that quality circles represent only 5–10 per cent of the canvas of the Japanese success. The rest is concerned with understanding quality, its related costs and the organization and techniques necessary for achieving customer satisfaction.

Given the right sort of commitment by top management, introduction, and environment in which to operate, quality circles can produce the 'shop floor' motivation to achieve quality performance at that level. Circles should develop out of an understanding and knowledge of quality on the part of senior management. They must not be introduced as a desperate attempt to do something about poor quality.

*The structure of a quality circle organization*

The unique feature about quality circles is that people are asked to join and not told to do so. Consequently, it is difficult to be specific about the structure of such a concept. It is, however, possible to identify four elements in a circle organization:

- Members.
- Leaders.
- Facilitators or co-ordinators.
- Management.

*Members* form the prime element of the programme. They will have been taught the basic problem solving and quality control techniques and, hence, possess the ability to identify and solve work related problems.

*Leaders* are usually the immediate supervisors or foremen of the members. They will have been trained to lead a circle and bear the responsibility of its success. A good leader, one who develops the abilities of the circle members, will benefit directly by receiving valuable assistance in tackling nagging problems.

*Facilitators* are the managers of the quality circle programmes. They, more than anyone else, will be responsible for the success of the concept, particularly within an organization. The facilitator must co-ordinate the meetings, the training and energies of the leaders and members, and form the link between the circles and the rest of the organization. Ideally the facilitator will be an innovative industrial teacher, capable of communicating with all levels and with all departments within the organization.

*Management* support and commitment are necessary to quality circles, or, like any other concept, they will not succeed. Management must retain its prerogatives, particularly regarding acceptance or nonacceptance of recommendations from circles, but the quickest way to kill a programme is to ignore a proposal arising from it. One of the most difficult facts for management to accept, and yet one forming the cornerstone of the quality circle philosophy, is that the real 'experts' on performing a task are those who do it day after day.

*Training quality circles*

The training of circle leaders and members is the foundation of all successful programmes. The whole basis of the training operation is that the ideas must be easy to take in and be put across in a way that facilitates understanding. Simplicity must be the key word, with emphasis being given to the basic techniques. Essentially there are eight segments of training:

1 Introduction to quality circles.
2 Brainstorming.
3 Data gathering and histograms.
4 Cause and effect analysis.
5 Pareto analysis.
6 Sampling.
7 Control charts.
8 Presentation techniques.

Managers should also be exposed to some training in the part they are required to play in the quality circle philosophy. A quality circle programme can only be effective if management believes in it and is supportive and, since changes in management style may be necessary, managers' training is essential.

*Operation of quality circles*

There are no formal rules governing the size of a quality circle. Membership usually varies from three to fifteen people, with an average of seven to eight. It is worth remembering that, as the circle becomes larger than this, it becomes increasingly difficult for all members of the circle to participate.

Meetings must be held away from the work area, so that members are free from interruptions, and are mentally and physically at ease. The room should be arranged in a manner conducive to open discussion, and any situation that physically emphasizes the leader's position should be avoided.

Meeting length and frequency are variable, but new circles meet for approximately one hour once per week. Thereafter, when training is complete, many circles continue to meet weekly; others extend the interval to 2 or 3 weeks. To a large extent the nature of the problems selected will determine the interval between meetings, but this should never extend to more than 1 month, otherwise members will lose interest and the circle will cease to function.

Great care is needed to ensure that every meeting is productive, no matter how long it lasts or how frequently it is held. Any of the following activities may take place during a circle meeting:

- Training – initial or refresher.
- Problem identification.
- Problem analysis.
- Preparation and recommendation for problem solution.
- Management presentations.
- Quality circle administration.

A quality circle usually selects a project to work on through discussion within the circle. The leader then advises management of this choice and, assuming that no objections are raised, the circle proceeds with the work. Other suggestions for projects come from management, quality assurance staff, the maintenance department, various staff personnel, and other circles.

It is sometimes necessary for quality circles to contact experts in a particular field, e.g. engineers, quality experts, safety officers, maintenance personnel. This communication should be strongly encouraged, and the normal company channels should be used to invite specialists to attend meetings and offer advice. The experts may be considered to be 'consultants', the quality circle retaining responsibility for solving the particular problem. The overriding purpose of quality circles is to provide the powerful motivation of allowing people to take some part in deciding their own actions and futures.

### Kaizen teams

Kaizen is a philosophy of continuous improvement of all the employees in an organization, so that they perform their tasks a little better each day. It is a never-ending journey centred on the concept of starting anew each day with the principle that methods can always be improved. Using this approach, it is reported that Pratt and Whitney reduced reject rates on one process from 50 per cent to 4 per cent, and in 12 months eliminated overdue deliveries on a key sub-assembly.

*Kaizen Teian* is a Japanese system for generating and implementing employee ideas. Japanese suggestion schemes have helped companies to improve quality and productivity, and reduced prices to increase market share. They concentrate on participation and the rates of implementation, rather than on the 'quality' or value of the suggestions. The emphasis is on encouraging everyone to make improvements.

Kaizen Teian suggestions are usually small scale ones, in the worker's own area, and are easy and cheap to implement. Key points are that the rewards given are small, and implementation is rapid, which results in many small improvements that accumulate to massive total savings and improvements.

Throughout a total quality organization each process oriented team must develop its own conscience, and focus its efforts on quality improvement. Each needs to be given the encouragement, tools, and responsibility to achieve the requirements at the next interface. Clearly, the organizational issues discussed in this chapter will have great impact on the ease with which that is brought about.

## Chapter highlights

### People and the organizational structure

- The only point at which true responsibility for quality can lie is with the person or group actually doing the job. Separate, elite inspectors and checkers can cause abdication of this responsibility.

- The Chief Executive must take responsibility for quality. The quality function's role is the provider of systems and guidance.

## Responsibilities and performance management

- Positive quality policy objectives must be accompanied by clear allocation of responsibilities within the management structure, particularly at the levels of senior executive and first line supervision.
- Progress in quality improvement must have the full co-operation and commitment of all employees. This means their participation in process design, operation, and control.
- Managers are in control only when their subordinates can exercise self-control. The process of performance management, then, consists of clarifying responsibilities, developing performance indicators and objectives, and preparing action plans.
- It is desirable to introduce or sustain a TQM initiative without direct financial incentives. Where they do exist, the long-term full potential of TQ requires a planned withdrawal of incentives that focus on output volume only.

## Departmental purpose analysis

- DPA helps to define the real purpose of each department, with the objective of improving performance and breaking down barriers. It leads to an understanding and agreement on the key processes of each group.
- The departmental manager runs the exercise and must understand DPA. The basic steps are form DPA group; list all departmental tasks; agree five main tasks; define position and role of manager; identify task customer(s) and supplier(s), and consult, review and brainstorm improvements; prioritize; implement plan; review progress and repeat DPA.

## The quality function and the quality director or manager

- The quality function should be the organization's focal point of the integration of the business interests of customers and suppliers into the internal dynamics of the organization.
- Its role is to encourage and facilitate quality improvement; monitor and evaluate progress; promote the quality chains; plan, manage, audit and review systems; plan and provide quality training, counselling and consultancy; and give advice to management.

- In larger organizations a quality director will contribute to the prevention strategy. Smaller organizations may appoint a member of the management team to this task on a part-time basis. An external TQM adviser is usually required.

### Selection of people

- To obtain the appropriate people for the organization and to carry out the tasks necessary for TQM, a comprehensive selection procedure is needed.
- The procedure should include the phase of development of a person specification; screening and selection, through the collection of predictive information; comparison for 'fit'; and decision.

### Councils, committees and teams

- In devising and implementing TQM for an organization, it may be useful to ask first if the managers have the necessary authority, capability and time to carry it through.
- A disciplined and systematic approach to continuous improvement may be established in a quality council (QC), whose members are the senior management team.
- Reporting to the QC are the process quality teams (PQTs) or any site steering committees, which in turn control the quality improvement teams (QITs) and quality circles.
- A QIT is a group brought together by management to tackle a particular problem on a project basis. The running of QITs includes several team factors: selection and leadership, objectives, meetings, assignments, dynamics, results and reviews.
- A quality circle is a group of people who do similar work meeting voluntarily, regularly, in normal working time, to identify, analyse and solve work related problems, under the leadership of their supervisor. They make recommendations to management.
- Kaizen is a philosophy of small step continuous improvement, by all employees. In Kaizen teams the suggestions and rewards are small but the implementation is rapid.

# 12 Culture change through teamwork for quality

## 12.1 The need for teamwork

The complexity of most of the processes that are operated in industry, commerce and the services places them beyond the control of any one individual. The only efficient way to tackle process improvement or problems is through the use of some form of teamwork. The use of the team approach to problem solving has many advantages over allowing individuals to work separately:

* A greater variety of complex problems may be tackled – those beyond the capability of any one individual or even one department – by the pooling of expertise and resources.
* Problems are exposed to a greater diversity of knowledge, skill, experience, and are solved more efficiently.
* The approach is more satisfying to team members, and boosts morale and ownership through participation in problem solving and decision making.
* Problems that cross departmental or functional boundaries can be dealt with more easily, and the potential/actual conflicts are more likely to be identified and solved.
* The recommendations are more likely to be implemented than individual suggestions, as the quality of decision making in *good teams*, is high.

Most of these factors rely on the premise that people are willing to support any effort in which they have taken part or helped to develop.

When properly managed and developed, teams improve the process of problem solving, producing results quickly and economically. Teamwork throughout any organization is an essential component of the implementation of TQM, for it builds trust, improves communications and develops interdependence. Much of what has been taught previously in management has led to a culture in the West of indepen-

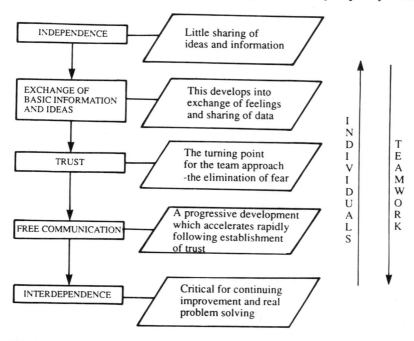

**Figure 12.1** *Independence to interdependence through teamwork*

dence, with little sharing of ideas and information. Knowledge is very much like organic manure – if it is spread around it will fertilize and encourage growth, if it is kept closed in, it will eventually fester and rot.

Teamwork devoted to quality improvement changes the independence to interdependence through improved communications, trust and the free exchange of ideas, knowledge, data and information (Figure 12.1). The use of the face-to-face interaction method of communication, with a common goal, develops over time the sense of dependence on each other. This forms a key part of any quality improvement process, and provides a methodology for employee recognition and participation, through active encouragement in group activities.

Teamwork provides an environment in which people can grow and use all the resources effectively and efficiently to make continuous improvements. As individuals grow, the organization grows. It is worth pointing out, however, that employees will not be motivated towards continual improvement in the absence of:

- Commitment to quality from top management.
- The organizational quality 'climate'.
- A mechanism for enabling individual contributions to be effective.

All these are focused essentially at enabling people to feel, accept, and discharge responsibility. More than one organization has made this part of their quality strategy – to 'empower people to act'. If one hears from employees comments comments such as 'We know this is not the best way to do this job, but if that is the way management want us to do it, that is the way we will do it', then it is clear that the expertise existing at the point of operation has not been harnessed and the people do not feel responsible for the outcome of their actions. Responsibility and accountability foster pride, job satisfaction, and better work.

Empowerment to act is very easy to express conceptually, but it requires real effort and commitment on the part of all managers and supervisors to put into practice. Recognition that only partially successful but good ideas or attempts are to be applauded and not criticized is a good way to start. Encouragement of ideas and suggestions from the workforce, particularly through their part in team or group activities, requires investment. The rewards are total commitment, both inside the organization and outside through the supplier and customer chains.

Teamwork for quality improvement has several components. It is driven by a strategy, needs a structure, and must be implemented thoughtfully and effectively. The strategy that drives the quality improvement teams at the various levels was outlined in Chapter 1, and will be dealt with in more detail in the final chapter of this book, but in essence it comprises:

- The mission of the organization.
- The critical success factors.
- The key processes.

The structure of having the top management team in a quality council, and the key processes being owned by process quality teams, which manage quality improvement projects through QITs and quality circles was detailed in Chapter 11 on the organizational requirements for quality. The remainder of this chapter will concentrate on some theories of teamwork and its implementation.

## 12.2 Some theories and models for teamwork: action-centred leadership

Over the years there has been much academic work on the psychology of teams and on the leadership of teams. Three points on which all authors are in agreement are that teams develop a personality and culture of their own, respond to leadership, and are motivated according to criteria usually applied to individuals.

Key figures in the field of human relations, like Douglas McGregor, Abraham Maslow and Fred Hertzberg, all changed their opinions on group dynamics over time as they came to realize that groups are not the democratic entity that everyone would like them to be, but respond to individual, strong, well directed leadership, both from without and within the group, just like individuals. Much of their original work goes back to the 1950s and 1960s, but it is necessary to look again at these basic ideas, which are often neglected in the management of teams.

### McGregor

Initial work by Mayo – the famous Hawthorne Experiments[1] – and McGregor with 'T-Groups' was largely replaced by later work. McGregor, when he eventually became a manager himself (college president), formed the hypothesis that when a manager carried out his/her responsibilities, (s)he based actions on a series of assumptions or theories, whether these were implicit or explicit. While there will clearly be many individual variations, McGregor maintained that there are basically two theories about human nature used by managers in general. These he labelled Theory X and Theory Y, the major points of which are:

*McGregor's theory X*

1 The average human being has an inherent dislike of work and will avoid it if possible.
2 Because of this human characteristic of dislike of work, most people must be forced, bribed, coerced, controlled, directed, or threatened with punishment to get them to put forth adequate effort toward the achievement of organizational objectives.
3 The average human being prefers to be directed, wishes to avoid responsibility, and has relatively little ambition.
4 Human beings are motivated mainly by money, or by anxiety about their security.

5 Most humans have little creativity, except when it comes to finding ways around management rules.

*McGregor's theory Y*

1 The expenditure of physical and mental effort in work is as natural as play or rest, and is necessary to humans' psychological growth.
2 External control and the threat of punishment are not the only means for bringing about effort toward organizational objectives. Humans will exercise self-direction and self-control in the service of objectives to which they are committed.
3 Commitment to objectives is a function of the rewards associated with their achievement, and under the right conditions humans will enjoy their work.
4 The average human being learns, under the right conditions, not only to accept but to seek responsibility, and will direct him/herself towards an accepted target.
5 The capacity to exercise a relatively high degree of imagination, ingenuity and creativity in the solution of organizational problems is widely, not narrowly, distributed in the population. (But this capacity may be grossly under-used in most job situations.)
6 The discipline a human exerts on him/herself is more effective and can be more severe than any imposed on him/her because, under the right conditions, humans are motivated by a desire to realize their own potential.

**Maslow**

Abraham Maslow hypothesized that human beings have a hierarchy of needs that tend to have to be satisfied in the given order, and that, as a lower order of needs is satisfied at least partially, the aims and drives in a particular individual will shift to those appropriate to the higher order needs (Figure 12.2). In summary the needs are:

1 *Physiological* – these are the needs for food, drink, shelter, warmth, sleep, etc.
2 *Safety* – the need to belong and to have a place in the family, the work group, other groups or all of these; to provide security and protection from danger.
3 *Social* – the need to have affectionate relationships with people; to avoid feeling lonely, rejected, estranged.
4 *Esteem* – the need for a stable, firmly based, usually high evaluation of oneself, self-respect, self-esteem and esteem of others.

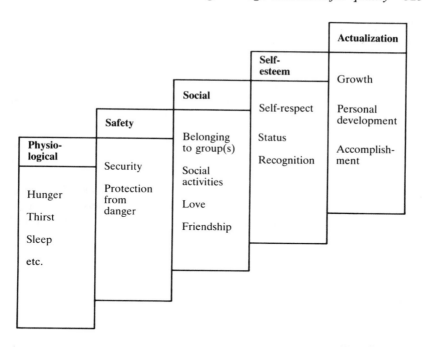

**Figure 12.2** *Maslow's theories of motivation – the hierarchy of individual needs*

The esteem needs Maslow classified into two subsidiary sets.

(a) The desire for strength, achievement, adequate mastery, competence, in the face of the world, and for independence and freedom.
(b) The desire for reputation, prestige (esteem of others) status, fame, dominance, recognition, dignity, appreciation. The thwarting of these needs causes feelings of inferiority, weakness and helplessness, leading to basic discouragement or compensatory neurotic trends.

5 *Self-actualization* – 'What a man can be he must be', the desire for self-fulfilment, the tendency to actualize what he is potentially. Maslow seemed to differentiate these needs from the other four by suggesting that, when self-actualizing, people are propelled by growth motivation rather than by a deficiency motivation.

The important thing to realize about Maslow's hierarchy of needs, of course, is that a change in circumstances, e.g. threat of redundancy, can cause an individual to slip back down the scale rapidly from self-realization to the basic physiological needs. Indeed the model should be seen as a dynamic one, in which individuals move up and down the hierarchy, depending on circumstances. It is worth pointing out that the satisfied lower order needs may well become underestimated by the individuals and the team. In addition, subsequent theorists have recognized that hierarchical ordering of human needs greatly underestimates the tremendous range and variability of individual needs. Maslow did, however, relate his hypothesis to other theories and the development of people in general.

### Hertzberg

Professor Hertzberg carried out investigations into the factors affecting job attitudes. From an analysis of his findings, he hypothesized that the things that lead to *satisfaction or dissatisfaction* are not equal and opposite. He labelled the satisfying factors *motivators*, and the dissatisfying factors *hygiene*.

The *hygiene* needs may be summarized as:

- How people are treated at work.
- Salary.
- Supervision.
- Working conditions.

The hygiene factors merely keep people from being unhappy, they do not motivate people.

The *motivators* are:

- Achievement.
- Recognition for achievement.
- Meaningful, interesting work.
- Increased responsibility.
- Growth and advancement at work.

To be motivated people need ability, which may require some training, and the opportunity to use that ability. According to Hertzberg, job enrichment, feedback, self-checking, and direct communication all aid the motivators.

Hertzberg concluded that when managers say *mea culpa* – 'It's my fault' – owning up to not being such capable managers, who make mistakes once in a while – then a new understanding and culture will develop in the organization. 'The biggest problem in industry is creating the opportunity for people to use their abilities,' said Hertzberg. His major conclusions were that:

1 All jobs should be a learning experience – a growth experience that is inherent in the job.
2 What makes people happy and motivated at work, is what they do.
3 What makes people unhappy is the situation in which they do it.

## Adair

During the 1960s John Adair was senior lecturer in Military History and the Leadership Training Advisor at the Military Academy, Sandhurst. Later, when assistant director of the Industrial Society, he developed what he called the action-centred leadership model, based on his experiences at Sandhurst, where he had the responsibility to ensure that results in the cadet training did not fall below a certain standard. He had observed that some instructors frequently achieved well above average results, owing to their own natural ability with groups and their enthusiasm. He developed this further into a team model, which is the basis of the approach of the author and his colleagues to this subject.

In developing his model for teamwork and leadership John Adair related the three main approaches of McGregor, Maslow and Hertzberg. He brought out clearly that for any group or team, big or small, to respond to leadership, they need a clearly defined *task*, and the response and achievement of that task are interrelated to the needs of the *team* and the separate needs of the *individual members* of the team (Figure 12.3).

The value of the overlapping circles is that it emphasizes the unity of leadership and the interdependence and multifunctional reaction to single decisions affecting any of the three areas.

*Leadership tasks*

Drawing upon the discipline of social psychology, John Adair developed and applied to training the functional view of leadership. The essence of this he distilled into the three interrelated but distinctive requirements of a leader. These are to define and achieve the job or task, to build up and co-ordinate a team to do this, and to develop and satisfy the individuals within the team (Figure 12.4):

1 *Task needs.* The difference between a team and a random crowd is that a team has some common purpose, goal or objective, e.g. a football team. If a work team does not achieve the required results or meaningful results, it will become frustrated. Organizations have to make a profit, to provide a service, or even to survive. So anyone

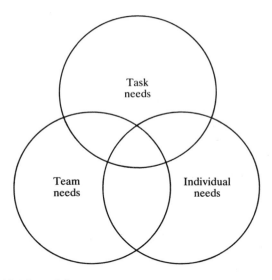

**Figure 12.3** *Adair's model*

who manages others has to achieve results; in production, marketing, selling or whatever. Achieving objectives is a major criterion of success.

2　*Team needs.* To achieve these objectives, the group needs to be held together. People need to be working in a co-ordinated fashion in the same direction. Teamwork will ensure that the team's contribution is greater than the sum of its parts. Conflict within the team must be used effectively; arguments can lead to ideas or to tension and lack of co-operation.

3　*Individual needs.* Within working groups, individuals also have their own set of needs. They need to know what their responsibilities are, how they will be needed, how well they are performing. They need an opportunity to show their potential, take on responsibility and receive recognition for good work.

The task, team and individual functions for the leader are as follows:

(a) *Task functions*　　Defining the task.
　　　　　　　　　　　Making a plan.
　　　　　　　　　　　Allocating work and resources.
　　　　　　　　　　　Controlling quality and tempo of work.
　　　　　　　　　　　Checking performance against the plan.
　　　　　　　　　　　Adjusting the plan.

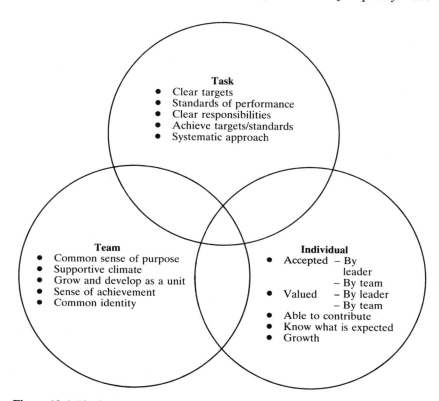

**Figure 12.4** *The leadership needs*

(b) *Team functions*  Setting standards.
Maintaining discipline.
Building team spirit.
Encouraging, motivating, giving a sense
of purpose.
Appointing sub-leaders.
Ensuring communication within the group.
Training the group.

(c) *Individual functions* Attending to personal problems.
Praising individuals.
Giving status.
Recognizing and using individual abilities.
Training the individual.

The team leader's or facilitator's task is to concentrate on the small central area where all three circles overlap. In a business that is introducing TQM this is the 'action to change' area, where the leaders are attempting to manage the change from *business as usual*, through total quality management, to *TQM equals business as usual*, using the cross-functional quality improvement teams at the strategic interface.

In the action area the facilitator's or leader's task is similar to the task outlined by John Adair. It is to try to satisfy all three areas of need by achieving the task, building the team, and satisfying individual needs. If a leader concentrates on the task, e.g. in going all out for production schedules, while neglecting the training, encouragement and motivation of the team and individuals, (s)he may do very well in the short term. Eventually, however, the team members will give less effort than they are capable of. Similarly, a leader who concentrates only on creating team spirit, while neglecting the task and the individuals, will not receive maximum contribution from the people. They may enjoy working in the team but they will lack the real sense of achievement that comes from accomplishing a task to the utmost of the collective ability.

So the leader/facilitator must try to achieve a balance by acting in all three areas of overlapping need. It is always wise to work out a list of required functions within the context of any given situation, based on a general agreement on the essentials. Here is Adair's original Sandhurst list, on which one's own adaptation may be based:

- *Planning*, e.g. seeking all available information.
  Defining group task, purpose or goal.
  Making a workable plan (in right decision-making framework).
- *Initiating*, e.g. briefing group on the aims and the plan.
  Explaining why aim or plan is necessary.
  Allocating tasks to group members.
  Setting group standards.
- *Controlling*, e.g. maintaining group standards.
  Influencing tempo.
  Ensuring all actions are taken towards objectives.
  Keeping discussion relevant.
  Prodding group to action/decision.
- *Supporting*, e.g. expressing acceptance of persons and their contribution.
  Encouraging group/individuals.
  Disciplining group/individuals.
  Creating team spirit.
  Relieving tension with humour.
  Reconciling disagreements or getting others to explore them.

- *Informing*, e.g. clarifying task and plan.
  Giving new information to the group,
  i.e. keeping them 'in the picture'.
  Receiving information from group.
  Summarizing suggestions and ideas coherently.
- *Evaluating*, e.g. checking feasibility of an ideal.
  Testing the consequences of a proposed solution.
  Evaluating group performance.
  Helping the group to evaluate its own performance against standards.

A checklist (Table 12.1) should assist the team leader to measure the progress against the required functions of fulfilling the task, maintaining the team and growing the people.

**Team processes**

The team process is like any other process; it has inputs and outputs. High-performing teams have three main attributes: high task fulfilment, high team maintenance, and low self-orientation. These may be subdivided as follows:

*TASK FULFILMENT*

| | |
|---|---|
| INITIATING | Ideas, solutions, defining problems, suggesting procedures, proposing tasks or goals. |
| INFORMATION-SEEKING | Facts, opinions, suggestions, ideas. |
| INFORMATION-GIVING | Facts, opinions, suggestions, ideas. |
| CLARIFYING | Analysing implications of information or ideas, interpreting, defining terms, indicating alternatives. |
| SUMMARIZING | Reviewing, drawing together ideas/information. |
| TESTING FOR CONSENSUS | Checking readiness for decision, checking agreements. |

*TEAM MAINTENANCE*

| | |
|---|---|
| ENCOURAGING | Supporting contributions, stimulating contributions, being friendly and responsive. |
| SETTING STANDARDS | Suggesting standards for group working, reviewing against these, evaluating group success. |

**Table 12.1** *Task – team – individual checklist*

| | |
|---|---|
| *Task* | 1 Are the targets clearly set out? |
| | 2 Are there clear standards of performance? |
| | 3 Are available resources defined? |
| | 4 Are responsibilities clear? |
| | 5 Are resources fully utilized? |
| | 6 Are targets/standards being defined? |
| | 7 Is a systematic approach being used? |
| | |
| *Team* | 1 Is there a common sense of purpose? |
| | 2 Is there a supportive climate? |
| | 3 Is the unit growing and developing? |
| | 4 Is there a sense of corporate achievement? |
| | 5 Is there a common identity? |
| | 6 Does the team know and respond to the leader's vision? |
| | |
| *Individual* | 1 Is each individual accepted by the leader/team? |
| | 2 Is each individual made part of the team by leader/team? |
| | 3 Is each individual able to contribute? |
| | 4 Does each individual know what is expected in relation to the task and by the team? |
| | 5 Does each individual feel a part of the team? |
| | 6 Does each individual feel valued by the team? |
| | 7 Is there evidence of individual growth? |

| | |
|---|---|
| EXPRESSING GROUP FEELINGS | Observing, understanding and expressing group emotions, reducing tension, mediating, recognizing conflicts and encouraging exploration of differences. |
| COMPROMISING | Giving weight to others' views, commitment to best solution. |
| GATEKEEPING | Keeping communications open, facilitating participation, suggesting procedures for sharing discussion. |

### SELF-ORIENTATION

| | |
|---|---|
| BLOCKING | Interposing a difficulty without alternative or reasoning |
| AGGRESSIVENESS | Attacking, over-painting the picture to stir up feelings, exaggerating. |
| DOMINATING | Asserting authority or superiority in manipulating group, refusing to budge. |
| FORMING CLIQUES | Forming sub-groups for protection or support. |
| SPECIAL PLEADING | Speaking for special interests as a cover for personal interest. |
| SEEKING SYMPATHY | Drawing attention, attempting to gain sympathy. |
| WITHDRAWING | Opting out or getting behind stronger members. |
| WASTING TIME | Various diversions for self-orientated reasons. |
| NOT LISTENING | Ignoring suggestions or closing off hearing when others are speaking. |

These may be used in various ways to construct a 'team behaviour checklist', which may be used by team facilitators or observers to rate the team performance. A second review document (see Table 12.2) may be used by individuals to rate the various aspects of a team meeting.

**Situational leadership**

In dealing with the task, the team, and with any individual in the team, a style of leadership appropriate to the situation must be adopted. The teams and the individuals within them will, to some

**Table 12.2** *Team meeting review*

| Good points | | Bad points |
|---|---|---|

|  | 10      5      0 |  |
|---|---|---|
| 1 Goal clear and agreed | ⊔⊔⊔⊔⊔⊔⊔⊔⊔⊔ | Goal unclear |
| 2 Previous agreements complete | ⊔⊔⊔⊔⊔⊔⊔⊔⊔⊔ | Partially or not at all |
| 3 We listen to each other | ⊔⊔⊔⊔⊔⊔⊔⊔⊔⊔ | No awareness of listening |
| 4 Right people present | ⊔⊔⊔⊔⊔⊔⊔⊔⊔⊔ | Team not correctly composed |
| 5 Leadership needs creatively met | ⊔⊔⊔⊔⊔⊔⊔⊔⊔⊔ | Drifting or dominating |
| 6 Open and trusting atmosphere | ⊔⊔⊔⊔⊔⊔⊔⊔⊔⊔ | Distrust and defensiveness |
| 7 Time used efficiently | ⊔⊔⊔⊔⊔⊔⊔⊔⊔⊔ | Time wasted |
| 8 Systematic tools used | ⊔⊔⊔⊔⊔⊔⊔⊔⊔⊔ | Lack of systematic approach |
| 9 Agreements reached (what/who/when) and documented | ⊔⊔⊔⊔⊔⊔⊔⊔⊔⊔ | Verbal agreements or none |
| 10 Consensus decisions | ⊔⊔⊔⊔⊔⊔⊔⊔⊔⊔ | Authoritarian or other |
| 11 I was able to express my opinion | ⊔⊔⊔⊔⊔⊔⊔⊔⊔⊔ | No opportunity |
| 12 Opinions could be questioned | ⊔⊔⊔⊔⊔⊔⊔⊔⊔⊔ | Opinions untouchable |
| 13 Opinions distinguished from facts | ⊔⊔⊔⊔⊔⊔⊔⊔⊔⊔ | Mixed and not aware of it |
| 14 Everyone participating | ⊔⊔⊔⊔⊔⊔⊔⊔⊔⊔ | Some not participating |
| 15 Challenging, rewarding, committed atmosphere | ⊔⊔⊔⊔⊔⊔⊔⊔⊔⊔ | Flat and lifeless |

| UNACCEPTABLE | 0 |
|---|---|
| MUST BE IMPROVED | 1, 2, 3 |
| FAIR | 4, 5, 6 |
| GOOD | 7, 8, 9 |
| EXCELLENT | 10 |

extent, start 'cold', but they will develop and grow in both strength and experience. The interface with the leader must also change with the change in the team, according to the Tannenbaum and Schmidt model (Figure 12.5).[2]

Initially a very directive approach may be appropriate, giving clear instructions to meet agreed goals. Gradually, as the teams become more experienced and have some success, the facilitating team leader will move through coaching and support to less directing and eventually a less supporting and less directive approach – as the more interdependent style permeates the whole organization.

This equates to the modified Blanchard model[2] in Figure 12.6, where directive behaviour moves from high to low as people develop and are more easily empowered. When this is coupled with the appropriate level of supportive behaviour, a directing style of leadership can move through coaching and supporting to a delegating style. It must be

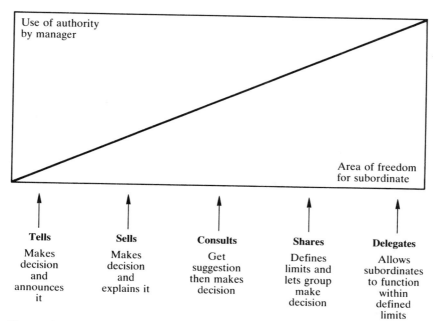

**Figure 12.5** *Continuum of leadership behaviour*

stressed, however, that effective delegation is only possible with developed 'followers', who can be fully empowered.

One of the great mistakes in recent years has been the expectation by management that teams can be put together with virtually no training or development (S 1 in Figure 12.6) and that they will perform as a mature team (S4). The Blanchard model emphasizes that there is no quick and easy 'tunnel' from S1 to S4. The only route is the laborious climb through S2 and S3.

## 12.3   Stages of team development

Original work by Tuckman[2] suggested that when teams are put together, there are four main stages of team development, the so-called forming (awareness), storming (conflict), norming (co-operation), and performing (productivity). The characteristics of each stage and some key aspects to look out for in the early stages are given below:

(High)                    The four leadership styles

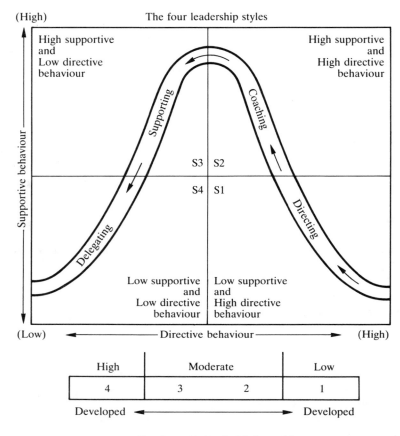

**Figure 12.6** *Situational leadership – progressive empowerment through TQM*

**Forming – awareness**

Characteristics:

- Feelings, weaknesses and mistakes are covered up.
- People conform to established lines.
- Little care is shown for others' values and views.
- There is no shared understanding of what needs to be done.

Watch out for:

- Increasing bureaucracy and paperwork.
- People confining themselves to defined jobs.
- The 'boss' is ruling with a firm hand.

### Storming – conflict

Characteristics:

- More risky, personal issues are opened up.
- The team becomes more inward-looking.
- There is more concern for the values, views and problems of others in the team.

Watch out for:

- the team becomes more open, but lacks the capacity to act in a unified, economic, and effective way.

### Norming – co-operation

Characteristics:

- Confidence and trust to look at how the team is operating.
- A more systematic and open approach, leading to a clearer and more methodical way of working.
- Greater valuing of people for their differences.
- Clarification of purpose and establishing of objectives.
- Systematic collection of information.
- Considering all options.
- Preparing detailed plans.
- Reviewing progress to make improvements.

### Performing – productivity

Characteristics:

- Flexibility.
- Leadership decided by situations, not protocol.
- Everyone's energies utilized.
- Basic principles and social aspects of the organization's decisions considered.

The team stages, the task outcomes, and the relationship outcomes are shown together in Figure 12.7. This model, which has been modified from Kormonski and Mozenter,[2] may be used as a framework for the assessment of team performance. The issues to look for are:

1  How is leadership exercised in the team?
2  How is decision making accomplished?
3  How are team resources utilized?
4  How are new members integrated into the team?

Teams which go through these stages successfully should become effective teams and display the following attributes.

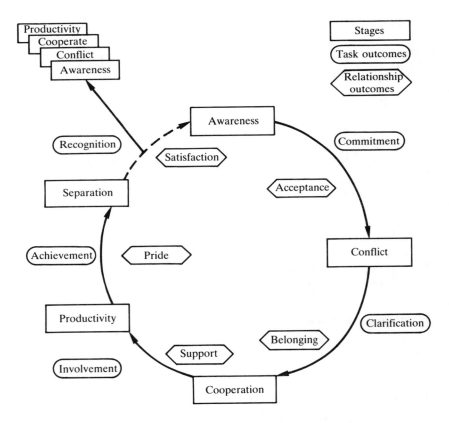

**Figure 12.7** *Team stages and outcomes. (Derived from Kormanski and Mozenter, 1987)*[2]

## Attributes of successful teams

*Clear objectives and agreed goals*

No group of people can be effective unless they know what they want to achieve, but it is more than knowing what the objectives are. People are only likely to be committed to them if they can identify with and have ownership of them – in other words, objectives and goals are agreed by team members.

Often this agreement is difficult to achieve but experience shows that it is an essential prerequisite for the effective group.

*Openness and confrontation*

If a team is to be effective, then the members of it need to be able to state their views, their differences of opinion, interests and problems, without fear of ridicule or retaliation. No teams work effectively if there is a cutthroat atmosphere, where members become less willing or able to express themselves openly; then much energy, effort and creativity are lost.

*Support and trust*

Support naturally implies trust among team members. Where individual group members do not feel they have to protect their territory or job, and feel able to talk straight to other members, about both 'nice' and 'nasty' things, then there is an opportunity for trust to be shown. Based on this trust, people can talk freely about their fears and problems and receive from others help they need to be more effective.

*Co-operation and conflict*

When there is an atmosphere of trust, members are more ready to participate and are committed. Information is shared rather than hidden. Individuals listen to the ideas of others and build on them. People find ways of being more helpful to each other and the group generally. Co-operation causes high morale – individuals accept each other's strengths and weaknesses and contribute from their pool of knowledge of skill. All abilities, knowledge and experience are fully utilized by the group; individuals have no inhibitions about using other people's abilities to help solve their problems, which are shared.

Allied to this, conflicts are seen as a necessary and useful part of organizational life. The effective team works through issues of conflict and uses the results to help achieve objectives. Conflict prevents teams from becoming complacent and lazy, and often generates new ideas.

### Good decision making

As mentioned earlier, objectives need to be clearly and completely understood by all members before good decision making can begin. In making decisions effective, teams develop the ability to collect information quickly then discuss the alternatives openly. They become committed to their decisions and ensure quick action.

### Appropriate leadership

Effective teams have a leader whose responsibility it is to achieve results through the efforts of a number of people. Power and authority can be applied in many ways, and team members often differ on the style of leadership they prefer. Collectively, teams may come to different views of leadership but, whatever their view, the effective team usually sorts through the alternatives in an open and honest way.

### Review of the team processes

Effective teams understand not only the group's character and its role in the organization, but how it makes decisions, deals with conflicts, etc. The team process allows the team to learn from experience and consciously to improve teamwork. There are numerous ways of looking at team processes – use of an observer, by a team member giving feedback, or by the whole group discussing members' performance.

### Sound inter-group relationships

No human being or group is an island; they need the help of others. An organization will not achieve maximum benefit from a collection of quality improvement teams that are effective within themselves but fight among each other.

### Individual development opportunities

Effective teams seek to pool the skills of individuals, and it necessarily follows that they pay attention to development of individual skills and try to provide opportunities for individuals to grow and learn, and of course have FUN.

Once again, these ideas are not new but are very applicable and useful in the management of teams for quality improvements, just as Newton's theories on gravity still apply!

## 12.4 Team roles and personality types

No one person has a monopoly of 'good' characteristics. Attempts to list the qualities of the ideal manager, for example, demonstrate why that paragon cannot exist. This is because many of the qualities are mutually exclusive, for example:

| | | |
|---|---|---|
| Highly intelligent | *v* | Not *too* clever |
| Forceful and dominant | *v* | Sensitive to people's feelings |
| Dynamic | *v* | Patient |
| Fluent communicator | *v* | Good listener |
| Decisive | *v* | Reflective |

Although no individual can possess all these and more desirable qualities, a team often does.

The overwhelming majority of behavioural research has been concerned with the individual. Since the early 1980s, however, some very valuable work has at least been done on teams, including that of Dr Meredith Belbin. Through observation over many years, both in industry and in the world of management training, Belbin identified a set of eight 'roles' which, if all present in a team, give that team the best possible chance of success. Indeed the eight roles are the only ones available in a team.

A preponderance of a few of these roles and the absence of some within the team are a pretty good guarantee of failure, whatever the intelligence, motivation, etc., of the individuals concerned.

Although the roles have misleading names, they are, together with their characteristics, behaviours, and team roles, the following:

*CO-ORDINATOR* (formerly Chairman)

*Characteristics*    Stable, dominant, extrovert, at least normally intelligent but not brilliant. Has 'character'. Is not original.

*Behaviours*    Preoccupied with objectives. Exerts personal authority and self-discipline. Is dominant, but not domineering. Has an instinct for trusting people. Through seeing people's strengths and weaknesses is able to focus people on what they do best. Communicates (including listening) well.

*Team roles*   Clarifies group objectives and sets its agenda. Establishes priorities and selects problems for consideration, but does not dominate the discussion. Tends to ask questions rather than assert or propose. Listens, sums up, and articulates. Is decisive – but lets everyone have their say.

## SHAPER

*Characteristics*   Anxious, dominant, extrovert, outgoing and emotional, impulsive and impatient, easily frustrated. The most prone to paranoia of the whole team. Wants action, and wants it now, Personally competitive and intolerant of woolliness, vagueness and muddled thinking.

*Behaviours*   Quick to challenge, and quick to respond to challenge. Often has rows, but does not harbour grudges. Exudes self-confidence, but only results can give reassurance.

*Team roles*   To give 'shape' to the application of the team effort, often supplying a heavy personal input. Looks for a pattern in discussion and practical considerations as regards single feasible project. Can 'steamroller' the team, but gets results.

## PLANT

*Characteristics*   Dominant, very high IQ, introvert. Can be prickly. Very original and creative thinker, the vital spark of creativity in a team. Thrusting and uninhibited, radical thinking.

*Behaviours*   Has brilliant ideas, but can cause offence if criticized. May sulk if ideas are dissected or rejected. Needs to be handled carefully and even flattered to give his/her best. Very concerned with major issues, and may miss out on details, making careless mistakes.

*Team roles*   The source of original ideas, suggestions, and proposals. Others have ideas, but the plant's are original and radical. Is the one who is most likely to start searching for completely new answers if the team gets bogged down.

## MONITOR – EVALUATOR

*Characteristics*   High IQ, stable, introvert. A bit of a cold fish. Serious and not very exciting. Not noted for enthusiasm and euphoria, therefore free of ego-involvement. Highly objective mind. Not tactful or ambitious but fair and open to change. Judgement is rarely wrong.

*Behaviours*     Objective but unequivocal critic. Slow to make up his mind, and does not like to be rushed. Skilled at assimilating and interpreting complex written material, the ME can also analyse problems and judge and assess the contributions of others. Sometimes tactless and disparaging, and has no sense of timing or delivery in discussion. Solid and dependable, but lacking in jollity and warmth. Can compete, often with co-ordinator or plant.

*Team roles*     Contributions lie in measured and dispassionate analysis and an ability, through objectivity, to stop the team from committing itself to a misguided task.

## IMPLEMENTOR (formerly Company Worker)

*Characteristics*     Stable and controlled. Strength of character and a disciplined approach. Needs stability and stable structures. Efficient, systematic and methodical. High sincerity, integrity and trust.

*Behaviours*     Not easily deflated or discouraged but sudden changes of plan are likely to upset the implementation. Always tries to build stable structures. A little inflexible and intolerant of imprecise ideas.

*Team roles*     Turns decisions and strategies into defined and manageable tasks. Sorts out objectives and pursues them logically. Willing to trim and adapt personal schedules to fit into agreed plans and systems. If you don't know what is being decided or what you are supposed to be doing, go to the implementor to find out.

## RESOURCE INVESTIGATOR

*Characteristics*     Stable, dominant, extrovert, relaxed, sociable and gregarious. Interest easily aroused. Positive and enthusiastic, quick to see the relevance of new ideas, although rarely initiates them.

*Behaviours*     Makes friends easily, having masses of outside contacts. Loves to explore new possibilities in the wide world outside. When not in contact with others, can easily become bored, demoralized and ineffective. Enthusiasms are sometimes short-lived.

*Team roles*    The one that goes outside the group and brings ideas, information and developments back to it. The team's salesperson, diplomat, liaison officer and explorer. Encourages innovation in others, improvises and is active under pressure. Can over-relax when pressure eases, or waste time on interesting irrelevancies.

## TEAMWORKER

*Characteristics*    Stable, extrovert, low in dominance. The most sensitive in the team. Aware of individuals' needs and worries, and perceptive to emotional undercurrents in the group. Sympathetic, understanding and loyal. Uncompetitive.

*Behaviours*    Builds on the ideas of others, a good and willing listener and communicator, encouraging others to do likewise. A promoter of unity and harmony, counterbalancing the discord of others. Dislikes personal confrontation, avoiding it and 'cooling down' others.

*Team roles*    A force operating against division and disruption in the team. Likeable, popular and unassertive, the 'cement' of the team, loyal to the team as a unit. Although the TW's value may not be immediately visible, its absence is very noticeable in times of stress and pressure.

## FINISHER

*Characteristics*    Anxious, introvert. Worries about what might go wrong. Maintains a sense of urgency. Self-control and strength of character.

*Behaviours*    Compulsive to meet deadlines and fulfil schedules. Never at ease until every detail has been personally checked, everything has been done and nothing overlooked.

*Team roles*    Not an assertive member of the team, but maintains a permanent sense of urgency. Can be intolerant of more casual team members. The finisher can annoy and depress, get bogged down in detail, but the relentless follow-through is a great asset.

A few additional general points are worth making about team roles:

- The term 'plant' is used because this type, if 'planted' in a bogged-down group, will get it going again.
- All roles have value, and are missed when not in a team. There are no 'stars' or 'extras'.
- In small teams people can and do assume more than one role.
- The roles divide generally into outward- and inward-looking groups:

| *Outward-looking* | *Inward-looking* |
|---|---|
| Co-ordinator | Implementor |
| Plant | Monitor–evaluator |
| Resource investigator | Team worker |
| Shaper | Finisher |

- The team role for an individual is determined by the completion and analysis of Belbin's self-administered questionnaire.

**Using team roles**

Eight people are not required for a team, but people who are aware and capable of carrying out the roles should be present. A team will not perform so effectively if there is not a good match between the attributes of team members and their responsibilities, e.g., if the co-ordinator is actually a shaper.

Most people play different roles to suit different situations. The natural or *main* role for an individual may be a shaper, but if there is already a strong shaper in the group, it may be advisable for him/her to develop a *secondary* role.

Some roles represent *active characteristics*, e.g. the shaper 'makes things happen' and the implementor 'converts plans into tasks'. Other roles are *passive descriptions* of personality, e.g., the teamworker 'dislikes friction and confrontation' and the plant is 'forthright' and 'independent'. Groups need active members. They are not necessarily people who talk too much and dominate a meeting, but people who make a positive contribution to the proceedings.

Analysing existing groups and their performance or behaviour, using the team roles concept, can lead to improvement, e.g.

- Underachievement demands a good co-ordinator or finisher.
- Conflict within the group requires a teamworker or strong co-ordinator.
- Mediocre performance can be improved by a resource investigator, innovator or shaper.
- Error prone groups need a clever evaluator and an able organizer.

Stable organizations need a different mix of people to those operating in areas of rapid change. Different roles are more important in particular circumstances. For example, new groups need a strong shaper to get started, competitive situations demand an innovator with good ideas, and in areas of high risk a good evaluator may be needed. Teams should be analysed therefore, both in terms of what team roles members can play, and also in relation to what team skills are most needed.

The Belbin team roles concept has the merit of simplicity. The author and his colleagues believe, however, that a more complete, understandable, and helpful approach is provided by the use of the personality type indicator described in the following section.

### Understanding and valuing team members – the MBTI

A powerful aid to team development is the use of the Myers-Briggs Type Indicator (MBTI).[2] This is based on an individual's preferences on four scales for:

- Giving and receiving 'energy.'
- Gathering information.
- Making decisions.
- Handling the outer world.

Its aim is to help individuals understand and value themselves and others, in terms of their differences as well as their similarities. It is well researched and non-threatening when used appropriately.

The four MBTI preference scales, which are based on Jung's theories of psychological types, represent two opposite preferences:

- *Extroversion – Introversion* – how we prefer to give/receive energy or focus our attention.
- *Sensing – iNtuition* – how we prefer to gather information.
- *Thinking – Feeling* – how we prefer to make decisions.
- *Judgement – Perception* – how we prefer to handle the outer world.

To understand what is meant by preferences, the analogy of left and right-handedness is useful. Most people have a preference to write with either their left or their right hand. When using the preferred hand, they tend not to think about it, it is done naturally. When writing with the other hand, however, it takes longer, needs careful concentration, seems more difficult, but with practice would no doubt become easier.

Most people *can* write with and use both hands, but tend to prefer one over the other. This is similar to the MBTI psychological preferences: most people are able to use both preferences at different times, but will indicate a preference on each of the scales.

In all, there are eight possible preferences – E or I, S or N, T or F, J or P, i.e. two opposites for each of the four scales. An individual's *type* is the combination and interaction of the four preferences. It can be assessed initially by completion of a simple questionnaire. Hence, if each preference is represented by its letter, a person's type may be shown by a four letter code – there are sixteen in all. For example, ESTJ represents an *extrovert* (E) who prefers to gather information with *sensing* (S), prefers to make decisions by *thinking* (T) and has a *judging* (J) attitude towards the world, i.e. prefers to make decisions rather than continue to collect information. The person with opposite preferences on all four scales would be an INFP, an introvert who prefers intuition for perceiving, feelings or values for making decisions, and likes to maintain a perceiving attitude towards the outer world.

The questionnaire, its analysis and feedback must be administered by a qualified MBTI practitioner, who may also act as external facilitator to the team in its forming and storming stages.

*Type and teamwork*

With regard to teamwork, the preference types and their interpretation are extremely powerful. The *extrovert* prefers action and the outer world, whilst the *introvert* prefers ideas and the inner world.

*Sensing–thinking* types are interested in facts, analyse facts impersonally, and use a step-by-step process from cause to effect, premise to conclusion. The *sensing–feeling* combinations, however, are interested in facts, analyse facts personally, and are concerned about how things matter to themselves and others.

*Intuition–thinking* types are interested in possibilities, analyse possibilities impersonally, and have theoretical, technical, or executive abilities. On the other hand, the *intuition–feeling* combinations are interested in possibilities, analyse possibilities personally, and prefer new projects, new truths, things not yet apparent.

*Judging* types are decisive and planful, they live in orderly fashion, and like to regulate and control. *Perceivers*, on the other hand are flexible, live spontaneously, and understand and adapt readily.

As we have seen, an individual's type is the combination of four preferences on each of the scales. There are sixteen combinations of the preference scales and these may be displayed on a *type table* (Figure 12.8). If the individuals within a team are prepared to share

| ISTJ | ISFJ | INFJ | INTJ |
|------|------|------|------|
| ISTP | ISFP | INFP | INTP |
| ESTP | ESFP | ENFP | ENTP |
| ESTJ | ESFJ | ENFJ | ENTJ |

**Figure 12.8** *MBTI type table form. Source: Isabel Briggs Myers, Introduction to Type[2]*

with each other their MBTI preferences, this can dramatically increase understanding and frequently is of great assistance in team development and good team working. The similarities and differences in behaviour and personality can be identified. The assistance of a qualified MBTI practioner is absolutely essential in the initial stages of this work.

*Problem solving using type preferences*

The MBTI preferences may be used by an individual or a team in a step-by-step process for problem solving. The problem solving model, represented in Figure 12.9, is straightforward, but can be difficult to use, because people tend to skip over those steps that require them to use their non-preferences. For example, information tends to be gathered by the preferred function (S or N) and decisions made by the preferred function (T or F). A strongly ST type will spend much time gathering facts (S) and thinking logically through the decision process (T), with perhaps insufficient attention being given to other possibilities (N) and the impact on people (F). If the size of each letter repre-

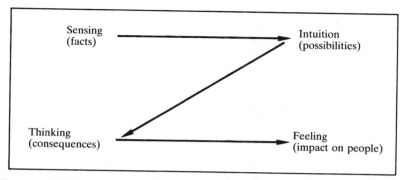

**Figure 12.9** *Team task analysis: the problem-solving model. Source: Sandra Krebs Hirsh and Jean M. Kummerow, Introduction to Type in Organisational settings*[2]

sents a unit of time, the ST's problem solving method may be represented in Figure 12.10, in which the Z pattern of the model is not followed. Problems, solutions, and decisions are likely to be improved if *all* the preferences are used. Until individuals master the process of spending time in their non-preferred funtions, i.e. type development, it may be wise to consult others of opposite preference when tackling important problems or making vital decisions.

Clearly, this has great implications for teamwork and requires that team members share their MBTI preferences or types.

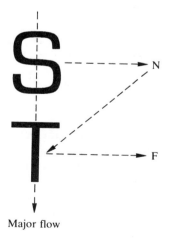

Major flow

**Figure 12.10** *Relative time spent on each aspect of problem solving model by 'ST type'*

### The five 'A' stages for teamwork

For any of these models or theories to benefit a team, the individuals within it need to become *aware* of the theory, e.g. the MBTI. They then need to *accept* the principles as valid, *adopt* them for themselves in order to *adapt* their behaviour accordingly. This will lead to individual and team *action* (Figure 12.11).

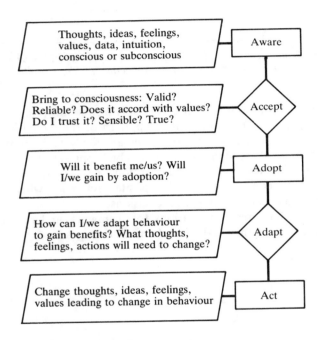

**Figure 12.11** *The five 'A' stages for teamwork*

In the early stages of team development particularly, the assistance of a skilled facilitator to aid progress through these stages is necessary. This is often neglected, causing failure in so many team initiatives. In such cases the net output turns out to be lots of nice warm feelings about 'how good that team workshop was a year ago', but the nagging reality that no action came out and nothing has really changed.

## 12.5   Implementing teamwork for quality improvement – the 'drive' model

The author and his colleagues have developed a model for a structured approach to problem solving in teams, the *DRIVE* model. The mnemonic provides landmarks to keep the team on track and in the right direction:

*Define*       – the problem. *Output*: written definition of the task and its success criteria.

*Review*       – the information. *Output*: presentation of known data and action plan for further data.

*Investigate* – the problem. *Output*: documented proposals for improvement and action plans.

*Verify*        – the solution. *Output*: proposed improvements that meet success criteria.

*Execute*     – the change. *Output*: task achieved and improved process documented.

The DRIVE model fits well with the MBTI Z-shaped problem-solving approach. Figure 12.12 shows how the stages relate to the S–N–T–F path.

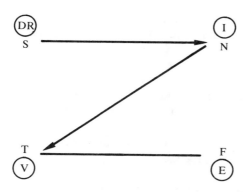

**Figure 12.12** *The DRIVE model and MBTI-based problem-solving*

The various stages are discussed in detail below. Some of the steps may be omitted if they have already been answered or are clearly not relevant to a particular situation.

**Define**

At this stage the team is concerned with gaining a common understanding and agreement within the groups of the task that it faces, in terms of the problem to be solved and the boundaries of the process or processes that contain it. It is necessary to generate at the outset a means of knowing when the team has succeeded. There is no concern at this stage with solutions. The key steps are:

1 *Look at the task*
   Typical questions:
   (a) What is the brief?
   (b) Is it understood?
   (c) Is there agreement with it?
   (d) Is it sufficiently explicit?
   (e) Is it achievable?
   There may be a need for clarification with the 'sponsor' at this stage, and possibly some redefinition of the task.
2 *Understand the process*
   (a) What processes 'contain' the problem?
   (b) What is wrong at present?
   (c) Brainstorm – ideas for improvement.
   (d) Perhaps draw a rough flowchart to focus thinking.
3 *Prioritize*
   (a) Set boundaries to the investigation.
   (b) Make use of ranking, Pareto, matrix analysis etc., as appropriate.
   (c) Review and gain agreement in the team of what is 'do-able'.
4 *Define the task*
   (a) Produce a written description of the process or problem area that can be confirmed with the team's sponsor.
   (b) Confirm agreement in the team.
   (c) This step may generate further questions for clarification by the sponsor of the process.
5 *Agree success criteria*
   (a) List possible success criteria. How will the team know when it has succeeded?
   (b) Choose and agree success criteria in the team.
   (c) Discuss and agree time scales for the project.
   (d) Agree with 'sponsor'.
   (e) Document the task definition, success criteria and time scale for the complete project.

## Review

This stage is concerned with finding out what information is already available, gathering it together, structuring it, identifying what further information might be needed, and agreeing in the team WHAT is needed, HOW it is going to be obtained, and WHO is going to get it.

1 *Gather existing information*
   (a) Locate sources – verbal inputs, existing files, charts, quality records, etc.
   (b) Go and collect, ask, investigate.
2 *Structure information*
   Information may be available but not in the right format.
3 *Define gaps*
   (a) Is enough information available?
   (b) What further information is needed?
   (c) What equipment is affected?
   (d) Is the product/service from one plant or area?
   (e) How is the product/service at fault?
4 *Plan further data collection*
   (a) Use any data already being collected.
   (b) Draw up checksheet(s).
   (c) Agree data-collection tasks in the team – WHO, WHAT, HOW, WHEN.
   (d) Seek to consult others, where appropriate. Who actually has the information? Who really understands the process?
   (e) This is a good opportunity to start to 'extend the team' in preparation for the *Execute* stage later on.

## Investigate

This stage is concerned with analysing all the data, considering all possible improvements, and prioritizing these to come up with one or more solutions to the problem, or improvements to the process, which can be verified as being the answer which meets the success criteria.

1 *Implement data collection action plan*
   Check at an early stage that the plan is satisfying the requirements.
2 *Analyse data*
   (a) What picture is the data painting?
   (b) What conclusions can be drawn?
   (c) Use all appropriate tools to give a clearer picture of the process.

3 *Generate potential improvements*
  (a) Brainstorm improvements.
  (b) Discuss all possible solutions.
  (c) Write down all suggestions (have there been any from outside the team?)
4 *Agree proposed improvements*
  (a) Prioritize possible proposals.
  (b) Decide what is achievable in what time scales.
  (c) Work out how to test proposed solution(s) or improvement(s).
  (d) Design check sheets to collect all necessary data.
  (e) Build a checking/verifying plan of action.

**Verify**

This stage is concerned with testing the plans and proposals to make sure that they work before any commitment to major process changes. This may require a relatively short discussion round a table in a meeting or lengthy pilot trials in a laboratory, office or even a main operations area or production plant.

1 *Implement action plan*
  Carry out the agreed tests on the proposals.
2 *Collect data*
  (a) Consider the use of questionnaires, if appropriate.
  (b) Make sure the check sheets are accumulating the data properly.
3 *Analyse data*
4 *Verify that success criteria are met*
  (a) Compare performance of new or changed process with success criteria from *Define* stage.
  (b) If success criteria are not met, return to appropriate stage in drive model (usually the *Investigate*) stage.
  (c) Continue until the success criteria have been met. For difficult problems, it may be necessary to go a number of times round this loop.

**Execute**

This stage is concerned with selling the solution or process improvement to others, e.g., the process owner, who may not have taken part in the investigation but whose commitment is vital to ensure success. Part of this stage may well be the need to address the existing documented quality management system, especially in the case of BS5750/ISO9000-registered organizations.

1 *Develop implementation plan to gain commitment*
   (a) Is there commitment from others? Consider all possible impacts.
   (b) Actions?
   (c) Timing?
   (d) Selling required?
   (e) Training required for new or modified process?
2 *Review appropriate system paperwork/documentation*
   (a) Who should do this? The team? The activity/process owner?
   (b) What are the implications for other systems?
   (c) What controlled documents are affected?
3 *Gain agreement to all facets of the execution plan from the process-owner*
4 *Implement the plan*
5 *Monitor success*
   (a) Extent of original team involvement? Initially perhaps and then at intervals?
   (b) 'Delegate' to process owner/department concerned? At what stage?
6 *Responsibility*
   Balance between team taking responsibility for meeting its agreed project success criteria and ownership within the organization of processes and continuous improvement. In the case of registered firms, responsibility for continued monitoring can be delegated to the quality management.

The problem solving tools (see Chapter 9) most likely to be used at each of the DRIVE stages are shown in Figure 12.13. The position of the DRIVE system in the breakdown of the most critical processes is represented in Figure 12.14.

**An example of the DRIVE model used in practice**

The example below shows how the DRIVE model for a particular project worked out in practice. The sort of responses made by the team are given in quotes thus ' '.
*Stated task*: 'We lose orders because our response time in making quotations is too long. We must significantly reduce our response time'.

1 *Define stage*
   (a) Look at the task:
       (i) Can we accept the problem as stated? 'Yes, this is generally known to be a problem area.'

| | D E F I N E | R E V I E W | I N V E S T I G A T E | V E R I F Y | E X E C U T E |
|---|---|---|---|---|---|
| Brainstorming | ● | ● | ● | | |
| Cause and effect diagrams | ● | | | | |
| Pareto | ● | ● | | ● | ● |
| Matrix analysis | ● | ● | ● | | |
| Check sheets | | ● | ● | ● | ● |
| Flowcharts | | ● | ● | | ● |
| Forcefield | | ● | | | ● |
| Scatter diagram | | ● | | ● | |
| Histograms | | ● | | | |
| Charts | | ● | ● | ● | ● |
| Project bar chart | | | | ● | ● |

**Figure 12.13** *Likely tools in the DRIVE model*

(ii) Does this apply to all customers, or to specific product lines? 'All customers.'

(iii) Does anyone measure response time at the moment? 'There was a one-off assessment a long time ago but it is not routinely measured.'

(iv) Have we the right expertise in our team to tackle it? 'Not really sure until we understand the problem.'

(v) Can we succeed with this problem? 'Yes, if we don't let it get too big.'

(b) Understand the process

(i) What processes 'contain' this problem? 'Customer visits by sales reps, telephone enquiries system, telex/fax enquiries, development department (technical vetting and provision of samples) pricing department', etc.

(ii) What is wrong at present? 'No real liaison between departments, labs have other priorities, visit reports are not explicit.'

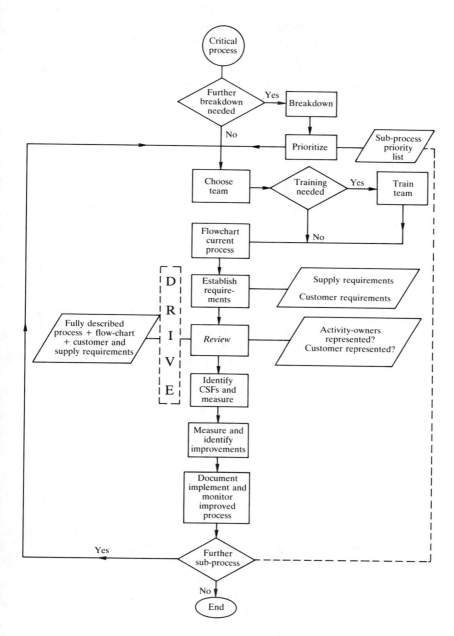

**Figure 12.14** *Critical processes and the DRIVE model*

(c) Prioritize
    (i) What should be the boundaries of our investigation? 'Enquiries arising from direct sales visits to customers compose about 70 per cent of all enquiries. We will restrict our project to this area initially.'
    (ii) Is it do-able? 'Yes, but now we realize we need someone from the Development Department on the team.'
(d) Define the task.
(e) Agree success criteria.
(f) In response to d) and e) the team finally documented:

'Customer quotations project:

Our task is to investigate and reduce delays in the handling of those customer enquiries which arise from direct visits by our salesforce. The project will be conducted in three phases:

1 (a) To establish the average time (in days) between the salesperson's visit and receipt by the customer of our quotation.
  (b) To agree a target reduction in the average response time to enquiries.
2 To make recommendations that will enable the target reduction in response time to be achieved.
3 To implement the recommendations and monitor response times on a sample basis to demonstrate that the desired reduction has been achieved.

Milestones for the completion of each phase, measured from the formal go-ahead date for these proposals, are

Phase 1 – 1 month
Phase 2 – 4 months
Phase 3 – 8 months'

2 *Review stage*
The team was not able to locate the original study report, but did discover a memo that gave the following summary:

- Average time to process a quotation request:     17 days
- Average time of quotations judged 'too late':    20 days
- Percentage of quotations 'too late':             30%

From this, the team concluded that the average time would have to be reduced to about 9 days to give a frequency of exceeding 20 days of only 1 in 100, i.e., only 1 per cent of quotations 'too late'.

### 3 *Investigate stage*

The team constructed flowcharts of the various stages of the process. Major 'grey areas' occurred in dealing with quotations for new(er) products or new customers, where more technical vetting by the laboratory was required, because (a) customer requirements were not clear, and (b) salesmen were not authorized to offer new specifications without checking with the technical department. It was in these areas that the sales visit reports were not sufficiently specific.

The flowchart of the process was changed to include a path giving early warning to the technical department of requirements from 'new business areas', by identifying specifically named customers and product types. Quotations in these areas were treated with priority.

A check sheet to measure quotation turn-round times was designed.

### 4 *Verify stage*

- The modified process was implemented.
- The check sheet was used to gather data.
- A 'c chart' was used to monitor the average turn-round time in days for each week's orders, with the new procedure introduced at week 10. Action and warning lines for the chart were based on a target average of 9 days. The ensuing chart is shown in Figure 12.15.

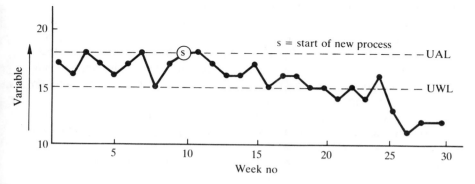

**Figure 12.15** *Charting the effects of the improvement through DRIVE*

5 *Execute stage*

- The above data was presented to a meeting of the Sales and Technical Departments.
- The changed procedures were agreed, documented and circulated, including the list of current customers and products for special vetting.
- A procedure, which was documented, called for *all* quotations for new customers and products to be added to the special list and retained until familiarity enabled them to become 'standard'. They were then removed from the list for special attention.
- Continued monitoring, using the chart in Figure 12.15, showed the average turn-round time reduce eventually to 10 days. Only 2 per cent of quotations were then taking longer than 20 days.

**Steps in the introductions of teams**

The idea of introducing problem solving groups, quality circles or quality improvement teams often makes its way into an organization through the awareness of successful results in other organizations or companies. There is no fixed methodology for starting a teamwork programme, but there are certain key points that must be considered:

1 The concept should be presented to (or come from) management and supervision, and their commitment and support enlisted. It should be possible at this stage to engage the interest and support of potential team leaders.
2 Projects should be started slowly and on a small scale. Ideally a pilot scheme, run by the most enthusiastic candidates and in the most promising areas, should be launched. Early teething troubles, doubts and worries may then be identified and resolved.
3 Selected or volunteer team or circle leaders must be trained in all aspects of group leadership, and the appropriate techniques, and they should subsequently help train the team members in the techniques required in effective problem solving. The techniques of statistical process control (SPC) should be introduced, particularly brainstorming, cause and effect analysis, Pareto analysis and charting. These concepts lay the groundwork for analysing problems in a systematic fashion, and show that the majority of the problems are concentrated into a few areas.
4 Once the causes have been determined, a solution can be proposed. This solution may affect any of the components of the process: equipment, procedures, training, input requirements or output

requirements. The proposed solution should be tested by the team or circle, particularly if procedures are affected.

6 If the test of a solution proves successful, full-scale implementation can then be carried out. In the case of procedures, full documentation of the solution and management approval should be obtained. The procedure can then be communicated to all personnel concerned. Full-scale changes in equipment and other processes should occur in the same manner. The team should monitor implementation of the solution, plotting the appropriate data until the criteria for solution are met.

With the initial problems declared solved, the circle or team may then tackle another problem, and another, or be disbanded and new teams formed. The record of successful solutions will motivate other teams within the organization, and ideas should spread. As the number of teams in a company grows, new opportunities arise for stimulating interest. Some large companies organize in-house conferences of their quality improvement teams and quality circles, providing the opportunity for the publication of results and for recognition. Experience has shown that very significant improvements in areas such as energy reduction, productivity, and cost-effectiveness, in addition to quality, may be achieved by the project team approach.

One of the problems of the team approach to problem identification and solving is that sometimes the teams are organized because it is the fashionable thing to do. They either exist on paper only, or the meetings are social gatherings where nothing is learned, no projects are initiated, and people do not grow. Another common problem is that the teams attempt to solve problems without first learning the necessary techniques: enthusiasm outruns ability. Teams have enormous potential for helping to solve an organization's problems, but for them to be successful, they must follow a disciplined approach to problem solving, using proven techniques.

The team approach to problem solving works. It taps the skills and initiative of all personnel engaged in a process. This may mean a change in culture, which must be supported by management through its own activities and behaviour.

**Adding the teams to the TQM model**

In part 1 of this book the foundations for TQM were set down. The core of customer/supplier chains and, at every interface, a process were surrounded by the 'soft' outcomes of culture, communications, and commitment. In Parts 2 and 3 were added the hard management necessities of systems and tools. We are now ready to complete the model with the necessity of teams – the councils, the PQTs, QITs, quality circles, DPA groups, etc., which work on the processes – using the tools – to bring about continuous improvements in the systems that manage them. (Figure 12.16).

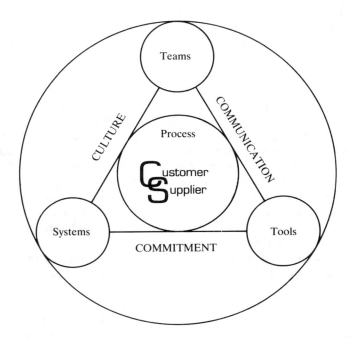

**Figure 12.16** *Total quality management – teamwork added to complete the model*

The author is grateful for the significant contribution to this chapter made by his colleagues in O & F Quality Management Consultants Ltd, Stephen Mathews, Development Director and John Glover, Senior Consultant.

## Chapter highlights

### The need for teamwork

• The only efficient way to tackle process improvement or complex problems is through teamwork. The team approach allows individuals and organizations to grow.

- Employees will not engage continual improvement without commitment from the top, a quality 'climate', and an effective mechanism for capturing individual contributions.
- Teamwork for quality improvement is driven by a strategy, needs a structure, and must be implemented thoughtfully and effectively.

## Some theories and models for teamwork: action-centred leadership

- Early work in the field of human relations by McGregor (Theories X and Y), Maslow (Hierarchy of Needs) and Hertzberg (Motivators and Hygiene Factors) was useful to John Adair in the development of his model for teamwork and action-centred leadership.
- Adair's model addresses the needs of the task, the team, and the individuals in the team, in the form of three overlapping circles. There are specific task, team and individual functions for the leader, but (s)he must concentrate on the small central overlap area of the three circles.
- The team process has inputs and outputs. Good teams have three main attributes: high task fulfilment, high team maintenance, and low self-orientation.
- In dealing with the task, the team and its individuals, a situational style of leadership must be adopted. This may follow the Tannenbaum and Schmidt, and Blanchard models through directing, coaching, and supporting to delegating.

## Stages of team development

- When teams are put together, they pass through Tuckman's forming (awareness), storming (conflict), norming (co-operation), and performing (productivity) stages of development.
- Teams that go through these stages successfully become effective and display clear objectives and agreed goals, openness and confrontation, support and trust, co-operation and conflict, good decision-making, appropriate leadership, review of the team processes, sound relationships, and individual development opportunities.

## Team roles and personality types

- Valuable work on team behaviour by Belbin has identified eight team roles: co-ordinator, shaper, plant, monitor/evaluator, implementor, resource investigator, teamworker, finisher.
- Eight people are not required for a team, but the roles, either as the main or secondary individual functions, should be present.

Analysing existing groups and their performance or behaviour, using the team roles concept, can lead to improvement.

- The Belbin team roles have the merit of simplicity, but a more complete, understandable, helpful approach is provided by the Myers-Briggs Type Indicator (MBTI).
- The MBTI is based on individuals' preferences on four scales for giving and receiving 'energy' (extroversion–E or introversion–I), gathering information (sensing–S or intuition–N), making decisions (thinking–T or feeling–F) and handling the outer world (judging–J or perceiving–P).
- An individual's type is the combination and interaction of the four scales and can be assessed initially by completion of a simple questionnaire. There are sixteen types in all, which may be displayed for a team on a type table.
- The MBTI preferences may be used by an individual or a team in a Z-shaped stepwise problem-solving process: S–N–T–F.
- The five As: for any of the teamwork models and theories, the individuals must become aware, need to accept, adopt and adapt, in order to act. A skilled facilitator is always necessary.

### Implementing teamwork for quality improvement – the DRIVE model

- A structured approach to problem solving is provided by the DRIVE model: define the problem, review the information, investigate the problem, verify the solution, and execute the change.
- After initial problems are solved, others should be tackled – successful solutions motivating new teams. In all cases teams should follow a disciplined approach to problem-solving, using proven techniques.
- Teamwork may mean a change in culture, which must be supported by management through its activities and behaviour.

### Adding the teams to the TQM model

The third and final hard management – the teams – are added to the tools and systems to complete the TQM model.

### References

1  These experiments were conducted by Mayo on the shopfloors of Western Electric's Hawthorne plant. These showed that the attention paid to the employees, not the plant conditions, had a beneficial effect.

2  See references under *TQM through people and teamwork* heading in Bibliography, pages 452–453.

# Part Five
# TQM – The Implementation

All words, and no performance.
  *Philip Massinger*, 1583–1640 from 'The Unnatural Combat', ca 1619

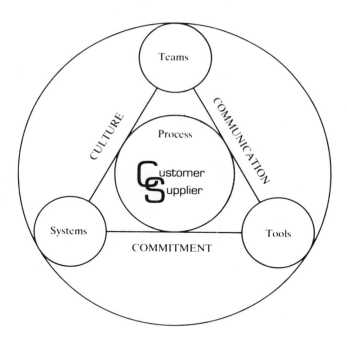

# 13 Communications for quality

## 13.1 Communicating the total quality strategy

People's attitudes and behaviour clearly can be influenced by communication; one has to look only at the media or advertising to understand this. The essence of changing attitudes to quality is to gain acceptance for the need to change, and for this to happen it is essential to provide relevant information, convey good practices, and generate interest, ideas and awareness through excellent communication processes. This is possibly the most neglected part of many organizations' operations, yet failure to communicate effectively creates unnecessary problems, resulting in confusion, loss of interest and eventually in declining quality through apparent lack of guidance and stimulus.

Total quality management will significantly change the way many organizations operate and 'do business'. This change will require direct and clear communication from the top management to all staff and employees, to explain the need to focus on processes. Everyone will need to know their roles in understanding processes and improving their performance.

Whether a strategy is developed by top management for the direction of the business/organization as a whole, or specifically for the introduction of TQM, that is only half the battle. An early implementation step must be the clear widespread communication of the strategy.

An excellent way to accomplish this first step is to issue a total quality message that clearly states top management's commitment to TQM and outlines the role everyone must play. This can be in the form of a quality policy (see Chapter 2) or a specific statement about the organization's intention to integrate TQM into the business operations. Such a statement might read:

The Board of Directors (or appropriate title) believe that the successful implementation of Total Quality Management is critical to achieving and maintaining our business goals of leadership in quality, delivery and price competitiveness.

We wish to convey to everyone our enthusiasm and personal commitment to the Total Quality approach, and how much we need your support in our mission of process improvement. We hope that you will become as convinced as we are that process improvement is critical for our survival and continued success.

We can become a Total Quality organization only with your commitment and dedication to improving the processes in which you work. We will help you by putting in place a programme of education, training, and teamwork development, based on process improvement, to ensure that we move forward together to achieve our business goals.

The quality director or TQM co-ordinator should then assist the quality council to prepare a directive. This must be signed by all business unit, division, or process leaders, and distributed to everyone in the organization. The directive should include the following:

* Need for improvement.
* Concept of total quality.
* Importance of understanding business processes.
* Approach that will be taken.
* Individual and process group responsibilities.
* Principles of process measurement.

The systems for disseminating the message will be covered in detail in sections 13.2 and 3, but should include all the conventional communication methods of seminars, departmental meetings, posters, newsletters, etc. First line supervision will need to review the directive with all the staff, and a set of questions and answers may be suitably pre-prepared in support.

Once people understand the strategy, the management must establish the infrastructure (see Chapter 11). The required level of individual commitment is likely to be achieved, however, only if everyone understands the aims and benefits of TQM, the role they must play, and how they can implement process improvements. For this understanding a constant flow of information is necessary, including:

1 When and how individuals will be involved.
2 What the process requires.
3 The successes and benefits achieved.

The most effective means of developing the personnel commitment required is to ensure people know what is going on. Otherwise they will feel left out and begin to believe that TQM is not for them, which will lead to resentment and undermining of the whole process. The first line of supervision again has an important part to play in ensuring key messages are communicated and in building teams by demonstrating everyone's participation and commitment.

Effective TQM communications, then, have two essential components:

(a) General information about the TQM process.
(b) Regular meetings between employees and managers/supervisors.

These equate respectively to the:

(a) 'Technical' aspects of the TQM framework or model.
(b) Human and organizational aspects of launching the whole process.

TQM will clearly have a profound effect on all tasks, activities, and processes throughout the organization. It should change management style and integrate the process inputs of information, people, machines, and materials. One aspect of the communication process worthy of particular attention in this context is that between departments or functions. This is essential for establishing up-to-the-minute customer-oriented goals and building the 'house of quality' around the business processes.

The language used between departmental or functional groups will need attention in many organizations. Reducing the complexity and jargon in written and spoken communications will facilitate comprehension. When written business communications cannot be read or understood easily, they receive only cursory glances, rather than the detailed study they require. *Simplify and shorten* must be the guiding principles. The communication model illustrated in Figure 13.1 indicates the potential for problems through environmental distractions, mismatches between sender and receiver (or, more correctly, decoder) in terms of attitudes – towards the information and each other – vocabulary, time pressures, etc.

All levels of management should introduce and stress 'open' methods of communication, by maintaining open offices, being accessible to staff/employees, and taking part in day-to-day interactions and the detailed processes. This will lay the foundation for improved interactions *between* staff and employees, which is essential for information flow and process improvement. Opening these lines of communication may lead to confrontation with many barriers and much resistance. Training and the behaviour of supervisors/managements should be

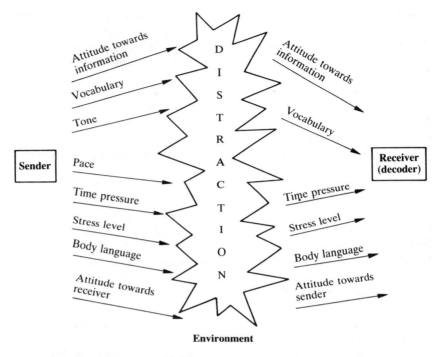

**Environment**

**Figure 13.1** *Communication model*

geared to helping people accept responsibility for their own behaviour, which often creates the barriers, and for breaking the barriers down by concentrating on the process rather than 'departmental' needs.

Resistance to change will always occur and is to be expected. Again, first line management must be trained to help people deal with it. This requires an understanding of the dynamics of change and the support necessary – not an obsession with forcing people to change. Opening up lines of communication through a previously closed system, and publicizing people's efforts to change and their results, will aid the process. Change can be – even should be – exciting if employees start to share their development, growth, suggestions, and questions. Management must encourage and participate in this by creating the most appropriate communication systems.

### Communicating the quality message

The people in most organizations fall into one of four 'audience' groups, each with particular general attitudes towards TQM:

- *Senior managers*, who should see TQM as an opportunity, both for the organization and themselves.
- *Middle managers*, who may see TQM as another burden without any benefits, and may perceive a vested interest in the status quo.
- *Supervisors* (first-line or junior managers), who may see TQM as another 'flavour of the period' or campaign, and who may respond by trying to keep heads down so that it will pass over.
- *Other employees*, who may not care, so long as they still have jobs and get paid, though these people must be the custodians of the delivery of quality to the customer and own that responsibility.

Senior management must ensure that each group sees TQM as being beneficial to them. Total quality training material and support (whether internal from a quality director and team or from external consultants) will be of real value only if the employees are motivated to respond positively to them. The implementation strategy must then be based on two mutually supporting aspects:

1 'Marketing' the TQM initiative.
2 A positive, logical process of communication designed to motivate.

There are of course a wide variety of approaches to, and methods of, TQM. Any individual organization's TQ strategy must be designed to meet the needs of its own structure and business, and the state of commitment to continuous improvement activities. These days very few organizations are starting from a green-field site. The key is that groups of people must feel able to 'join' the TQM process at the most appropriate point for them. This way TQM will be owned, not bought into. For middle managers to be convinced that they must participate, TQM must be presented as the key to help them turn the people who work for them into total quality employees.

The noisy, showy, hype-type activity is not appropriate to any aspect of TQM. TQM 'events' should of course be fun, because this is often the best way to persuade and motivate, but the value of any event should be judged by its ability to contribute to understanding and the change to TQM. Key words in successful exercises include 'discovery', affirmation, participation, and team-based learning. In the difficult area of dealing with middle and junior managers, who can and will prevent change with ease and invisibility, the recognition that progress must change from being a threat to a promise will help. In the workshops designed for them managers and supervisors should be made to feel recognized, not victimized. The workshop programme should be delivered by specially trained people, and the environment and conduct of the workshops must demonstrate the organization's concern for quality.

The key medium for motivating the employees and gaining their commitment to TQM is face-to-face communication and *visible* management commitment. Much is written and spoken about leadership, but it is mainly about communication. If people are good leaders, they are invariably good communicators. Leadership is a human interaction depending on the communications between the leaders and the followers. It calls for many skills that can be *learned* from education and training, but must be **acquired** through practice.

## 13.2    Types of communication

It may be useful to consider why people learn. They do so for several reasons, some of which are:

(a)  Self-betterment.
(b)  Self-preservation.
(c)  Need for responsibility.
(d)  Saving time or effort.
(e)  Sense of achievement.
(f)  Pride in work.
(g)  Curiosity.

So communication and training can be a powerful stimulus to personal development at the workplace, as well as achieving improvements for the organization. This may be useful in the selection of the appropriate method(s) of communication, the principal ones being:

- *Verbal communication* either between individuals or groups, using direct or indirect methods, such as public address and other broadcasting systems, and tape recordings.
- *Written communication* in the form of notices, bulletins, information sheets, reports and recommendations.
- *Visual communication* such as posters, films, video tapes, exhibitions, demonstrations, displays and other promotional features. Some of these also call for verbal communication.
- *Example*, through the way people conduct themselves and adhere to established working codes and procedures, through their effectiveness as communicators and ability to 'sell' good quality practices.

The characteristics of each of these methods should be carefully examined before they are used in communicating the quality messages.

## 1 Direct verbal communication

The requirements of this method are for:

- Careful preparation.
- Good individual communication and presentation skills.
- A broad knowledge of the subject matter.
- Ability to control and answer questions or seek answers.
- Credibility with the audience or group,
- The encouragement of participation and commitment.

Its strengths are:

1 Direct impact on individuals or the group.
2 Permits assessment of reactions and allows discussion or presentations to be modified accordingly.
3 Permits use of plain words easily understood by groups or individuals.
4 Audience can ask questions and get answers.
5 Permits presenter to check assimilation through, for example, asking questions.
6 Allows for reiteration, recapitulation and special emphasis, as necessary.
7 'Personalizes' quality and improvement.
8 Can secure commitment from groups and individuals.

But it has limitations, for it:

(a) Depends upon the individual's ability to communicate effectively.
(b) Uses only *one* of the senses through which people acquire knowledge.
(c) Requires time to prepare carefully in proportion to the complexity of the subject.
(d) Does not guarantee uniformity of content and understanding between groups unless based on a common agenda.
(e) Is time consuming and usually most effective for small groups.

The art of speaking to people effectively should be learned and practised at all levels of the communication framework.

## 2   Indirect verbal communication

This method is limited in its effectiveness in communicating quality. It suffers from many deficiencies. For example, many internal broadcasting systems are periodically overwhelmed by noise, so there is no guarantee that the message has been even received – much less understood. It is often difficult to check that everyone has heard the message, and checking understanding is often impractical. Furthermore, it is inflexible and cannot adapt easily to individual requirements.

## 3   Written communication

The requirements of written methods are:

- Ability to express the message in words clearly and concisely.
- Ability to make words interesting to read.
- Ability to say exactly what is meant, unambiguously.
- Sense of 'timing' – good administrative arrangements for circulation.
- Awareness of limitations and deployment only in appropriate situations.

Its strengths are:

1 Same message goes to everyone,
2 Speed.
3 Careful timing of 'release' can ensure that message is received by everyone at the same time.
4 Useful for dealing with large numbers in a short span of time.
5 Useful for giving 'non-critical' information.
6 Can be circulated by a number of routes, e.g. in pay packets, individual letters, notices, etc., simultaneously,
7 Helpful – and sometimes essential – in backing up verbal communication, particularly if subject is complicated.
8 Regularizes and records actions, procedures, systems, rules, etc.
9 Usual form for submitting reports and recommendations.

The limitations are:

(a) Not everyone chooses to – or can – read; therefore no guarantee that message has 'got through'.
(b) Written words may mean different things to different people, according to vocabulary.

(c) Words may be ambiguous and create confusion and misunder-standing.

(d) No opportunity for clarification; people cannot easily ask questions, get replies or discuss.

(e) Difficult to convey relative importance and emphasis and give topic 'light and shade'.

(f) Lacks animation, depersonalizes communication processes and reduces opportunity for personal contact.

(g) Reduces sense of participation and precludes exchanges of information and views.

## 4 Visual communication

People learn through their senses, but by far the highest percentage of what they take in is through sight. It is estimated that the five senses contribute to the learning process in the following percentages:

| | |
|---|---|
| Sight (visible) | 75 |
| Hearing (audible) | 13 |
| Feeling (tactile) | 6 |
| Smell (olfactory) | 3 |
| Taste (gustatory) | 3 |

This clearly means that visible methods of communication can be extremely successful, especially when combined with other methods, such as verbal in the form of films, video tapes, audio visual presentations, or demonstrations. It also has implications for training sessions and group discussions, in which visual aids should be used as liberally and dramatically as possible. The use of simple flip charts and felt-tip pens, which allow everyone to communicate on an equal footing, can be a very effective visual aid to most discussions.

## 5 Communication by example

Showing videos, displaying posters, discussion groups, speaking or writing are not the only ways of communicating quality. Personal example is a powerful medium for getting across the messages. This can be done by:

• People's general positive attitude and alertness to quality.
• The way people conduct themselves at the workplace.
• Adherence to rules, procedures, systems, standard operations, and practices.

- Standards of housekeeping and hygiene.
- The way in which people are inclined to help others appreciate and avoid potential problems.
- People learning how to relate to, communicate with and influence others to gain their commitment to quality.
- The way in which people exude enthusiasm, pride, and confidence in themselves and the organization for which they work.

Written words, however well written, have no value unless backed by appropriate management behaviour. This is a most important means of communication, which should proceed with continual emphasis on employee participation.

**Counselling and coaching**

If people do have to be corrected at work, it is important for managers and supervisors to remember that the objective is to help staff to understand and identify with their process problems and prevent recurrence of mistakes. It is necessary to be objective always, and supervision should try to find out *what* has gone wrong rather than *who* has gone wrong. This will lead to a reliance on facts rather than opinions and 'hunches'. Managers and supervisors should be trained to create a good atmosphere, be patient, listen, and be prepared to respond to other ideas and initiatives. When correction of operating staff is necessary, supervision should:

1  Choose the place and the time carefully.
2  'Talk straight' but not humiliate the listener, especially in front of an audience.
3  Never be punitive or retaliatory.
4  Be open and adapt to changing situations.
5  Recapitulate progress and gain commitment to any improvement, and anticipated future steps agreed.

## 13.3   Ten methods of communication for quality improvement

Below are given a few ideas which are in current use in many TQM-driven organizations.

## 1 Suggestion schemes

If one already exists, it may be used for periods when only quality suggestions can be accepted. Such an event, which should be used sparingly to gain maximum impact, must be given lively publicity. If special prizes are to be awarded, presentations to the best suggestions should be made with the appropriate publicity.

## 2 'Departmental' talk-ins

This method, often known descriptively as 'huddles' in the USA or team briefings, calls for gathering people together for brief but organized periods to discuss quality issues relevant to the department. Time is usually short (by arrangement it may be attached to a tea or meal break, or shift change, for administrative simplicity), so an 'agenda' should be prepared and the sessions should be 'punchy' to make significant points with impact.

## 3 Induction and vocational training

'Quality consciousness' begins when a new employee enters the organization. Induction training in quality alerts people to requirements, codes of practice, conduct, procedures, and the quality culture. It should also capture interest and imagination, make people take quality seriously, and encourage them to hear more about it.

Vocational training for specific jobs should satisfy the employees' interest in quality created during the induction phase. Further training in methods and techniques for problem solving may need to be formal and off-the-job, but quality training should be integrated with operational training, as the opportunities occur, by relating the consequences of mal-operation to quality as well as production/operations and safety.

## 4 Poster campaigns

Some organizations have found that posters or similar devices can form an important part of the quality communication message from the very beginning. The first posters should be simple and may carry very straightforward statements such as:

**Quality starts here**
**The next person who checks your work will be your customer**
**Get it right the first time and avoid waste**

with suitable cartoon drawings or photographs, if appropriate.

There are hundreds of available quality posters, but many are often displayed with less effect than is possible. It is useless to simply stick them up at random. A poster campaign must be carefully planned, organized and 'managed'. The key question is 'What do you want to achieve with the campaign?' When that is answered, carefully select the most relevant and impact-provoking posters. Next, look at the locations. Will people stop, look and think? A well lit and prominent location that does not interfere with traffic is required. Posters should be centred about eye level, but a few gimmicky locations sometimes arouse interest. Keep quality posters separate and away from competition or 'clutter'. Integrate posters with other interests – particularly at holiday times. Holiday posters or notices can often be made to carry quality messages with some added impact. Home made posters can be even more effective than 'bought-in' ones, and a 'quality poster' competition may stimulate even more interest.

The posters should change to match the changing awareness, as the quality poster campaign matures. They may begin to reflect the breadth of the subject by referring to computer-integrated-manufacture, just-in-time concepts, and quality in the 'non-producing' areas. The success of a quality poster campaign will be enhanced by continually freshening the communication messages with new posters – say every 3 months.

## 5   Point-of-work reminders

The energy crisis gave birth to a good example of the point-of-work reminder with the 'Save it' stickers. This idea may be developed for highlighting special problems and to encourage careful working practices, particularly where these have been neglected in the past.

## 6   Competitions

A competition may be at the company/organization level with, say, a determined attempt to win a national or continental 'quality award', such as the Malcolm Baldrige National Quality Award in the USA or the European Quality Award (see Chapter 6), or arranged internally on an inter-departmental basis. Quality competitions are no substitute for training – they simply raise interest and levels of awareness. If they fail to generate interest and improvement, they are worthless. Many quality competitions are based on error or defect rates over a finite period of time. To make the competition even between departments with dissimilar risks, some 'modifier' must be brought into the calculations. To take account of uneven effects, results could be judged on, say:

(a) The percentage reduction in each department's defect rates from a previous base period.
(b) Error frequencies modified by a 'handicap' based on the relativity of the risk weightings between departments. Thus, 'high risk' areas would not be disadvantaged in the competition by those with a lower risk.

Some organizations have experience of quality competitions in which each department is 'assessed' by a team on a set number of occasions within the duration of the competition at random intervals. Marks are allocated under a number of different headings relative to the customer satisfaction being measured.

## 7  Prizes and formal presentations

If presentations to process quality teams, quality improvement teams, or quality circles are part of the recognition process, it is a good idea to award some sort of certificate of recognition to allow people to display their success. Photographs and reports of such award 'ceremonies' provide a colourful method of publicity. Different organizations have used various reward devices, from copper-etched plaques to weekends in Paris, for successful individual contributions. If lunches and 'external' senior executives are used as the medium for presentation of these rewards, the commitment and support from the top is visually demonstrated. A 'Chief Executive's Award' may be the major glittering prize for the best presentation made during the year.

## 8  Demonstrations and exhibitions

Static exhibitions of certain aspects of quality can be a focal point of interest, and a powerful way of making an impact.

## 9  House magazines or newsletters/posters

Local or organization-specific newspapers have a role to play if regular communication is to be achieved on a broad scale. These may feature articles on quality success stories and, in particular, should be used as a 'shop window' for quality improvement teams and/or quality circles. Publication of project findings, changes resulting from them, and measured improvements or savings, in newsletter form, is a powerful motivator that should not be underestimated. If done properly, it also encourages the 'me too' syndrome, which can generate the excitement and momentum so essential for successful TQM. There are a considerable number of possibilities for getting the message across by taking space in the company publication. But it must be interesting, eye-catching and newsworthy. If it is not read or fails to make an impact, it is worthless.

**10   Opinion or attitude surveys**

In some companies employee opinion or attitude surveys are conducted by questionnaire as part of TQM. If these are designed carefully, they should measure the employee perception of the programme. It is the author's experience that, in companies which have embraced TQM and carried out surveys properly, the results confirm a positive response. In one company:

- 83 per cent of the workforce were in favour of their manager's attitude to quality.
- 86 per cent believed that the quality of service provided by their department had increased.
- 73 per cent were convinced that the output of their department had improved.

One danger with this sort of counting is the development of complacency. TQM demands continuous improvement, and each achievement should set targets for further improvement in the future. Another danger is that TQM raises perceptions and expectations, and the second survey, in a series begun before the introduction of TQM, may indicate that things have worsened. What has actually happened of course is that the *awareness* of problems has been raised through the training and education processes.

It is not intended that this list should be exhaustive, relevant to every situation, or the most important way of communicating quality. It is given only as an indicator to the sort of possibilities there are for bringing the quality message 'alive' – even for the cynics.

## 13.4   Communication skills

If TQM is to succeed in any organization, it is important for all managers, supervisors and staff to recognize the value and influence of good communication as vital links in creating and maintaining standards for quality. Moreover, they must learn the characteristics of the various methods of communication and select the one most appropriate for the situation. This process is very much accelerated by an appreciation of how people learn to assimilate knowledge, since this will encourage people to make use of all the senses when communicating.

All communication and training exercises must be planned like military operations, leaving nothing to chance. When dealing with people – particularly when checking or counselling – managers and supervisors must be sensitive to the effect they have. They may need to be trained to communicate with people in a way that will help everyone feel more capable, more necessary and more worthwhile.

Effective communication is a two-way exercise. We were designed with two ears and one tongue. Could it be we were meant to listen twice as much as we speak? Listening with attention, interest, and courtesy, and carrying on listening, do not come naturally to many people, and they may need to be reminded, in their training, teamwork, or counselling activities, to listen 'openly'.

**Communicating in teams**

The starting point for any problem-solving team is brainstorming, during which a team member records all the ideas on a chart – possibly as a cause and effect diagram (see Chapter 9). The purpose and rules of brainstorming are directed at achieving agreement on action plans. The agreement to be reached among team members, with regard to action plans, will force the consideration of all aspects of a problem, and will make everyone alert to possible objections to the chosen courses of action. A useful device along this path to consensus of opinion is to allow the team some 'thinking time' before, during and after brainstorming sessions.

If conflict occurs, as is inevitable in any teamwork, it must be managed so that it assists rather than hinders the team to achieve its objectives. The team leader has an important role in such situations and it will help to:

- Recognize all contributors of ideas, not just those whose ideas are used.
- Stress that both the organization *and* the individuals benefit, if improvements are made.
- Clarify what is expected of each team member, in terms of the common goals *and* individually assigned tasks.

- Mediate when dominating members cause others to feel inadequate or suppressed.
- Remind members who make personal references that the group is in existence to reach agreement and find solutions.
- Endorse the positive traits of members, such as co-operation, openness, listening, contribution, etc.
- Discourage criticism, defensiveness, aggressiveness, closed-mindedness, interrupting, etc.

**Talking to people**

If anyone has to speak to a group of people, they should use the following checklist as an aid to structuring and presenting the talk:

1 What is the *objective* of the talk – what has to be conveyed?
2 What *key points* must be included to achieve the objective?
3 In what *sequence* should these be arranged for maximum impact and smooth 'flow'?
4 Who will comprise the *audience*? What is their occupation, status level, experience, etc.? And how many will there be?
5 What *method* of presentation will be most effective for the particular purpose to be achieved and audience to be addressed? For example, will it be a talk or a discussion?
6 Will *visual aids* be required, and, if so, how will they be used? The saying 'one picture is worth 1,000 words' should remind people of the value of illustrating talks or discussions.
7 How much *time* is available and how will it be allocated?
8 In which *location* is the talk to be given? Is it suitable? Is it correctly appointed?
9 How will *assimilation* of the message be checked? Will some form of test and/or questions be used to check *understanding*?
10 What *follow-up* is planned to reinforce the message and ensure *implementation*?

In presenting a case or point of view in a meeting, you will need to show people how to perform to maximum effect. The key points here are to encourage presenters to:

- Try, by taking a little time and by making introductions, to take the stress out of any 'negotiating' situations and create the right 'atmosphere'.
- Speak slowly, simply and with variation in pitch and tone, using pauses to aid assimilation, and avoiding jargon and clichés.

- Present points of view logically and with clarity and precision, so that all understand the substance of the case.
- Interest the audience through the content and presentation style, and let them participate whenever possible.
- Keep an open mind and an open ear – listen carefully to what other people are saying.
- Keep alert and try to read the 'language' of the situation.
- Be flexible in outlook – adapt to new situations and take advantage of new avenues of approach.
- Build on the best points of any particular case and diminish the weaknesses.
- Make constructive proposals but prevent people from being 'cornered' inextricably.
- Maintain discipline over the team or group to control discussions, cover the agenda, keep to the point, and keep cool!
- Keep the objective in mind throughout, and do not try to cover too many points in one go.
- 'Manage' the time of the meeting.
- Be sure that both sides **understand** what has been agreed before the meeting closes.
- Communicate outcomes quickly and accurately to all interested parties.

Training in presentation skills at all levels is never a waste of resources.

### Reports and writing generally (including flowcharts)

A good report should be readable, interesting, informative, well-presented and be no longer than is necessary. Recipients are likely to be busy people, and will welcome a concise report from which they can grasp the essentials. Therefore, when constructing a report, consider the following questions:

- Why has the report been requested?
- What are the terms of reference and objectives?
- What messages need to be conveyed?
- What type of information is required? For example, is it factual information based on observation or research, conclusions drawn from facts, or recommendations as to future courses of action?
- Is it arranged in a logical sequence, such as:

   Title.
   Contents.

Introduction or terms of reference.
Summary.
Data and information.
Analysis/discussion.
Conclusions and recommendations.
Action plans.
Supplementary information, (e.g. appendices)

- Will the subject and presentation capture the interest of the reader?
- Is it as short and easy to read as possible?
- Can some of the text be explained in diagrammatic form where this will aid understanding?
- Is it intelligible to the reader?
- Is it free of 'shorthand' expressions, departmental 'code words' and technical jargon?
- Does it take account of minority views or dissenting opinions?
- Have factual information and personal comments been distinguished to provide a sufficiently objective report?
- Do the conclusions and recommendations match the requirements of the terms of reference? Do they follow logically from the information and analysis contained in the main body of the report?

Report writing requires a particular skill in expression and some experience to do well. These notes are only a few clues to the more obvious considerations and are not exhaustive. There are many full texts on this subject.

Flowcharts paint written 'pictures' of processes that any group of people can understand and use (see Chapter 4). Any process will have its own communication system, with its own separate and distinct flow. This should be recognized, flowcharted and understood as an integral part of the process, and it may be superimposed on the flowchart of activities.

### Leading discussions

For those who have to lead discussions, including quality council chairmen, and leaders of quality improvement teams and quality circles, this plan may help:

| | |
|---|---|
| *Make an outline* | Determine the objectives and what is to be covered. |
| | Decide the 'key points' for discussion and how much time there will be available. |

Select areas of priority from 'key points' relative to the time available.

Plan the session in the imagination.

*Plan the approach*  Decide how the topic will be introduced.

Move the discussion along from one point to the next.

Determine how people will be brought into the discussion.

*Plan the physical*  Make sure everyone can be made comfortable.
*arrangements*  Ensure that everyone can see and hear.

Check the heating, ventilation, lighting, etc.

Make sure all the necessary visual aids are available and that they are all serviceable.

*Introduce the session*  Review the background to the discussion.

Announce the topic briefly and concisely and emphasize the relevance to the background.

Explain how the discussion should proceed and gain commitment to this approach.

Lead into the discussion smoothly and logically.

*Control the discussion*  Encourage participation; draw out ideas by asking questions, encouraging the exchange of views and opinions.

Encourage the reluctant contributors and prevent monopolization by the more vocal members.

Distribute the questions evenly and avoid bias.

Keep the discussions to the point and always moving forward.

Stimulate thought and discussion if necessary.

Handle irrelevancies tactfully.

Summarize frequently, particularly at key stages of the discussion.

*Summarize the*  Summarize the various outputs from the
*discussion and*  discussion, the ideas and experiences, etc. that
*document*  came to light.

Restate the objective.

Arrive at conclusions or solutions and restate as an achievement.

Give credit for effective contributions.

Issue a written statement of the main points and conclusions, with action plans, if appropriate.

## Chairing meetings

Many factors make a good chairman of a meeting. The following points should help people charged with such tasks to improve their performance:

1 If members of the group do not know each other, introduce them.
2 Create a good 'atmosphere', in which the meeting can proceed smoothly. Remain calm and cool. Be impartial.
3 State the intentions of the meeting and 'ground rules' for its conduct. Gain tacit acceptance of this 'methodology'.
4 Maintain a good natured discipline over the meeting; control casual conversations and damp down emotional outbursts. Bring all the members present into discussions.
5 Be courteous, patient and understanding. Not all individuals are articulate – help them to overcome their problems of self-expression so that their views, ideas and experience are not disregarded.
6 Keep an eye on the clock and make sure that time is allocated usefully.
7 Be flexible. If the meeting is getting 'bogged down', allow discussions a little freedom, but do not lose sight of the objectives or the time in the process. A little humour applied at the right time may help to revive a flagging meeting. Adjust the speed of debate up or down according to the situation.
8 Cover the agenda and achieve the intentions. Make interim summaries. Indicate progress, refocus off-track discussions, highlight or confirm important points, clarify and restate points that are not clear.
9 Encourage all members of the group to participate; generate discussion to reach solutions and decide options, according to requirements.
10 Summarize the consensus views.

In planning all communication activity, answering six basic questions will help the process get off to a flying start.

- *Who* should we communicate with?
- *Why* should we communicate?
- *What* should we communicate?
- *When* should we communicate?
- *Where* should we communicate?
- *How* should we communicate?

The more known and the better the information gathered in response to these questions, the more effective will be the communications.

## Chapter highlights

### Communicating the total quality strategy

- People's attitudes and behaviour can be influenced by communication, and the essence of changing attitudes is to gain acceptance through excellent communication processes.
- The strategy and changes to be brought about through TQM must be clearly and directly communicated from top management to all staff/employees. The first step is to issue a 'Total quality message'. This should be followed by a signed TQM directive.
- People must know when and how they will be brought into the TQM process, what the process is, and the successes and benefits achieved. First-line supervision has an important role in communicating the key messages and overcoming resistance to change.
- The complexity and jargon in the language used between functional groups must be reduced in many organizations. Simplify and shorten are the guiding principles.
- 'Open' methods of communication and participation must be used at all levels. Barriers may need to be broken down by concentrating on process rather than 'departmental' issues.
- There are four audience groups in most organizations – senior managers, middle managers, supervisors, and employees – each with different general attitudes towards TQM. The senior management must ensure that each group sees TQM as being beneficial.
- Good leadership is mostly about good communications, the skills of which can be learned through training but must be acquired through practice.

### Types of communication

- There are four principal types of communication: verbal (direct and indirect), written, visual, and by example. Each has its own requirements, strengths, and weaknesses.
- In counselling and coaching, the objective is to help staff to prevent process problems.

### Ten methods of communication for quality improvement

* The ten methods are: suggestion schemes, 'departmental' talk-ins, induction and vocational training, poster campaigns, point-of-work reminders, competitions, prizes and formal presentations, demonstrations and exhibitions, house magazines/newsletters/papers, and opinion or attitude surveys. This is not an exhaustive list.

### Communication skills

* All communication and training exercises must be planned and operated to leave nothing to chance. Managers will need training in communicating skills, particularly with respect to communicating in teams, talking to people, reporting and writing (including flowcharts), leading discussions and chairing meetings.
* In planning all communication activity Kipling's 'six honest serving men' questions should be asked – Who, Why, What, When, Where and How?

# 14  Training for quality

## 14.1  It's Wednesday – it must be training

It is the author's belief that training is the single most important factor
in actually improving quality, once there has been commitment to do
so. For training to be the effective, however, it must be planned in a
systematic and objective manner. Quality training must be continuous
to meet not only changes in technology but also changes in the environment in which an organization operates, its structure, and perhaps
most important of all the people who work there.

### Training cycle of improvement

Quality training activities can be considered in the form of a cycle of
improvement (Figure 14.1), the elements of which are the following.

*Ensure training is part of the quality policy*

Every organization should define its policy in relation to quality (see
Chapter 2). The policy should contain principles and goals to provide
a framework within which training activities may be planned and operated. This policy should be communicated to all levels.

*Allocate responsibilities for training*

Quality training must be the responsibility of line management, but
there are also important roles for the quality manager and his function.

*Define training objectives*

The following questions are useful first steps when identifying training
objectives:

* How are the customer requirements transmitted through the organization?

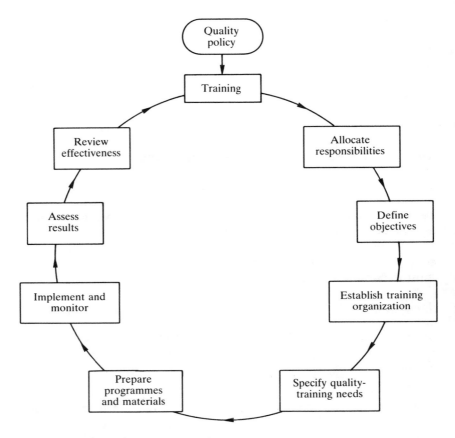

**Figure 14.1** *The quality training circle*

- Which areas need improved performance?
- What changes are planned for the future?
- What new procedures and provisions need to be drawn up?

When attempting to set training objectives three essential requirements must be met:

1 Senior management must ensure that objectives are clarified and priorities set.
2 Defined objectives must be realistic and attainable.
3 The main problems should be identified for all functional areas in the organization. Large organizations may find it necessary to promote a phased plan to identify these problems.

*Establish training organization*

The overall responsibility for seeing that quality training is properly organized must be assumed by one or more designated senior executives. All managers have a responsibility for ensuring that personnel reporting to them are properly trained and competent in their jobs. This responsibility should be written into every manager's job description. The question of whether line management requires specialized help should be answered when objectives have been identified. It is often necessary to use specialists, who may be internal or external to the organization.

*Specify quality training needs*

The next step in the cycle is to assess and clarify specific quality training needs. The following questions need to be answered:

(a) Who needs to be trained?
(b) What competences are required?
(c) How long will training take?
(d) What are the expected benefits?
(e) Is the training need urgent?
(f) How many people are to be trained?
(g) Who will undertake the actual training?
(h) What resources are needed, e.g. money, people, equipment, accommodation, outside resources?

*Prepare training programmes and materials*

Quality management should participate in the creation of draft programmes, although line managers should retain the final responsibility for what is implemented, and they will often need to create the training programmes themselves.

Quality-training programmes should include:

• The training objectives expressed in terms of the desired behaviour.
• The actual training content.
• The methods to be adopted.
• Who is responsible for the various sections of the programme.

*Implement and monitor training*

The effective implementation of quality training programmes demands considerable commitment and adjustment by the trainers and trainees alike. Training is a progressive process, which must take into account the learning problems of the trainees.

*Assess the results*

In order to determine whether further training is required, line management should themselves review performance when training is completed. However good the quality training may be, if it is not valued and built upon by managers and supervisors, its effect can be severely reduced.

*Review effectiveness of training*

Senior management will require a system whereby decisions are taken at regular fixed intervals on:

• The quality policy.
• The quality training objectives
• The training organization.

Even if the quality policy remains constant, there is a continuing need to ensure that new quality training objectives are set either to promote work changes or to raise the standards already achieved.

The purpose of system audits and reviews is to assess the effectiveness of an organization's quality effort. Clearly, adequate and refresher training in these methods is essential if such checks are to be realistic and effective. Audits and reviews can provide useful information for the identification of changing quality training needs.

The training organization should similarly be reviewed in the light of the new objectives, and here again it is essential to aim at continuous improvement. Training must never be allowed to become static, and the effectiveness of the organization's quality training programmes and methods must be assessed systematically.

## 14.2    A systematic approach to quality training

Training for quality should have, as its first objective, an appreciation of the personal responsibility for meeting the 'customer' requirements by everyone from the most senior executive to the newest and most junior employee. Responsibility for the training of employees in quality rests with management at all levels and, in particular, the person nominated for the co-ordination of the organization's quality effort. Quality training will not be fully effective, however, unless responsibility for the quality policy rests clearly with the Chief Executive. One objective of this policy should be to develop a *climate* in which everyone is quality conscious and acts with the needs of the immediate customer in mind. Quality objectives should be stated in relation to the activities and the place of training in their achievement.

The main elements of effective and systematic quality training may be considered under four broad headings:

- Error/defect/problem prevention.
- Error/defect/problem reporting and analysis.
- Error/defect/problem investigation.
- Review.

The emphasis should obviously be on error, defect, or problem prevention, and hopefully what is said under the other headings maintains this objective.

### Error/defect/problem prevention

The following contribute to effective and systematic training for prevention of problems in the organization:

1 An issued quality policy.
2 A written quality system.
3 Job specifications that include quality requirements.
4 An effective quality council or committee including representatives of both management and employees.
5 Efficient housekeeping standards.
6 Preparation and display of flow diagrams and charts for all processes.

### Error/defect/problem reporting and analysis

It will be necessary for management to arrange the necessary reporting procedures, and ensure that those concerned are adequately trained in these procedures. All errors, rejects, defects, defectives, problems, waste, etc., should be recorded and analysed in a way that is meaningful for each organization, bearing in mind the corrective action programmes that should be initiated at appropriate times.

**Error/defect/problem investigation**

The investigation of errors, defects, and problems can provide valuable information that can be used in their prevention. Participating in investigations offers an opportunity for training. The following information is useful for the investigation:

(a) Nature of problem.
(b) Date, time and place.
(c) Product/service with problem.
(d) Description of problem.
(e) Causes and reasons behind causes.
(f) Action advised.
(g) Action taken to prevent recurrence.

Effective problem investigation requires appropriate follow-up and monitoring of recommendations.

**Review of quality training**

Review of the effectiveness of quality training programmes should be a continuous process. However, the measurement of effectiveness is a complex problem. One way of reviewing the content and assimilation of a training course or programme is to monitor behaviour during quality audits. This review can be taken a stage further by comparing employees' behaviour with the objectives of the quality training programme. Other measures of the training processes should be found to establish the benefits derived.

**Training records**

All organizations should establish and maintain procedures for the identification of training needs and the provision of the actual training itself. These procedures should be designed (and documented) to include all personnel. In many situations it is necessary to employ professionally qualified people to carry out specific tasks, e.g. accountants, lawyers, engineers, chemists, etc., but it must be recognized that all other employees, including managers, must have or receive from the company the appropriate education, training and/or experience to perform their jobs. This leads to the establishment of training records.

Once an organization has identified the special skills required for each task, and developed suitable training programmes to provide competence for the tasks to be undertaken, it should prescribe how the competence is to be demonstrated. This can be by some form of examination, test or certification, which may be carried out in-house or by a recognized external body. In every case, records of personnel qualifications, training, and experience should be developed and maintained. National vocational qualifications (NVQs) have an important role to play here.

At the simplest level this may be a record of tasks and a date placed against each employee's name as he/she acquires the appropriate skill through training. Details of attendance on external short courses, in-house induction or training schemes complete such records. What must be clear and easily retrievable is the status of training and development of any single individual, related to the tasks that he/she is likely to encounter. For example, in a factory producing contact lenses that has developed a series of well defined tasks for each stage of the manufacturing process, it should be possible, by turning up the appropriate records, to decide whether a certain operator is competent to carry out a lathe-turning process. Clearly, as the complexity of jobs increases and managerial activity replaces direct manual skill, it becomes more difficult to make decisions on the basis of such records alone. Nevertheless, they should document the basic competency requirements and assist the selection procedure.

## 14.3 Starting where and for whom?

Training needs occur at four levels of an organization:

- *Very senior management* (strategic decision-makers).
- *Middle management* (tactical decision-makers or implementors of policy).
- *First level supervision and quality team leaders* (on-the-spot decision-makers).
- *All other employees* (the doers).

Neglect of training in any of these areas will, at best, delay the implementation of TQM. The provision of training for each group will be considered in turn, but it is important to realize that an integrated training programme is required, one that includes follow-up activities and encourages exchange of ideas and experience, to allow each transformation process to achieve quality at the supplier/customer interface.

**Very senior management**

The Chief Executive and his team of strategic policy makers are of primary importance, and the role of training here is to provide awareness and instil commitment to quality. The importance of developing real commitment must be established; and often this can only be done by a free and frank exchange of views between trainers and trainees. This has implications for the choice of the trainers themselves, and the fresh-faced graduate, sent by the 'package consultancy' operator into the lion's den of a boardroom, will not make much impression with the theoretical approach that he or she is obliged to bring to bear. The author recalls thumping many a boardroom table, and using all his experience and whatever presentation skills he could muster, to convince senior managers that without the TQM approach they would fail. It is a sobering fact that the pressure from competition and customers has a much greater record of success than enlightenment, although dragging a team of senior managers down to the shop floor to show them the results of poor management was successful on one occasion.

Executives responsible for marketing, sales, finance, design, operations, purchasing, personnel, distribution, etc. must all be helped to understand quality. They must be shown how to define the quality policy and objectives, how to establish the appropriate organization for quality, how to clarify authority, and generally how to create the atmosphere in which total quality will thrive. This is the only group of people in the organization that can ensure that adequate resources are provided and they must be directed at:

1 Meeting customer requirements – internally and externally.
2 Setting standards to be achieved – zero failure.
3 Monitoring of quality performance – quality costs.
4 Introducing a good quality management system – prevention.
5 Implementing process control methods – SPC.
6 Spreading the idea of quality throughout the whole workforce – TQM.

**Middle management**

The basic objectives of management quality training should be to make managers conscious and anxious to secure the benefits of the total quality effort. One particular 'staff' manager will require special training – the quality manager, who will carry the responsibility for management of the quality system, including its design, operation, and review.

## Training for quality managers

The selection of a person of the right calibre to advise management on quality is a key part of any TQM programme. His/her training must be related to the kind of job he/she is expected to do, the number of people employed, and the nature of the processes and materials handled. In smaller companies a senior manager may perform the function of 'quality manager' as part of his/her normal duties.

The quality manager and subordinates will require training in how to assist colleagues in the design and operation of management systems, within their own functions, which allow them to discharge their duties adequately and to liaise effectively with other parts of the organization. For example, the purchasing manager may require assistance with setting up a system of receiving goods of the correct standard from suppliers. The quality manager should be shown how to provide this help without assuming responsibility for the system itself. Similarly, the quality manager should be shown how to encourage the 'ownership' of an SPC system within production/operations. Usually the most effective way to train a quality manager in these tasks is to enlist the services of a *good* specialist quality management consultant to carry out a quality system advisory project, and provide almost 'on-the-spot' training through the implementation phase of the consultancy.

## Training for other middle management

The building-in of quality requires the commitment of the direct operating managers. This can only be engaged if the most senior managers effectively communicate their own feelings and devotion to total quality. Only then will it be possible to bring to life the quality policy through an effective management system.

The middle managers should be provided with the technical skills required to design, implement, review, and change the parts of the quality system that will be under their direct operational control. It will be useful throughout the training programmes to ensure that the responsibilities for the various activities in each of the functional areas are clarified. The presence of a highly qualified and experienced quality manager must not allow abdication of these responsibilities, for the internal 'consultant' can easily create not-invented-here feelings by writing out procedures without adequate consultation of those charged with implementation.

Middle management must receive comprehensive training on the philosophy and concepts of teamwork, and the techniques and applications of statistical process control (SPC). Without the teams and tools, the quality system will lie dormant and lifeless. It will relapse into a paper generating system, fulfilling the needs of only those who thrive on bureaucracy.

**First-level supervision**

There is a layer of personnel in many organizations which plays a vital role in their inadequate performance – foremen and supervisors – the forgotten men and women of industry and commerce. Frequently promoted from the 'shop floor' (or recruited as graduates in a flush of conscience and wealth!), these people occupy one of the most crucial managerial roles, often with no idea of what they are supposed to be doing, without an identity, and without training. If this behaviour pattern is familiar and is continued, then TQM is doomed.

The first level of supervision is where the implementation of total quality is actually 'managed'. Supervisors' training should include an explanation of the principles of TQM, a convincing exposition on the commitment to quality of the senior management, and an explanation of what the quality policy means for them. The remainder of their training should then be devoted to explaining their role in the operation of the quality system, teamwork, SPC etc., and to gaining *their* commitment to the concepts and techniques of total quality.

It is often desirable to involve the middle managers in the training of first line supervision in order to:

- Ensure that the message they wish to convey through their tactical manoeuvres is not distorted.
- Indicate to the foreman level that the organization's whole management structure is serious about quality, and intends that everyone is suitably trained and concerned about it too. One display of arrogance towards the training of supervisors and the workforce can destroy such careful planning, and will certainly undermine the educational effort.

**All other employees**

Awareness and commitment at the point of production or operation is just as vital as at the very senior level. If it is absent from the latter, the TQM programme will not begin; if it is absent from the shop floor, total quality will not be implemented. The training here must include the basics of quality, and particular care should be given to using easy reference points for the explanation of the terms and concepts. Most people can relate to quality and how it should be managed, if they can think about the applications in their own lives and at home. Quality is really such commonsense that, with sensitivity and regard to various levels of intellect and experience, little resistance should be experienced.

All employees should receive detailed training in the quality procedures relevant to their own work. Obviously they must have appropriate technical or 'job' training, but they must also understand the requirements of their customers. This is frequently a difficult concept to introduce, particularly in the non-manufacturing areas, and time and follow-up assistance must be given if TQM is to take hold. It is always bad management to ask people to follow instructions without understanding why and where they fit into their own scheme of things.

## 14.4 Training programmes and their design

The series of integrated programmes described in this section are centred around the basic principles of understanding the processes operating throughout the organization. Training in TQM does not lend itself to conference-style, mass-education methods, and the number of people attending each of the seminars or workshops should be limited to about twenty. Six is rather a small number and thirty is far too many. Somewhere in between allows a U-shape arrangement of seating, possibly in team 'islands', so that the tutor can get 'close' to the participants, and the group(s) can begin to knit together through face-to-face discussions as the training progresses.

### Senior management (8–20 hours of seminars)

The following recommendations represent the minimum requirement for an introduction of TQM to the most senior executives of an organization:

1 The foundations necessary for effective quality management and improvement should be examined in a free ranging discussion. This may take the form of a case study illustrating the relations between commitment, organization, culture, quality, and cost.
2 A presentation of the case for a company-wide approach to the control of quality should be made, showing how the functions of marketing, finance, research and development, production/operations,

distribution, etc. must interface well for good management. There should be some discussion on the effects of quality on market share, if appropriate.

3 An understanding of quality and its costs is essential for good marketing–operations relations. A consideration of the economics of quality should provide the basis for further discussions. Some discussion should also take place at this stage on quality management systems, using an international standard as the foundation.

4 A brief introduction to teamworking, communications, and the systematic techniques associated with quality improvement should be given. These are part of the essential 'toolkit' for senior managers interested in benefits of process development. Understanding of the meaning of a 'process' and knowledge of process capabilities is an essential requirement for senior management, if the needs of the customers are to be met.

The tutors should have considerable experience with similar organizations in the design and implementation of total quality management programmes, so that, in the final session, the recommended training/communication programmes and action plans can be discussed to ensure that the senior management of the organization benefits to the full from the brief exposure to the latest thinking in quality management. The culture change can then begin.

**Middle management (20–30 hours of seminars)**

This 'workshop' should introduce, through a series of practical case studies and exercises, the concepts of quality management. It should illustrate the importance and application of quality systems, teamwork and statistical methods of process control (SPC), using simple concepts and elementary statistics. The seminars should include a wide range of applications of TQM concepts and techniques, and give guidance on how they might be introduced most effectively and with least resistance. The emphasis should be on practical problem solving rather than acquiring theoretical perfection, and the course should be very participative.

The course programme should include the following:

1 An introduction to quality and total quality management – understanding, commitment, policy, costs, supplier/customer interface, processes, etc.
2 Quality systems – content, design, implementation, operation, etc.

3 Systematic quality control – basic tools and techniques such as Pareto and cause–effect analysis, flowcharting, and their introduction.
4 Process capability and market requirements – a 'process', measurement of capability, concept of in-control, capability indices, etc.
5 Process control charts for variables and attributes – grouping of data, mean and range, np, p, c, u, cusum charts, etc.
6 Control of the organization's own processes – application of the techniques to local data.
7 Process quality teams and quality improvement teams – their role, use, establishment, training requirements, etc.
8 Implementation of TQM – recommended programmes, follow-up workshops, projects, action plans, reading, etc.

Throughout the programme, exercises, video tapes, etc., should be used to ilustrate the application of the principles, concepts and techniques introduced in the workshop sessions. Suitable periods of time should also be devoted to applying the methods and techniques to the participants' own processes and data. To derive maximum benefit from the programme, the delegates should bring with them to the sessions flowcharts of operations that highlight the people involved, data-collection points, typical data, and descriptions of current inspection procedures.

**First level supervision and quality team leaders (30–40 hours of seminars with follow-up workshops)**

Supervisors should be trained in the correct, efficient, and safe operation and maintenance of plant and processes, the management of people and the establishment of the correct work procedures. They must know and accept their role in ensuring that these are understood and adhered to by their managers, colleagues and subordinates. This of course requires that people should be allocated to jobs for which they are mentally and physically suitable.

Quality training for first level supervisors should include knowledge and appreciation of the quality policy, error and waste prevention, and investigation methods of communicating with and motivating the workforce, and the quality system and procedures. The 'foreman' is the key link in the training that is given to all the other employees. They must be given intensive training, perhaps over 40 hours, not only to teach them about the control of quality, but also to equip them to communicate their knowledge to the shop floor.

The seminars should illustrate the importance and application of

TQM methods in the supervisors' own environment. By means of simple concepts and examples, they should indicate, through the practical nature of the seminars, the wide range of applications of TQM techniques, and give guidance on how they might be introduced. The purpose of the courses should be to provide practical training and to place the emphasis on process control.

A quality team leader or facilitator training programme should be developed which must avoid the twin dangers of becoming too simplistic or overspecialized. The emphasis should be on practice. In addition to problem solving methods, group dynamics, and meetings management, team leadership will need to be addressed specifically. A course programme should include the following modules:

1 *Quality philosophy* – in which is covered all the relevant theories, concepts, and definitions pertinent to a competent working knowlege in the field of quality. It may be necessary to explain why change is needed, and to explain the organization's quality policy. The basic ideas of customer focus, design, detection vs prevention, consistency, continuous improvement and quality system protocol will require detailed attention.

2 *Quality tools* – in which will be explained the array of tools available for quality management and improvement. The topics must include the seven basic tools (Chapter 9), control charts, process capability studies and any special topics required, such as FMECA or Taguchi methods.

3 *Team leadership* – to provide knowledge of elements of 'group processes', and corresponding skills to ensure a quick start-up of the team work. Specific topics include:

(a) *Leadership skills and style*

   (i) Skills needed for team leaders and members.
   (ii) Assessment of team leader's style.
   (iii) Assessment of team members' styles.
   (iv) Fitting the styles and skills together.

(b) *Forming new teams*

   (i) Defining projects.
   (ii) Selecting appropriate teams.
   (iii) Team organization and role of members.
   (iv) Starting up tasks or assignments.
   (v) Stages of team development.

(c) *Running effective meetings*

- (i) Clarifying terms of reference and objectives.
- (ii) Gaining commitment to and willingness to participate in projects.
- (iii) Sharing leadership.
- (iv) Managing the agenda and other documentation.
- (v) Assuring follow-up.

(d) *Managing group dynamics*

- (i) Predicting behaviour (natural and expected).
- (ii) Characteristics of effective teams.
- (iii) Managing the group 'process' and problem solving skills.
- (iv) Action planning.

(e) *Leading teams through difficult situations*

- (i) Handling conflict.
- (ii) Difficult behaviour.
- (iii) Team leader traps and their release.
- (iv) Problems originating outside the team.

Other course possibilities include 'whole team' training, which provides the opportunity for the leader to practise training skills and strengthen his/her capability to manage. Good team leadership skills training is essential if an organization is to integrate TQM throughout.

## All other employees

It is difficult to set down here specific training programmes for this group, since it is vital that their quality education process is closely related to their jobs. The people in the typing pool will require a different approach and content for their introduction to TQM from, say, the chemical process operators. Clearly, there is a need to train every employee in the general principles of company-wide quality achievement, and much of the first part of the training given to first level supervision is appropriate for this purpose. It is recommended, however, that the training of the workforce is spread over a period of time – perhaps a half day per week for 6 weeks – and that the formal sessions are interspersed with small projects or assignments in which the participants are engaged in activities such as:

1 Listing their immediate 'customers' and the corresponding requirements.
2 Listing their immediate 'suppliers' and their own requirements.
3 Identifying the various processes with which they are involved, and listing the inputs and outputs for each.
4 Flowcharting the processes.
5 Designing check sheets for gathering data and collecting data from processes, including inputs and outputs.
6 Analysing data by simple methods, such as histograms, Pareto and cause/effect analysis, and recommending action for improvement.
7 Using simple charts and process capability analysis techniques, for control and improvement and to aid decision making.
8 Being useful team members and valuing people for their differences.

These projects almost create their own training programme, which must be very relevant to the individuals taking part. This aspect cannot be over-emphasized. The improvement projects outlined above help employees to acquire the necessary technical expertise, and sow the seeds of quality improvement teams, which are such an essential component of the successful TQM effort.

Analysis of jobs and tasks will identify the specific quality training needs. Where such analysis has not been completed, and there is an appreciable risk of problems, errors or defects being produced, an analysis should be kept under continuous review, and retraining undertaken when the nature of a job changes. Operating instructions should cover the use of materials, plant and equipment (including maintenance). Operators should receive instruction about the potential risks for error and waste that have come to light from either past operation of the process or customer feedback.

One aspect of quality training programmes that is all too often missing is corrective action. Written procedures are introduced, control charts are explained, and posters appear, but when things do not go according to plan, nobody is sure what to do. The actions of the workforce at this stage are absolutely vital, for it is here that their training and expertise have to be used to the full to design corrective action procedures and controls that rapidly analyse and remove the causes of failure. These principles apply equally to people employed in offices, laboratories, warehouses, computer rooms, etc.

*New entrants*

The acceptance and understanding of the total quality philosophy and practices by new entrants are of paramount importance. Quality should be included in all training and induction programmes for new employees.

*Shift workers*

Where it is difficult to obtain the release of a sufficient number of people to form a group of a reasonable size for training, it may be possible to release people singly for programmed learning sessions. Various institutions and organizations specialize in these methods, and advice and information may be obtained directly from them.

## 14.5   Follow-up and quality counselling

### Follow-up

For the successful implementation of TQM, training must be followed up during the early stages. Follow-up can take many forms, but the managers must provide the lead through the design of improvement projects and 'surgery' workshops.

In introducing statistical methods of process control, for example, the most satisfactory strategy is to start small and build up a bank of knowledge and experience. Sometimes it is necessary to introduce SPC techniques alongside existing methods of control (if they exist), thus allowing comparisons to be made between the new and old methods. When confidence has been established from these comparisons, the SPC methods will almost take over the control of the processes themselves. Improvements in one or two areas of the organization's operations, by means of this approach will quickly establish the techniques as reliable methods of controlling quality.

The author and his colleagues have found that a successful formula is the in-company training course plus follow-up workshops. Usually a 20-hour seminar on TQM is followed within a few weeks by an 8–10 hour workshop at which participants on the initial training course present the results of their efforts to improve processes, and use the various methods. The presentations and specific implementation problems may be discussed. A series of such workshops will add continually to the follow-up, and can be used to initiate quality improvement teams. Wider company presence and activities should be encouraged by the follow-up activities.

**Counselling**

It will usually be found that external help is required to introduce and
establish the necessary components of TQM. The author has lost
count of the number of occasions on which, following a presentation
in a boardroom of a company, he has been challenged by the quality
manager claiming that he has been repeating for years all the points
and suggestions he has just heard the 'outsider' pronounce with such
authority. The difference of course is that the company is now going
to do something about it. It is not clear why this happens – perhaps it
is about presentation skills, perhaps the prophet is never accepted in
his own country, but the fact remains that external advice is often
heeded and therefore needed.

If external consultants and trainers are used, and both large and
small companies buy in skills in this field, it is essential to select and
control the counselling carefully. The dangers of not doing so are:

* The creation of a paperwork system that is not operational.
* The 'not-invented-here' effect of buying in someone else's methods.
* A mismatch of the consultant's approach and the unique requirements of the company, its style, operations and the business environment in which it lives.

Any of these will render the system unworkable.

The fact that a consultant is 'known to operate' in an industry is not
quite the same as the consultant knowing what the quality requirements of the industry or company are, and how they differ from those
of other industries. Many consultancies have failed to provide good
advice because they did not possess the depth of knowledge of both
quality management issues and their application in special processes.
For example, the application of statistical process control (SPC) methods in continuous polymer production is not simply a question of
changing widgets for polyolefins; it requires a fundamentally different
approach, one derived from the direct experience of the consultant and
his/her understanding of the nature of the process or industry.

The two requirements, for knowledge of the industry and for knowledge of quality management, should give rise to a crude initial choice
of consultant, which perhaps could operate on the basis of qualifications and membership of professional bodies. For example, a consultant with a technical or professional qualification *and* membership of a
learned society devoted to quality should pass the first hurdle for
inclusion on the shortlist.

The consultants should have worked with many different companies in the industry, helping them to implement total quality management. This does not prevent the introduction of new consultants into the field, provided their training is adequate and supervised by experienced professionals. The acquisition of outside help can become a minefield for the unsuspecting organization, but the establishment of professional bodies – such as the Association of Quality Management Consultants (AQMC) in the UK, which carefully vets and qualifies its members with designatory letters – should enable clients to acquire the correct expertise and skills, whether in seminar presentation or direct consultancy.

## Chapter highlights

### It's Wednesday – it must be training

- Training is the single most important factor in improving quality, once commitment is present. Quality training must be objectively, systematically, and continuously performed.
- All training should occur in an improvement cycle of ensuring training is part of quality policy, allocating responsibilities, defining objectives, establishing training organizations, specifying needs, preparing programmes and materials, implementing and monitoring, assessing results, and reviewing effectiveness.

### A systematic approach to quality training

- Responsibility for quality training of employees rests with management at all levels. The main elements should include error/defect/problem prevention, reporting and analysis, investigation, and review.
- Training procedures and records should be established. These should show how job competence is demonstrated.

### Starting where and for whom?

- Needs for integrated quality training occur at four levels of the organization: very senior management, middle management, first level supervision and quality team leaders, and all other employees.

**Training programmes and their design**

- Quality training programmes should centre round the basic principles of understanding processes, and the seminars/workshops should be carried out in small groups.

**Follow-up and quality counselling**

- All quality training should be followed up with improvement projects and 'surgery' workshops.
- External help is often required to introduce TQM. Consultants should be selected carefully on the basis of qualifications, knowledge, experience, and demonstrated practical success in the 'industry'.

# 15 Implementation of TQM and the management of change

## 15.1 TQM and the management of change

The author recalls the managing director of a large transportation company who decided that a major change was required in the way the company operated if serious competitive challenges were to be met. The Board of Directors went away for a weekend and developed a new vision for the company and its 'culture'. A personnel director was recruited and given the task of managing the change in the people and their 'attitudes'. After several 'programmes' aimed at achieving the required change, including a new structure for the organization, a staff appraisal system linked to pay, training programmes to change attitudes, and questionnaire surveys, very little change in actual organizational behaviour had occurred.

Clearly something had gone wrong somewhere. But what, who, where? Everything was wrong, including what needed changing, who should lead the changes, and, in particular, how the changes should be brought about. This type of problem is very common in organizations desiring to change the way they operate to deal with increased competition, a changing market place, and different business rules. In this situation many companies recognize the need to move away from an autocratic management style, with formal rules and hierarchical procedures, and narrow work demarcations. Some have tried to create teams, to delegate (perhaps for the first time), and to improve communications.

Some of the senior managers in such organizations recognize the need for change to deal with the new realities of competitiveness, but they lack an understanding of how the change should be implemented. They often believe that changing the formal organizational structure, having vision or mission statements, 'culture change' programmes, training courses, and new payment systems will, by themselves, make the transformations.

In much research work carried out at the European Centre for

TQM, at Bradford University Management Centre, it has been shown that there is almost an inverse relationship between successful change and having formal organization-wide change This is particularly true if one functional group, such as personnel, 'owns' the programme.

In several large organizations in which total quality has been used successfully to effect change, the senior management did not focus on formal structures and systems, but set up *process-management* teams to solve real business or organization problems. The key to success in this area is to align the employees of the business, their roles and responsibilities with the organization and its *processes*. This is the core of process mapping or total quality alignment. When an organization focuses on its key processes, that is the activities and tasks themselves, rather than on abstract issues such as 'culture' and 'participation', then the change process can begin in earnest.

An approach to change, based on process alignment, and starting with the mission statement, analysing the critical success factors, *and* moving on to the key or critical processes, is the most effective way to engage the staff in an enduring change process. Many change programmes do not work because they begin trying to change the knowledge, attitudes and beliefs of individuals. The theory is that changes in these areas will lead to changes in behaviour throughout the organization. It relies on a form of religion spreading through the people in the business.

What is required, however, is virtually the opposite process, based on the recognition that people's behaviour is determined largely by the roles they have to take up. If we create for them new responsibilities, team roles, and a process driven environment, a new situation will develop, one that will force their attention and work on the processes. This will change the culture. *Teamwork* is an especially important part of the TQ model in terms of bringing about change. If changes are to be made in quality, costs, market, product or service development, close co-ordination among the marketing, design, production/operations and distribution groups is essential. This can be brought about effectively only by multifunctional teams working on the processes and understanding their interrelationships. *Commitment* is a key element of support for the high levels of co-operation, initiative, and effort that will be required to understand and work on the labyrinth of processes existing in most organizations. In addition to the knowledge of the business as a whole, which will be brought about by an understanding of the mission→CSF→process breakdown links, certain *tools*, *techniques*, and *interpersonal skills* will be required for good *communication* around the processes. These are essential if people are to identify and solve problems as teams.

If any of these elements are missing the total quality underpinned change process will collapse. The difficulties experienced by many organizations' formal change processes is that they tackle only one or two of these necessities. Many organizations trying to create a new philosophy based on teamwork fail to recognize that the employees do not know which teams to form or how they should function as teams. Recognition that effective teams need to be formed round their process, which they begin to understand together – perhaps for the first time – and further recognition that they then need to be helped as individuals through the forming–storming–norming–performing sequence, will generate the interpersonal skills and attitude changes necessary to make the new 'structure' work.

**Obstacles to implementation**

Some of the obstacles to TQM implementation are that it can be seen as time-consuming, bureaucratic, formalistic, rigid, impersonal, and/or the property of a specialist group. Frequently found is the so-called middle management resistance, particularly where there is a fear of openness.

Some of the resistance to TQM is typical resistance to any change. This may be more severe if the organization is successful, if there is a particularly deep-seated culture, if there has been a great deal of change already, or if the change lacks legitimacy.

The methods of overcoming resistance to change have largely been the subject of this book, but they include:

• Education and communication.
• Participation and involvement
• Facilitation and support.
• Negotiation and agreement.

For successful change to occur of course, there must be the perceived need for it, appropriate resources, and a supportive culture.

**Choosing the right approach**

There are basically two approaches to TQM implementation (Figure 15.1) and the correct choice of method is important to minimize resistance. The two types are:

1 The 'blitz' approach, in which the whole organization, in its current 'business as usual' state, is exposed very rapidly to TQM, and mass

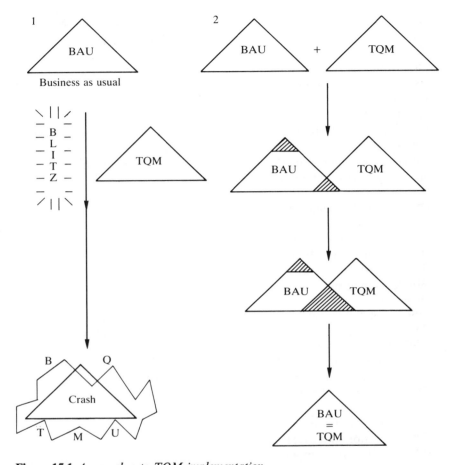

**Figure 15.1** *Approaches to TQM implementation*

education, or even hype, is started. This can lead to many problems associated with not knowing what to do next (or first), and some organizations have suffered indigestion by trying to swallow the 'elephant' whole, instead of a bite each time. The reader will observe that such 'programmes' can lead to a situation that is neither TQM nor business as usual.

2 The slow, planned, purposeful approach causes a gradual change to take place, so that 'business as usual' becomes total quality management. An important first stage in this process is the convincing and converting of senior management to TQM, so that it can permeate the organization with support from the very top.

## 15.2  Integrating TQM into the strategy of the business

Organizations will avoid the problems of 'change programmes' by con-centrating on 'process alignment' – recognizing that people's roles and responsibilities must be related to the processes in which they work. Senior managers may begin the task of process alignment by a series of seven distinct but clearly overlapping steps. This recommended path develops a self-reinforcing cycle of *commitment*, *communication*, and *culture* change. The order of the steps is important because some of the activities will be inappropriate if started too early. In the introduction of total quality for managing change, timing can be critical.

### Step 1  Gain commitment to change through the organization of the top team

Process alignment requires the starting point to be a broad review of the organization and the changes required by the top management team. By gaining this shared diagnosis of what changes are required, what the 'business' problems are, and/or what must be improved, the most senior executive mobilizes the initial commitment that is vital to begin the change process. An important element here is to get the top team working as a team, and techniques such as MBTI and/or Belbin team roles will play an important part (see Chapter 12).

### Step 2  Develop a shared 'mission' or vision of the business or of what change is required

Once the top team is committed to the analysis of the changes required, it can develop a mission statement that will help to define the new process alignment, roles and responsibilities. This will lead to a co-ordinated flow of analysis of process that crosses the traditional functional areas at all levels of the organization, without changing formal structures, titles, and systems which can create resistance (Figure 15.2).

The mission statement gives a purpose to the organization or unit. It should answer the questions 'What are we here for?' or 'What is our basic purpose?' and therefore must define the boundaries of the business in which the organization operates (Figure 15.2a). This will help to focus on the 'distinctive competence' of the organization, and to orient everyone in the direction of what has to be done. The mission must be documented, agreed by the top management team, sufficiently explicit to enable its eventual accomplishment to be verified, and

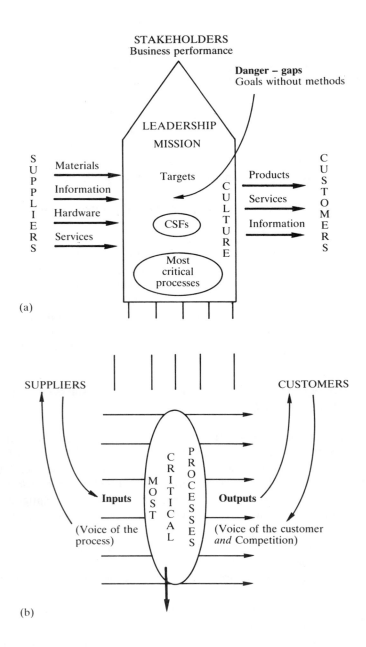

**STAKEHOLDERS**
Business performance

**Danger – gaps**
Goals without methods

LEADERSHIP
MISSION

S
U
P
P
L
I
E
R
S

Materials

Information

Hardware

Services

Targets

CSFs

Most
critical
processes

C
U
L
T
U
R
E

Products

Services

Information

C
U
S
T
O
M
E
R
S

(a)

SUPPLIERS

CUSTOMERS

M
O
S
T

C
R
I
T
I
C
A
L

P
R
O
C
E
S
S
E
S

Inputs

(Voice of the
process)

Outputs

(Voice of the customer
*and* Competition)

(b)

**Figure 15.2** (and opposite)   *From mission to process breakdown*

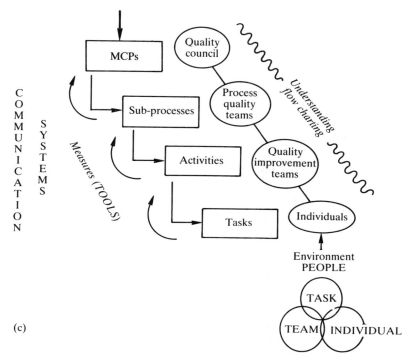

(c)

ideally be no more than four sentences. The statement must be under-standable, communicable, believable, and usable.

Some questions that may be asked of a mission statement are:

- Does it contain the need that is to be fulfilled?
- Is the need worthwhile in terms of admiration and identification, both internally and externally?
- Does it take a long term view, leading to, for example, commitment to new product or service development, or training of personnel?
- Does it take into account all the 'stakeholders'?
- Will the purpose remain constant despite changes in top manage-ment?

It is important to establish in some organizations whether or not the mission is survival. This does not preclude a longer term mission, but the short term survival mission must be expressed, if it is relevant. The management team can then decide whether it wishes to continue long term strategic thinking. If survival is a real issue, the author and his colleagues would advise against concentrating on the long term plan-ning initially.

There must be open and spontaneous discussion during generation of the mission, but there must in the end be convergence on one statement. If the mission statement is wrong, everything that follows will be wrong too, so a clear understanding is vital.

### Step 3    Define the measurable objectives, which must be agreed by the team, as being the quantifiable indicators of success in terms of the mission

The mission provides the vision and guiding light and sets down the core values, but it must be supported by measurable objectives that are tightly and inarguably linked to it. These will help to translate the directional and sometimes 'loose' statements of the mission into clear *targets*, and in turn to simplify management's thinking. They can later be used as evidence of success for the team, in every direction, internally and externally.

### Step 4    Develop the mission into its critical success factors (CSFs) to coerce and move it forward

The development of the mission is clearly not enough to ensure its implementation. This is the 'danger gap' into which many companies fall, because they do not foster the skills needed to translate the mission through its CSFs into the critical processes. Hence they have 'goals without methods', and TQM is not integrated properly into the business. At this stage of the process strong leadership from the top is crucial. Commitment to the change, whatever it may be, is always imbalanced; some senior managers may be antagonistic, some neutral, others enthusiastic or worried about the proposed changes.

Once the top managers begin to list the CSFs, they will gain some understanding of what the mission or the change requires. The first step in going from mission to CSFs is to brainstorm all the possible impacts on the mission. In this way thirty to fifty items, ranging from politics to costs, from national cultures to regional market peculiarities, may be derived.

The CSFs may now be defined – what the organization must accomplish to achieve the mission, by examination and catergorization of the impacts. There should be no more than eight CSFs, and no more than four if the mission is survival. They are the minimum key factors or subgoals that the organization *must have* or *need*, and which together will achieve the mission. They are not the how, and are not directly manageable – they may be in some cases statements of hope or fear – but they provide direction and the success criteria. In CSF determination a management team should follow the rule that each CSF is *necessary*, and that together they are *sufficient* for the mission to be achieved.

Some examples of CSFs may clarify understanding:

* We must have right-first-time suppliers.
* We must have motivated, skilled people.
* We need new products that satisfy market needs.
* We need new business opportunities.
* We must have best-in-the-field product quality.

The list of CSFs should be an agreed balance of strategic and tactical issues, each of which deals with a 'pure' factor, the use of *and* being forbidden. It will be important to know when the CSFs have been achieved, but the more important next step is to use the CSFs to enable the identification of the *processes*.

### Step 5 Break down the critical success factors into the key or critical process and gain process ownership

This is the point at which the top management team have to consider how to institutionalize the mission or the change in the form of processes that will continue to be in place, after any changes have been effected (Figure 15.2b).

The key, critical, or business processes describe what actually is or needs to be done so that the organization meets its CSFs. As with the CSFs and the mission, each process *necessary* for a given CSF must be identified, and together the processes listed must be *sufficient* for the CSFs to be accomplished. To ensure that *processes* are listed, they should be in the form of verb plus object, such as 'research the market', 'recruit competent staff', or 'measure supplier performance'.

Each business process should have an owner who is a member of the management team that agreed the CSFs. The business processes identified frequently run across 'departments' or functions, yet they must be measurable.

The questions will now come thick and fast. Is the process currently carried out? By whom? When? How frequently? With what performance and how well compared with competitors? The answers to these will force process ownership into the business. The process owner should form a process quality team to take the next steps in quality improvement. Some form of prioritization, by means of process 'quality' measures, is necessary at this stage to enable effort to be focused on the key areas for improvement. This may be carried out by a form of matrix analysis[1] or some other means. The outcome should be a set of 'most critical processes' (MCPs), which receive priority attention for improvement.

The first stage in understanding the critical processes is to produce a set of processes of a common order of magnitude. Some processes identified by the quality council may break into two or three critical processes; others may be already at the appropriate level. This method will ensure that the change becomes entrenched, the critical processes are identified and that the right people are in place to own or take responsibility for them; and it will be the start of getting the process-team organization up and running.

### Step 6  Break down the critical processes into sub-processes, activities and tasks and form improvement teams around these.

Once an organization has defined and mapped out the critical processes, people need to develop the skills to understand how the new process structure will be analysed and made to work. The very existence of new process quality teams (PQTs) with new goals and responsibilities will force the organization into a learning phase. The changes should foster new attitudes and behaviours.

An illustration of the breakdown from mission through CSFs and critical processes to individual tasks may assist in understanding the process required:

| Mission |
| --- |

Two of the statements in a well known quality management consultancy's mission statement are: 'Gain and maintain a position as Europe's foremost management consultancy in the development of organizations through the management of change' and 'provide the consultancy, training and facilitation necessary to assist with making the continuous improvement of quality an integral part of our customers' business strategy.'
↓

| Critical success factor |
| --- |

*One* of the CSFs that clearly relates to this is 'We need a high level of awareness of our company in the market place'.
↓

| Critical process |
| --- |

*One* of the critical processes that clearly must be done particularly well to achieve this CSF is to 'Promote, advertise, and communicate the company's business capability'.

↓

---
Sub-process
---

*One* of the sub-processes resulting from a breakdown of this critical process is 'Prepare the company's information pack'.
↓

---
Activity
---

*One* of the activities contributing to this sub-process is 'Prepare *one* of the subject booklets, i.e. TQM, SPC or quality systems'.
↓

---
Task
---

*One* of the tasks that contributes to this is 'Write the detailed leaflet for any particular seminar', e.g.: 'One-day or three-day seminars on TQM or SPC, or quality system advisory project'.

### Individuals, tasks, and teams

Having broken down the processes into sub-processes, activities, and tasks in this way, we can now link them with the Adair model of action-centred leadership and teamwork.

The *tasks* are performed, at least initially, by individuals. For example, some*body* has to sit down and draft out the first version of a seminar leaflet. There has to be an understanding by the individual of the task and its position in the hierarchy of processes. Once the initial task has been performed, the results must be checked against the activity of co-ordinating the promotional booklet – say for TQM. This clearly brings in the team, and there must be interfaces between the needs of the *tasks*, the *individuals* who performed them and the *team* concerned with the *activities*.

Using the hierarchy of processes, it is possible to link this with the hierarchy of quality teams. Hence:

Quality council – mission – CSFs – critical processes.
Process quality teams – critical processes.
Quality improvement (or functional) teams (QITs) – sub-processes.
QITs – activities.
QITs and quality circles/Kaizen teams/individuals – tasks.

### Performance measurement and metrics

Once the processes have been analysed in this way, it should be possible to develop *metrics* for measuring the performance of the processes, sub-processes, activities, and tasks. These must be meaningful in terms of the *inputs* and *outputs* of the processes, and in terms of the *customers* of and *suppliers* to the processes (Figure 15.2c).

At first thought, this form of measurement can seem difficult for processes such as preparing a sales brochure or writing leaflets advertising seminars, but, if we think carefully about the *customers* for the leaflet-writing tasks, these will include the *internal* ones, i.e. the consultants, and we can ask whether the output meets their requirements. Does it really say what the seminar is about, what its objectives are and what the programme will be? Clearly, one of the 'measures' of the seminar leaflet-writing task could be the number of typing errors in it, but is this a *key* measure of the performance of the process? Only in the context of office management is this an important measure. Elsewhere it is not.

The same goes for the *activity* of preparing the subject booklet. Does it tell the 'customer' what TQM or SPC is and how the consultancy can help? For the *sub-process* of preparing the company brochure, does it inform people about the company and does it bring in enquiries from which customers can be developed? Clearly, some of these measures require *external market research*, and some of them *internal research*. The main point is that metrics must be developed and used to reflect the *true performance* of the processes, sub-processes, activities, and tasks. These must involve good contact with external and internal customers of the processes. The metrics may be quoted as *ratios*, e.g. number of customers derived per number of brochures mailed out. Good data-collection, record-keeping, and analysis are clearly required.

It is hoped that this illustration will help the reader to:

• Understand the breakdown of processes into sub-processes, activities, and tasks.
• Understand the links between the process breakdowns and the task, individual and team concepts.
• Link the hierarchy of processes with the hierarchy of quality teams.
• Begin to assemble a cascade of flowcharts representing the process breakdowns, which can form the basis of the quality system and communicate what is going on throughout the business.
• Understand the way in which metrics must be developed to measure the true performance of the process, and their links with the customers, suppliers, inputs and outputs of the processes.

This whole concept/structure is represented in Figure 15.2c. The changed patterns of co-ordination, driven by the process maps, should increase collaboration and information sharing.

Clearly the senior and middle managers must provide the right support. Once employees, at all levels, identify what kinds of new skill are needed, they will ask for the formal training programmes in order to develop those skills further. This is a key area, because the teamwork around the processes will ask more of employees, so they will need increasing support from their managers.

This has been called 'just-in-time' training, which describes very well the nature of the process required. Such training is quite different from the blanket or carpet-bombing training associated with many unsuccessful change programmes, which targets competencies or skills but does not change the organization's patterns of collaboration and co-ordination.

**Step 7   Monitor and adjust the process alignment in response to difficulties in the change process.**

Change must create something that did not exist before, namely a 'learning organization' capable of adapting to a changing competitive environment. One must also learn how to monitor and modify the new behaviour to maintain the change-sensitive environment.

Some people will, of course, find great difficulty in accepting the changes, and perhaps will be incapable of doing so, in spite of all the direction, support, and peer pressure brought about by the process alignment. There will come a time to replace those managers and staff who cannot function in the new organization, after they have had a good opportunity to make the changes. These decisions are of course never easy, especially where valuable technical skills are owned by the people who have difficulty working in the new participatory, process-driven organization.

When people  begin to understand what kind of manager and employee/staff the new organization needs, and this often develops slowly and from experience of seeing individuals succeed and fail, they should begin to accept the need to replace or move people to other parts of the organization.

## Summarizing the steps

If a top-management team has attended at least a 1-day workshop on TQM (see Chapter 14), the initial key steps may be summarized in Figure 15.3, together with their links to commitment, communications and culture change, through project work and correct follow-up. This

| | | |
|---|---|---|
| **C** | | Initial key steps following one day seminar for top management |
| **O** | | • Formation of quality council (Top-management team) |
| **M** | | • TQM 'Attitude' survey<br>– Profile of organization<br>– Quality costs |
| **M** | **C** | – Strengths/weaknesses |
| **I** | **O** | • Two-day strategic planning workshop (quality council) |
| **T** | **M** | – Charter<br>– Mission statement |
| **M** | **M** | – Quality policy<br>– Critical success factors |
| **E** | **U** | – Critical processes<br>– Implementation action plan |
| **N** | **N** | • Formation of process quality teams and/or site steering committees |
| **T** | **I** | • Teamwork seminar for quality council (may precede strategic planning workshop) |
| | **C** | • Identify team facilitators |
| | **A** **C** | • Run specific training and team-forming workshops |
| | **T** **U** | • Company-wide awareness training on customer/supplier interfaces |
| | **I** **L** | • Implementation/improvement projects for quality policy deployment |
| | **O** **T** | – Quality costing |
| | **N** **U** | – Customer/supplier framework<br>– DPA |
| | **R** | – Systems<br>– Techniques |
| | **E** | • Feedback/follow-up workshops throughout implementation |

**Figure 15.3** *TQM implementation*

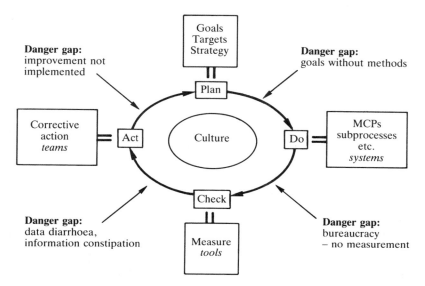

**Figure 15.4** *TQM implementation – all done with the Deming continuous improvement cycle*

must all be done within the continuous improvement cycle to avoid the 'danger gaps' shown in Figure 15.4. The training/implementation flow-chart of Figure 15.5 maps out this sequence, in which the rectangles are the training/workshop inputs and the rings are the project work.

**The goal-translation process**

One of the keys to integrating total quality into the business strategy is a formal 'goal-translation' process. If the mission and measurable goals have been analysed in terms of critical success factors and critical processes, then the organization has begun to understand how to achieve the mission. Goal-translation ensures that the WHATS are converted into HOWS right down through the organization, by means of the quality function deployment (QFD) process (see Chapter 3). The method is best described by an example.

At the top of an organization in the chemical process industries, five measurable goals have been identified. These are listed under the heading WHAT in Figure 15.6. The top team listens to the 'voice of the customer' and tries to understand HOW these business goals will be achieved. It realizes that product consistency, on-time delivery and speed or quality of response are the keys. These CSFs are placed along

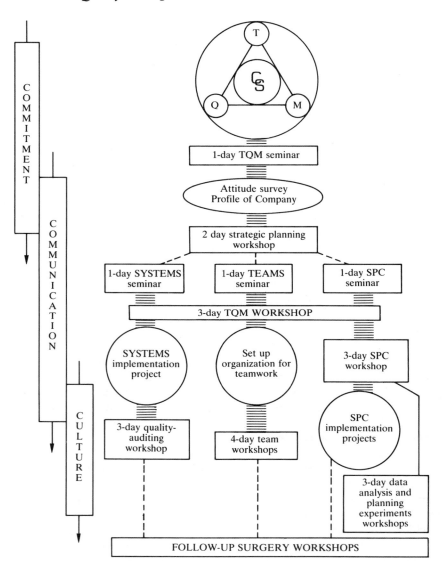

**Figure 15.5** *Training implementation flowchart*

the first row of the matrix, and the relationships between the WHAT and the HOW estimated as strong, medium or weak. A measurement target for the hows is then specified.

The HOW becomes the WHAT for the next layer of management.

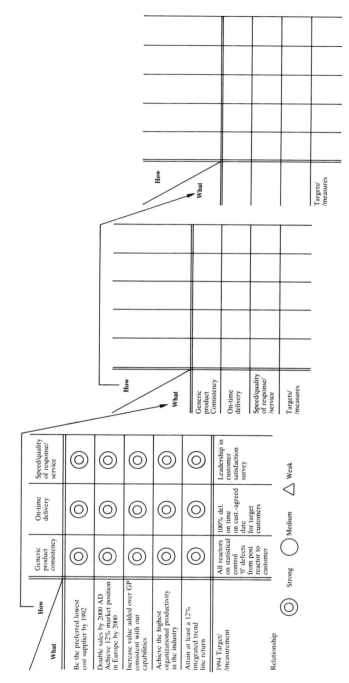

**Figure 15.6** *Goal-transition process*

The top team shares its goals with its immediate subordinates at a meeting, and asks them to determine their HOWS, indicate the relationship, and set measurement targets. The process continues down the organization until the senior-management goals have been translated through the WHAT/HOW→WHAT/HOW→WHAT/HOW matrices to the individual tasks within the organization. This provides a good discipline to support the breakdown and understanding of the business process mapping described previously in Figure 15.2.

## 15.3   Planning the implementation of TQM

The task of implementing TQM can be daunting, and the Chief Executive faced with this may draw little comfort from the so-called 'gurus'. The first decision is where to begin, and this can be so difficult that many organizations never get started. This has been called TQP – total quality paralysis!

This book has been written to help senior management bring total quality into existence. The preliminary stages of understanding, commitment, and leadership are vital steps that also form the foundation of the whole TQM structure (Figure 15.7). Too many organizations ignore these phases, believing that they have the right attitude and awareness, when in fact there are some fundamental gaps in their 'quality credibility'. These gaps will soon lead to insurmountable difficulties and collapse of the edifice.

While an intellectual understanding of quality provides a basis for TQM, it is clearly only the planting of the seed. The understanding must be translated into commitment, policies, plans and actions for TQM to germinate. Making this happen requires not only commitment, but a competence in the mechanics of quality management, and in making changes. Without a strategy to implement TQM through systems, capability and control, the expended effort will lead to frustration. Poor quality management can become like poor gardening – a few weeds are pulled up, only for others to appear in their place days later, *plus* additional weeds elsewhere. Problem solving is very much like weeding; tackling the root causes, often by digging deep, is essential for better control.

Individuals working on their own, even with a plan, will never generate optimum results. The individual effort is required in improvement but it must be co-ordinated with the efforts of others to be truly effective. The implementation begins with the drawing up of the mission statement, and the establishment of the appropriate organizational structure, both for managing and encouraging acceptance of quality

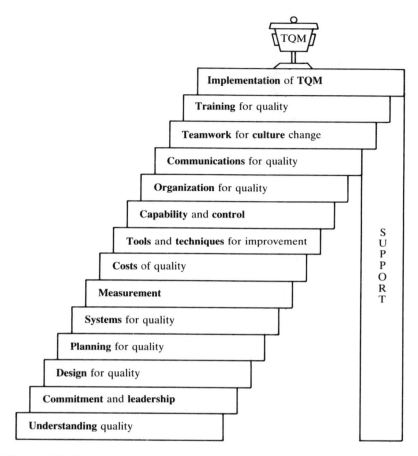

**Figure 15.7** *The steps to TQM*

through teamwork. Collecting information on how the organization operates, including the costs of quality, helps to identify the prime areas in which improvements will have the largest impact on performance. Designing and planning improvement should be the job of all managers, but a crucial early stage is putting quality management systems in place to drive the improvement process and make sure that problems remain solved forever, by means of structured corrective action procedures and techniques.

Once the plans and systems have been put into place, the need for continued education, training and communication becomes paramount. Organizations that try to change the quality culture, but operate systems, procedures, or control methods without effective, honest, two-

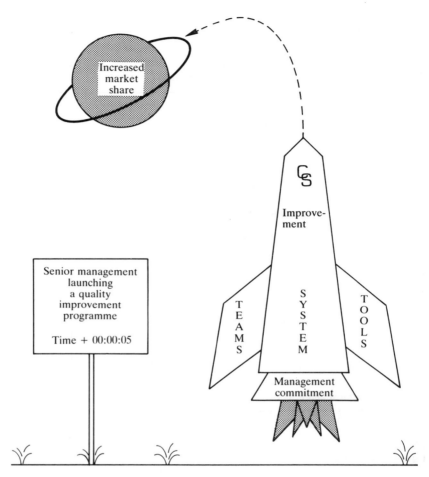

**Figure 15.8** *Launching quality improvement*

way communication, will experience the frustration of being 'cloned' types of organizations, which can function but inspire no confidence in being able to survive the changing environment in which they live.

An organization may of course have already taken several steps on the road to TQM. If good understanding of quality and how it should be managed already exists, and there is top management commitment, a written quality policy and a satisfactory organizational structure, then the strategic planning stage may begin straight away. When implementation is contemplated, priorities among the various projects must be identified. For example, a quality system that conforms to the requirements of ISO 9000 may already exist, and the systems step will not be a major task, but introducing a measurement or quality related costing system may well be. It is important to remember that a review of the current performance in all the areas, even when well established, should be part of normal operations to ensure continuous improvement.

Education and training must be continuous, and draw together the requirements of all the steps into a cohesive programme of introduction. The timing of the training inputs, follow-up sessions, and advisory work should be co-ordinated and reviewed, in terms of their effectiveness, on a regular basis. It will be necessary at various stages of the implementation to develop checks to establish the true progress. For example, before moving from understanding to trying to obtain top management commitment, one should obtain objective evidence to show that the next stage is justified.

The launch of quality improvement requires a balanced approach, and the three 'hard' management components must be 'fired' to lift the campaign off the ground (Figure 15.8). If teams are started before the establishment of a good system of management, there will be nothing to which they can adhere. Equally, if SPC is introduced without a good system of data recording and standard operating procedures, the techniques will simply measure how bad things are. A quality system on its own will give only a weak thrust; it must have the boost of improvement teams and SPC to make it come 'alive'.

Effective co-ordination of these three components will result in quality improvement through increased capability. This should in turn lead to consistently satisfied customers, and, where appropriate, an increase in or preservation of market share.

An excellent example of the principles in this book being applied in practice is provided by Tetrapak, which has flowcharted the process under five headings for internal training purposes:

- How total quality projects are decided (Figure 15.9).
- How total quality project teams are formed (Figure 15.10).
- How total quality projects are run (Figure 15.11).
- How your training will help you take one step further towards total quality (Figure 15.12).
- How total quality techniques are applied to business as usual (Figure 15.13).

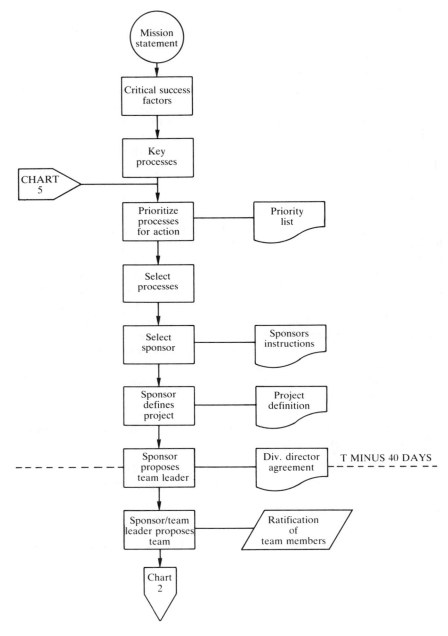

**Figure 15.9** *Flowchart 1 – how total quality projects are decided*

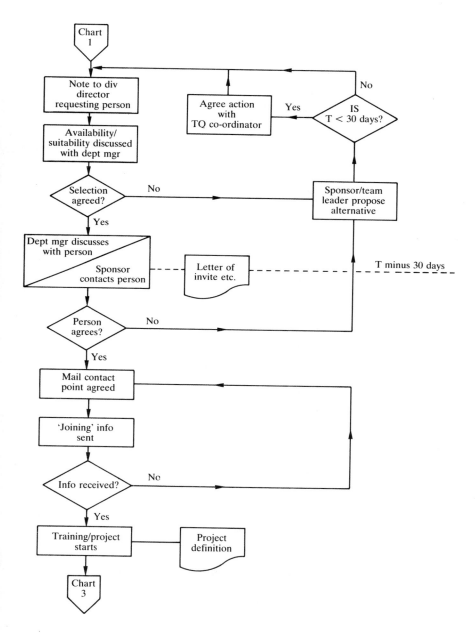

**Figure 15.10** *Flowchart 2 – how total quality project teams are formed*

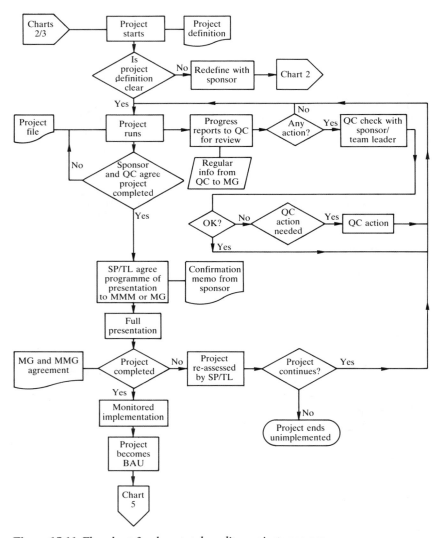

**Figure 15.11** *Flowchart 3 – how total quality projects are run*

## 15.4   Continuous improvement and the TQM model

Never ending or continuous improvement is probably the most powerful concept to guide management. It is a term not well understood in
many organizations, although that must begin to change if those organizations are to survive. To maintain a wave of interest in quality, it is

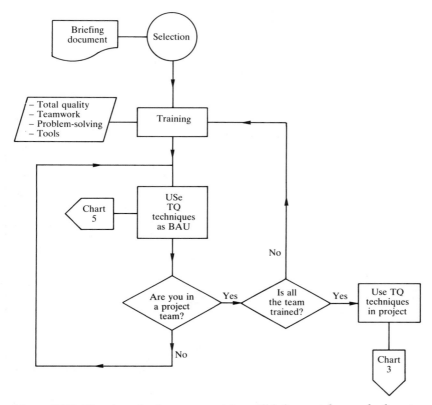

**Figure 15.12** *Flowchart 4 – how your training will help you take one further step towards total quality*

necessary to develop generations of managers who not only understand but are dedicated to the pursuit of never-ending improvement in meeting external and internal customer needs.

The concept requires a systematic approach to quality management that has the following components:

- *Planning* the processes and their inputs.
- *Providing* the inputs.
- *Operating* the processes.
- *Evaluating* the outputs.
- *Examining* the performance of the processes.
- *Modifying* the processes and their inputs.

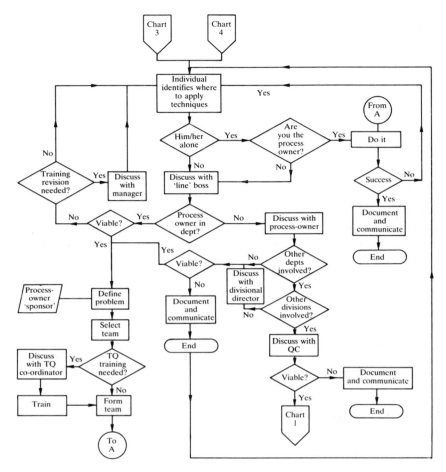

**Figure 15.13** *Flowchart 5 – how total quality techniques are applied to business as usual (BAU)*

This system must be firmly tied to a continuous assessment of customer needs, and depends on a flow of ideas on how to make improvements, reduce variation, and generate greater customer satisfaction. It also requires a high level of commitment, and a sense of personal responsibility in those operating the processes.

The never-ending improvement cycle ensures that the organization learns from results, standardizes what it does well in a documented quality management system, and improves operations and outputs from what it learns. But the emphasis must be that this is done in a planned, systematic, and conscientious way to create a climate – a way of life – that permeates the whole organization.

There are three basic principles of never-ending improvement:

* Focusing on the *customer*.
* Understanding the *process*.
* All *employees* committed to quality.

## 1   Focusing on the customer

An organization must recognize, throughout its ranks, that the purpose of all work and all efforts to make improvements is to serve the customers better. This means that it must always know how well its outputs are performing, in the eyes of the customer, through measurement and feedback. The most important customers are the external ones, but the quality chains can break down at any point in the flows of work. Internal customers therefore must also be well served if the external ones are to be satisfied.

## 2   Understanding the process

In the successful operation of any process it is essential to understand what determines its performance and outputs. This means intense focus on the design and control of the inputs, working closely with suppliers, and understanding process flows to eliminate bottlenecks and reduce waste. If there is one difference between management/ supervision in the Far East and the West, it is that in the former management is closer to, and more involved in, the processes. It is not possible to stand aside and manage in never-ending improvement. TQM in an organization means that everyone has the determination to use their detailed knowledge of the processes and make improvements, and to use appropriate statistical methods to analyse and create action plans.

## 3   All employees committed to quality

Everyone in the organization, from top to bottom, from offices to technical service, from headquarters to local sites, must play their part. People are the source of ideas and innovation, and their expertise, experience, knowledge, and co-operation have to be harnessed to get those ideas implemented.

When people are treated like machines, work becomes uninteresting and unsatisfying. Under such conditions it is not possible to expect quality services and reliable products. The rates of absenteeism and of staff turnover are measures that can be used in determining the strengths and weaknesses, or management style and people's morale, in any company.

The first step is to convince everyone of their own role in total quality. Employers and managers must of course take the lead, and the most senior executive has a personal responsibility for quality. The degree of management's enthusiasm and drive will determine the ease with which the whole workforce is motivated.

Most of the work in any organization is done away from the immediate view of management and supervision, and often with individual discretion. If the co-operation of some or all of the people is absent, there is no way that managers will be able to cope with the chaos that will result. This principle is extremely important at the points where the processes 'touch' the outside customer. Every phase of these operations must be subject to continuous improvement, and for that everyone's co-operation is required.

Never-ending improvement is the process by which greater customer satisfaction is achieved. Its adoption recognizes that quality is a moving target, but its operation actually results in quality.

**A model for total quality management**

The concept of total quality management is basically very simple. Each part of an organization has customers, whether within or without, and the need to identify what the customer requirements are, and then set about meeting them, forms the core of a total quality approach. This requires the three hard management necessities: a good quality management system, tools such as statistical process control (SPC), and teamwork. These are complementary in many ways, and they share the same requirement for an uncompromising commitment to quality. This must start with the most senior management and flow down through the organization. Having said that, teamwork, SPC, or the quality system, or all three, may be used as a spearhead to drive TQM through an organization. The attention to many aspects of a company's operations – from purchasing through to distribution, from data recording to control chart plotting – which are required for the successful introduction of a good quality system, or the implementation of SPC, will have a 'Hawthorne effect', concentrating everyone's attention on the customer/supplier interface, both inside and outside the organization.

Total quality management calls for consideration of processes in all

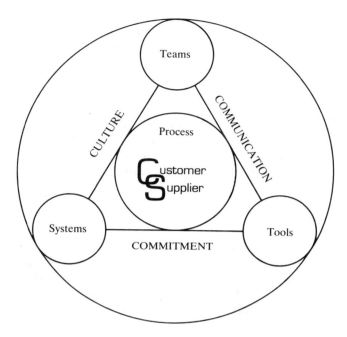

**Figure 15.14** *Total quality management model*

the major areas: marketing, design, procurement, operations, distribution, etc. Clearly, these each require considerable expansion and thought, but if attention is given to all areas, using the concepts of TQM, then very little will be left to chance. Much of industry and commerce would benefit from the improvements in quality brought about by the approach represented in Figures 15.2 and 15.14. This approach will ensure the implementation of the management commitment represented in the quality policy, and provide the environment and information base on which teamwork thrives.

## 15.5   How long can TQM survive?

During the introduction of TQM, or several years into its implementation, problems may arise. Companies have experienced different types of difficulty but the major ones are:

- Management is not fully committed and reverts to meeting short-term gains.

- Scepticism due to lack of integration and organizational focus on quality.
- Loss of credibility for TQM, which becomes last month's or last year's flavour.
- Teams become bogged down in trivia instead of tackling the important problems.

After several years of TQM, organizations may find it useful to carry out surveys to ensure that real commitment at the top is still present. The quality council or senior management should be interrogated regarding commitment, strategies, teamwork, problems and results, and development.

### Survey of commitment

The survey should examine the success of the initial drive towards management commitment and its current level. Senior managers may be, or perceive themselves to be, fully committed, at least to the TQM ideology, but middle managers need to have the right attitude, *and* be sure of the practical implications. This approach should draw attention to a number of problems, including staff struggling owing to lack of direction.

The remainder of the people may be committed to the concept to a far greater degree than management believes, but they may doubt the sincerity of management's application. Work in companies using the survey approach has shown that:

- Communication is the key to the programme.
- Commitment from the workforce is tied to the amount of training they receive.
- Belief in the system is linked directly to the changes that actually take place.

### Survey of strategies

The strategy for TQM implementation is often underdeveloped. This can lead to intermittent tactics and 'add-on' fads, which contribute greatly to a 'flavour of the month' reputation for TQM. The lack of long term strategies, objectives, and targets will cause the scheme to lose credibility with the people. If, for example, teams are formed, meet and make presentations to management without really knowing the ultimate purposes or aims of their operation, or the goalposts are moved during a project, frustration and even anger will destroy the TQM drive very quickly.

It is vital for the strategic planning to develop proper measurement indices for all processes, including those in 'administration'. Another valuable aid is to obtain an outside, independent view to help with and develop the strategy. This will usually be seen, by top management and the people, as a positive step to keep up the momentum.

**Survey of teamwork**

Some basic misconceptions may develop during the first few years of operating TQM. The perception of the status of the various teams – PQTs, QITs and quality circles – may become distorted. In one organization, for example, it was found that the workforce felt that QITs were for professional staff and quality circles for the rest of the workforce. There was also a belief that teams worked best in a production environment, because the progress of results could be measured against definite parameters. This led to teams not being formed in the administration departments as quickly as hoped. Communications were also poor in those areas, since half the staff did not know about the scheme, or had not been asked to join a team. When people did find out about the teams, they asked for training and wanted to take part.

**Survey of problems and results**

Everyone in an organization that is, say, 5 years into TQM will realize that it is not without its problems. The application of measurement to administrative practices, for example, may cause a number of headaches. Other problems that have been seen blocking the road to TQM include:

- No formal strategy.
- Failure to provide incentives by recognition.
- Lack of effective communication.
- Narrowly based training.

These can be major causes of lack of penetration. One approach that should definitely not be used to try to correct these difficulties is a financial incentive – it does not form part of the TQM culture, and would defeat many of the objectives. Recognition and the chance to participate are the only effective incentives.

The successes of TQM may be measured on a number of dimensions:

1   *Stakeholders* (business measures)
Increased market share/reduced loss in market share.
Increased profit.

2   *Customers*
More contact with and recognition by external customers.
Better understanding of their requirements.
Reduced complaints, lost orders, claims, goodwill, etc.

3   *Outputs/products/services*
Less defects, errors, returns, repairs (costs).

4   *Suppliers*
Better liaison and partnerships with external suppliers.
They have better understanding of requirements and cause less
problems.
Reductions in total costs of dealing with suppliers.

5   *Inputs*
Fewer returns to suppliers, defects, errors.

6   *Inside organization*
Clearer leadership.
Clearer strategy and deployment.
Improvement in internal processes:
(a) Reduction in scrap, rework (generally: internal quality waste
    problems), time, etc.
(b) Better understanding of processes.
(c) Better internal communications.
(d) More rapid innovation – greater scope.
(e) Better/quicker decisions, based on teamwork.
(f) More productive/smoother operations and systems.
(g) Better scheduling of resources.
(h) Better conditions.

7   *People*
Happier/more contented or fulfilled staff.
Improved 'industrial relations'/morale/attitudes.
Release of employee 'energy' into the business.
More participation from people in all processes, including innova-
tion.
More teamwork.
Facilitation of management of change.

**Survey of development**

Following a review of progress by surveys or other means, thought
must be given to how TQM is to develop in the organization.
Suggestions for consideration may include:

- Development of the long-term TQM strategies.
- Re-emphasis of the TQM culture.
- Reorganization of the TQM structure.
- Increase in QITs and quality circles or Kaizen team membership.
- Additional training and resources.
- Improvements in measurement – especially for administration areas.
- Improvements in communication of progress, results, and successes.
- Improvements in the recognition process.

The most important thing is that management and the people must want TQM to continue because they recognize the benefits. The organization may realize through progress reviews that, although it is getting a number of things right, it has a long way to go before the quality management can be considered to be *total*. The emphasis may, for example, move from achieving assessment of the quality system by an independent body to new initiatives aimed at getting the backing of *all* the people, such as the various quality award criteria (see Chapter 6).

The basic lessons that those companies with most success in TQM have learned can be summarized as follows:

1 TQM is hard work.
2 To establish TQM takes longer than first thought.
3 TQM needs to be driven by the strategy through the whole business.
4 Top and middle-management commitment is vital.
5 TQM champions must balance their enthusiasm with practicability.
6 Sceptics are not always a hindrance – they can be beneficial.

### Caution – this concept can damage your wealth (or even health!)

The author has forgotten who first said that there is nothing as inevitable as an idea whose time has come. TQM is in this fortunate situation. *But*, there is also nothing as inevitable as the rejection of ideas that do not fulfil their promise. In the 1990s this is still the greatest danger facing TQM.

TQM, or any other good idea, will not succeed by itself – it must be carefully managed. To avoid TQD – total quality disillusionment – several things must be done by all concerned:

- Avoid overstating the benefits of TQM (disillusionment is often caused by unrealistic expectations – anyone who has played golf will certainly know this!).
- Avoid understanding the commitment required when trying to gain acceptance for the quality strategy.

- Emphasize the long, slow journey to TQM to prevent it being consigned to the scrap heap of discarded magic management ointments or fads.
- Avoid creating the impression that quality is a finite task that once installed will last forever, with only minimum maintenance.
- Prevent TQM being used as an instant solution to a particular problem.
- Emphasize that quality improvement requires an ongoing, never-ending commitment for the lasting benefits to be obtained.

One of the greatest tangible benefits of TQM for a commercial organization is the increased market share that results, rather than just reductions in quality costs. The evidence for this can be seen already in some of the major consumer and industrial markets of the world. Quality can also be converted into premium prices, and it clearly correlates with profit, but the less tangible benefit of greater employee commitment to quality is equally, if not more, important in the longer term. The pursuit of continual improvement must become a way of life for everyone in an organization if it is to succeed in today's increasingly competitive environment.

## Chapter highlights

### TQM and the management of change

- Senior managers in some organizations recognize the need for change to deal with increasing competitiveness, but lack an understanding of how to implement the changes.
- Successful change is effected not by focusing on formal structures and systems, but by aligning process management teams. This starts with writing the mission statement, analysis of the critical success factors (CSFs) and understanding the critical or key processes.
- Some of the obstacles to TQM implementation and resistance to change may be overcome through education, communication, participation, facilitation, and support. The 'blitz' or rapid change approach should be rejected in favour of a slow, planned purposeful one, starting at the top.

### Integrating TQM into the strategy of the business

- Senior management may begin the task of process alignment through seven steps to a self-reinforcing cycle of commitment, communication, and culture change.

- The first three steps are gain commitment to change, develop a shared mission or vision of the business or desired change, and define the measurable objectives.
- The remaining four steps comprise developing the mission into its CSFs; understanding the key or critical processes and gaining ownership; breaking down the critical processes into sub-processes, activities and tasks; and monitoring and adjusting the process alignment in response to difficulties in the change process.
- Goal translation then ensures that the WHATs are converted into HOWs, using a quality function deployment matrix-based process.

## Planning the implementation of TQM

- Making quality happen requires not only commitment but competence in the mechanics of TQM. Crucial early stages will comprise establishment of the appropriate organization structure; collecting information, including quality costs; teamwork; quality systems; and training.
- The launch of quality improvement requires a balanced approach, through systems, teams and tools.
- The steps may be flowcharted as: how total quality projects are decided, how teams are formed, how projects are run, how training helps, and how techniques are applied.

## Continuous improvement and the TQM model

- Managers must understand and pursue never-ending improvement. This should cover planning and operating processes, providing inputs, evaluating outputs, examining performance, and modifying processes and their inputs.
- There are three basic principles of continuous improvement: focusing on the customer, understanding the process, and seeing that all employees are committed to quality.
- In the model for TQM the customer–supplier chains form the core, which is surrounded by the hard management necessities of a good quality system, tools, and teamwork.

## How long can TQM survive?

- Some of the problems experienced by TQM practitioners include lack of full commitment, lack of integration, loss of focus, loss of credibility, and failure in the ability to tackle the important issues.

- Surveys may be useful to 'check' progress in terms of commitment, strategies, teamwork, problems and results, and TQM development.
- Successful organizations using TQM have learned that it is hard work, takes a long time, needs to be driven by the strategy through the whole business, relies on top and middle management commitment, and enthusiastic practical champions.
- Emphasize the need for a never-ending commitment to improvement.

**Reference**

1   See, for example, Hardaker, M. and Ward, B. K., 'Getting Things Done – how to make a team work', *Harvard Business Review*, Nov/Dec. 1987, pp. 112–119.

# Appendix A  Three American gurus

A small group of American quality experts or 'gurus' has been advising industry throughout the world on how it should manage quality. The approaches of Philip B Crosby, W Edwards Deming, and Joseph M Juran, their similarities and differences, are presented briefly here.

## Philip B Crosby

Crosby has four absolutes of quality:

- Definition – conformance to requirements.
- System – prevention.
- Performance standard – zero defects.
- Measurement – price of non-conformance.

He offers management fourteen steps to improvement:

### Crosby's fourteen steps to quality improvement
1 Make it clear that management is committed to quality.
2 Form quality improvement teams with representatives from each department.
3 Determine where current and potential quality problems lie.
4 Evaluate the cost of quality and explain its use as a management tool.
5 Raise the quality awareness and personal concern of all employees.
6 Take actions to correct problems identified through previous steps.
7 Establish a committee for the zero defects programme.
8 Train supervisors to actively carry out their part of the quality improvement programme.
9 Hold a 'zero defects day' to let all employees realize that there has been a change.
10 Encourage individuals to establish improvement goals for themselves and their groups.

11  Encourage employees to communicate to management the obstacles they face in attaining their improvement goals.
12  Recognize and appreciate those who participate.
13  Establish quality councils to communicate on a regular basis.
14  Do it all over again to emphasize that the quality improvement programme never ends.

## W Edwards Deming

*Deming has fourteen points for management*

1  Create constancy of purpose towards improvement of product and service.
2  Adopt the new philosophy. We can no longer live with commonly accepted levels of delays, mistakes, defective workmanship.
3  Cease dependence on mass inspection. Require, instead, statistical evidence that quality is built in.
4  End the practice of awarding business on the basis of price tag.
5  Find problems. It is management's job to work continually on the system.
6  Institute modern methods of training on the job.
7  Institute modern methods of supervision of production workers. The responsibility of foremen must be changed from numbers to quality.
8  Drive out fear, so that everyone may work effectively for the company.
9  Break down barriers between departments.
10  Eliminate numerical goals, posters, and slogans for the workforce asking for new levels of productivity without providing methods.
11  Eliminate work standards that prescribe numerical quotas.
12  Remove barriers that stand between the hourly worker and his right to pride of workmanship.
13  Institute a vigorous program of education and retraining.
14  Create a structure in top management that will push every day on the above thirteen points.

## Joseph M Juran

*Juran's ten steps to quality improvement*

1  Build awareness of the need and opportunity for improvement.
2  Set goals for improvement.

3 Organize to reach the goals (establish a quality council, identify problems, select projects, appoint teams, designate facilitators).
4 Provide training.
5 Carry out projects to solve problems.
6 Report progress.
7 Give recognition.
8 Communicate results.
9 Keep score.
10 Maintain momentum by making annual improvement part of the regular systems and processes of the company.

**A comparison**

One way to compare directly the various approaches of the three American gurus is in tabular form. Table A.1 shows the differences and similarities, classified under 12 different factors.

**Table A.1** *The American quality gurus compared*

| | *Crosby* | *Deming* | *Juran* |
|---|---|---|---|
| Definition of quality | Conformance to requirements | A predictable degree of uniformity and dependability at low cost and suited to the market | Fitness for use |
| Degree of senior-management responsibility | Responsible for quality | Responsible for 94% of quality problems | Less than 20% of quality problems are due to workers |
| Performance standard/motivation | Zero defects | Quality has many 'scales'. Use statistics to measure performance in all areas. Critical of zero defects | Avoid campaigns to 'do perfect work' |
| General approach | Prevention, not inspection | Reduce variability by continuous improvement. Cease mass inspection | General management approach to quality – especially 'human' elements |
| Structure | Fourteen steps to quality improvement | Fourteen points for management | Ten steps to quality improvement |
| Statistical process control (SPC) | Rejects statistically acceptable levels of quality | Statistical methods of quality control must be used | Recommends SPC but warns that it can lead to 'tool-driven' approach |

| | | |
|---|---|---|
| **Improvement basis** | A 'process', not a programme. Improvement goals | Continuous to reduce variation. Eliminate goals without methods | Project-by-project team approach. Set goals |
| **Teamwork** | Quality improvement teams. Quality councils | Employee participation in decision-making. Break down barriers between departments | Team and quality circle approach |
| **Costs of quality** | Cost of non-conformance. Quality is free | No optimum – continuous improvement | Quality is not free – there is an optimum |
| **Purchasing and goods received** | State requirements. Supplier is extension of business. Most faults due to purchasers themselves | Inspection too late – allows defects to enter system through AQLs. Statistical evidence and control charts required | Problems are complex. Carry out formal surveys |
| **Vendor rating** | Yes *and* buyers. Quality audits useless | No – critical of most systems | Yes, but help supplier improve |
| **Single sources of supply** | | Yes | No – can neglect to sharpen competitive edge. |

# Appendix B    TQM Bibliography

## General quality management and TQM

Bank, J., *The Essence of Total Quality Management*, Prentice Hall, Hemel Hempstead (UK), 1992.

Caplen, R. H., *A Practical Approach to Total Quality Control* (5th edn), Business Books, London, 1988.

Crosby, P. B., *Quality is Free*, McGraw-Hill, New York, 1979.

Crosby, P. B., *Quality Without Tears*, McGraw-Hill, New York, 1984.

Dale, B. G. and Plunkett, J. J. (eds), *Managing Quality*, Philip Allan, Hemel Hempstead (UK), 1990.

Deming, W. E., *Our of the Crisis*, MIT, Cambridge, Mass. (USA), 1982.

Edosomwam, J. A., *Productivity and Quality Improvement*, IFS, Bedford (UK), 1988.

Feigenbaum, A. V., *Total Quality Control* (3rd edn, revised), McGraw-Hill, New York, 1991.

Garvin, D. A., *Managing Quality: the strategic competitive edge*, The Free Press (Macmillan), New York, 1988.

Hakes, C. (ed), *Total Quality Improvement: the key to business improvement*, Chapman & Hall, London, 1991.

Hutchins, D., *In Pursuit of Quality*, Pitman, London, 1990.

Hutchins, D., *Achieve Total Quality*, Director Books, Cambridge (UK), 1992.

Ishikawa, K. (translated by D. J. Lu), *What is Total Quality Control? – the Japanese Way*, Prentice-Hall, Englewood Cliffs, NJ (USA), 1985.

Macdonald, J. and Piggot, J., *Global Quality: the new management culture*, Mercury Books, London, 1990.

Mann, N. R., *The Keys to Excellence: the story of the Deming philosophy*, Prestwick Books, Los Angeles, CA (USA), 1985.

Murphy, J. A., *Quality in Practice*, Gill and MacMillan, Dublin, 1986.

Popplewell, B. and Wildsmith, A., *Becoming the Best*, Gower, Aldershot (UK), 1988.

Price, F., *Right Every Time*, Gower, Aldershot (UK), 1990.

Sarv Singh Soin, *Total Quality Control Essentials – key elements, methodologies and managing for success*, McGraw-Hill, New York, 1992.
Wille, E., *Quality: achieving excellence*, Century Business, London, 1992.
Zairi, M., *Total Quality Management for Engineers*, Woodhead, Cambridge (UK), 1991.

## Leadership and commitment

Adair, J., *Not Bosses but Leaders: how to lead the successful way*, Talbot Adair Press, Guildford (UK), 1987.
Adair, J., *The Action-Centred Leader*, Industrial Society, London, 1988.
Adair, J., *Effective Leadership* (2nd edn), Pan Books, London, 1988.
Crosby, P. B., *Running Things*, McGraw-Hill, New York, 1986.
Juran, J. M., *Juran on Leadership for Quality: an executive handbook*, The Free Press (Macmillan), New York, 1989.
Townsend, P. L. and Gebhardt, J. E., *Commit to Quality*, J. Wiley Press, New York, 1986.
Townsend, P. L. and Gebhardt, J. E., *Quality in Action – 93 lessons in leadership, participation and measurement*, J. Wiley Press, New York, 1992.

## Customers, suppliers and service

Albin, J. M., *Quality Improvement in Employment and other Human Services – managing for quality through change*, Paul Brookes Pub. (USA), 1992.
Cook, S., *Customer Care – implementing total quality in today's service driven organization*, Kogan Page, London, 1992.
Groocock, J. M., *The Chains of Quality*, John Wiley, Chichester (UK), 1986.
King Taylor, L., *Quality: total customer service* (a case study book), Century Business, London, 1992.
Lash, L. M., *The Complete Guide to Customer Service*, J. Wiley Press, New York, 1989.
Mastenbrock, W. (ed.), *Managing for Quality in the Service Sector*, Basil Blackwell, Oxford (UK), 1991.
Zeithaml, V. A., Parasuraman, A. and Berry, L. L., *Delivering Quality Service: balancing customer perceptions and expectations*, The Free Press (Macmillan), New York, 1990.

## Design, innovation, and QFD

Adair, J., *The Challenge of Innovation*, Talbot Adair Press, Guildford (UK), 1990.
Juran, J. J., *Juran on Quality by Design*, Free Press, New York, 1992.
Marsh, S., Moran, J., Nakui, S. and Hoffherr, G. D., *Facilitating and Training in QFD*, ASQC, Milwaukee, WI (USA), 1991.
Zairi, M., *Management of Advanced Manufacturing Technology*, Sigma Press, Wilmslow (UK), 1992.

## Quality planning, JIT, and POM

Ansari, A. and Modarress, B., *Just-in-time Purchasing*, The Free Press (Macmillan), New York, 1990.
Bineno, J., *Implementing JIT*, IFS, Bedford (UK), 1991.
Harrison, A., *Just-in-Time Manufacturing in Perspective*, Prentice-Hall, Englewood Cliffs, NJ (USA), 1992.
Hutchins, D., *Just-in-Time*, Gower, Aldershot (UK), 1988.
Juran, J. M. (ed), *Quality Control Handbook*, McGraw-Hill, New York, 1988.
Juran, J. M. and Gryna, F. M., *Quality Planning and Analysis* (2nd edn), McGraw-Hill, New York, 1980.
Muhlemann, A. P., Oakland, J. S. and Lockyer, K. G., *Production and Operations Management* (6th edn), Pitman, London, 1992.
Voss, C. A. (ed), *Just-in-Time Manufacture*, IFS Publications, Bedford (UK), 1989.

## Quality systems

Dale, B. G. and Oakland, J. S., *Quality Improvement Through Standards*, Stanley Thornes, Cheltenham (UK), 1991.
Hall, T. J., *The Quality Manual – the application of BS5750 ISO 9001 EN 29001*, John Wiley, Chichester (UK), 1992.
Rothery, B., *ISO 9000*, Gower, Aldershot (UK), 1991.
Stebbing, L., *Quality Assurance: the route to efficiency and competitiveness* (2nd edn), John Wiley, Chichester (UK), 1989.

## The Baldrige Award criteria

Brown M. G., *Baldrige Award Winning Quality: how to interpret the Malcolm Baldrige Award criteria* (2nd edn), ASQC, Milwaukee, WI (USA), 1992.

Hart, W. L. and Bogan, C. E., *The Baldrige: what it is, how it's won, how to use it to improve quality in your company*, McGraw-Hill, New York, 1992.

Mills Steeples, M., *The Corporate Guide to the Malcolm Baldrige National Quality Award*, ASQC, Milwaukee, WI (USA), 1992.

NIST (US Dept. of Commerce, National Institute of Standards and Technology), *Malcolm Baldridge National Quality Award Criteria*, 1993.

## Quality costing, measurement and benchmarking

Camp, R. C., *Benchmarking: the search for industry best practices that lead to superior performance*, ASQC Quality Press, Milwaukee, WI (USA), 1989.

Dale, B. G. and Plunkett, J. J., *Quality Costing*, Chapman and Hall, London, 1991.

Dixon, J. R., Nanni, A. and Vollmann, T. E., *The New Performance Challenge – measuring operations for world class competition*, Business One Irwin, Homewood (USA), 1990.

Hall, R. W., Johnson, H. Y. and Turney, P. B. B., *Measuring Up – charting pathways to manufacturing excellence*, Business One Irwin, Homewood (USA), 1991.

Kaplan, R. W. (ed), *Measures for Manufacturing Excellence*, Harvard Business School Press, Boston, Mass. (USA), 1990.

Kinlaw, D. C., *Continuous Improvement and Measurement For Total Quality – a team-based approach*, Pfieffer & Business One (USA), 1992.

Porter, L. J. and Rayner, P., 'Quality costing for TQM', *International Journal of Production Economics*, **27**, pp. 69–81, 1992.

Spendolini, M. J., *The Benchmarking Book*, ASQC, Milwaukee, WI (USA), 1992.

Talley, D. J., *Total Quality Management: performance and cost measures*, ASQC, Milwaukee, WI (USA), 1991.

Zairi, M., *Competitive Benchmarking*, TQM Practitioner Series, Technical Communications (Publishing), Letchworth (UK), 1992.

Zairi, M., *TQM-Based Performance Measurement*, TQM Practitioner Series, Technical Communications (Publishing), Letchworth (UK), 1992.

## Tools and techniques of TQM (including SPC)

Bhote, K. R., *World Class Quality – using design of experiments to make it happen*, AMACOM, New York (USA), 1991.

Carlzon, J., *Moments of Truth*, Ballinger, Cambridge, Mass. (USA), 1987.

Caulcutt, R., *Data Analysis in the Chemical Industry, Vol. 1: Basic Techniques*, Ellis Horwood, Chichester (UK), 1989.

Caulcutt, R., *Statistics in Research and Development* (2nd edn)., Chapman and Hall, London, 1991.

Neave, H., *The Deming Dimension*, SPC Press, Knoxville (USA), 1990.

Oakland, J. S. and Followell, R. F., *Statistical Process Control: a practical guide* (2nd edn), Butterworth-Heinemann, Oxford (UK), 1990.

Price, F., *Right First Time*, Gower, London, 1985.

Ryuki Fukuda, *CEDAC – a tool for continuous systematic improvement*, Productivity Press, Cambridge, Mass (USA), 1990.

## Shingo and Taguchi methods

Bendell, T., Wilson, G. and Millar, R. M. G., *Taguchi Methodology with Total Quality*, IFS, Bedford (UK), 1990.

Lagothetis, N., *Managing for Total Quality – from Deming to Taguchi and SPC*, Prentice-Hall, Englewood Cliffs, NJ (USA), 1992.

Ranjit, Roy, *A Primer on the Taguchi Method*, Van Nostrand Reinhold, New York, 1990.

Shingo, S., *Zero Quality Control: source inspection and the Poka-yoke system*, Productivity Press, Stamford, Conn. (USA), 1986.

## TQM through people and teamwork

Adair, J., *Effective Teambuilding* (2nd edn), Pan Books, London, 1987.

Aubrey, C. A. and Felkins, P. K., *Teamwork: involving people in quality and productivity improvement*, ASQC, Milwaukee, WI (USA), 1988.

Belbin, R. M., *Management Teams: why they succeed or fail*, Butterworth-Heinemann, Oxford (UK), 1981.

Blanchard, K. and Hersey, P., *Management of Organizational Behaviour: Utilizing Human Resources* (4th edn), Prentice-Hall, Englewood Cliffs, NJ (USA), 1982.

Briggs Myers, I., *Introduction to Type: a description of the theory and applications of the Myers Briggs Type Indicator*, Consulting Psychologists Press, Palo Alto (USA), 1987.

Choppin, J., *Quality Through People: a blueprint for proactive total quality management*, IFS, Kempston (UK), 1991.

Collard, R., *Total Quality: success through people*, Institute of Personnel Management, Wimbledon (UK), 1989.

Dale, B. G. and Cooper, C., *Total Quality and Human Resources – an executive guide*, Blackwell, Oxford (UK), 1992.

Hutchins, D., *The Quality Circle Handbook*, Gower, Aldershot (UK), 1985.

Kormanski, C., 'A situational leadership approach to groups using the Tuckman Model of Group Development', *The 1985 Annual: Developing Human Resources*, University Associates, San Diego (USA), 1985.

Kormanski, C. and Mozenter, A., 'A new model of team building: a technology for today and tomorrow', *The 1987 Annual: Developing Human Resources*, University Associates, San Diego (USA), 1987.

Krebs Hirsh, S., *MBTI Team Building Program, Team Member's Guide*, Consulting Psychologists Press, Palo Alto, CA (USA), 1992.

Krebs Hirsh, S. and Kummerow, J. M., *Introduction to Type in Organizational Settings*, Consulting Psychologists Press, Palo Alto, CA (USA), 1987.

McCaulley, M. H., 'How individual differences affect health care teams', *Health Team News*, **1** (8), pp. 1–4, 1975.

Masaaki, I., *Kaizen: the key to Japanese competitive success*, McGraw-Hill, New York, 1986.

Robson, M., *Quality Circles, a practical guide* (2nd edn), Gower, Aldershot (UK), 1989.

Scholtes, P. R., *The Team Handbook*, Joiner Associates, Madison, NY (USA), 1990.

Shetty, Y. K. and Buehler, V. M. (eds), *Productivity and Quality Through People* (case studies), Quorum Books, London, 1985.

Tannenbaum, R. and Schmidt, W. H., 'How to choose a leadership pattern', *Harvard Business Review*, May–June, 1973.

Tuckman, B. W. and Jensen, M. A., 'Stages of small group development revisited', *Group and Organizational Studies*, **2** (4), pp. 419–427, 1977.

Wellins, R. S., Byham, W. C. and Wilson, J. M., *Empowered Teams*, Jossey Bass, Oxford (UK), 1991.

Whitley, R., *The Customer Driven Company*, Business Books, London, 1991.

## Cross-functional process improvement

Dimaxcescu, D., *The Seamless Enterprise – making cross-functional management work*, Harper Business, New York, 1992.

Francis, D., *Unblocking the Organisational Communication*, Gower, Aldershot (UK), 1990.

Harrington, H. J., *Business Process Improvement*, McGraw-Hill, New York, 1991.

Rummler, G. A. and Brache, A. P., *Improving Performance: how to manage the white space on the organisation chart*, Jossey-Bass Publishing, San Francisco, CA (USA), 1990.

## Implementing TQM

Atkinson, P. E., *Creating Culture Change: the key to successful total quality management*, IFS, Bedford (UK), 1990.

Ciampa, D., *Total Quality – a user's guide for implementation*, Addison-Wesley, Reading, Mass. (USA), 1992.

Crosby, P. B., *The Eternally Successful Organization*, McGraw-Hill, New York, 1988.

Cullen, J. and Hollingham, J., *Implementing Total Quality*, IFS (Publications), London, 1987.

Fox, R., *Six Steps to Total Quality Management*, McGraw-Hill, NSW (Australia), 1991.

Gitlow, H. S., and Gitlow, S. J., *The Deming Guide to Quality and Competitive Position*, Prentice-Hall, New Jersey (USA), 1987.

Hardaker, M. and Ward, B. K., 'Getting things done – how to make a team work', *Harvard Business Review*, pp. 112–119, Nov/Dec. 1987.

Hiam, A., *Closing the Quality Gap – lessons from America's leading companies*, Prentice-Hall, Englewood Cliffs, NJ (USA), 1992.

Munro-Faure, L. and Munro-Faure, M., *Implementing Total Quality Management*, Pitman, London, 1992.

Saylor, J. H., *Total Quality Management Field Manual*, McGraw-Hill, New York, 1992.

Scherkenbach, W. W., *The Deming Route to Quality and Productivity: road maps and road blocks*, Mercury Press/Fairchild Publications, Rockville, Md (USA), 1986.

Scherkenbach, W. W., *Deming's Road to Continual Improvement*, SPC Press, Knoxville (USA), 1991.

Schuler, R. S. and Harris, D. L., *Managing Quality – the primer for middle managers*, Addison-Wesley, Reading, Mass. (USA), 1992.

Spenley, P., *World Class Performance Through Total Quality*, Chapman and Hall, London, 1992.

Tennor, A. R. and De Toro, I. J., *Total Quality Management – three steps to continuous improvement*, Addison-Wesley, Reading, Mass. (USA), 1992.

Tunks, R., *Fast Track to Quality*, McGraw-Hill, New York, 1992.

## British Standards related to TQM

BS 600:1935 'The application of statistical methods to industrial standardisation and quality control'

BS 2564: 1955 'Control chart technique when manufacturing to a specification, with special reference to articles machined to dimensional tolerances'

BS 2846:Parts 1 to 7:1976–1991 (ISO 2602, Part 2; ISO 3207, Part 3; ISO 2854, Part 4; ISO 3494, Part 5; ISO 3301, Part 6; ISO 5479, Part 7) 'Guide to statistical interpretation of data'

BS 4891:1972 'A guide to quality assurance'

BS 5700:1984 'Guide to process control using quality control chart methods and cusum techniques'

BS 5701:1980 'Guide to number-defective charts for quality control'

BS 5703:Parts 1 to 4:1980–1982 'Guide to data analysis and quality control using cusum techniques'

BS 5750:Parts 0 to 13 (with gaps):1987 to 1991 (ISO 9001, Part 1; ISO 9002, Part 2; ISO 9003, Part 3; ISO 9004–2, Part 8; ISO 900–3, Part 13) 'Quality systems'

BS 5760:Parts 0 to 7:1981–1991 'Reliability of systems, equipment and components'

BS 5781:Parts 1 to 2:1988 'Measurement and calibration systems'

BS 6000:1972 (ISO 2859) 'Guide to the use of BS 6001, sampling procedures and tables for inspection by attributes'

BS 6001:Parts 1 to 3:1984 to 1991 (ISO 2859–1) 'Sampling procedures for inspection by attributes'

BS 6002:1979 (ISO 2859–2) 'Specification for sampling procedures and charts for inspection by variables for per cent defective'

BS 6143:Parts 1 to 2:1990–1992 (ISO 2859–3) 'Guide to the economies of quality'

BS 7000:1989 'Guide to managing product design'

BS 7165:1991 'Recommendations for achievement of quality in software'

BS 7229:Parts 1 to 3:1991 (ISO 10011) 'Guide to quality systems auditing'

BS 7850:Parts 1 to 2:1992   'Total quality management'

BS 9000:Parts 1 to 8:1989–1991   'General requirements for a system for electronic components of assessed quality'

BS Published Document PD 3542:1991   'The role of standards in company quality management'

# Index

# Statistical Process Control
## Second edition

## John S. Oakland
and
## Roy F. Followell

In its first edition Professor Oakland's book sold over 12,000 copies worldwide (including 3500 in the USA) and became recognized as a particularly practical and effective guide to the control of product or service quality.

Recent and continuing changes in the business and commercial world are forcing companies to concentrate more and more on the prevention of quality control problems rather than on how to identify and fix them. With his colleague Roy Followell, John Oakland has completely rewritten his book in this second edition. Still based firmly in real-life studies, it reflects the authors' recent work with all types of industry in refining SPC techniques and applying them to a variety of processes. The explanations stress key issues such as the meaning and use of process capability indices and the application of SPC to the non-manufacturing enterprise.

'Professor Oakland. . . demonstrates the variety of potential applications. . . . It is certainly a well-produced, well-written, instructive guide to the subject.'                                                *Quality News*

**Contents**
- Quality, processes and control
- Understanding the process
- Data collection and presentation
- Process problem solving
- Variables and process variation
- Process control using variables
- Process capability for variables and its measurement
- Other types of control charts for variables
- Random variation and its management
- Managing out-of-control processes
- Process control by attributes
- Cumulative sum charts
- Designing the process control system
- SPC in non-manufacturing
- The implementation of SPC
- Appendices; Index

**Statistical Process Control** is for anyone who needs to understand and implement modern SPC techniques. It is a useful textbook for self or group instruction of production and inspection supervisors, engineers, scientists and technologists and of managers in both the production and service sectors of industry. For students on courses leading to qualifications in science, engineering and management it is a useful and comprehensive guide to quality assurance techniques and practices.

ISBN 0 7506 0797 1    444 pages    145 diagrams    hardback